Street by Street

GW00419245

BRISTOL,
CLEVEDON, PORTISHEAD,
WESTON-SUPER-MARE, YATE

Avonmouth, Bradley Stoke, Chipping Sodbury, Congresbury, Keynsham, Kingswood, Long Ashton, Mangotsfield, Nailsea, Pucklechurch, Thornbury, Yatton

3rd edition November 2008
© Automobile Association Developments Limited 2008

Original edition printed May 2001

 This product includes map data licensed from Ordnance Survey® with the permission of the Controller of Her Majesty's Stationery Office. © Crown copyright 2008. All rights reserved. Licence number 100021153.

The copyright in all PAF is owned by Royal Mail Group plc.

 Information on fixed speed camera locations provided by RoadPilot © 2008 RoadPilot® Driving Technology.

Published by AA Publishing (a trading name of Automobile Association Developments Limited, whose registered office is Fanum House, Basing View, Basingstoke, Hampshire RG21 4EA. Registered number 1878835).

Produced by the Mapping Services Department of The Automobile Association. (A03728)

A CIP Catalogue record for this book is available from the British Library.

Printed by Oriental Press in Dubai

Key to map pages	ii-iii
Key to map symbols	iv-1
Enlarged map pages	2-7
Main map pages	7-127
Index – towns & villages	128
Index – streets	129-151
Index – featured places	151-154
Acknowledgements	154

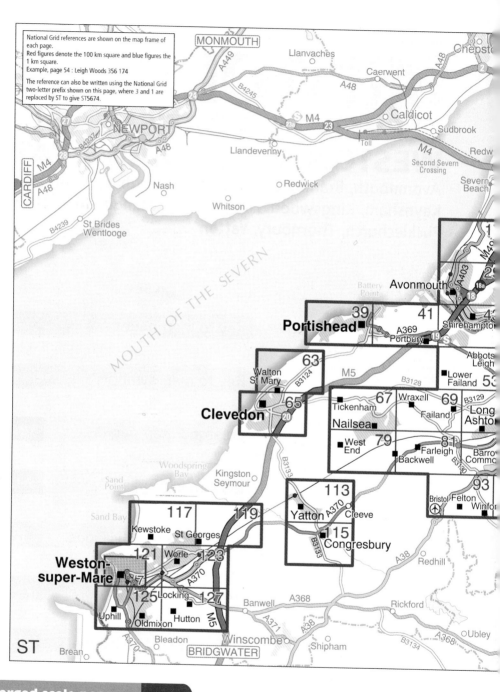

National Grid references are shown on the map frame of each page.
Red figures denote the 100 km square and blue figures the 1 km square.
Example, page 54 : Leigh Woods 356 174

The reference can also be written using the National Grid two-letter prefix shown on this page, where 3 and 1 are replaced by ST to give ST5674.

MONMOUTH
Llanvaches
Chepsto
A449
Caerwent
A48
A48
B4245
Caldicot
M4
Sudbrook
NEWPORT
A48
23
Second Severn Crossing
Redw
CARDIFF
M4
A48
Llandevenny
Toll
M4
Severn Beach
Nash
Redwick
B4239
Whitson
St Brides Wentlooge

MOUTH OF THE SEVERN

Battery Point
Avonmouth
A403
18a
18
39
41
Shirehampton
Portishead
A369
Portbury
19
4
63
Abbots Leigh
Walton St Mary
B3124
M5
Lower Failand
55
B3128
65
67
Wraxall
69
B3129
Long Ashto
Clevedon
20
Tickenham
Nailsea
Failand
79
West End
81
Farleigh
Barro Commo
Backwell
B3130
Woodspring Bay
Kingston Seymour
B3133
113
93
Sand Point
Yatton
A370
Cleeve
Bristol Felton
Winfor
Sand Bay
117
119
115
Kewstoke
St Georges
Congresbury
B3133
Weston-super-Mare
121
Worle
123
A38
Redhill
125
Locking
127
Banwell
A368
Rickford
Uphill
Oldmixon
Hutton
M5
A371
A38
Ubley
Bleadon
Winscombe
A368
Brean
BRIDGWATER
Shipham
B3134

ST

Enlarged scale pages   1:10,000   6.3 inches to 1 mile

0   1/4   miles   1/2
0   1/4   1/2   kilometres   3/4   1

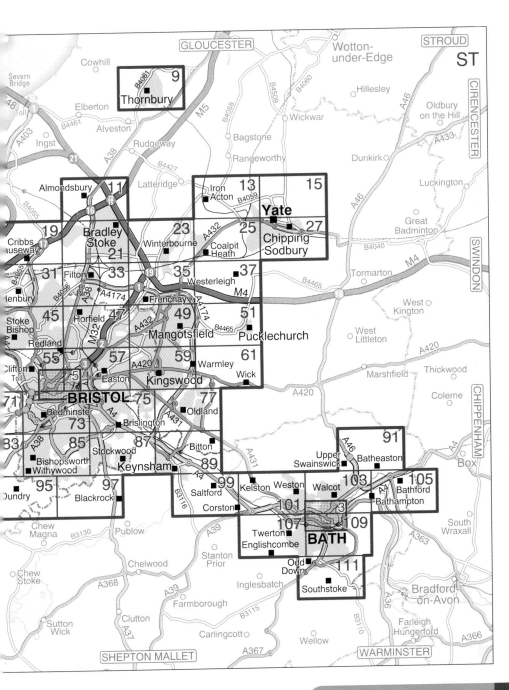

iv

Junction 9	Motorway & junction			Railway & minor railway station
Services	Motorway service area			Underground station
	Primary road single/dual carriageway			Light railway & station
Services	Primary road service area			Preserved private railway
	A road single/dual carriageway		LC	Level crossing
	B road single/dual carriageway			Tramway
	Other road single/dual carriageway			Ferry route
	Minor/private road, access may be restricted			Airport runway
	One-way street			County, administrative boundary
	Pedestrian area			Mounds
	Track or footpath		**17**	Page continuation 1:15,000
	Road under construction		**3**	Page continuation to enlarged scale 1:10,000
	Road tunnel			River/canal, lake, pier
30	Speed camera site (fixed location) with speed limit in mph			Aqueduct, lock, weir
V	Speed camera site (fixed location) with variable speed limit		465 ▲ Winter Hill	Peak (with height in metres)
40	Section of road with two or more fixed camera sites; speed limit in mph or variable			Beach
50→ ←50	Average speed (SPECS™) camera system with speed limit in mph			Woodland
P	Parking			Park
P+	Park & Ride			Cemetery
	Bus/coach station			Built-up area
	Railway & main railway station		IKEA®	IKEA store

Symbol	Description	Symbol	Description
	Industrial/business building		Abbey, cathedral or priory
	Leisure building		Castle
	Retail building		Historic house or building
	Other building	Wakehurst Place NT	National Trust property
	City wall	M	Museum or art gallery
A&E	Hospital with 24-hour A&E department		Roman antiquity
PO	Post Office		Ancient site, battlefield or monument
	Public library		Industrial interest
i	Tourist Information Centre		Garden
i	Seasonal Tourist Information Centre		Garden Centre Garden Centre Association Member
	Petrol station, 24 hour Major suppliers only		Garden Centre Wyevale Garden Centre
†	Church/chapel		Arboretum
	Public toilet, with facilities for the less able		Farm or animal centre
PH	Public house AA recommended		Zoological or wildlife collection
	Restaurant AA inspected		Bird collection
Madeira Hotel	Hotel AA inspected		Nature reserve
	Theatre or performing arts centre		Aquarium
	Cinema	V	Visitor or heritage centre
	Golf course		Country park
▲	Camping AA inspected		Cave
	Caravan site AA inspected		Windmill
	Camping & caravan site AA inspected		Distillery, brewery or vineyard
	Theme park	•	Other place of interest

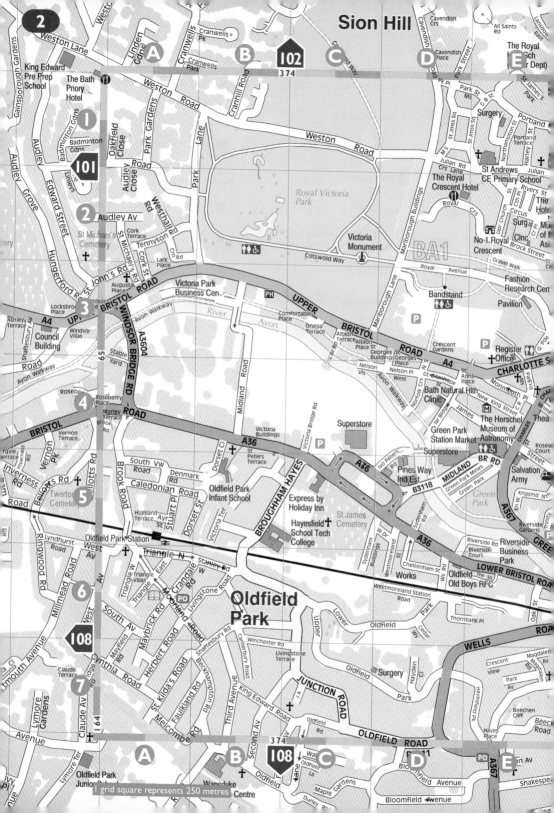

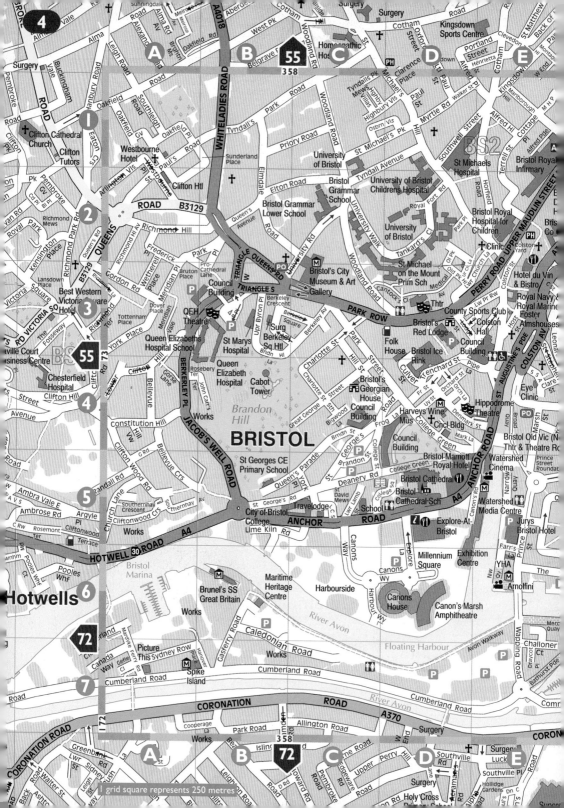

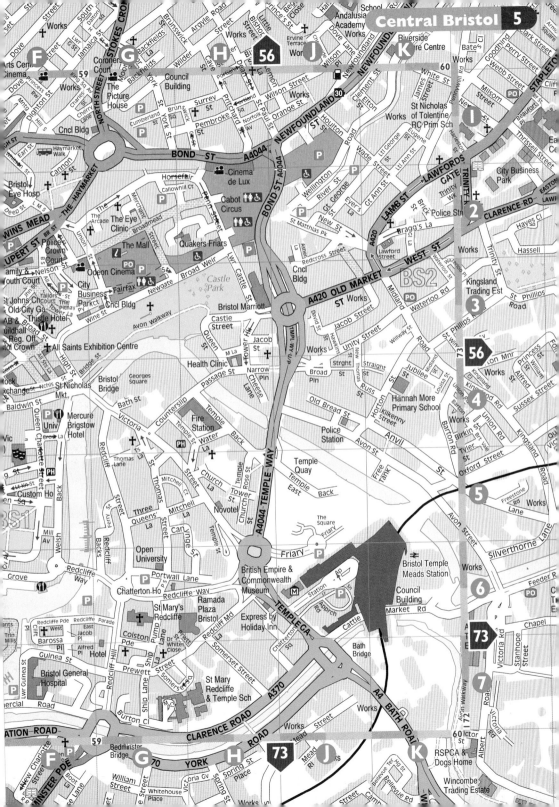

WESTON-SUPER-MARE

Weston Bay

Grand Pier

Model Yacht Pond

SeaQuarium

Tropicana Leisure Complex

6

Further Education

Birkett Rd
Camp Rd
Trinity Rd
South Road
South Road
South Rd
Cecil Rd

A B **120** C D E

Atlantic Road
Highbury Road
Tower Wlk
ery Avenue
St Matthew's Close
Grove Park Road
132

Madeira Rd
Paragon Rd
Atlantic Road South
Hamilton Road
Shrubbery Ter
Shrubbery Road
St Peter's Av

Daunce Hotel
1
62
Birnbeck Road
Atlantic Business Park
New Birchfield Hotel
Shrubbery Complex
PO
Upper Church Road
Victoria Park
St John's Close
Queen's Rd
All Saints' Road
Tichborne Road
Bristol Rd
Coombe Rd
Lang

Anchor Head Hotel
New Ocean Hotel
Manilla Crescent
P
Park Place
Royal Crs
Lower Church Rd
Grove La
Edinburgh Place
Connaught Place
Victoria Qdt
South

Marine Lake
Greenfield Pl
Knightstone Road
P
Vctr Pl
South Crs
The Arosfa Hotel
Grove Rd
High Street
Playhouse Thr
Surgery
Twoll Pl

2
Old Knightstone Theatre
Knightstone Cswy
P
Weston College
Heritage Cen
West Street
Worthy Pl
Worthy La
Boule

3
Royal Parade
The Royal Hotel
South Pde
Waterloo Street
PO
Palmer Rw
Palmer St
North Somerset Museum
Meadow
St M Ter
Winter Gardens & Pavilion
Palmer St
Cambridge Place
North Street
Burlington St
Tim

4
V Sq
Salisbury Terrace
P
Sovereign Shopping Centre
Regent St
Weston-super-Mare Co Court
Alexandra Parade
Orchard St
Back Street
Alma Street
Alfred

MARINE PDE
Regent St
Richmond St
High Street
Works
Meadow St
Union St
Odeon Cinema
P PO
Regent St
Wallscote Rd
Supers
Hildesheim Court

P
7
P
Oxford St
Town Hall
CAB
Dolphin Square Shopping Centre
Indoor Market
AMF Bowling
Cncl Bldg
Union St

5
161
Carlton St
Salvation Army
Birkbeck
Walliscote Primary School
P
Walliscote Road
Magistrates Court
Police Station
Beaconsfield Rd
Surgery
Graham Rd
W C
Neva

6
Ashbrook House School
P
Ellenborough Park North
Ellenborough Park
Ellenborough Crs
Ellenborough Park Road
Albert Avenue

Ellenborough Park South
A370
Marine Parade
BEACH ROAD

7
Corpus Christi RC Primary School
Albert Road
Clevedon Road
Walliscote Road
Pitma Road
Newton

331

A B **124** C D E

Model Yacht Centre
P
32fton Road
Whitecross Road
Severn Road
PO

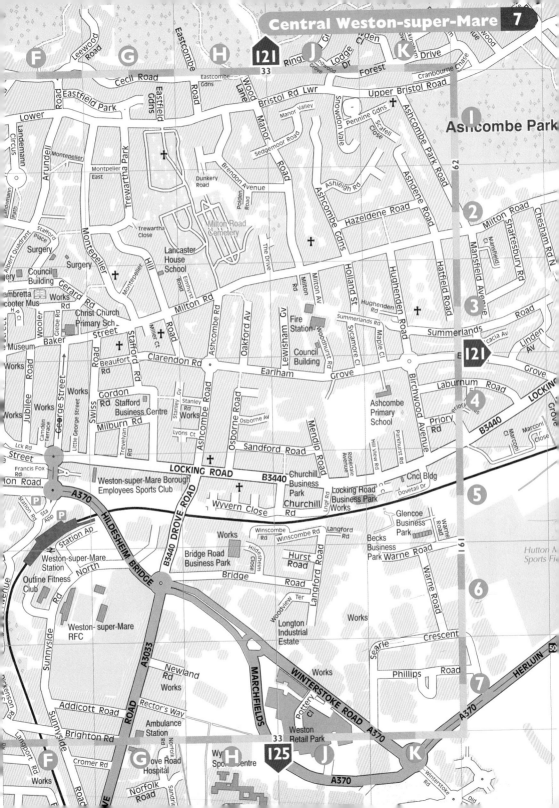

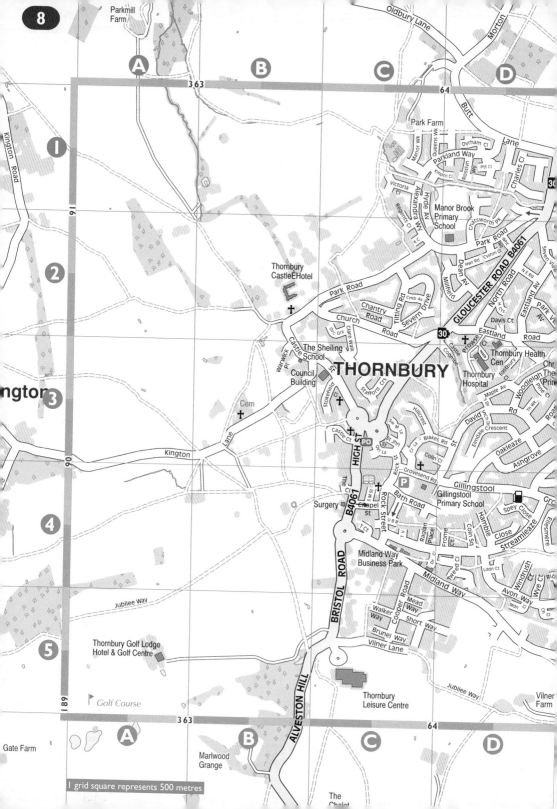

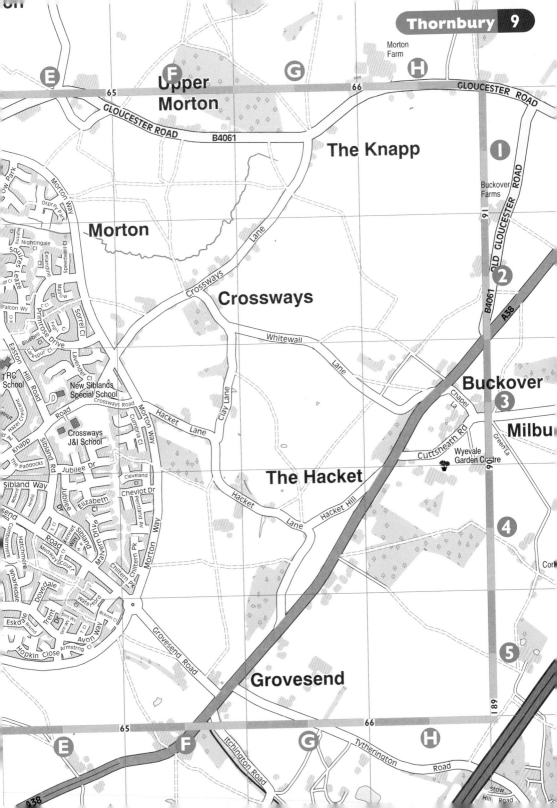

Morton Farm

E

F
**Upper
Morton**

G

H

65   GLOUCESTER ROAD   66   GLOUCESTER ROAD

GLOUCESTER ROAD

B4061

The Knapp

I

Buckover
Farms

Morton

91

OLD GLOUCESTER ROAD

Osprey Park

Morton Way

Nightingale Cl

Celandine Cl

Squires Leaze

Speedwell Dr

Crossways Lane

Falcon Wy

Mallow Cl

Bluebell Dr

Primrose Drive

Sorrel Cl

Lavender Cl

Fern Cl

Larkspur Cl

Crossways

2

B4061

A38

Whitewall   Lane

RC
School

Easton Hill Road

Hazel Cres

Walnut

New Siblands
Special School

Crossways Road

Clay Lane

Hacket   Lane

Morton Way

Cumbria Cl

Buckover

3

Chapel La

Green La

Milbu

Knapp
Road

Sibland Rd

The Paddocks

Jubilee Dr

**Crossways
J&I School**

Cleveland Cl

Cheviot Dr

Pentland Av

Cuttsheath Rd

Wyevale
Garden Centre

96

Sibland Way

Jubilee Dr

Elizabeth
Cl

The Hacket

Hacket   Lane

Hacket Hill

4

Grovesend Road

Combermere

Hatchmere

Wharfedale

Kennet Way

Sibland Way

Medway Court

Maven Drive

Chiltern Pk

Chiltern Pk

Morton Way

Dovedale

Trent Dr

Watchford

Slade Wy

Bckmm Cl

Eskdale

Brkmd

Avon Way

Armstrng Cl

Hopkin Close

5

Grovesend

189

E

F

G

H

65   66

Itchington Road

Tytherington   Road

A38

Stow
Hill Road

Cor

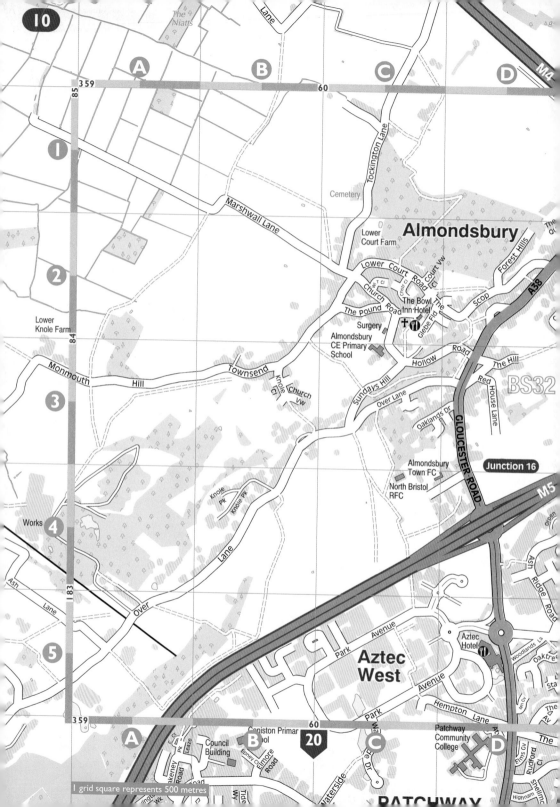

Woodhouse
Down

Woodhouse Avenue
Ferr Cl
Woodhouse Close
Woodhouse South Road
E
F
G
H

62
63
85

Hortham Wood

I

Old Aust Road
Bishop's Wood
GLOUCESTER ROAD
Hortham Lane
Hickory La
Hortham Farm
Hortham Lane
M5

Cope Pk
...nce ...ttock Dr
...Park

2

84

Woodlands Lane

Junction 20/15

3

Golf Course

Brothersvd
Ct
St J's Ct
Woodlands
Apex
Ct
Eagles Wood Business Park
New Leaze
Great Pk Rd
Eagles Wd
Hawkley Dr
Almondsbury Business Cen

4

M4

Woodlands Pk Lane
The Park
Ottrells Mead
Cooks Close
Cooks
Trench Lane
Crows Grove
Foxfield Avenue
Pye Ct
Paddock Cl
Woodlands Golf & Country Club

83

Apeleys Md
Pear Tree
Br Ct
Chessel Cl
Rush Cl
Westfield Way
Trench La

Grange
PO
Orchard Ga
Bradley Stoke Way
Mallard Cl
Lapwing Cl
Bowsland
Way

St Marys RFC
West Country Water Park

5

...shaws Close
Crescent
Ferndene
Bradley
Stoke Way
Tesham
Bowsland Green Primary School
Ellicks Close
Ormonds Close
Trench Lane

...1 The Close
Common
E
The Common East
Harvest Cl
Wheatfield Drive
F
Stoke Way
21
Savage's Wood
G
H

Cranham Dr
St Chads Patchway CE
Cornfield Dr
Wheatfield Primary School
Brook
Dewfalls Dr

62
63

12

A 3 67 B 68 C D

85

1

B4059

LC

84

2

Acton Court

Ladden Brook

3

LC

B4058

Laddenside Farm

Elm Farm

4

Hoover's Lane

83

5

A 3 67 B 68 24 C Tub Bottom D

Northmead Lane

Patch Elm Lane

Mudgedown Farm

Acton Lodge

Iron Acton

Hill House

B4058

WOTTON ROAD

YATE ROAD

Latteridge Rd

Park St

High Street

Police Station

Wotton Road

Iron Acton CE Primary School

Holly Hill

Cem

Chilwood Cl

YATE ROAD

Nibley Lane

Station Road

Algars Manor

Frome valley walkway

Frome valley walkway

River Frome

n End Rd

OL ROAD

ROAD

1 grid square represents 500 metres

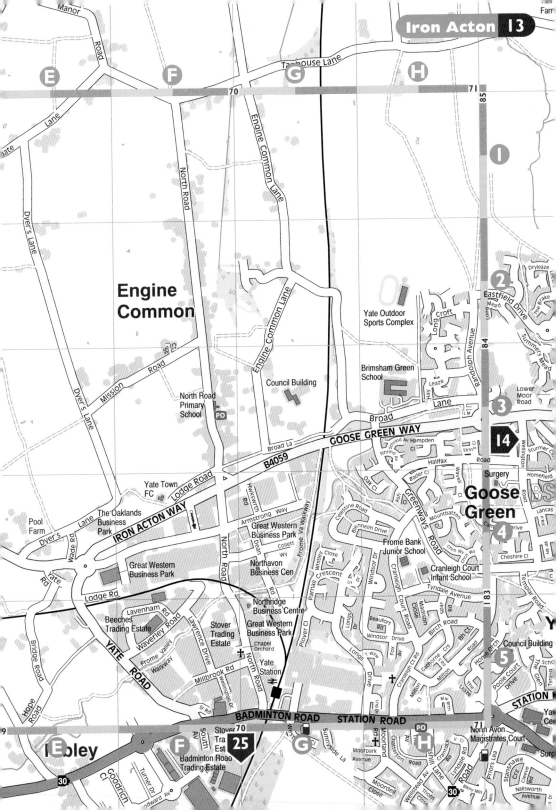

Farn

Manor

Road

E F G H

Tanhouse Lane

70 71 85

Engine Common Lane

North Road

Dyer's Lane

I

Engine
Common

Dryleaze

Mead

2
Eastfield Drive

The Brake

Summer's Mead

Long Croft

Randolph Avenue

Yate Outdoor
Sports Complex

Hay
Leaze

Cross

Mission Road

Dyer's Lane

Lane

Council Building

Brimsham Green
School

Lower
Moor
Road

3

North Road
Primary
School
PO

Broad

Broad La

B4059

GOOSE GREEN WAY

Sthrind Av Hampden

Sthrind Cl

Sthrind Av Cl

Halifax

Wellington Road

Homefield

14

Bader Cl

Oak Cl

Ash

Waverly Rd

Surgery

Lancas

BS

**Goose
Green**

Pool
Farm

Dyer's

Yate Town
FC

The Oaklands
Business Park

IRON ACTON WAY

Lodge Road

Wade Rd

Lane

Hawksworth Rd

Armstrong Way

Dean

Collett

Wy

Frome Via Walkway

Celestine Road

Blenheim Drive

Greenways Road

Mountbatten

Chch Wy Wy

Cheshire Cl

Camp Drive

4

Great Western
Business Park

Northavon
Business Cen

Frome Bank
Junior School

Cranleigh Court
Infant School

Tyndale Avenue

Yate
Rd

Lodge Rd

North Road

Parnall Crescent

Whitley Close

Windsor Dr

Cranleigh Cl

Cranleigh Court Road

Madison
Close

Birch Road

BH Cl

Great Western
Business Park

Lavenham
Rd

Beeches
Trading Estate

Waverley Road

Lawrence Drive

Frome valley
Walkway

Stover
Trading
Estate

Northridge
Business Centre

Great Western
Business Park

Chapel
Orchard

Plover Cl

Beaufort
Rd

Windsor
Drive

Longs

Fox
Cl

Longs

Tilly

Drive

Milton

Cranleigh Ct Rd

Cathorne Crs

Milton

Cl

Birch

Milton Cl

Home Orch

The
Leaze

Council Building

Poole Court
Drive

The Glen

5

Bridge Road

Hope
Road

YATE ROAD

Millbrook Rd

Wellington Dr

St Rd

North Road

Chapel
Orchard

Yate Station

Cranleigh Ct Rd

Poole Court
Drive

STATION

Yate
Cen

E Ebley

F

25

South Av

Goodrich
Cl

Turner Dr

Badminton Road
Trading Estate

Stover
Tra
Est

70

BADMINTON ROAD

West Cl

Sunnyside La

STATION ROAD

Moorland Rd

PO

Moorpark
Avenue

Chatterton
Road

Lyndale Rd

Shill Lane

Cranock
Cl

G

H

North Avon
Magistrates Court

Priors Lea

Stanshawe

Cleeve

Yate
Cen

Sur

30

Moordell
Close

Wellstead Av

Moordell Close

Thorn

Nailsworth
Avenue

Blley Mills

Cres

30

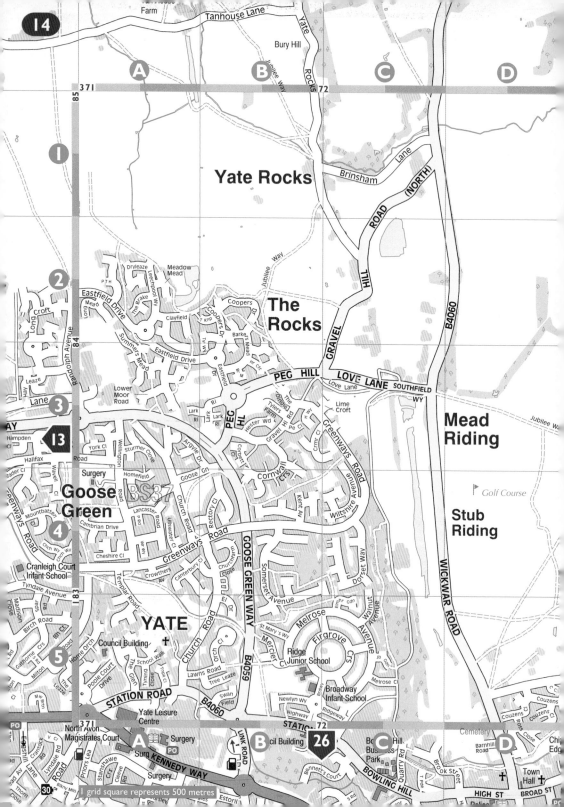

E   F   G   H

74   75

85

Horton Bushes

Bushes

1

Mapleridge Lane

Ho

2

Totteroak

84

Horton Road

Little Sodbury End

3

†

Sodbury Common

Chipping Sodbury Golf Club

Monarch's Way

4

Lit

Great House Farm

83

Horton Road

Jubilee Way

5

Portway Lane

Portway Lan

Trinity Lane

Harwoodgate Farm

St   Johns

Horton Rd

Collins Close

Brookfield Cl

Manor Way

Way

Vayre Close

Grace Close

Hatters' Lane

Rogers Ct

Bn Ct

Frome Rd

Walshe Av

Brandash Rd

TT Trading Estate

ng St

3

E   F   **27**   G   H

74   75

Park's Farm

Commonmead

Jubilee Way

Lar

CHIPPING

16

A   B   C   D

351   52

1

82

2

3

81

Fuel Depot

4

Rockingham
Works

5

180

351   52

A   B   **28**   C   D

Fuel Depot

Kings Weston Lane
Stores

LANE

SMOKE

Poplar

Way

A403

Dean Rd

Burcott Road

Humber Wy

Bank Road

Worthy

ST ANDREW'S ROAD

Ironchurch Road

Severnside
Trading
Estate

1 grid square represents 500 metres

South Gloucestershire
City of Bristol

E   F   G   H

Severnside
Works

54   55

I

Crook's
Marsh

Abieton La

Philblack
Works

2

Abieton La

Minor's

Gas
Works

Severn Road

Docks
Ind Est

Lane

3

18

Washingpool

Lane

CHITTENING ROAD

Severn Road

M49

A403

4

Moorend
Farm
Av

Hallen
Marsh

Severn Road

Berwick Ct

Berwick Lan

5

Poplar Way East

West

Moorhouse   Lane

Lawrence

Halle

Windsor Crs

80

54   29   55

E   F   G   H

Weston

Moorhouse

Moor
House   Lane

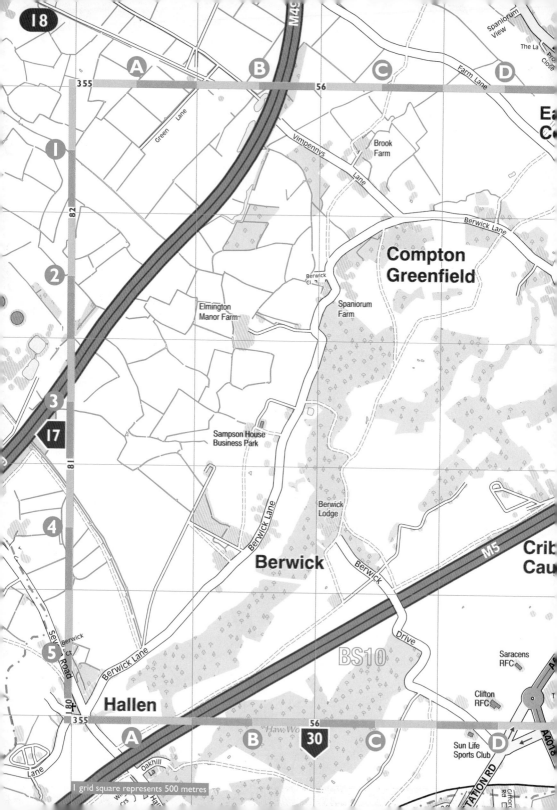

18

A   B   C   D

355   56   Farm Lane

Green Lane

Vimpennys

Spaniorum View

The La

Clo

1

82

Brook Farm

Ea
Co

Lane

Berwick Lane

Berwick Cl.

Compton Greenfield

2

Elmington Manor Farm

Spaniorum Farm

3

81

17

Sampson House Business Park

4

Berwick Lodge

M5

Crib
Cau

Berwick

Berwick Lane

Berwick

Berwick

Drive

5

Berwick Ct.

Severn Road

101

BS10

Saracens RFC

Clifton RFC

Hallen

Berwick Lane

355   56

Lane

Haw Wo

A

B   **30**   C

Sun Life Sports Club

D

STATION RD

A4018

Oakhill La

Gifford
Rd

I grid square represents 500 metres

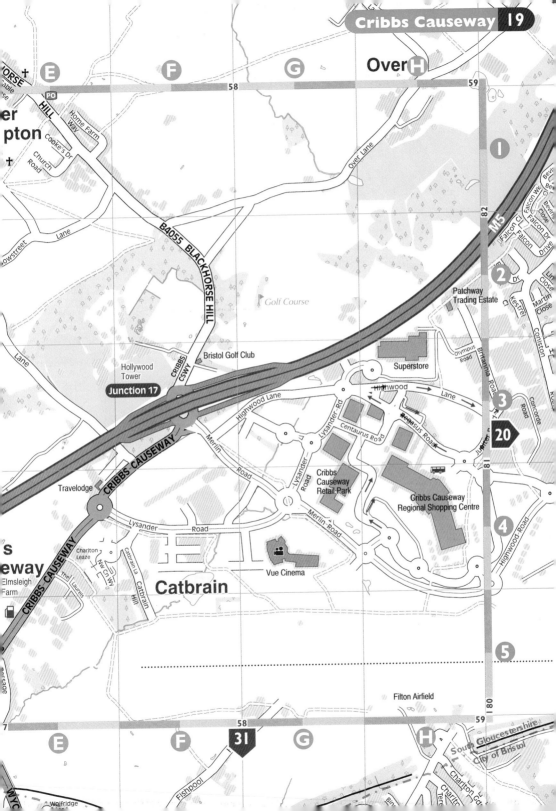

E **F** **G** Over **H**

I

58 59

PO

E HILL

Home Farm Way

Cooke's Dr

er pton

Church Road

B4055 BLACKHORSE HILL

Over Lane

M5 82

Falcon Wk
Falcon Cl
Falcon
Falcon Dr
Falcon Drive

Bevin
Bevir

Kestrel

Lin Close
Martin Close

2 Dr

Conliston

Patchway Trading Estate

Golf Course

Olympus Road

Britannia Road

Concorde Road

Bristol Golf Club

Hollywood Tower

CRIBBS CSWY

Junction 17

Superstore

Highwood Lane

Highwood Lane

Pegasus Road

Centaurus Road

Lysander Rd

3

81

20 ►

Merlin Road

Lysander Road

Cribbs Causeway Retail Park

Cribbs Causeway Regional Shopping Centre

Highwood Road

4

Travelodge

CRIBBS CAUSEWAY

Lysander Road

Charlton Leaze

NW Ch Wy

Catbrain La

Catbrain Hill

Merlin Road

Vue Cinema

eway

Elmsleigh Farm

The Laurels

Catbrain

5

80

Filton Airfield

7 58 59

E **F** **31** **G** **H** South Gloucestershire
City of Bristol

Charlton
Charter

Fishpool

WYC

Wolfridge

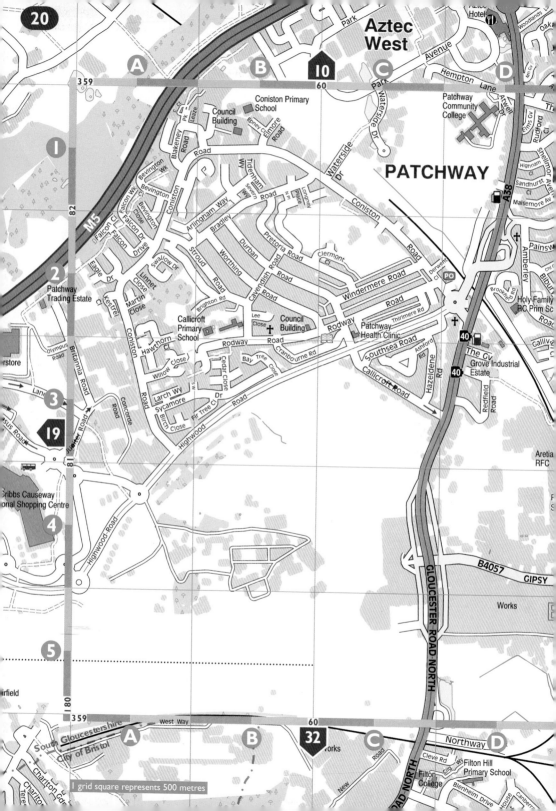

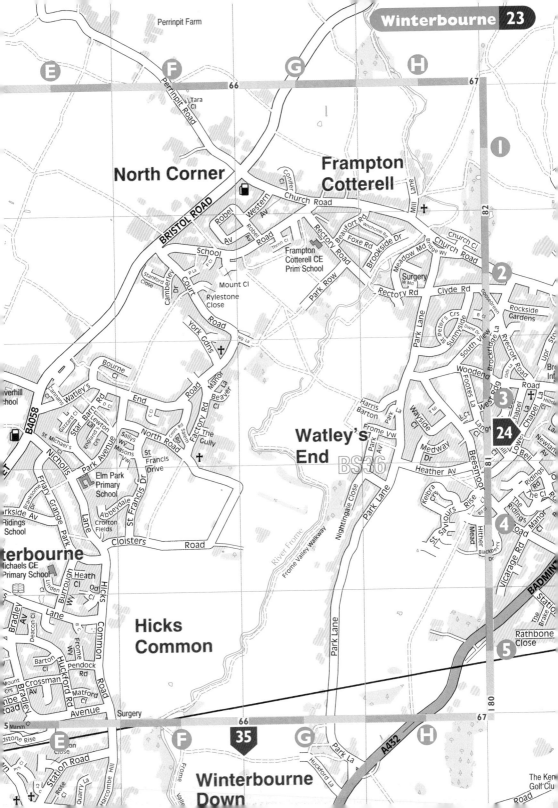

Perrinpit Farm

E F G H

Perrinpit Road

66

67

I

82

Tara Cl

North Corner

Frampton Cotterell

Conifer

Church Road

Mill Lane

BRISTOL ROAD

Robel Av

Western Av

Church Cl

Robel Av

Church Road

Beaufort Rd

Wnchcmb Rd

Robel Road

Foxe Rd

2

Rectory Road

Brookside Dr

School

Thrmn Cl

Camberley Dr

P Cl

Meadow Md

Surgery

Bridge Wy

Stanford Close

Court

Frampton Cotterell CE Prim School

W Md

Clyde Rd

Crossgreen

Rockside Gardens

Mount Cl

P La

Park Row

Rectory Rd

Ryecroft Road

Rylestone Close

St Peter's Crs

Sunnyside

Upr

Road

York Gdns

Np La

Brockridge La

B Cl

Bro Inf

Bourne Cl

Manor

Woodend

Dwnr Dr

West Pdg

3

Lct

Chapel La

Hillside

Watley's

Road

End

Beaver

Footes La

B4058

Cammans

Star Barn Cl

Lewton

Gazzard Cl

England Crs

End

B Cl

Factory Rd

Cl

The Gully

Harris Barton

Frome Vw

Wayside Cl

Park La

South View

Langle

Chapel La

Lower Bell

Newlan

24

St Michael's

North Road

Comm Rd

Sallys Wy

Masons Vw

Park Av

Medway Dr

Saviours Rise

Beesmoor Road

The Ridings

The Cl

Nicholls

Park Avenue

St Francis Drive

Sallen

Watley's End

BS 36

Heather Av

Kelbra Crs

Hither Mead

Manor Road

4

Elm Park Primary School

Friary Grange Park

Abbeydale

Crofton Fields

St Francis Dr

Blackberry

Vicarage Rd

The Ridings

Rd

Brook

Parkside Av

Ridings School

Cloisters

Road

River Frome

Frome Valley Walkway

Park Lane

St

BADMIN

terbourne

Michaels CE Primary School

Heath Cl

Hicks

Linden Cl

od

Park Lane

Station

The Brake

Rd

Bradley

Burrough Wy

Cl

Hicks Common

Nightingale Close

Rathbone Close

5

Deacon Cl

Frome Wy

Barton Cl

Pendock Rd

Huckford Road

Matford Rd

80

Mount Crs

B

Crossman Av

Surgery

Mapley

Avenue

67

5 Marsh

E

66

35

F

G

A432

H

Station Road

Harcombe Hill

Rose La

Quarry La

Prg Cl

Winterbourne Down

Huckford La

Frome

Park La

The Ken Golf Clu

Road

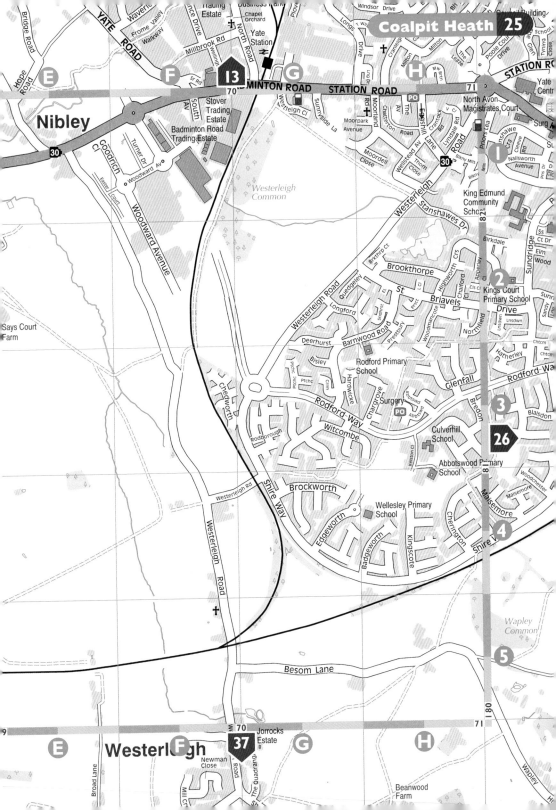

Portway Lane

Trinity Lane

Portway Lane

Johns

E

Horton Rd

Brookfield Cl

Way

F

15

Harwoodgate Farm

G

H

Portway Lane

74

75

Commonmead

Park's Farm

Jubilee Lane

I

Vavre Close

Grace Close

Frome Rd

Walshe Av

Rogers

Brandash Rd

Ridings

CHIPPING SODBURY

82

Cl

Hartley Cl

Gorlands Road

St Johns

Trading Estate

Bn Ct

Cesson Close

Frome valley way

2

Hayes Farm

HORSE STREET

Mead Rd

Kingrove Crs

Jenner Cl

Wickham

Colts Gn

Ridings Road

B4060

Woodmans Road

Wdmns Cl

Wdmns V

A432 BADMINTON ROAD

BADMINTON ROAD

A432

PO

Smarts Green

Green Hayes

Blanchards

Station Cl

New

Way

Colt's Green

Chapel Lane

3

Monarch's

81

Kingrove Common

Mill Lane

Chapel Lane

4

Coomb' End

Dodington Lane

5

Dodington Manor

Dodington

80

3

74

75

E

F

G

H

Lydes

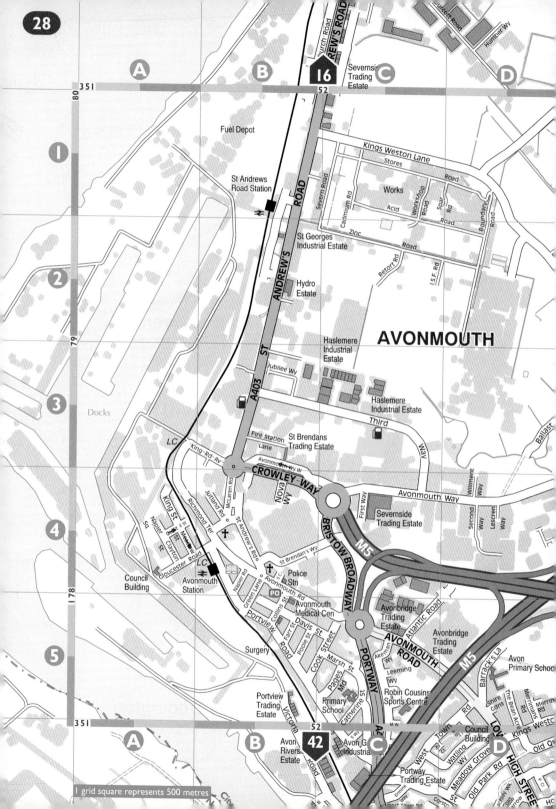

A B C D

351
80

16

Severnside Trading Estate

I

Fuel Depot

St Andrews Road Station

Kings Weston Lane

Stores

Severn Road

Works

Cadmium Rd

Acid

Zinc

Road

Workshop Road

Spar Rd

Boundary Road

Road

St Georges Industrial Estate

2
79

Hydro Estate

Retort Rd

I.S.F. Rd

Road

AVONMOUTH

Haslemere Industrial Estate

Docks

3

A403

Jubilee Wy

ST ANDREW'S ROAD

Haslemere Industrial Estate

Third Way

Ballast

LC

King Rd Av

Fire Station Lane

St Brendans Trading Estate

Avonmouth Wy W

CROWLEY WAY

Nova Wy

Avonmouth Way

Willment Way

McLaren Rd

First Way

Severnside Trading Estate

Second Way

Lescren Wy

4
178

King St

Richmond Ter

Jutland Rd

E St

Clayton St

Napier St

Sq

Meadow

Gloucester Road

St Andrew's Rd

St Brendan's Wy

BRISTOW BROADWAY

M5

Atlantic Road

Avonbridge Trading Estate

Avonbridge Trading Estate

Avon Primary Sch

LC

Council Building

Avonmouth Station

Police Stn

PO

Avonmouth Rd

Green Lane

Napier Rd

Collins St

Avonmouth Medical Cen

AVONMOUTH ROAD

Akeman Wy

Leeming Wy

PORTWAY

M5

Barrack's La

Shire Gdns

The Bean Acre

Merrimans Rd

Merrim St

5

Surgery

Portway Road

Davis St

Farr St

Poole St

Cook Street

Marsh St

Pages Rd

Robin Cousins Sports Centre

Avon Primary Sch

Old Park Rd

Meadow Grove

Kings Westo

Portview Trading Estate

Victoria

Primary School

Catherine St

Council Building

HIGH STREET

Low

351

A B

42
52

C D

Avon Riverside Estate

Avon G Industrial

Portway Trading Estate

West Town Rd

Watling

West Town

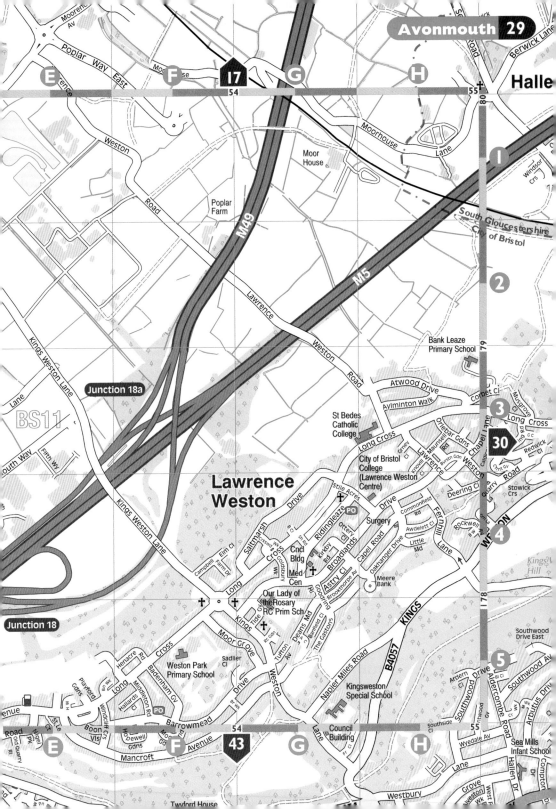

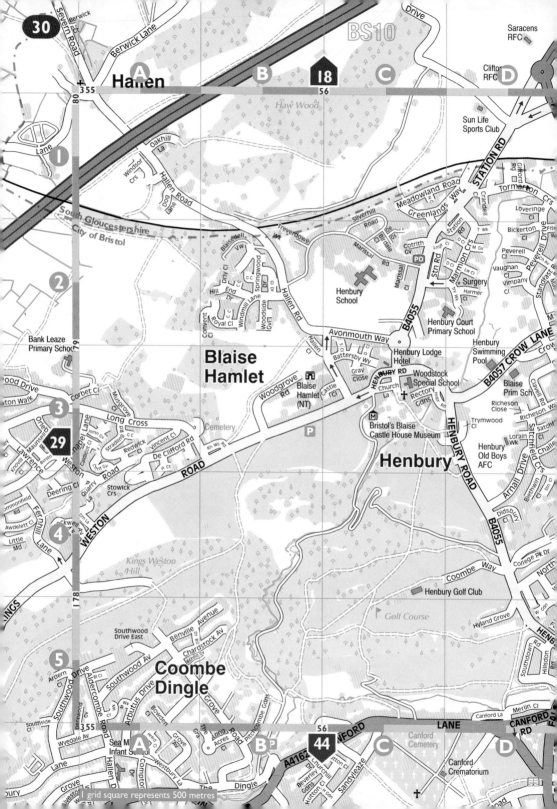

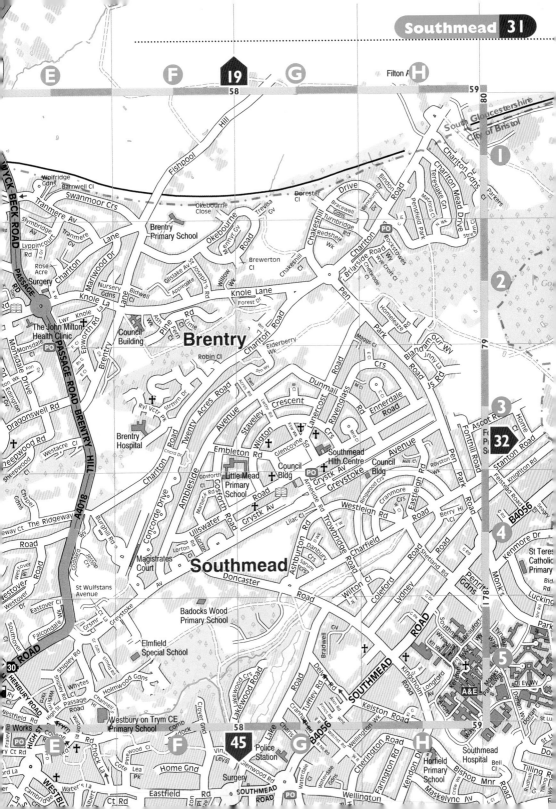

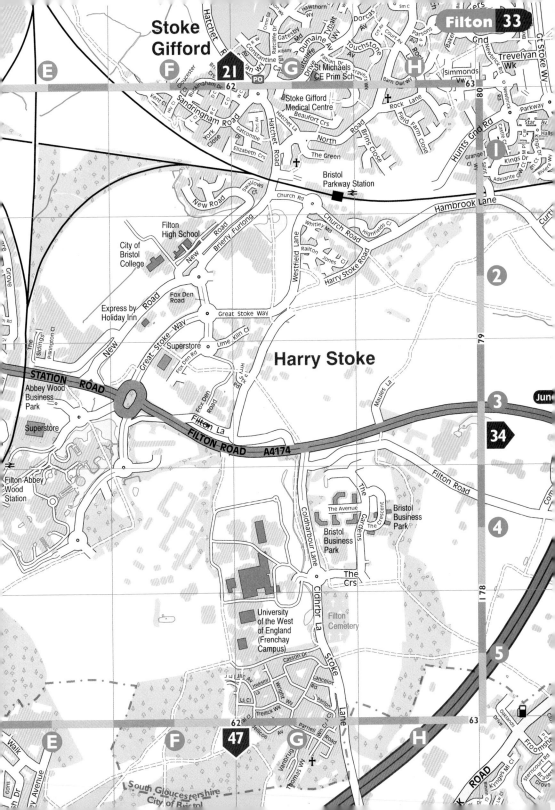

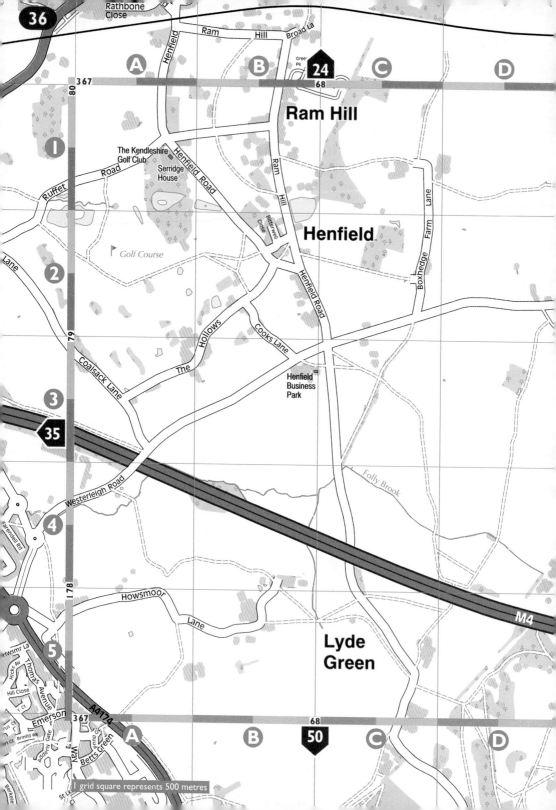

A   B   C   D

3 43   44

1

77

2

3

76

4

5

175

Black
Nore

Portishead
Lifeboat Station

Black Nore
Point

Riverleaze

Se
Nicho
Rd

Nr Ct

Svrn
Ct

Nore Pk Dr

Glenwood Rd

Brecklenwood

Cdns

Somerset
Rd

Den

Devonshire
Dr

Hawthorn
Cl

Marconi
Road

Knw

Nwp
Ct

Mnm
Ct

Mhm Ct

MGW

Woodside
Cdns

Beechwood
Rd

Sage
Cl

Hillcrest

Road

King's Rd

PK
Lindsey

Merlin

Me

Gaunts
Cl

Rnchry's

Cl

Gn
Cl

PK
Cl

Hang
Rock

Hallwell
Rd

Little Halt

Road

Hillside

Newhaven
Pl

Nore Road

Seaview Road

Queens
Rd

Queens
Wy

St Augustine's
Close

Harmony
Dr

Weatherley Drive

Redcliff
Bay

Newhaven Road

Pembroke
Rd

Cedarnurst Rd

Road

HCct

Rdc Cl

Down

Chestle
Wy

Brock
End

Chesterfield

Badger Rise

B W

Wtnd Pk

Hillside Road

Northfield
Rd

Highfield

Drive

Brock End

Brock End

Nightingale Rise

Redcliff Bay

Charlcombe
Bay

charlcome
Rise

Down
Rd

3 43   44

A   B   C   D

ston
Down

Blackberry
La

alton

1 grid square represents 500 metres

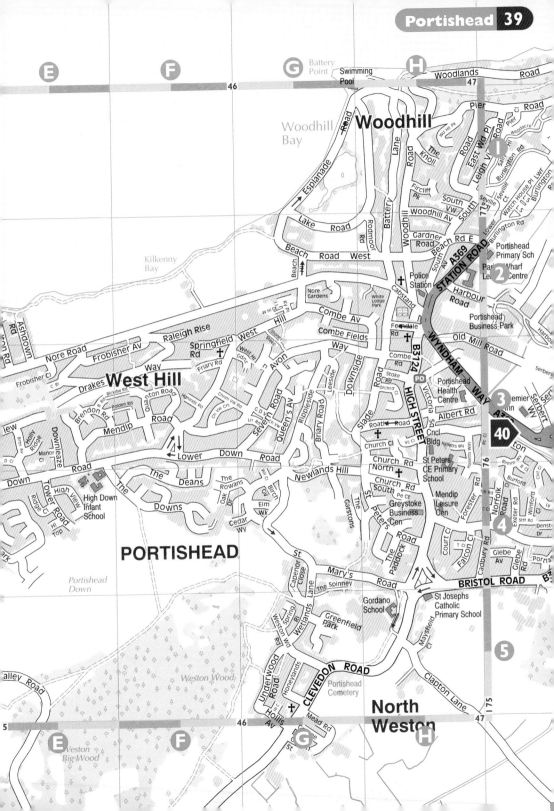

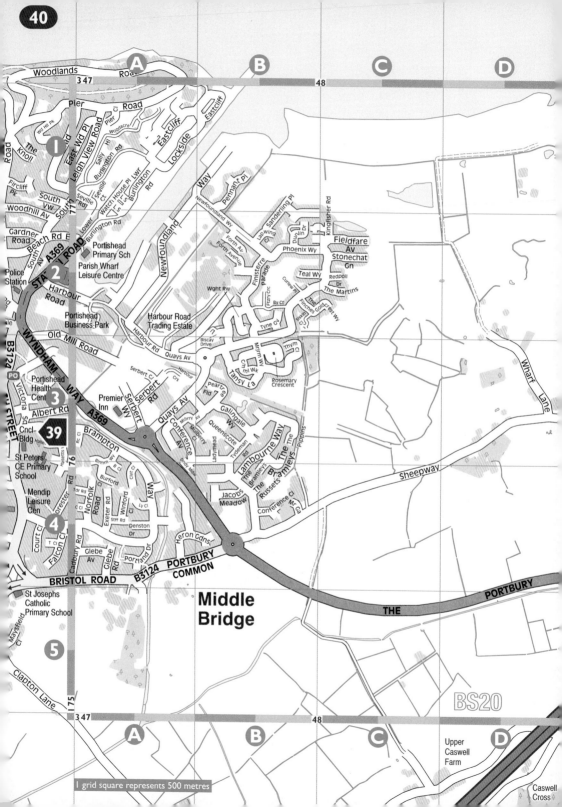

A 3 47 **B** 48 **C** **D**

Woodlands Road

Pier Road

Wd Hill Pk

The Knoll

Pier Road
Woodacre

Fircliff Pk

Eastcliff
Lockside
Eastcliff

East Wd Pl
Leigh View Road
Sally Hl
Burlington Ct
Seville
Watch House Pl Lwr
Seville Rd
Lower Burlington Rd
S Ls Burlington Rd
Burlington Rd
Woodacre Rd

Way

Pennant Pl

Newfoundland Wy

South Vw
Woodhill Av
South 71

Gardner Road

Beach Rd E
South Rd
STATION ROAD
A369

Portishead Primary Sch

Parish Wharf Leisure Centre

Police Station
B3124

Finisterre Parade
Forth Av
Forth Avenue

La Wing
Sanderling Pl
Dublin Dr

Phoenix Wy

Kingfisher Rd

Fieldfare Av
Stonechat Gn
Redpoll Dr

Teal Wy

2

Harbour Road

Portishead Business Park

Harbour Road Trading Estate

Harbour Rd

Wght Rw

Fizzy Crc
By Ct

Curlew Rd

The Martins

The Finches
Sea Wl
Goldcrest Wy

Newfoundland

Old Mill Road

WYNDHAM WAY

Quays Av

Harbour Crs

Biscay Drive

Tyne Gv

Mrnm Wk
Cml Wk

Thym

Rosemary Crescent

PO

Portishead Health Cent

Serbert Cl
Serbert Rd
Serbert Wy

Harbour

Pearce Fld

Tansy La

Galingale Wy

3
Albert Rd A369

Victoria Sq

Premier Inn

Quays Av
Conference Av

Milbry Av
Mulberry

Queenscote
Ladymead
Tydeman Rd

Pippins

Lambourne Way

The Bramleys
The Russets

39

Cncl Bldg
Halletts

Brampton

RC Cl

76

Forrester Rd
Hayletts

Way

Norfolk Road
Blrmm Wy
B Cl
CWt

Burford
Binmm Wy

Conference Cl
Mr Ga

Jacobs Meadow

Sheepway

St Peters CE Primary School

Mendip Leisure Cen

4

Court Cl
Falcon Cl
Cadbury Rd

Tdr Rd
Ly Cl

Exeter Rd
Stff Rd

Winford
Denston Dr

Glebe Rd
Glebe Av
Portland Dr

Heron Gdns

PORTBURY COMMON
B3124

5

BRISTOL ROAD

St Josephs Catholic Primary School

Maysfield

Clapton Lane

175

Middle Bridge

THE PORTBURY

BS20

Upper Caswell Farm

Caswell Cross

A 3 47 **B** 48 **C** **D**

1 grid square represents 500 metres

The Royal Portbury Dock

E   F   G   H

50   51

Normans Wy

St George's Road

Gordano Road

Portbury Sawmills Industrial Estate

Redland Av

Marsh Lane

Royal Portbury Dock Road

The Drove

First Avenue

Garonor Way

Sheepway

Portbury Way

Gordano Way

Barnyard Road

Bradley Road

Royal Portbury Dock Road

The Dro

Station Road

Junction 19

Days Inn

Gordano Service Area

A369 THE PORTBURY HUNDRED

M5

A369

Priory Rd

Priory Farm Trading Estate

St Marys CE VA Primary School

Church La

Church

High   Street

St George

Portbury

High St

Forge End

Hillside

Brittan Place

Gordano RFC

M5

E   F   G   H

50   51

Mill Close

Mill Lane

Portb

1   2   3   42   4   5

77   76   175

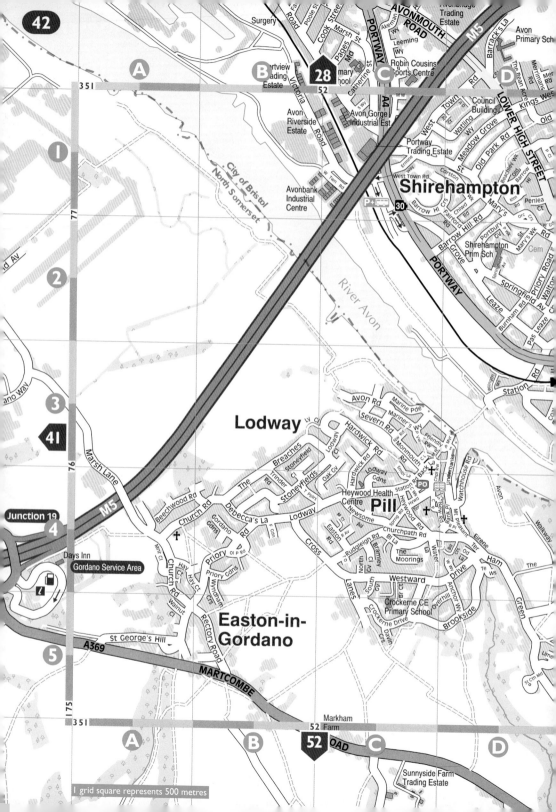

Weston Park Primary School

Kingsweston Special School

Sadlier Cl

Council Building

Sea Mills Infant School

E

F

29

G

H

54

55

I

Barrowmead

Mancroft

Twyford Park House CC

Penpole

SHIREHAMPTON ROAD B4054

Shirehampton Park

Westbury

Sunny Hill

Portway Community School

Lane

Shirehampton CC

Golf Course

Sea Mills

PARK HILL B4054

Shirehampton Park Golf Club

STREET B4054

Clifford Gdns

2

SHIREHAMPTON

Park Road

A4162

Shirehampton Swimming Pool

Valerian Cl

A4

40

Woodleaze

Brookleaze

Woodwell Road

Sea Mills Junior Sch

Dursley

Nibley

Road

Chapel Pill Farm

3

City of Bristol
North Somerset

Avon Walkway

Manor Farm AFC

44

PORTWAY

City & Port of Bristol Social & Sports Club

Orchard View (Ham Green Hospital)

Pill

Lane

Sea Mills Station

4

Chapel

Roman

Ham Green

Macrae Rd

Hart

Fitzhardinge Road

5

St Katherines School

Leigh Court Business Centre

E

F

53

G

H

54

55

River

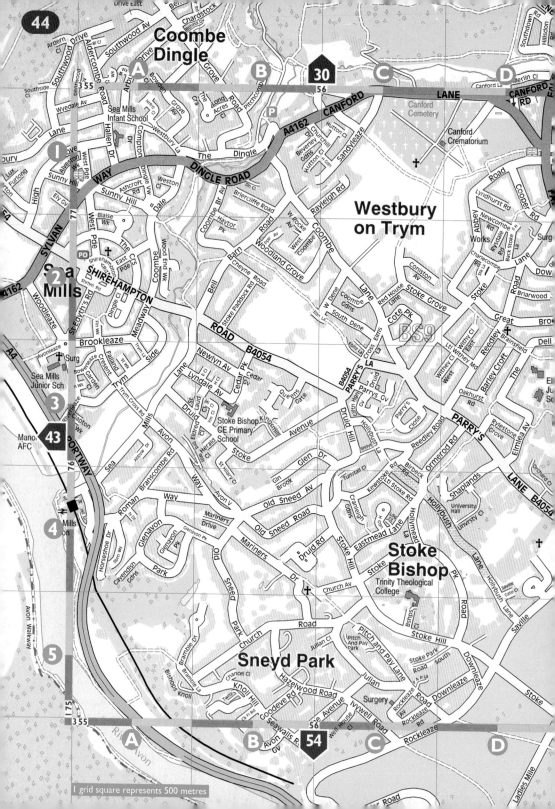

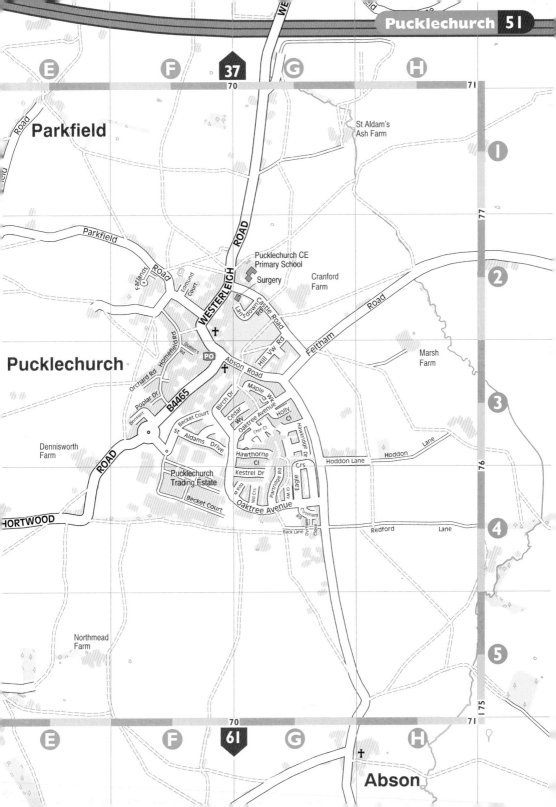

E F **37** G H

70 71

Road

Parkfield

St Aldam's
Ash Farm

Parkfield

Road

WESTERLEIGH   ROAD

Farlands   Road

Edmund
Court

Pucklechurch CE
Primary School

Surgery

Cranford
Farm

Feltham   Road

Marsh
Farm

Homefield   Rd

Queen's
Rd

Castle Rd

Laurs Down Cl

Castle   Road

Hill Vw Rd

Pucklechurch

Orchard Rd

PO

Abson   Road

Poplar Dr

Drinswrt

B4465

Maple
Wk

Birch Dr

Cedar
Wy

Holly
Cl

Oaktree Avenue

Chrr Ct

Hawkridge Rd

Hoddon   Lane

Hoddon

Lane

Becket Court

St
Aldams   Drive

**Dennisworth
Farm**

**Puck church
Trading Estate**

Hawthorne
Cl

Kestrel Dr

M Rdg

Wd Crs

Partridge Rd

M Td

Eagle
Crs

Redford   Lane

ROAD

Becket Court

Oaktree   Avenue

Back Lane

Cossham

Clock Dr

HORTWOOD

**Northmead
Farm**

Abson

I

77

2

76

3

4

175

5

70 71

E F **61** G H

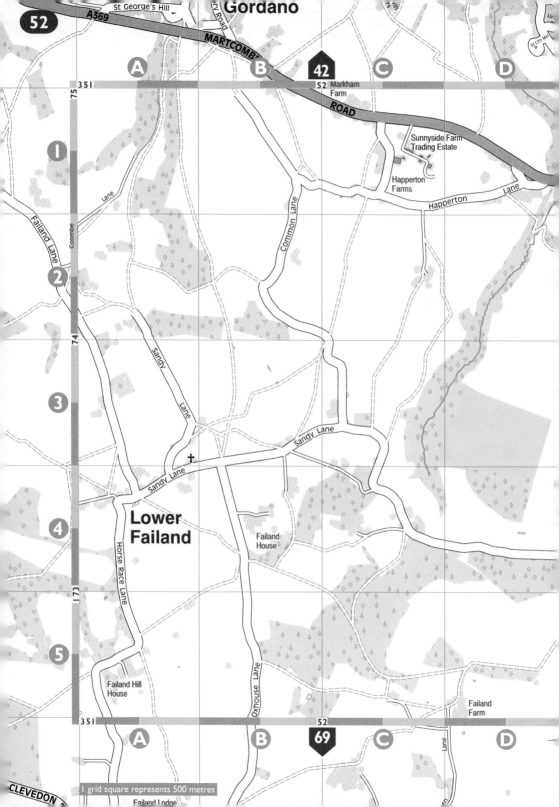

St Katherines
School

E   F   **43**   G   H

54

Road

Blackmoor

Road

Leigh Court
Business
Centre

ERFIELD HILL

A369 PILL ROAD

River Avon

I

2

3

54

4

Haberfield
Park Farm

Abbots Leigh

Church   Road

Monarch's   Way

Dennyview Road

Knightcott Rd

Glen
Av

Sandy Lane

Harris Lane

Manor Lane

The Mnr Cl

Manor
Road

Manor
House

A369

Home Farm   Road

Monarch's W

30 ABBOTS

Ashgrove
Av

LEIGH

Clifton
College
Sports Club

Glen
Farm

BS8

Manor Road

Upper
Farm

Cotham Park
RFC

BEGGAR BUSH LANE

B3129

5   Lei

Lei

E   F   **70**   G   H

54

Weir
Lane

Golf Course

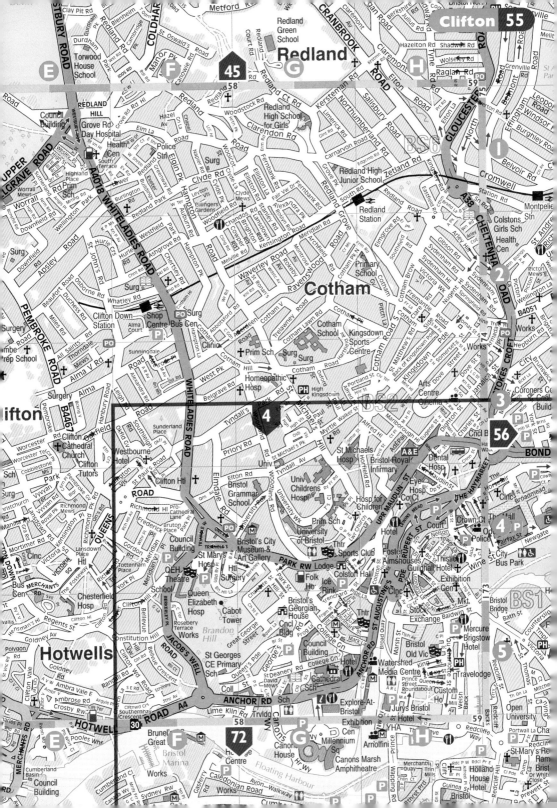

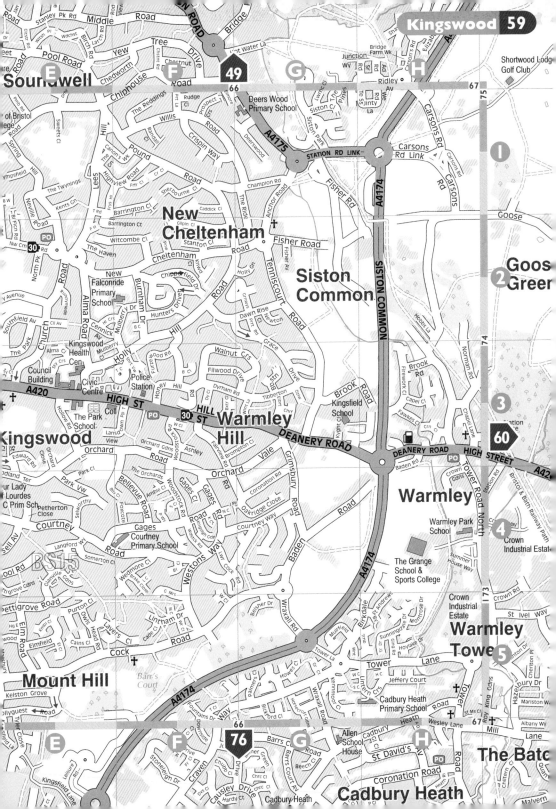

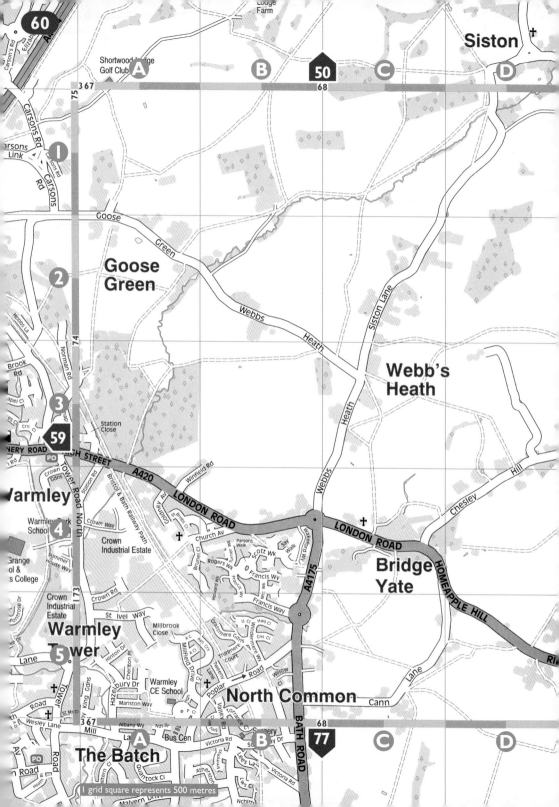

60

Siston

Shortwood Lodge
Golf Club **A**

B

50

C

D

I

Carsons Rd
Link

Carsons
Rd

Carsons Rd

3 67

75

2

Goose
Green

Goose

Green

Webbs

Heath

Webb's
Heath

74

Norman Rd

Brook
Rd

3

Station
Close

Siston Lane

Heath

59

PO

HIGH STREET

A420 LONDON ROAD

Winfield Rd

Webbs

LONDON ROAD

Chesley Hill

Warmley

Crown
Gdns

Tower Road North

Station Rd

Bristol & Bath Railway Path

Colthurst Av

Winfield Rd

Church Av

St Brids Cl

Parsons
Walk

Scott Wk

Sav
Walk

Wakeford Rd

A4175

LONDON ROAD

HOMEAPPLE HILL

Bridge
Yate

4

Warmley Park
School

Crown Way

Crown
Industrial Estate

Rogers Wk

Francis Wy

Summer
House Way

Grange
ol &
s College

Crown Rd

Crown
Industrial
Estate

173

St Ivel Way

Millbrook
Close

Howard Av

Brunel Wy

Francis Way

Francis Way

Windermere Wy

Grasmere Gdns

Cns Cl

Ws Cl

D

Cns Cl

Chesley Hill

5

Warmley
Tower

Lane

Hinton Cl

Cheriton Pl

King Gdns

Hazelbury Dr

Millfield Drive

Thirlmere
Court

Ash Cl

Torance Cl

Tweeny Rd

Willow
Road

Poplar Lane

Valley Rd

Cann Lane

Road

Montrose Dr

Wesley Lane

St Mcs Cl

Warmley
CE School

Mariston Way

PO

North Common

Cann Ri

3 67

A

B

77

BATH ROAD

C

D

The Batch

PO

Albany Wy

Nds Dr

Bus Cen

Quantock Cl

Victoria Rd

Victoria Rd

Lees La

Atheston

Summers

Lwr Cl

Lees Cl

ery Dr

Nchifts

Malvern

Av

Road

Road

Mill

La

1 grid square represents 500 metres

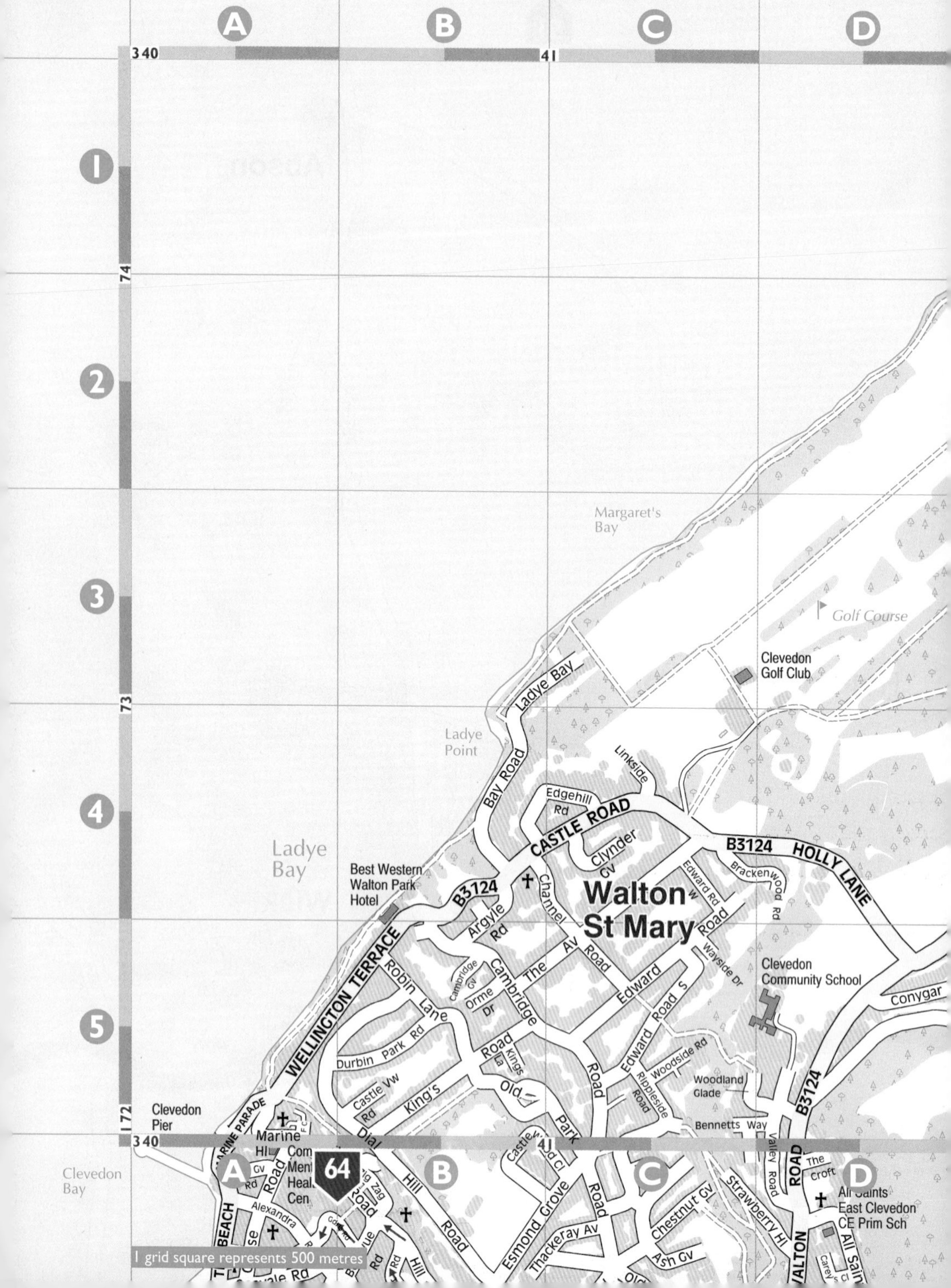

A   B   C   D

340   41

74

1

2

Margaret's
Bay

3

73

Golf Course

Ladye Bay

Clevedon
Golf Club

Ladye
Point

Ladye
Bay

Edgehill
Rd

Bay Road

Linkside

CASTLE ROAD

Clynder
GV

B3124   HOLLY LANE

4

Best Western
Walton Park
Hotel

B3124

Channel Road

Edward Rd

Brackenwood Rd

Walton
St Mary

Argyle Rd

Cambridge Road

Orme Dr

The Av

Road

Edward
Road

Wayside Dr

W

Clevedon
Community School

Conygar

WELLINGTON TERRACE

Robin Lane

Durbin Park Rd

Castle Vw Rd

King's Road

Edward Road S

Woodside Rd

Riddleside

Road

Edward Road

Woodland
Glade

B3124

5

172

Clevedon
Pier

MARINE PARADE

Kings Old Park

Castle Rd

Bennetts Way

VALLEY ROAD

The Croft

340   41

Clevedon
Bay

A   B   64   C   D

Marine
Hill

Com
Men
Heal
Cen

GV
Rd

Alexandra

BEACH

se

Dial

Hill Road

Esmond Grove

Castle Road

Chestnut GV

Strawberry HI

WALTON ROAD

All Saints
East Clevedon
CE Prim Sch

All Saint

Thackeray Av

Ash GV

Carey

E F G H

43 44

I

Walton
Bay

Heron Wk

Skylark
Avenue

Farley

Pigeon
House
Bay

Walton
Down

74

B3124

Hack's
Wood

2

3

Walton Moor

73

**Walton-in-
Gordano** †

Walton

Drove

Harley Lane

4

**Norton's
Wood**

Clevedon Lane

Nortons Wood Lane

M5

Cadbury Camp Lane West

5

Norton's
Wood

The
Warren

E **65** F G H

43 44 172 Orchard Av

Hill

Lane

CLEVEDON ROAD B31

Court Wood

Clevedon B3130

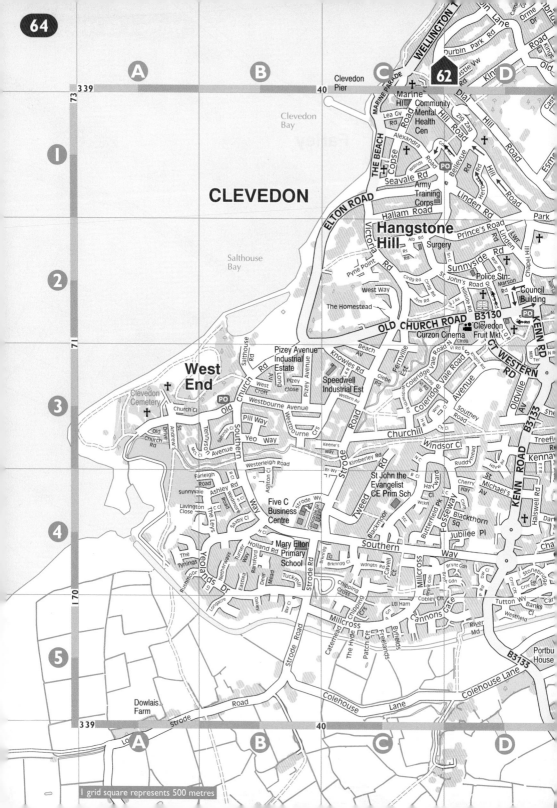

CLEVEDON

Clevedon Bay

Clevedon Pier

Clevedon Bay

Salthouse Bay

Marine Hill

Marine Community Mental Health Cen

Lea Gv Rd

Copse

Alexandra

Seavale Rd

Army Training Corps

Hallam Rd

Hangstone Hill

Surgery

Pyne Point

West Way

The Homestead

West End

Clevedon Cemetery

Church Cl

Salthouse Rd

West Croft

Pizey Close

Pizey Avenue

Pizey Avenue Industrial Estate

Knowles Rd

Speedwell Industrial Est

Westbourne Avenue

Westbourne Crs

Beach

Glebe

Fernville

Churchill

Windsor Cl

Coleridge Vale Road

Avenue

Southey Road

GT WESTERN RD

KENN RD

Old Church Rd

Pill Way

Yeo Way

Westerleigh Road

Keene's Way

Kimberley Rd

Br Wy

Strode Road

St John the Evangelist CE Prim Sch

St Michael's Av

Cherry Hay

Blackthorn Av

Farleigh Road

Sunnyvale

Ashley Rd

Wedmore

Saxby Cl

Lavington Close

Five C Business Centre

Hayward

Butterfield Pk

Fosseway

Jubilee Pl

The Leys

The Tynings

Yeolands Dr

Holland Rd

Mary Elton Primary School

Strode Rd

Southern Way

Millcross

Jubilee Pl

Turner Way

Ransford

Deer Mead

Tuckmill

Brknrdg

Wdngtn Rd

Cavell Ct

Cobley Cft

Cannons Gate

Dowlais Farm

Strode Road

Millcross

Catenhead

The Hyde

Patch Cft

Byfields

Freelands

Chipping Cross

Colehouse Lane

B3133

Portbu House

Colehouse Lane

OLD CHURCH ROAD

Curzon Cinema

Clevedon Fruit Mkt

B3130

Council Building

Police Stn

Sunnyside Rd

Prince's Road

Linden Rd

Park

Victoria Rd

ELTON ROAD

THE BEACH

Dial Hill Road

Wellington T

Durbin Park Rd

King Rd

Zig Zag

Bellevue

62

KENN ROAD

B3133

Oldville Av

Halswell Rd

Treefield

Kenna

St John's Road

Marson Rd

1 grid square represents 500 metres

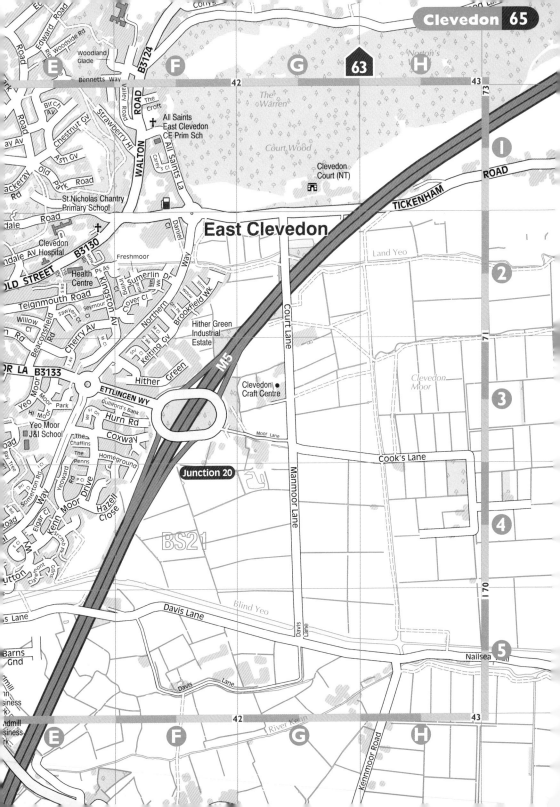

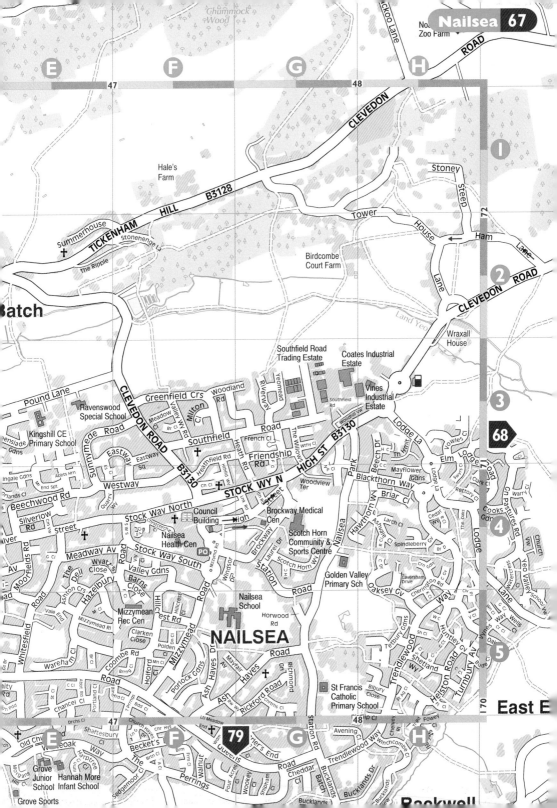

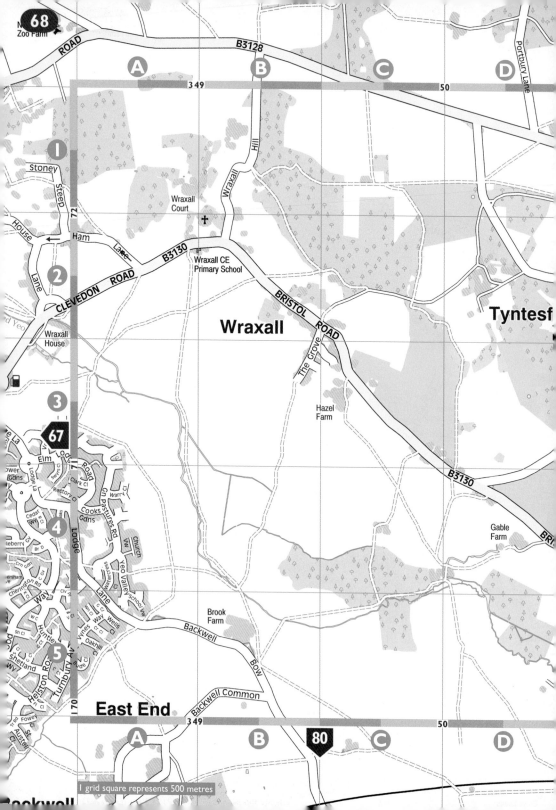

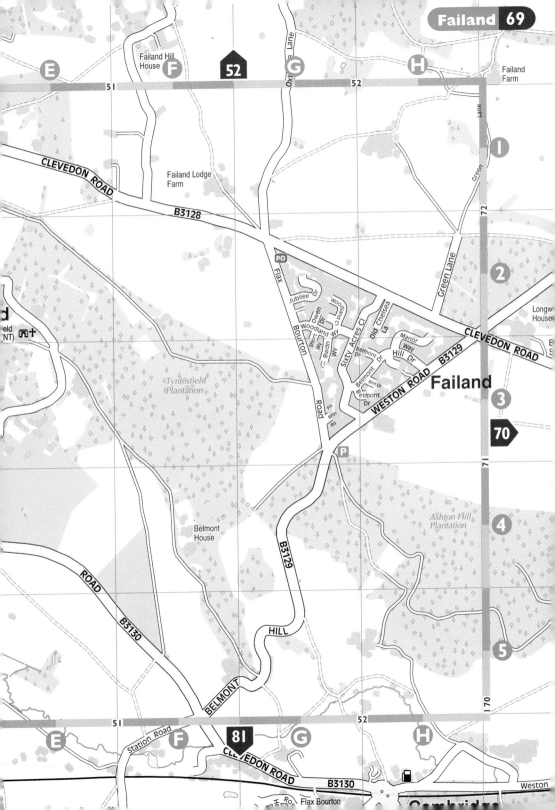

E   **F**   **52**   **G**   **H**

Failand Hill
House

Failand
Farm

I

CLEVEDON ROAD

Failand Lodge
Farm

B3128

72

2

PO

Flax

Jubilee Dr

Woodland Wy

Owen Dr

Short Wy

Bwdn Wy

Wood
land D

SIXTY ACRES CL

Old Chelsea La

Belmont Dr

Green Lane

CLEVEDON ROAD

Longw
House

Manor
Way

Hill Dr

Belmont Dr

Belmont
Dr

Tyntesfield
Plantation

Bourton

Road

B3129

WESTON ROAD

Failand

3

71

70

eld
(NT)

P

Belmont
House

Ashton Hill
Plantation

4

ROAD

B3130

B3129

HILL

BELMONT

5

170

51

E   Station Road   **F**   **81**   **G**   **H**

CLEVEDON ROAD

B3130

Weston

Flax Bourton

Cambridge

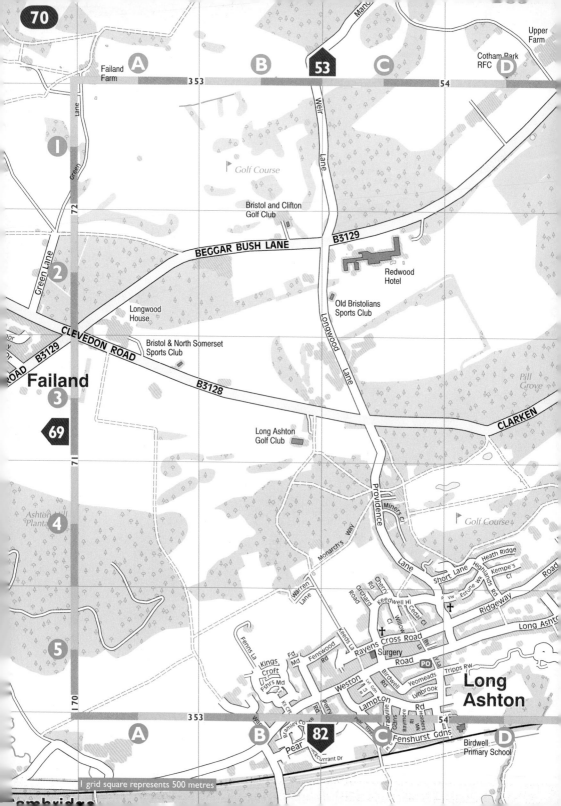

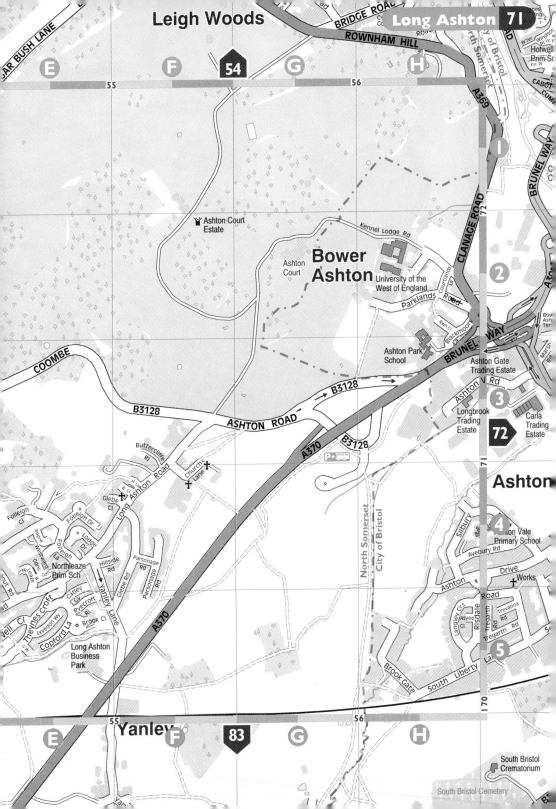

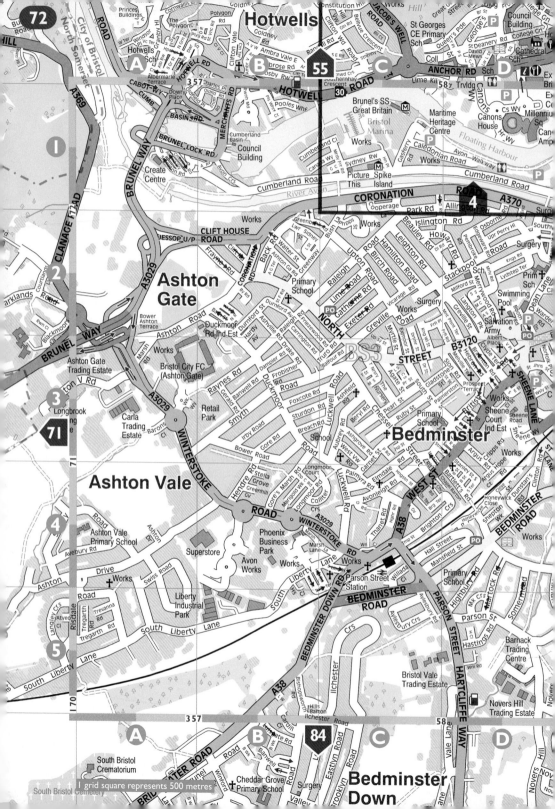

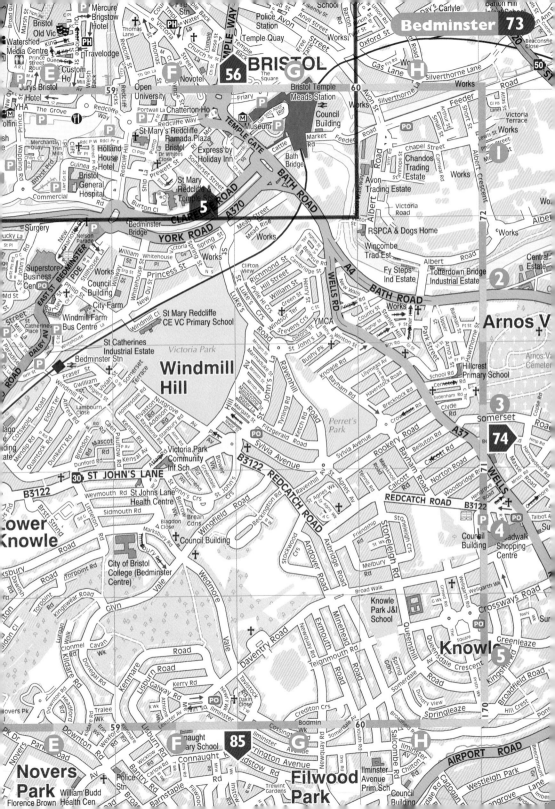

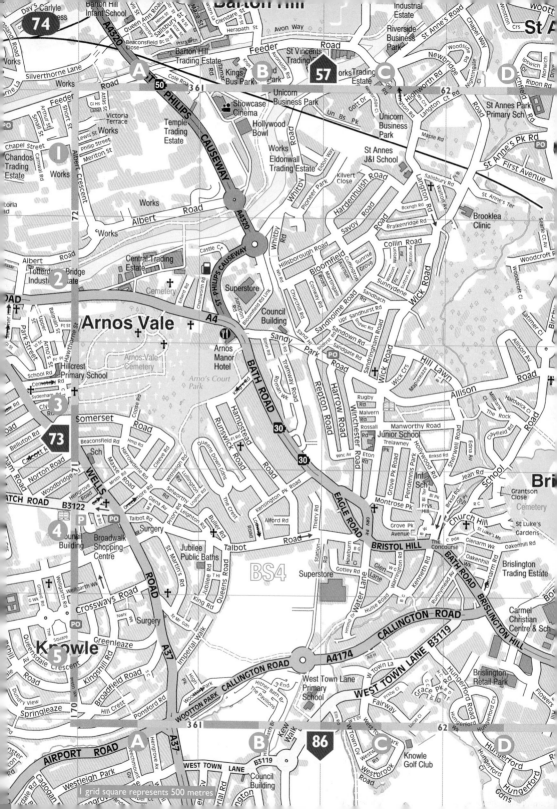

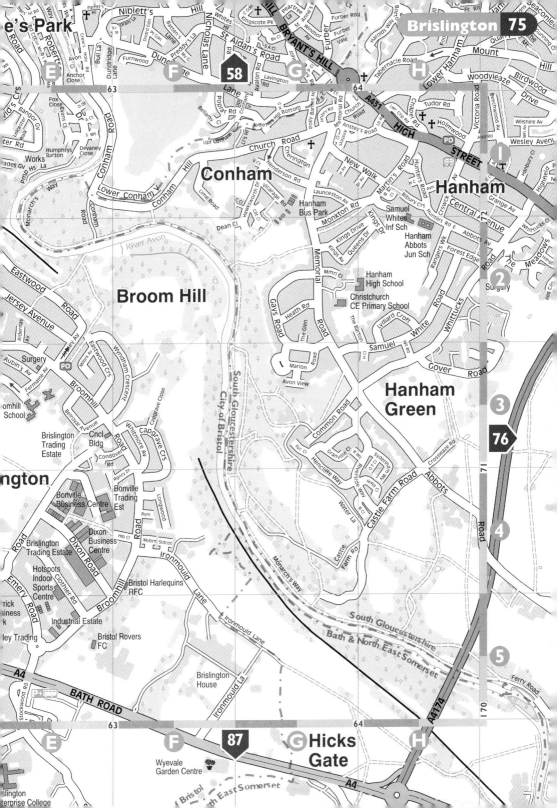

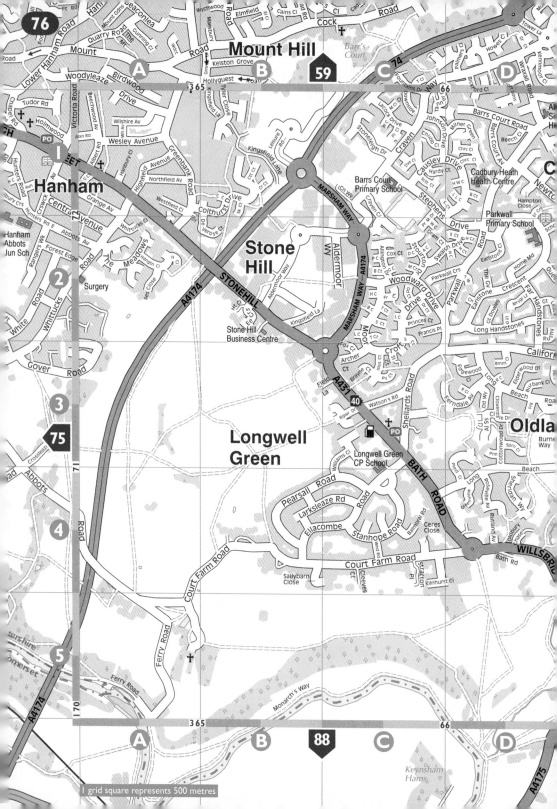

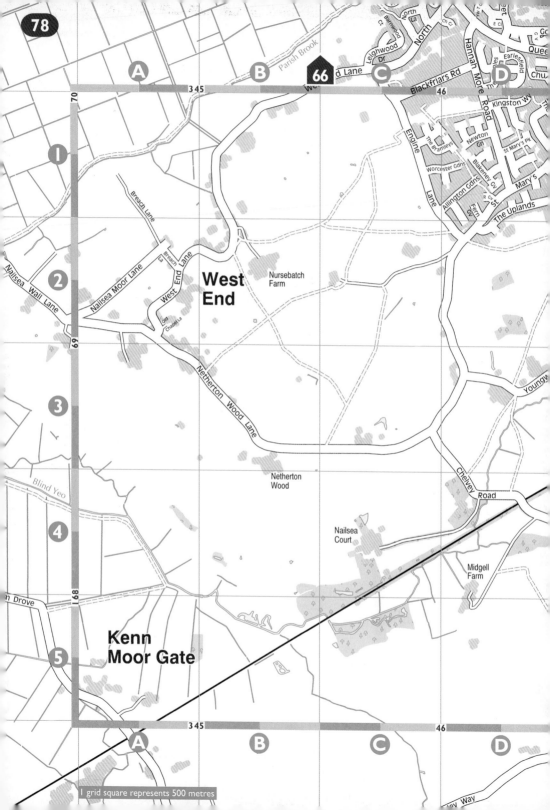

A
B
66
C
D

345
70
Parish Brook
d Lane
Blackfriars Rd
46
North
Leighwood Dr
Barnwood
North La
Ch Cl
Hannah More Road
Kingston Wy
Quee
Earlesfield
Chu

I
Engine Lane
The Bramleys
Newton Gn
St Mary's Pk
Worcester Gdns
Blakeney Gv
Allington Gdns
St Mary's
Fern Gv
The Uplands

Breach Lane
Nailsea Moor Lane
Breach La
West End Lane
West End
Nursebatch Farm
2
Nailsea Wall Lane
69
Old Chapel La

Netherton Wood Lane
3
Youngw

Blind Yeo
Netherton Wood
Chelvey Road
4
168
Nailsea Court
Midgell Farm

Drove
Kenn Moor Gate
5
345
46

A
B
C
D

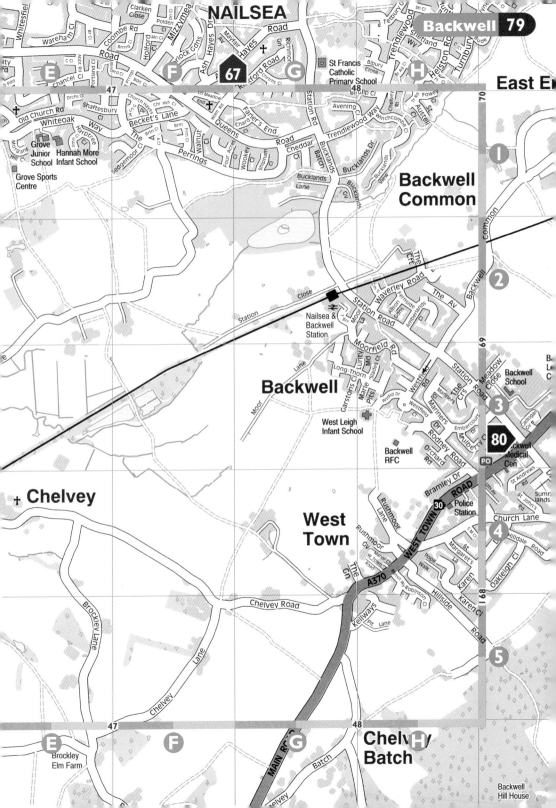

NAILSEA

East E

Backwell
Common

Nailsea &
Backwell
Station

Backwell

West Leigh
Infant School

Backwell
RFC

+ **Chelvey**

**West
Town**

Police
Station

Backwell
Medical
Cen

Church Lane

Chelvey Road

Brockley Elm Farm

Cheley
Batch

Backwell
Hill House

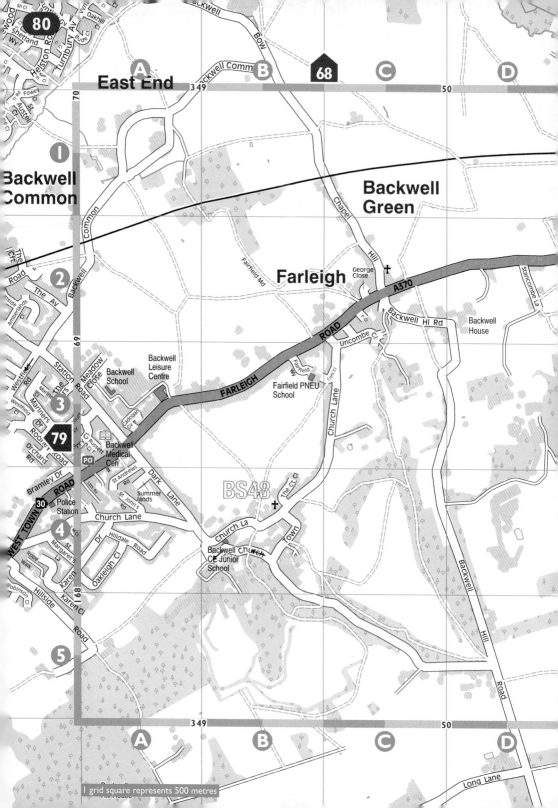

E   **F**   **G**   **H**

69 BELM

51   52   70

Station Road

CLEVEDON ROAD

B3130

I

Weston R

Flax Bourton CE
Primary
School

Orchard Cl

Head Cft

Rosemount Rd

Rd

Rosemount

Flax Bourton
Magistrates Court

**Cambridge
Batch**

Office La

Church Lane

Parsons Md

Br M

Old Weston Road

Redwood Lane

Land Yeo

ROAD   **MAIN**   **30**

A370

2

Bourton Combe

**Flax
Bourton**

B3130

Redwood La

Redwe
Farm

3

82

Barrow Court Lane

Vicarage   Lane

69

Bourton
Combe

†

Barrow
Court

BARROW

4

Scho

Home
Farm

168

Slade

Lane

**Ba
G**

5

51   52

E   **F**   **92**   **G**   **H**

Hyattswood

82

A B **70** C D

Long Ashton

Fenns La
Kings Croft
Ths Md
Keeds La
Fenswood Rd
Ravens Cross Road
Surgery
Cross Road
Weston
PO
Birdwell Rd
Yeomeads
Lynbrook
Tripps Rw
Lamb
Bradville Gdns
Holders
Raymore Av
Fenshurst Gdns

Warren La
Bamley Copse
Pear Tree Av
Blackcurrant Dr
Pear Tree Av

Birdwell
Primary School

I

**Cambridge
Batch**

Weston Road

Redwood Lane
Land Yeo

Wildcountry Lane

A370

2

Redwood La
Redwood Farm

Monarch's Way

Barrow
Hospital

3

81

Barrow
Wood

BARROW

4

STREET

School La

Lane

Wildcountry

Hern Lane

B3130

Reservoir

Barrow
Street

Barns
Close

**Barrow
Gurney**

5

Hobbs Lane

A B **93** C D

Reservoir

A38

Reservoir

BR

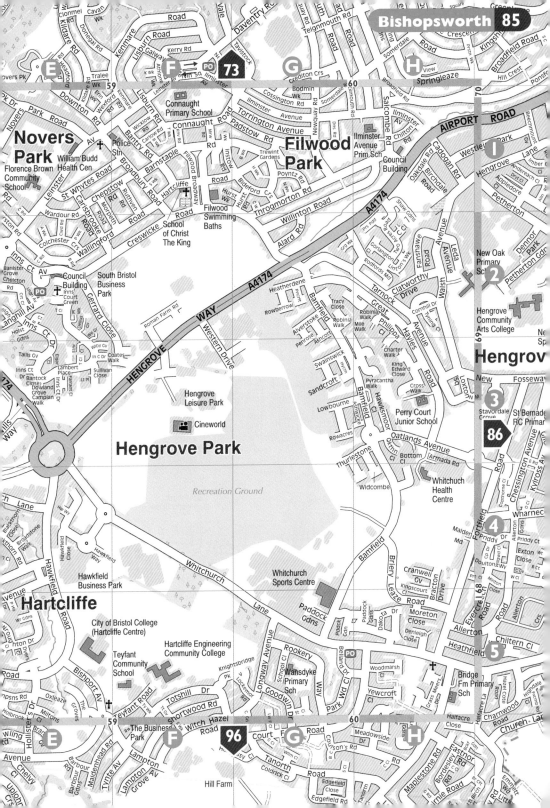

ey Trading

Bristol Rovers FC

A4

BATH ROAD

Stockwood Rd

P+R

E

63

F

Brislington House

75

Iron

G

64

H

A4174

70

I

Brislington Enterprise College

Scotland Lane

Wyevale Garden Centre

City of Bristol

Bath and North East Somerset

Hicks Gate

A4

Durley Hill

A4175

Durley

sham Cemetery

2

DURLEY HILL

Scotland Lane

Stockwood Open Space Nature Reserve

Stockwood Vale Golf Club

Golf Course

Stockwood Hill

Stockwood Vale

69

Broadlands School

Francis

3

88

St

St George

Warman Cl

Warman Rd

Road

Cottle Edge Rd

Derrick

Road

Matthews Close

Lane

Townsend

Townsend Road

Road

Copse

Bitfield

St

Winscombe Cl

Reeve

Selworthy

Mendip Close

Staple

Wheathill Close

Lockingwell

Road

Heathfield Close

4

Westfield Close

Charlton Road

Monmouth Rd

Ludlow Close

Barnard Walk

A4

Lays Drive

Queens

Lincoln Close

Caernarvon

Walton Close

Durham Grove

Caroline Cl

Lays Farm

Norfolk Grove

sworth Cl

Warwick

PO

5

Fareleigh

Corc

Longmeadow

Birch

Holmoak Road

Cedar

Maple Walk

Oak Tree Wk

Holly Wk

Bramfo

New

Walnut Close

63

E

F

64

G

H

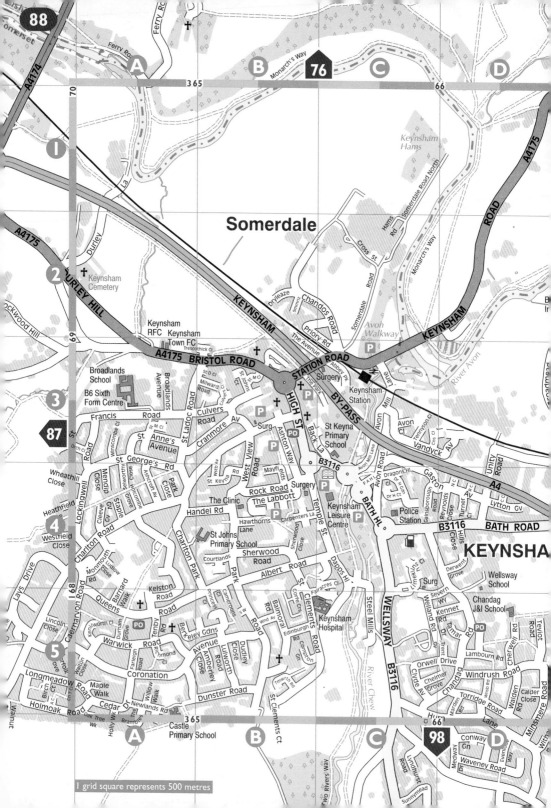

Keynsham **89**

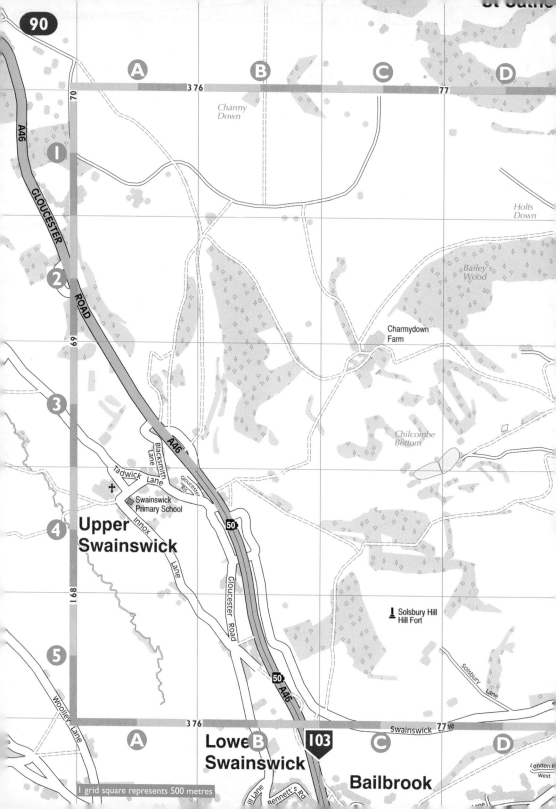

90

A 3 76 B C 77 D

70

A46

GLOUCESTER

1

ROAD

2

69

Charmy
Down

Holts
Down

Bailey's
Wood

Charmydown
Farm

3

A46

Blacksmith
Lane

Tadwick Lane

Gloucester Rd

Chilcombe
Bottom

Swainswick
Primary School

50

4

**Upper
Swainswick**

Innox Lane

68

Gloucester Road

Solsbury Hill
Hill Fort

5

Solsbury Lane

50

A46

Woolley Lane

A 3 76 B **103** swainswick 77 e C D

Lowe

B

Swainswick

ill Lane

Bennett's Rd

Bailbrook

London
West

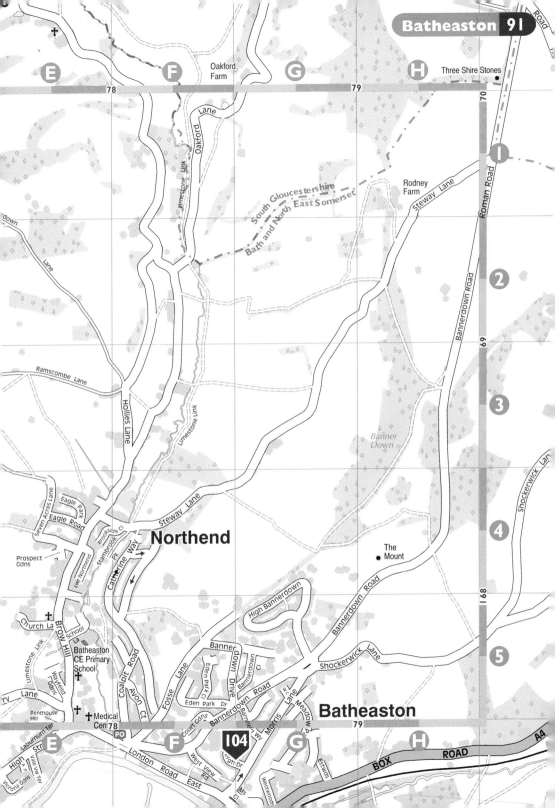

A 351 B 81 C 52 D

1

Hyattswood Farm

Hyatts Wood Road

67

Freemans Lane

2

3

Oatfield

66

Potters Hill

A38

Newditch Lane

Currells Lane

4

Coombe Dl

Downside Road

West Lane

Stanshalls Close

Hillview Gdns

Upper Pound Rd

Stanshalls Lane

Frog Lane

Orct Cl

Lulsgate Bottom

North Side Road

School La

St Katharine's Primary School

Road

i

N Side Road

Bristol International Airport

Felton Street

West Lane

5

65

Bath

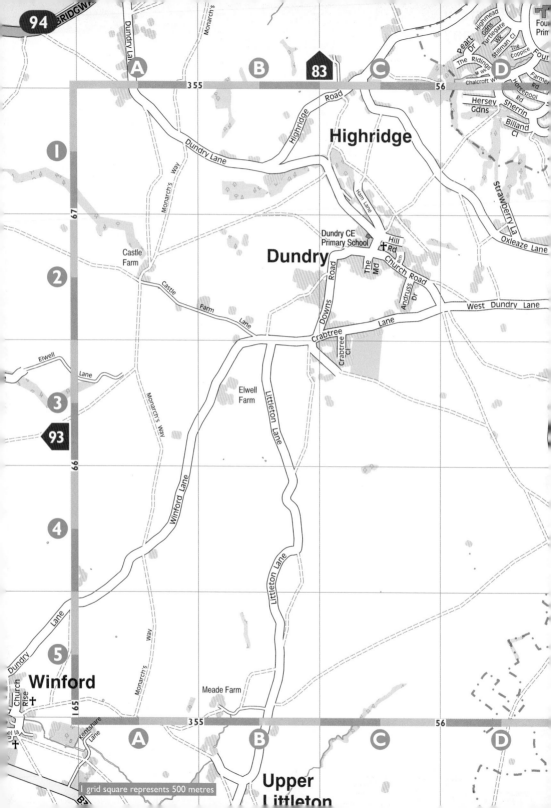

A B C D

1

67

Kelston

Manor
Farm †

A431

Kelston
Park

Dean Hill
House

Bristol & Bath Railway Path

2

Cotswold Way

Avon Walkway

3

River Avon

KELSTON

66

River Avon

Avon Walkway

4

Corston Lane

St Teresas
Private Hospital

The Orch

Goold
Cl

The Barton

PO

Meadlands

Bristol & Bath Railway Path

BRISTOL ROAD A4

BRISTOL ROAD

A4

Hill

5

165

† WELLS ROAD A39

PH

Corston Drive

A B C D

370

Pennyquid

71

Newton St Loe

I grid square represents 500 metres

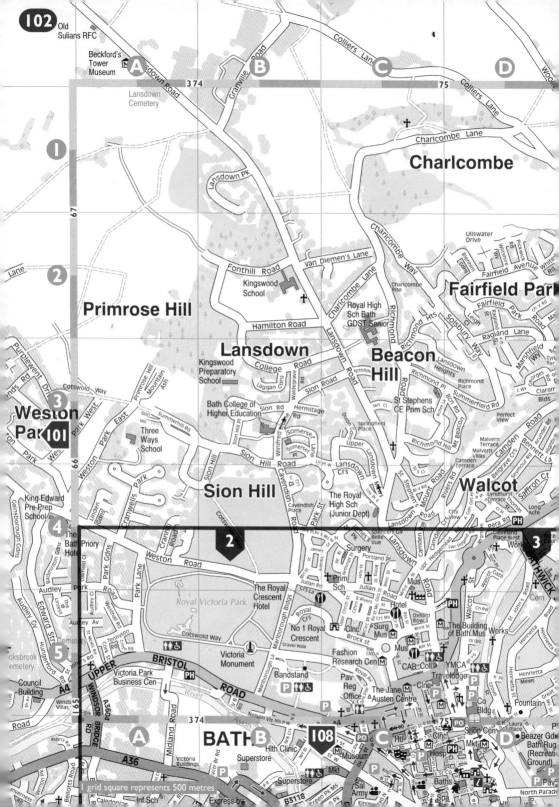

Batheaston CE Primary School

Banner
Shockerwick Lane

Limestone Link
Weyfield Gdns

Solsbury Lane **A**

Coalpit Road
Avon Ct
Lane
Eden Park Cl
Court Gdns
Eden Park
B Banner
Bannerdown Cl
Bannerdown Road
Morris
Westwoods
C Meadow Park
Estwds

Batheaston 79

D

Penthouse Hill
Medical Centre
378
PO

Laburnum Ter
Street
High
A
Vale View Ter
Victoria Gdns
London Road
West View Rd
Warleigh Dr
Elms Cl

London Road East

Ims

BOX ROAD

London Road West
1

67

Toll
Bridge Rd T Whrf
Toll

A4

Avon

50
Mill Lane

Bathford Hill
Ostlings Lane
A363
Church Cl
Church Street
Manor Dr
DVIS
PO
Bathford Prim Sch
Dovers Lane
Hig
As

2

LC

Bathampton Primary School
Church Cl
Tyning Road
Limestone Link
Mountain Wood
Dovers Park

Bathfor

Avon Walkway
PH

Court La Lane

Kennet Park
Half butts
High Street
Dark Lane
The Normans
Holcombe Vale
Down Lane
3

Lane
103
Devonshire Road
Holcombe
PO
Holcombe Close
Downside Ci
Holcombe Lane
Holcombe Farm

Pump Lane

BRADFORD ROAD
Warleigh Lane

Browns Folly Nature Reserve

4
Hantone Hill
Hantone Hill

Warleigh Lodge Farm

5

Bathampton Wood

Avon Walkway

A363

Bath and North East S...

1 65
378
A

WARMINST
B
ROAD
79
C
River Avon
D

Warleigh Manor

A36
Kennet &

1 grid square represents 500 metres

Box Bridge

BOX ROAD

E   80   F   G   81   H

A4

Golf Course

Ashley   Road

Kingsdown

Lower Kingsdown Road

I

Kingsdown Gv

Kingsdown Golf Club

Road

Garstons

reet

67

2

Farleigh Rise

Link Lane

3

Farleigh   Rise

66

Brown's Folly

4

Link Lane

PH

5

Monkton Farleigh & South Wraxall CE Primary School

PO

†

Broad Stones

Monkton Farleigh

65

Rush Farm

E   80   F   G   81   H

Butt's   Lane

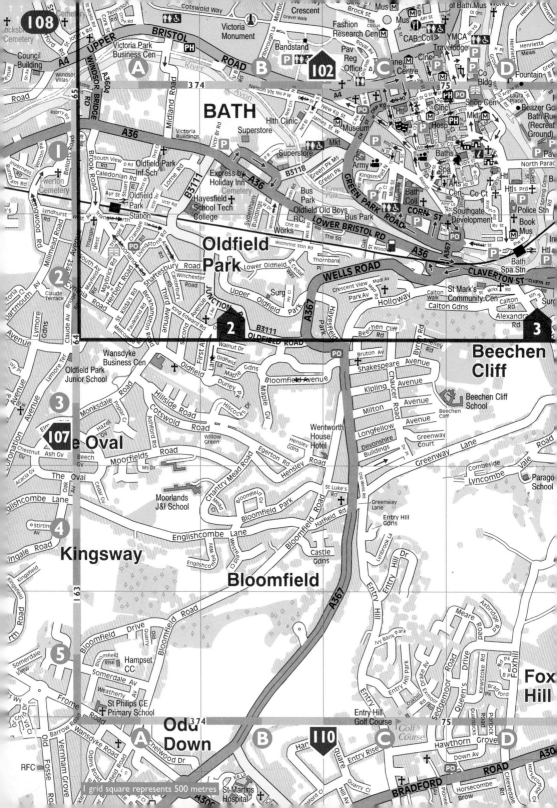

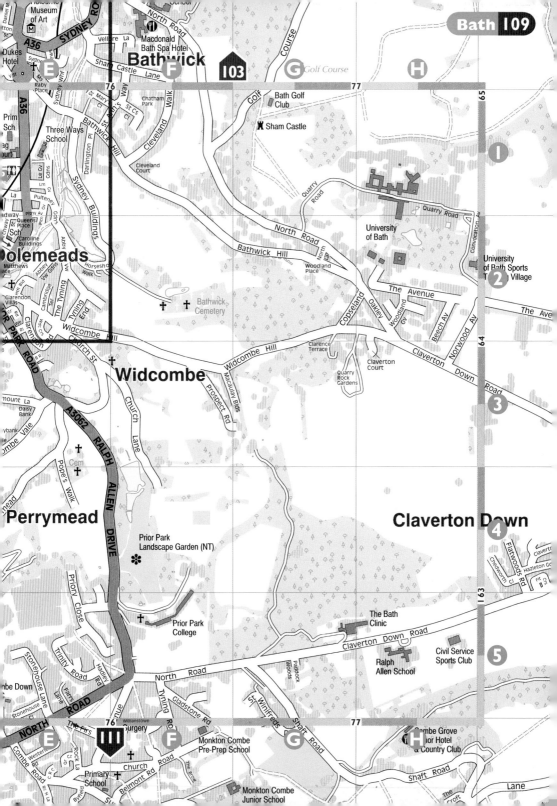

Rush Hill

Bloomfield

Hampset CC

Somerdale View

Somerdale Av

Weatherly

Bloomfield Rise

Odd Down

St Philips Primary School

Chelwood Dr

108

Entry Hill Golf Course

Entry Hill

Golf Course

Hansford

Hansford Square

Entry Rise

Quarry Cl

Hill Av

Hansford Cl

BRADFOR

Middlewood Close

Old Culverhaysians RFC

Barrow Road

Odins Road

Wansdyke Road

Upper Bloomfield Road

Frome Road

Old Fosse Road

Vernham Grove

Shickle Grove

Oolite Road

Stanway Cl

A3062 FROME ROAD

St Martins Hospital

St Martins Garden Prim Sch

Old Frome Rd

Southstoke Road

MIDFOR

Vernham Woods

Eastover Gv

Clare Rd

Colbourne Rd

WELLSWAY

A367 ROMAN RD

Oolite Gv

Banwell Road

Abington Gdns

Mendip Gardens

Wm Fosse

Ympsham Green

Cranmore Pl

St Martins Garden Prim Sch

The Link Centre

Three Ways School

Kilkenny Lane

Ce Hy La

St Gregorys Catholic College

Sulis Manor Road

Fullers Wy

Ridge Green Cl

Willow

Hazel Way

Alder Wy

Holly Dr

M Dr

Burnt House Road

P+

Odd Down FC

Poplar Rd

Sulis Manor

Rowley Wood

Old Sch Hl

PH

Sc

Combe Hay Lane

Hodshill

Hodshill

Week Farm

Avon Walkway

Avon Walkway

Pack

Rowley House

Brook Cam

Cemetery

PH

Twinhoe

1 grid square represents 500 metres

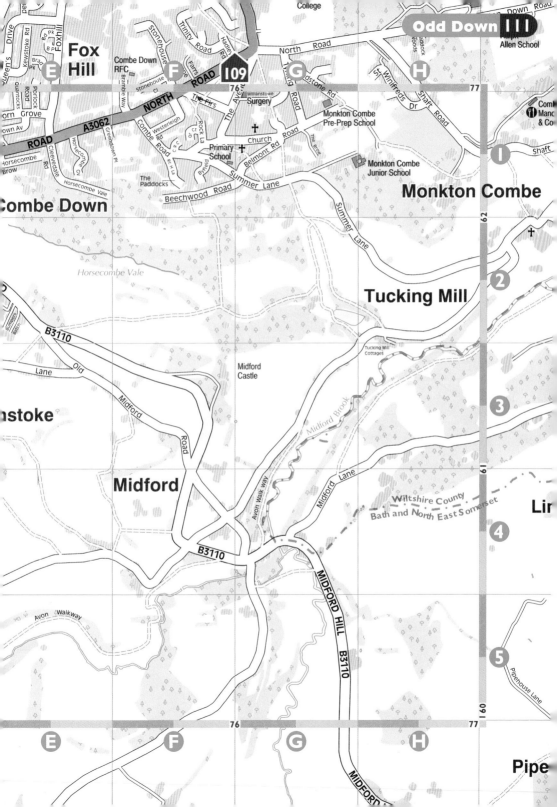

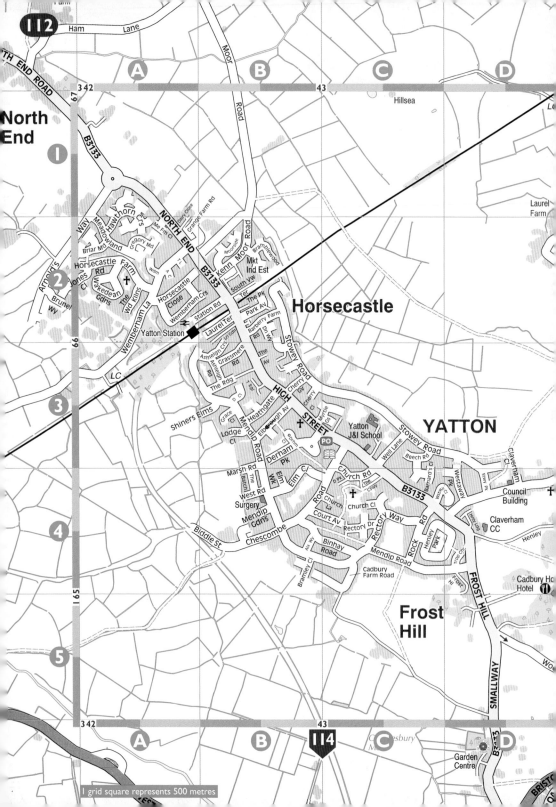

Brockley Way

Lower   Claverham

Mud Lane

Streamcross

Jasmine Lane

Brockley Way

Wd

High Street

Franklin's Wy

Claverham

Dunsters Dr

Orchard Ct

Chestnut

Broadcroft Rd

Broadcroft Cl

Claverham Rd

Claverham Pk

Streamcross

Court De Wyck Primary School

Hunt's Lane

Bishops   Road

Meetinghouse   Lane

Bishops Md

Graitney Cl

Wdw Dr

Cleeve Drive

Cleeve

Cleeve Court

Chapel Lane

Wht Hs Rd

Hollowmead Cl

Claverham Road

Hollowmead

Storybox Theatre

Millier Road

MAIN ROAD

Main Rd

A370

Plunder St

Chapel La

Cleeve Road

Warner Cl

Rhodyate La

La

BS49

Blind Lane

RHODYATE HILL

A370

King's Wood

Littlewood Lane

Hill

Woolmers

Wrington Rd

Wrington Road

The Woodlands

Wrington Lane

Ball Wood

Hill Pk   Weetwood

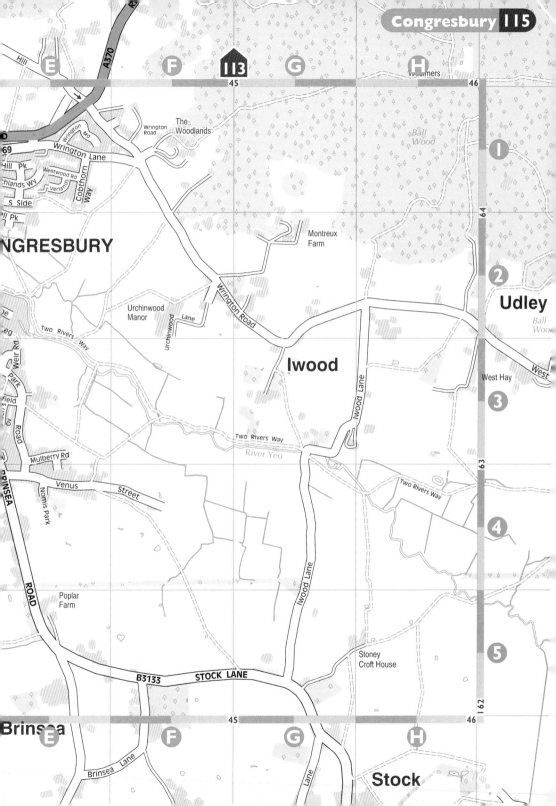

E F 113 G H

45 46

Hill

A370

Wrington Rd

Wrington Road

The Woodlands

Wrington Lane

69

Hill Pk

Weetwood Rd

chlands Wy

Cobthom Way

Verlands

S Side

ll Pk

Ball Wood

I

64

NGRESBURY

Montreux Farm

2

Udley

Ball Woo

Urchinwood Manor

Urchinwood Lane

Wrington Road

Two Rivers Way

Iwood

West Hay

West

3

e

g

Weir Rd

Park

field
Street

Iwood Lane

Two Rivers Way

River Yeo

Two Rivers Way

63

Mulberry Rd

PINSEA

Venus Street

Nomis Park

4

62

ROAD

Poplar Farm

Iwood Lane

Stoney Croft House

5

B3133 STOCK LANE

45 46

Brinsea

E F G H

Brinsea Lane

Lane

Stock

A   B   C   D

333   34

1

65

2

Sandbay
Farm

Sand
Farm
Lane   Sand
Farm

St. Bridges Close

Myrtle Tree
Crescent   Country View
Holiday Park

Sand 3
Bay

64

Beach Road

Court
Road

Beach
Rd

Kewstoke

4   Lane

Crookes   Sth Crs   Kewside

PO   Kewside
Gardens
Manor
Gardens
Orchard
Close   Lower Norton Lane

†   Kewstoke Road   Kewstoke
Primary School

Commodore
Hotel   P   Beach Road   Monks

5   Woodspring
Crescent

Woodspring Av

Toll   Furze
Road   Hill

Worlebury   Worlebury
Golf Club

Worlebury Park Road   Greenacre

163   333   34   Worlebu

A   B   **121**   C   lebury St
Pauls CE-VA
First Sch   D

Worlebury Park Road   iff
Road   Furz
Cl   Id's Cl   W Lnk Cl   Phm Cl   High
The
Crs   Milbury
Gdns

Milton

The Gln   Penrice
Close

Naunton
Wy   The
Crs   Tirley

Worlebury   Road

Sand Road

Elmsley Lane

Norton La

Golf Course

I grid square represents 500 metres

E F G H

I

2

3

4

5

M5

Little River

River Yeo

River

Oldbridge River

Tick Rd

LC

A370

West Hewish

Hewish

50 St Annes CE
Primary School

A370

Works

Maysgreen Lane

May's Green

May's Lane

Puxton Road

Road

Puxton

†

A370

Doubleton Farm

E F e G H

Cowslip

Road

Rolstone

Barn Lane

39 40

65

64

63

1

Birnbeck Island

Life Boat Station

Pier

Kewstoke Road

Worlebury Hill

Westcliff College of Further Education

Trinity Rd

2

Anchor Head

Dwhere Rd

Birkett Road

Atlantic Rd S

Atlantic Rd

New Birchfield Hotel

Dauncey's Hotel

Anchor Head Hotel

New Ocean Hotel

Upper

South Road

South Road

Shrubbery Avenue

Highbury Rd

S Ter

PO

6

St M Cl

Peter's Av

St John's Close

Grove Park Rd

Queen's Road

Cecil Road

All Saints' Rd

Tichborne Rd

Kew Road

Road Lower

Coombe Rd

Arundell Road

3

Marine Lake

Old Knightstone Theatre

Knightstone Causeway

Knightstone Road

Park Pl

Royal Crs

South Crs

Weston College

The Arosfa Hotel

Church

Lwr Church Rd

Ed Pl

Vctr

Southside

Lambretta Scooter Mus

Surg

WESTON-SUPER-MARE

Model Yacht Pond

Royal Parade

The Royal Hotel

High

Playhouse

Waterloo

St

Surgery Nrth

Somerset Museum

Bvd

Wer Rd

Blvd

Time Machine Mus

Baker Street

Works

Jubilee Road

George Street

Winter Gardens & Pavilion

Sovereign Shop Cen

P

North St

Palmer St

Meadow St

Orchard St

Back St

Alfred St

Alexandra Parade

Alfred Ct

Camden Ter

4

Grand Pier

MARINE PDE

A370

Cc Court Works

Oxford St

Orn Rd

Regent Street

PO

P

Cinema Superstore

Dolphin Square Shopping Centre

Salvation Army

Carlton St

CAB

Prim Sch

Mag Cts

Police Stn

Bcnsfld Rd

Graham Road

Surgery

Station Road

Neva Road

Albert Avenue

Ridgeway Av

Sunnyside Rd

Weston-super-Mare Str

Health & Fitness Club

SeaQuarium

ROAD

Ashbrook House Sch

Ellenborough Pk N

Ellenborough Park

Ellenborough Park S

Ellenborough Crs

Walliscote Road

Albert Rd

5

Weston Bay

Corpus Christi RC Primary School

Clevedon Road

Albert Road

P

P

P

Clifton Road

124

del ht nd

Parade

A370

BF

Walliscote

Severn Road

Clarence Road North

St Paul's

GV Rd

Avenue

Works

Ad

Clarence Park

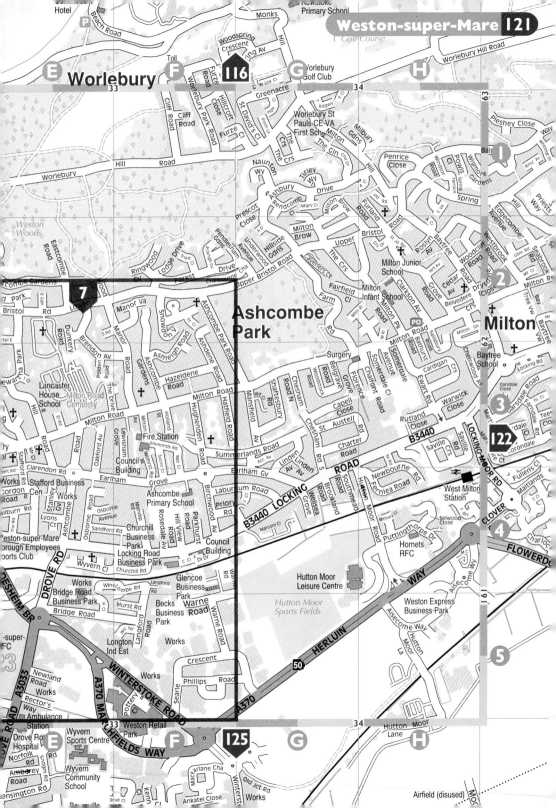

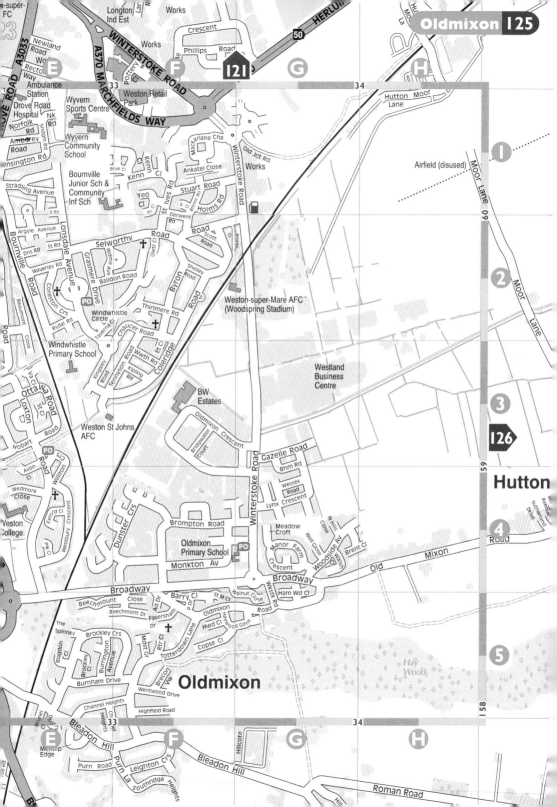

-super-FC
63

Longton Ind Est

Works

Crescent

Works

Phillips Road

HERLU...

50

WINTERSTOKE ROAD

A370 MARCHFIELDS WAY

Pottery Rd

E   **F**   **121**   **G**   **H**

33

34

Newland Road
Rector... Way
Ambulance Station
Drove Road
Norfolk Rd
Amberey Road
Kensington Rd

NK Rd
Snodom Rd

Wyvern Sports Centre
Wyvern Community School
Weston Retail Park

Bournville Junior Sch & Community Inf Sch

Brue Cl
Kenn Cl
Kenn

MacFarlane Cha

Ankatel Close
Stuart Road
Holms Rd
Birch...

Old Jct Rd
Works

Winterstoke Road

Airfield (disused)

Moor Lane

I

Stradling Avenue
Argyle Avenue
St Rd
Dns Rd

D Rd

Yeo Cl
St Ives Rd
A...

Derwent

Road
Road
Scott Road
Brone

2

Moor Lane

Bournville Road
Lonsdale Avenue
Waverley Rd
Beaumont Close

Coniston Crs
Grasmere Drive
Rydal Rd

Selworthy Road

Weme Ave
Balldon Road
PO
Windwhistle Circle
Thirlmere Rd
Tavena Cl

Byron Road

Shelley Road

Coleridge Road

Weston-super-Mare AFC (Woodspring Stadium)

Windwhistle Primary School

Kingsley Road
Tennyson Road
Chaucer Road
Wwth Rd
Et Cl
Kipling Rd

Westland Business Centre

3

Ottawa Road
Loxton Road
Va...
St Cl

PO
Williton
Crs

Avon Cl

126

59

Hutton

Weston St Johns AFC

BW Estates

Oldmixon Crescent

Bridgwater Court

Winterstoke Road

Gazelle Road

Bhm Rd

Wessex Road

Lynx Crescent

Wedmore Close

Weston College

Exford Cl
Westbury Crescent
Pik Cl

Dunster Crs

Brompton Road

Oldmixon Primary School
PO
Monkton Av

Meadow Croft

Manor Farm Crescent

N Hills Close
Well Close
Woodside Av
Walsh
Brent Cl

Old   **Mixon**   Road

4

Avenue
Sutherland Drive

Broadway

Broadway

Ham Wd Cl

Beechmount Close
Beechmont Dr

Barry Cl
Hd Dr
Faversham Dr

St M Ct

Walnut Close
Wstk Rd

The Spinney
Brockley Crs
Brockley Cl
Burlington Avenue
Bladgon Cl

Mast Cl
Rtr Cl

Oldmixon
Totterdown Lane
Hwd Cl
Hwood Gdns
Copse Cl

Hay Wood

5

58

Burnham Drive
Brecon VW
Wentwood Drive
Channel Heights
Highfield Road

Oldmixon

Brunel...
Bleadon Hill
Mendip Edge

33

E   **F**   Leighton Crs   **G**   **H**

34

Purn Road

Purn La
S'outhridge Heights

Bleadon Hill

Roman Road

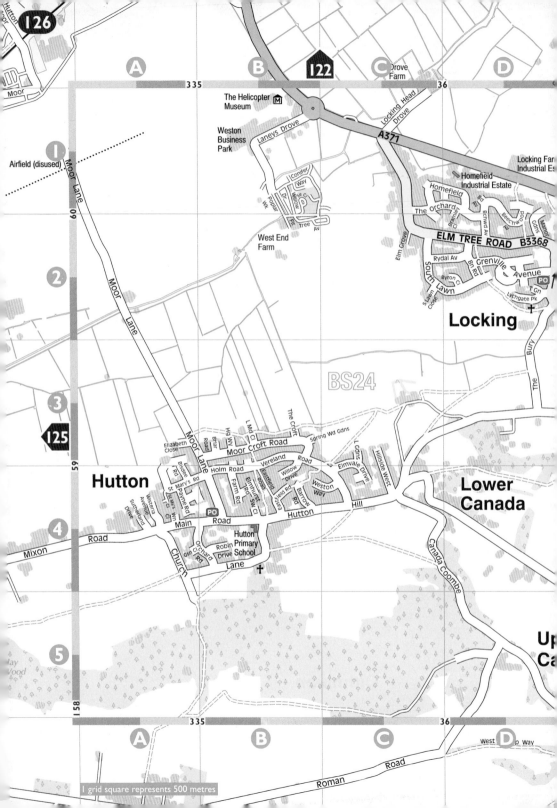

Abbots Leigh 53 H3	Coalpit Heath 24 B4	Hengrove Park 85 F3	New Cheltenham 59 F2	Thornbury 8 C3

Abbots Leigh 53 H3
Abson 61 H1
Almondsbury 10 C2
Arnos Vale 74 A2
Ashcombe Park 7 K1
Ashley Down 46 B4
Ashton Gate 72 A2
Ashton Vale 72 A4
Avonmouth 28 C2
Aztec West 10 C5
Backwell 79 C3
Backwell Common 79 H1
Backwell Green 80 C1
Bailbrook 103 G1
Barrow Common 83 E4
Barrow Gurney 82 A5
Barton Hill 57 E5
The Batch 77 E1
Bath 3 H5
Bathampton 103 H4
Batheaston 91 G5
Bathford 104 D2
Bathwick 103 F5
Bathwick 3 K5
Beacon Hill 102 C3
Bedminster 72 C3
Bedminster Down 84 C1
Beechen Cliff 3 G7
Berwick 18 B4
Bishopston 45 H4
Bishopsworth 84 A4
Bitton 89 H1
Blackhorse 49 F1
Blackrock 97 H4
Blaise Hamlet 30 E5
Bloomfield 108 B4
Bourton 118 D3
Bower Ashton 71 G2
Bradley Stoke 21 H2
Brentry 31 F2
Bridge Yate 60 C4
Brislington 74 D4
Bristol 4 B4
Bromley Heath 34 C3
Broom Hill 75 F2
Broomhill 47 G2
Buckover 9 H3
Burnett 98 C5
Cadbury Heath 76 D1
Cambridge Batch 81 H1
Catbrain 19 F4
Charlcombe 102 C1
Chelvey 79 E4
Chipping Sodbury 27 F1
Clarence Park 124 C1
Claverham 113 F2
Claverton Down 109 H4
Clay Hill 57 H1
Clays End 106 C1
Cleeve 113 H5
Clevedon 64 B1
Clifton 54 D3

Coalpit Heath 24 B4
Colt's Green 27 G2
Combe Down 111 E1
Compton Greenfield 18 C2
Congresbury 114 D2
Conham 75 F1
Coombe Dingle 30 A5
Corston 99 H4
Cotham 55 G2
Cowhorn Hill 77 F2
Crew's Hole 57 H4
Cribbs Causeway 18 D4
Crossways 9 F2
Dodington 27 G5
Dolemeads 3 H6
Dovenend 48 D1
Dundry 94 B2
East Clevedon 65 F2
East Dundry 95 G3
East End 88 A5
Easter Compton 18 D1
Eastfield 45 F1
Easton 57 E2
Easton-in-Gordano 42 B5
Eastville 47 E5
Ebdon 117 H2
Elborough 127 E3
Emerson's Green 49 H2
Engine Common 13 F2
Englishcombe 106 D5
Failand 69 H3
Fairfield Park 102 D2
Farleigh 80 B2
Farley 63 F1
Felton 93 E4
Filton 32 D2
Filwood Park 85 G1
Fishponds 47 H3
Flax Bourton 81 E2
Fox Hill 108 D5
Frampton Cotterell 23 G1
Frampton End 24 A2
Frenchay 34 B5
Frost Hill 112 C5
Golden Hill 45 H2
Goose Green 60 A2
Goose Green 13 H4
Great Stoke 22 A5
Grovesend 9 G5
The Hacket 9 G4
Hallen 18 A5
Hambrook 34 B4
Ham Green 43 E5
Hangstone Hill 64 C2
Hanham 75 H1
Hanham Green 75 H3
Harry Stoke 33 G5
Hartcliffe 85 E5
Headley Park 84 C2
Henbury 30 C3
Henfield 36 B2
Hengrove 85 H3

Hengrove Park 85 F3
Henleaze 45 G2
Hewish 119 H5
Hicks Common 23 F5
Hicks Gate 87 G1
Highridge 94 C1
Hillend 127 G4
Hillfields 48 B5
Holbrook Common 61 E3
Horfield 46 B2
Horsecastle 112 B2
Hotwells 55 E5
Hutton 126 A4
Iron Acton 12 B3
Iwood 115 G5
Kelston 100 B1
Kendleshire 35 G2
Kenn Moor Gate 78 A5
Kewstoke 116 B4
Keynsham 88 D4
Kingsdown 105 G1
Kingsway 107 H4
Kingswood 59 E3
The Knapp 9 G1
Knowle 73 H5
Lambridge 103 F2
Lansdown 102 B3
Larkhall 103 E2
Lawrence Weston 29 F4
Leigh Woods 54 A5
Little Sodbury End 15 H5
Little Stoke 21 E3
Locking 126 D2
Lockleaze 47 E1
Locksbrook 107 H1
Lodway 42 B5
Long Ashton 70 D5
Longwell Green 76 B3
Lower Canada 126 D4
Lower Failand 52 A4
Lower Knowle 73 E4
Lower Swainswick 103 F1
Lower Weston 101 H5
Luisgate Bottom 92 A4
Lyde Green 36 C5
Maiden Head 93 H4
Mangotsfield 49 F3
May's Green 119 G5
Mayshill 24 C1
Mead Riding 14 C3
Middle Bridge 40 B5
Midford 111 F4
Milton 122 A2
Monkton Combe 111 H1
Monkton Farleigh 105 G5
Montpelier 56 A1
Moorend 35 E2
Moorend 9 E2
Mount Hill 59 E5
Nailsea 67 F5
Netham 57 E5
Newbridge 101 F4

New Cheltenham 59 F2
Newton St Loe 106 C1
Nibley 25 E1
North Common 60 B5
North Corner 23 F1
Northend 91 F4
North Weston 39 H5
North Wick 95 H4
Norton 117 G4
Norton Malreward 96 D5
Norton's Wood 63 F4
Novers Park 85 E1
Odd Down 110 B1
Oldfield Park 2 B6
Oldland 76 D3
Oldland Common 77 G3
Oldmixon 125 F5
The Oval 107 H3
Parkfield 51 E1
Patchway 20 C1
Perrymead 109 E4
Pill 42 C4
Portbury 41 E5
Portishead 39 F4
Potters Hill 92 B3
Primrose Hill 102 A2
Pucklechurch 51 E3
Pye Corner 34 D2
Ram Hill 36 B1
Redcliff Bay 38 A5
Redland 45 G5
Ridgeway 47 H5
The Rocks 14 B2
Rush Hill 107 G5
St Anne's Park 57 G5
St George 58 A4
St Georges 118 A5
Saltford 99 E2
Sea Mills 43 H2
Sheepway 41 E3
Shirehampton 42 C1
Shortwood 50 B4
Sion Hill 102 B4
Siston 50 D5
Siston Common 59 G2
Sneyd Park 44 B5
Somerdale 88 B2
Soundwell 49 E5
Southdown 107 F4
Southmead 31 F4
South Stoke 110 D5
South Twerton 107 H2
Speedwell 58 A1
Staple Hill 49 E4
Stapleton 47 F4
Stockwood 86 C5
Stockwood Vale 87 G3
Stoke Bishop 44 C4
Stoke Gifford 21 F5
Stone-edge Batch 66 D2
Stone Hill 76 B2
Stub Riding 14 D4

Thornbury 8 C3
Tickenham 66 A2
Totteroak 15 G2
Tuckling Mill 111 H2
Twerton 58 B2
Two Mile Hill 58 D2
Tyntesfield 68 D2
Uphill 124 B4
Uphill Manor 124 D3
Upper Canada 126 D5
Upper Swainswick 90 A4
Upper Town 92 D4
Upper Weston 101 G1
Vinney Green 49 G1
Walcot 102 D4
Walton-in-Gordano 63 E3
Walton St Mary 62 C4
Warmley 59 H4
Warmley Hill 59 F5
Warmley Tower 59 H5
Watley's End 23 C3
Way Wick 123 H2
Webb's Heath 60 C3
Westbury on Trym 44 C1
Westbury Park 45 F4
West End 64 A3
West End 78 B2
Westerleigh 37 E1
Westerleigh Hill 37 H2
West Hewish 119 F3
West Hill 39 C3
Weston 101 F3
Weston Park 101 H3
Weston-super-Mare 6 A3
West Town 79 G4
West Wick 123 F2
Whitchurch 86 B5
Whitehall 57 E2
Whiteshill 34 C2
Whiteway 107 F3
Wick 61 H4
Wick St Lawrence 118 A1
Widcombe 109 F3
Willsbridge 77 E4
Windmill Hill 73 F3
Winford 93 H5
Winterbourne 24 B1
Winterbourne Down 35 F1
Withywood 84 A4
Woodhill 39 G1
Woolhampton Hills 123 H5
Worle 116 A5
Worlebury 116 A5
Wraxall 68 B2
Yanley 83 F1
Yate 14 A5
Yate Rocks 14 B1
Yatton 112 C3

USING THE STREET INDEX

Street names are listed alphabetically. Each street name is followed by its postal town or area locality, the Postcode District, the page number, and the reference in the square in which the name is found.

Standard index entries are shown as follows:

Abbey Gn *CBATH/BATHN* BA1 .... **3** G5

Street names and selected addresses not shown on the map due to scale restrictions are shown in the index with an asterisk:

Abbey St *CBATH/BATHN* BA1 * **3** G4

GENERAL ABBREVIATIONS

ACC	ACCESS	CTYD	COURTYARD	HLS	HILLS	MWY	MOTORWAY	SE	SOUTH EAST
ALY	ALLEY	CUTT	CUTTINGS	HO	HOUSE	N	NORTH	SER	SERVICE AREA
AP	APPROACH	CV	COVE	HOL	HOLLOW	NE	NORTH EAST	SH	SHORE
AR	ARCADE	CYN	CANYON	HOSP	HOSPITAL	NW	NORTH WEST	SHOP	SHOPPING
ASS	ASSOCIATION	DEPT	DEPARTMENT	HRB	HARBOUR	O/P	OVERPASS	SKWY	SKYWAY
AV	AVENUE	DL	DALE	HTH	HEATH	OFF	OFFICE	SMT	SUMMIT
BCH	BEACH	DM	DAM	HTS	HEIGHTS	ORCH	ORCHARD	SOC	SOCIETY
BLDS	BUILDINGS	DR	DRIVE	HVN	HAVEN	OV	OVAL	SP	SPUR
BND	BEND	DRO	DROVE	HWY	HIGHWAY	PAL	PALACE	SPR	SPRING
BNK	BANK	DRY	DRIVEWAY	IMP	IMPERIAL	PAS	PASSAGE	SQ	SQUARE
BR	BRIDGE	DWGS	DWELLINGS	IN	INLET	PAV	PAVILION	ST	STREET
BRK	BROOK	E	EAST	IND EST	INDUSTRIAL ESTATE	PDE	PARADE	STN	STATION
BTM	BOTTOM	EMB	EMBANKMENT	INF	INFIRMARY	PH	PUBLIC HOUSE	STR	STREAM
BUS	BUSINESS	EMBY	EMBASSY	INFO	INFORMATION	PK	PARK	STRD	STRAND
BVD	BOULEVARD	ESP	ESPLANADE	INT	INTERCHANGE	PKWY	PARKWAY	SW	SOUTH WEST
BY	BYPASS	EST	ESTATE	IS	ISLAND	PL	PLACE	TDG	TRADING
CATH	CATHEDRAL	EX	EXCHANGE	JCT	JUNCTION	PLN	PLAIN	TER	TERRACE
CEM	CEMETERY	EXPY	EXPRESSWAY	JTY	JETTY	PLNS	PLAINS	THWY	THROUGHWAY
CEN	CENTRE	EXT	EXTENSION	KG	KING	PLZ	PLAZA	TNL	TUNNEL
CFT	CROFT	F/O	FLYOVER	KNL	KNOLL	POL	POLICE STATION	TOLL	TOLLWAY
CH	CHURCH	FC	FOOTBALL CLUB	L	LAKE	PR	PRINCE	TPK	TURNPIKE
CHA	CHASE	FK	FORK	LA	LANE	PREC	PRECINCT	TR	TRACK
CHYD	CHURCHYARD	FLD	FIELD	LDG	LODGE	PREP	PREPARATORY	TRL	TRAIL
CIR	CIRCLE	FLDS	FIELDS	LGT	LIGHT	PRIM	PRIMARY	TWR	TOWER
CIRC	CIRCUS	FLS	FALLS	LK	LOCK	PROM	PROMENADE	U/P	UNDERPASS
CL	CLOSE	FM	FARM	LKS	LAKES	PRS	PRINCESS	UNI	UNIVERSITY
CLFS	CLIFFS	FT	FORT	LNDG	LANDING	PRT	PORT	UPR	UPPER
CMP	CAMP	FTS	FLATS	LTL	LITTLE	PT	POINT	V	VALE
CNR	CORNER	FWY	FREEWAY	LWR	LOWER	PTH	PATH	VA	VALLEY
CO	COUNTY	FY	FERRY	MAG	MAGISTRATE	PZ	PIAZZA	VIAD	VIADUCT
COLL	COLLEGE	GA	GATE	MAN	MANSIONS	QD	QUADRANT	VIL	VILLA
COM	COMMON	GAL	GALLERY	MD	MEAD	QU	QUEEN	VIS	VISTA
COMM	COMMISSION	GDN	GARDEN	MDW	MEADOWS	QY	QUAY	VLG	VILLAGE
CON	CONVENT	GDNS	GARDENS	MEM	MEMORIAL	R	RIVER	VLS	VILLAS
COT	COTTAGE	GLD	GLADE	MI	MILL	RBT	ROUNDABOUT	VW	VIEW
COTS	COTTAGES	GLN	GLEN	MKT	MARKET	RD	ROAD	W	WEST
CP	CAPE	GN	GREEN	MKTS	MARKETS	RDG	RIDGE	WD	WOOD
CPS	COPSE	GND	GROUND	ML	MALL	REP	REPUBLIC	WHF	WHARF
CR	CREEK	GRA	GRANGE	MNR	MANOR	RES	RESERVOIR	WK	WALK
CREM	CREMATORIUM	GRG	GARAGE	MS	MEWS	RFC	RUGBY FOOTBALL CLUB	WKS	WALKS
CRS	CRESCENT	GT	GREAT	MSN	MISSION	RI	RISE	WLS	WELLS
CSWY	CAUSEWAY	GTWY	GATEWAY	MT	MOUNT	RP	RAMP	WY	WAY
CT	COURT	GV	GROVE	MTN	MOUNTAIN	RW	ROW	YD	YARD
CTRL	CENTRAL	HGR	HIGHER	MTS	MOUNTAINS	S	SOUTH	YHA	YOUTH HOSTEL
CTS	COURTS	HL	HILL	MUS	MUSEUM	SCH	SCHOOL		

POSTCODE TOWNS AND AREA ABBREVIATIONS

ALMDB ....Almondsbury
AVONM ....Avonmouth
BATHSE ....Bath south & east
BLAG/CWMG/WR ....Blagdon/
Chew Magna/
Wrington
BMSTR ....Bedminster
BMSTRD/HC/WWD ....Bedminster
Down/Hartcliffe/
Withywood
BNWL ....Banwell
BOAV ....Bradford-on-Avon
BOS ....Burnham-on-Sea

BRSG/KWL/STAPK........ Brislington/
Knowle/St Anne's Park
BRSTK/PCHW ....Bradley Stoke/
Patchway
CBATH/BATHN ....Central Bath/
Bath north
CBRIS/FH ....Central Bristol/
Floating Harbour
CBRISNE ....Central Bristol
north & east
CFTN/FAIL ....Clifton/Failand
CHPMW/MSHF ......Chippenham west/
Marshfield

CLVDN..Clevedon
COR/BOX.......................... Corsham/Box
EVILLE/WHL............. Eastville/Whitehall
FRCTL/WBN ....Frampton Cotterell/
Winterbourne
HGRV/WHIT......Hengrove/Whitchurch
HNBRY/STHM........Henbury/Southmead
HNLZ/SM/SNYPK/WT ....Henleaze/
Sea Mills/Sneyd Park/
Westbury on Trym
HORF/LLZ ....Horfield/Lockleaze
KEYN ....Keynsham
KGWD/HNM........ Kingswood/Hanham

LGASH ....Long Ashton
MANG/FISH ....Mangotsfield/
Fishponds
MTN/WRL ....Milton/Worle
NAIL..Nailsea
OLD/WMLY/WICK ....Oldland/
Warmley/Wick
OMX/HUT/LCK ....Oldmixon/
Hutton-Locking
PLTN/PENS..............Paulton/Pensford
PTSHD/EG...........................Portishead/
Easton-in-Gordano
RDLND/MONT .... Redland/Montpelier

THNB/SVB ...Thornbury/Severn Beach
WSM ....Weston-super-Mare
WUE ....Wotton-under-Edge
YATE/CS ....Yate/Chipping Sodbury
YTN/CONG.........Yatton/Congresbury

Index - streets

Abb - Avo

A

Abbey Churchyard
  CBATH/BATHN BA1 .... 3 C5
Abbey Ct
  BRSG/KWL/STAPK BS4........ 75 E1
Abbeydale FRCTL/WBN BS36 ..... 23 E4
Abbey Gdns
  OMX/HUT/LCK BS24 .... 122 B3
Abbeygate St
  CBATH/BATHN BA1 .... 3 G5
Abbey Gn CBATH/BATHN BA1 ..... 3 G5
Abbey Pk KEYN BS31 .... 88 C3
Abbey Rd
  HNLZ/SM/SNYPK/WT BS9 ...... 44 D2
Abbey St CBATH/BATHN BA1 * 3 G2
Abbey Vw BATHSE BA2 .... 3 K6
Abbey View Gdns BATHSE BA2 ..... 3 K6
Abberwood Dr
  HNLZ/SM/SNYPK/WT BS9 ...... 44 A3
Abbots Av KGWD/HNM BS15 ..... 75 H2
Abbotsbury Rd NAIL BS48 .... 67 G5
Abbots CI MTN/WRL BS22 .... 117 H5
Abbots Ct MTN/WRL BS22 .... 96 D1
Abbotsford Rd
  RDLND/MONT BS6 .... 55 F2
Abbots Horn NAIL BS48 .... 67 E4
Abbots Leigh Rd
  CFTN/FAIL BS8 .... 53 H4
Abbots Rd KGWD/HNM BS15 ..... 75 H4
Abbots Wy
  HNLZ/SM/SNYPK/WT BS9 ...... 45 H2
Abbotswood KGWD/HNM BS15 ... 58 D4
  YATE/CS BS37 .... 25 H3
Aberdeen Rd
  RDLND/MONT BS6 .... 55 F2
Abingdon Gdns BATHSE BA2 ...... 110 B2
Abingdon Rd MANG/FISH BS16 ... 48 A5
Ableton La HNBRY/STHM BS10 ... 17 F2
Ableton Wk
  HNLZ/SM/SNYPK/WT BS9 ...... 43 H3
Abraham CI EVILLE/WHL BS5...... 56 D3
Abson Rd MANG/FISH BS16 .... 51 F5
Acacia Av MANG/FISH BS16 .... 61 G2
Acacia Av MANG/FISH BS16 .... 48 C4
  WSM BS23 .... 121 G3
Acacia CI MANG/FISH BS16 .... 48 C5
Acacia Ct KEYN BS31 .... 87 H5
Acacia Gv BATHSE BA2 .... 107 H4
Acacia Ms MANG/FISH BS16 * 48 D4
Acacia Rd MANG/FISH BS16 .... 48 D5
Acer Village HGRV/WHIT BS14 .... 86 D2
Acid Rd AVONM BS11 .... 28 C1
Aconite CI MTN/WRL BS22 .... 117 H3
Acorn Cv
  BMSTRD/HC/WWD BS13 .... 83 H5
Acraman's Rd BRSG/KWL/STAPK BS4 ... 72 D2
Acresbush CI
  BMSTRD/HC/WWD BS13 .... 84 B4
Acton Rd MANG/FISH BS16 .... 48 A5
Adams Hay
  BRSG/KWL/STAPK BS4 .... 74 C5
Adams Land FRCTL/WBN BS36 ... 24 A5
Adastral Rd
  OMX/HUT/LCK BS24 .... 127 C2
Adderly Ga MANG/FISH BS16 ...... 49 H1
Addicott Rd WSM BS23 .... 7 F2
Addiscombe Rd
  HGRV/WHIT BS14 .... 86 A4
  WSM BS23 .... 124 D2
Addison Rd BMSTR BS3 .... 73 H3
Adelaide PI EVILLE/WHL BS5 ...... 56 D5
  MANG/FISH BS16 .... 47 H4
Adelaide Ter
  MANG/FISH BS16 * 48 A4
Adelante CI BRSTK/PCHW BS34 ... 34 A1
Admiral CI MANG/FISH BS16 .... 47 F1
Agate St BMSTR BS3 .... 72 C3
Aiken St EVILLE/WHL BS5............ 56 D5
Ainslies Belvedere
  CBATH/BATHN BA1 .... 3 F1
Aintree Dr NAIL BS48 .... 53 F4
Air Balloon Rd EVILLE/WHL BS5.. 58 A4
Airport Rd HGRV/WHIT BS14 ...... 85 H4
Aisecome Wy MTN/WRL BS22 ... 121 H5
Akeman Wy AVONM BS11 .... 28 C5
Alanscourt
  OLD/WMLY/WICK BS30 *......... 77 E1
Alard Rd BRSG/KWL/STAPK BS4 . 85 E1
Albany Ga BRSTK/PCHW BS34..... 21 G5
Albany Rd BATHSE BA2 .... 107 G1
  RDLND/MONT BS6 .... 56 B2
Albany St KGWD/HNM BS15 ...... 58 C3
Albany Wy
  OLD/WMLY/WICK BS30 .... 77 F1
Albemarle Rw CFTN/FAIL BS8 ..... 54 D5
Albermarle Ter CFTN/FAIL BS8 ... 54 D5
Albert Av WSM BS23 .... 6 F7
Albert Crs CBRISNE BS2 .... 73 H1
Albert Gv South
  EVILLE/WHL BS5....................... 57 H3

KGWD/HNM BS15 .... 59 E2
Alma Road Av CFTN/FAIL BS8 ..... 55 F3
Alma St WSM BS23 .... 6 E4
Alma Vale Rd CFTN/FAIL BS8 ...... 55 E3
Almeda Rd EVILLE/WHL BS5........ 58 A5
Almond CI MTN/WRL BS22........ 122 D2
Almond Wy MANG/FISH BS16 ..... 49 F3
Almorah Rd BMSTR BS3 .... 73 F3
Alpha Rd BMSTR BS3 .... 73 H2
Alpine Gdns
  CBATH/BATHN BA1 .... 102 D4
Alpine Rd EVILLE/WHL BS5 .... 57 E2
Alsop Rd KGWD/HNM BS15 .... 58 D5
Alton Rd HORF/LLZ BS7 .... 46 B2
Altringham Rd
  EVILLE/WHL BS5....................... 57 F2
Alverstoke HGRV/WHIT BS14 ...... 85 G2
Alveston Wk
  HNLZ/SM/SNYPK/WT BS9 ...... 43 H1
Alwins Ct
  OLD/WMLY/WICK BS30 .... 76 C2
Amberey Rd WSM BS23 .... 125 E3
Amberlands CI NAIL BS48 .... 79 H2
Amberley CI KEYN BS31 .... 88 B5
  MANG/FISH BS16 .... 48 D1
Amberley Rd
  BRSTK/PCHW BS34 .... 20 D2
  MANG/FISH BS16 .... 48 D1
Amble CI KGWD/HNM BS15...... 59 F4
Ambleside Av
  HNBRY/STHM BS10 .... 31 F4
Ambleside Rd BATHSE BA2 .... 107 G5
Ambra Ter CFTN/FAIL BS8 * 55 E5
Ambra V CFTN/FAIL BS8 .... 55 E5
Ambra V East CFTN/FAIL BS8 ...... 55 E5
Ambra V West CFTN/FAIL BS8 .... 55 E5
Ambrose Rd CFTN/FAIL BS8 .... 55 E5
Ambury CBATH/BATHN BA1 .... 3 F6
Amercombe Wk
  HGRV/WHIT BS14 .... 86 C2
Amery La CBATH/BATHN BA1 .... 3 G5
Anchor CI
  BRSG/KWL/STAPK BS4............. 57 H5
Anchor Rd CBATH/BATHN BA1 ... 101 G3
  CBRIS/FH BS1 * 4 B6
  KGWD/HNM BS15 .... 59 G2
Anchor Wy PTSHD/EG BS20 .... 42 D4
Andereach CI HGRV/WHIT BS14 .. 86 A1
Andover Rd
  BRSG/KWL/STAPK BS4............. 73 G4
Andruss Dr LGASH BS41 .... 94 C2
Angers Rd
  BRSG/KWL/STAPK BS4............. 73 G2
Anglesea PI CFTN/FAIL BS8 .... 55 E1
Anglo Ter
  CBATH/BATHN BA1 * 102 D4
Ankatel CI WSM BS23 .... 125 F1
Annandale Av MTN/WRL BS22 .. 122 B2
Anson CI KEYN BS31 .... 99 E2
Anson Rd MTN/WRL BS22 .... 117 E4
  OMX/HUT/LCK BS24 .... 122 D5
Ansteys CI KGWD/HNM BS15 ..... 75 G1
Anstey's Rd KGWD/HNM BS15 ... 75 G1
Anstey St EVILLE/WHL BS5.......... 56 D2
Anthea Rd EVILLE/WHL BS5......... 57 G1
Antona Ct AVONM BS11 .... 42 D1
Antona Dr AVONM BS11 .... 42 D1
Antrim Rd
  HNLZ/SM/SNYPK/WT BS9 ...... 45 F2
Anvil Rd YTN/CONG BS49 * 113 F2
Anvil St CBRISNE BS2.................... 5 K4
Apex Ct ALMDB BS32 .... 11 F4
Apperley CI YATE/CS BS37 .... 25 H2
Appleby Wk
  BRSG/KWL/STAPK BS4............. 85 E2
Appledore CI HGRV/WHIT BS14.. 86 A1
Apple Farm La
  OMX/HUT/LCK BS24 .... 123 F2
Applegate HNBRY/STHM BS10 .... 31 F2
Appletree Ct MTN/WRL BS22 .... 123 E1
Applin Gn MANG/FISH BS16 .... 50 A2
Approach Rd CBRIS/FH BS1 * 5 K6
Appsley Ct MTN/WRL BS22 .... 121 H2
Apsley Ms CFTN/FAIL BS8 * 54 D1
Apsley Rd CBATH/BATHN BA1 ... 101 F5
  CFTN/FAIL BS8 .... 54 D1
Apsley St EVILLE/WHL BS5 .... 57 E1
Arbutus Dr
  HNLZ/SM/SNYPK/WT BS9 ...... 44 A1
The Arcade CBRIS/FH BS1 .... 5 G2
Archer Ct
  OLD/WMLY/WICK BS30 .... 76 C3
Archer Wk HGRV/WHIT BS14 ...... 86 D3
Archfield Rd RDLND/MONT BS6.. 55 G2
Archway St BATHSE BA2 .... 3 J6
Ardagh Ct HORF/LLZ BS7 * 46 B1
Ardenton Wk
  HNBRY/STHM BS10 .... 31 E2
Ardern CI
  HNLZ/SM/SNYPK/WT BS9 ...... 29 H5

Argus Ct BMSTR BS3..................... 72 D4
Argus Rd BMSTR BS3 .... 72 D3
Argyle Av WSM BS23 .... 125 E2
Argyle Dr YATE/CS BS37.............. 14 A3
Argyle PI CFTN/FAIL BS8 .... 55 E5
Argyle Rd CBRISNE BS2 .... 56 A3
  CLVDN BS21 .... 62 B5
  MANG/FISH BS16 .... 56 B2
Argyle St BATHSE BA2 .... 3 G4
  BMSTR BS3 .... 72 D3
  EVILLE/WHL BS5....................... 57 E1
Argyle Ter BATHSE BA2 * 107 H1
Arley HI RDLND/MONT BS6......... 55 H2
Arley Cots RDLND/MONT BS6 .... 55 H2
Arley Pk RDLND/MONT BS6......... 55 H2
Arley Ter EVILLE/WHL BS5 .... 57 G2
Arlingham Wy
  BRSTK/PCHW BS34 .... 20 A2
Arlington Rd
  BRSG/KWL/STAPK BS4............. 57 F5
Arlington Vls CFTN/FAIL BS8 .... 55 E4
Armada PI CBRISNE BS2 .... 56 B3
Armada Rd HGRV/WHIT BS14 ..... 85 H3
Armes Ct BATHSE BA2 .... 3 H7
Armidale Av RDLND/MONT BS6 .. 56 A2
Armoury Sq EVILLE/WHL BS5...... 56 C3
Armstrong Cl THNB/SVB BS35 ...... 9 E5
Armstrong Dr
  OLD/WMLY/WICK BS30 .... 77 E1
Armstrong Wy YATE/CS BS37 ...... 13 C4
Arnall Dr HNBRY/STHM BS10 ..... 30 D4
Arneside Rd
  HNBRY/STHM BS10 .... 31 G4
Arnold Rd MANG/FISH BS16 .... 49 H5
Arnor Ct MTN/WRL BS22 .... 117 H4
Arno's St
  BRSG/KWL/STAPK BS4............. 73 H2
Arrowfield CI HGRV/WHIT BS14 .. 96 D3
Artemesia Av MTN/WRL BS22 ... 122 B3
Arthurs CI MANG/FISH BS16 .... 50 A2
Arthur Skemp CI
  EVILLE/WHL BS5....................... 56 D4
Arthur St CBRISNE BS2................. 73 H1
  EVILLE/WHL BS5....................... 57 E3
Arthurswood Rd
  BMSTRD/HC/WWD BS13 .... 84 B5
Arundel CI
  BMSTRD/HC/WWD BS13 .... 84 C5
  CLVDN BS21 .... 64 D2
  HORF/LLZ BS7 .... 45 H5
Arundel Rd
  CBATH/BATHN BA1 .... 102 D3
  CLVDN BS21 .... 64 D2
  HORF/LLZ BS7 .... 45 H5
Ascot CI MANG/FISH BS16 .... 35 H5
Ascot Rd HNBRY/STHM BS10 ..... 31 H3
Ashbourne CI
  OLD/WMLY/WICK BS30 .... 60 A5
Ashburton Rd
  HNBRY/STHM BS10 .... 31 G4
Ashbury Dr MTN/WRL BS22 ...... 121 G1
Ash CI BRSTK/PCHW BS34 .... 21 F3
  MANG/FISH BS16 .... 48 C5
  MTN/WRL BS22 .... 123 C1
  YATE/CS BS37 .... 13 H4
Ashcombe CI
  OLD/WMLY/WICK BS30 .... 60 A5
Ashcombe Crs
  OLD/WMLY/WICK BS30 .... 60 A5
Ashcombe Gdns WSM BS23 .... 7 J2
Ashcombe Park Rd WSM BS23 ...... 7 K1
Ashcombe Rd WSM BS23 .... 7 H5
Ashcott HGRV/WHIT BS14 .... 85 G5
Ashcroft Av KEYN BS31 .... 88 A4
Ashcroft Rd
  HNLZ/SM/SNYPK/WT BS9 ...... 44 A1
Ashdene Av EVILLE/WHL BS5...... 47 H5
Ashdene Rd WSM BS23 .... 125 E1
Ashdown Rd PTSHD/EG BS20 ..... 39 E2
Asher La CBRISNE BS2 .... 5 J1
Ashfield PI RDLND/MONT BS6 .... 56 B2
Ashfield Rd BMSTR BS3 .... 72 C3
Ashfield Ter BMSTR BS3 * 72 C3
Ashford Dr
  OMX/HUT/LCK BS24 .... 125 F5
Ashford Rd BATHSE BA2 .... 108 A3
  BRSTK/PCHW BS34 .... 20 C3
Ash Gv BATHSE BA2 .... 107 H5
  CLVDN BS21 .... 64 D2
  EVILLE/WHL BS5....................... 48 C5
Ash Hayes Dr NAIL BS48 .... 67 F5
Ash Hayes Rd NAIL BS48 .... 67 F5
Ashland Rd
  BMSTRD/HC/WWD BS13 .... 84 A5
Ashleigh Crs YTN/CONG BS49 .... 112 B3
Ashleigh Rd WSM BS23 .... 7 J2

YTN/CONG BS49........................ 112 B3
Ashley KGWD/HNM BS15 .... 59 F3
Ashley Av CBATH/BATHN BA1 ... 101 H5
Ashley CI HORF/LLZ BS7 .... 46 B4
Ashley Court Rd HORF/LLZ BS7.. 56 B1
Ashley Down Rd HORF/LLZ BS7.. 46 A3
Ashley Grove Rd CBRISNE BS2 .... 56 B1
Ashley HI HORF/LLZ BS7 .... 46 A3
Ashley Pde CBRISNE BS2 .... 56 B1
Ashley Pk HORF/LLZ BS7 .... 46 B5
Ashley Rd CBATH/BATHN BA1 ... 104 D2
  CLVDN BS21 .... 64 B4
  COR/BOX SN13 .... 105 G1
  EVILLE/WHL BS5....................... 56 A2
Ashley St CBRISNE BS2 .... 56 C2
Ashley Ter
  CBATH/BATHN BA1 * 101 H5
Ashmans Yd
  CBATH/BATHN BA1 .... 107 G1
Ashmead Pk KEYN BS31 * 89 E4
Ashmead Rd KEYN BS31 .... 89 E4
Ashmead Wy CBRIS/FH BS1 * 72 A1
Ash Ridge Rd ALMDB BS32 .... 10 D4
Ash Rd BNWL BS29 .... 127 H2
  HORF/LLZ BS7 .... 46 A3
Ashton Av CBRIS/FH BS1 .... 72 B1
Ashton Dr BMSTR BS3.................. 71 H5
Ashton Gate Rd BMSTR BS3 .... 72 B2
Ashton Gate Ter BMSTR BS3 .... 72 B2
Ashton HI BATHSE BA2 .... 99 E4
Ashton Rd LGASH BS41 .... 71 F3
Ashton Vale Rd BMSTR BS3........ 71 H5
Ashton Wy KEYN BS31 .... 88 B5
Ashvale CI NAIL BS48 .... 67 H4
Ashville Rd BMSTR BS3................. 72 B2
Ash Wk HNBRY/STHM BS10 .... 31 F2
Ashwell CI HGRV/WHIT BS14 ...... 86 D3
Ashwicke HGRV/WHIT BS14 .... 85 G3
Aspen Park Rd
  MTN/WRL BS22 .... 122 B3
Aspley CI CBATH/BATHN BA1 ... 101 C5
Assembly Rooms La
  CBRIS/FH BS1 * 4 E5
Astry CI AVONM BS11 .... 29 G4
Atchley St EVILLE/WHL BS5......... 56 D4
Atherston
  OLD/WMLY/WICK BS30 .... 77 F1
Athlone Wk
  BRSG/KWL/STAPK BS4............. 73 F5
Atholl CI MTN/WRL BS22 .... 117 G5
Atkins Cl HGRV/WHIT BS14 .... 86 D3
Atlantic Rd AVONM BS11 .... 28 C5
  WSM BS23 .... 6 A5
Atlantic Rd South WSM BS23 .... 6 A4
Atlas CI EVILLE/WHL BS5............. 58 A1
Atlas Rd BMSTR BS3 .... 73 F3
Atlas St CBRISNE BS2.................... 74 A1
Atwell Dr ALMDB BS32 .... 20 D1
Atwood Dr AVONM BS11 .... 29 E3
Atyeo CI BMSTR BS3 .... 71 H5
Aubrey Meads
  OLD/WMLY/WICK BS30 .... 89 H1
Aubrey Rd BMSTR BS3 .... 72 C3
Aubrey Av
  OLD/WMLY/WICK BS30 .... 77 E3
Auburn Rd RDLND/MONT BS6.... 55 F1
Auckland CI WSM BS23 .... 125 E3
Auden Md HORF/LLZ BS7 .... 32 C5
Audley Av CBATH/BATHN BA1 ... 101 H5
Audley CI CBATH/BATHN BA1 ...... 2 A2
Audley Gv CBATH/BATHN BA1 ... 101 H5
Audley Park Rd
  CBATH/BATHN BA1 .... 101 H5
Audrey Wk
  HNLZ/SM/SNYPK/WT BS9 ...... 45 H2
Augusta PI CBATH/BATHN BA1 .... 2 A3
Austen Dr MTN/WRL BS22 .... 118 A4
Austen Gv HORF/LLZ BS7 .... 32 C5
Autumn Ms
  OMX/HUT/LCK BS24 .... 122 D3
Avalon Cl YTN/CONG BS49 .... 112 A2
Avalon La EVILLE/WHL BS5.......... 58 B5
Avalon Rd EVILLE/WHL BS5 .... 58 B5
Avebury Rd BMSTR BS3 .... 71 H4
Avening CI NAIL BS48................... 79 C1
Avening Rd KGWD/HNM BS15 .... 58 A3
The Avenue BATHSE BA2 .... 111 F1
  BRSTK/PCHW BS34 .... 21 E4
  BRSTK/PCHW BS34 .... 10 D5
  CFTN/FAIL BS8 .... 55 E5
  CLVDN BS21 .... 62 B5
  EVILLE/WHL BS5....................... 57 H4
  HNLZ/SM/SNYPK/WT BS9 ...... 45 H4
  HORF/LLZ BS7 .... 46 A4
  KEYN BS31 .... 88 B2
  MANG/FISH BS16 .... 33 G4
  NAIL BS48 .... 79 H2
  YATE/CS BS37 .... 25 H1
  YTN/CONG BS49 .... 112 B3
Averay Rd MANG/FISH BS16....... 47 E4
Avon CI EVILLE/WHL BS5 .... 57 H5

KEYN BS31 ....88 C3
WSM BS23 ....125 E4
Avon Ct CBATH/BATHN BA1 ...91 F5
Avon Crs CBRIS/FH BS1 ....72 B1
Avondale Blds
  CBATH/BATHN BA1 ....103 E2
Avondale Ct
  OLD/WMLY/WICK BS30 ....76 C4
Avondale Pl
  CBATH/BATHN BA1 ....104 A1
Avondale Rd
  CBATH/BATHN BA1 ....101 C5
Avondale Works
  KGWD/HNM BS15 ....58 C1
Avondown Cl
  HNBRY/STHM BS10 ....31 H5
Avondown Ct BRSTK/PCHW BS3 *...72 D4
Avon Gv
  HNLZ/SM/SNYPK/WT BS9 ....54 B1
Avonlea KGWD/HNM BS15 ....75 H1
Avonleaze
  HNLZ/SM/SNYPK/WT BS9 ....43 H5
Avonleigh Rd BMSTR BS3 ....72 C4
Avon Meads CBRISNE BS2 * 74 B1
Avon Mill La BMSTR BS3 ....88 C5
Avonmouth Rd AVONM BS11 ....28 B4
Avonmouth Wy AVONM BS11 ...28 C4
  HNBRY/STHM BS10 ....30 C2
Avonmouth Wy West
  AVONM BS11 ....28 B3
Avon Pk CBATH/BATHN BA1 ....101 F5
  EVILLE/WHL BS5 ....57 F4
Avon Rd
  BMSTRD/HC/WWD BS13 ....84 B3
  KEYN BS31 ....88 C4
  PTSHD/EG BS20 ....42 C3
Avonside Rd CBRISNE BS2 ....57 E5
Avonside Wy
  BRSG/KWL/STAPK BS4 ....57 H5
Avon St BATHSE BA2 ....3 F6
  CBRISNE BS2 ....5 J4
Avon V
  HNLZ/SM/SNYPK/WT BS9 ....44 B4
Avonvale Rd EVILLE/WHL BS5 ...57 E4
Avon Vw KGWD/HNM BS15 ......75 G3
Avon Walkway BATHSE BA2 .....110 C4
  BATHSE BA2 ....3 K4
  CBATH/BATHN BA1 ....4 D7
  CBRIS/FH BS1 ....5 K7
  CBRISNE BS2 ....99 H5
  KEYN BS31 ....89 G1
  PTSHD/EG BS20 ....39 G3
  THNB/SVB BS35 ....8 D4
Avon Wy EVILLE/WHL BS5 ....57 E5
  HNBRY/STHM BS10 ....31 H5
  HNLZ/SM/SNYPK/WT BS9 ....44 A3
  PTSHD/EG BS20 ....39 G3
  THNB/SVB BS35 ....8 D4
Avonwood Cl AVONM BS11 ....43 E2
Awdelett Cl AVONM BS11 ....29 H4
Axbridge Cl NAIL BS48 ....79 F1
Axbridge Rd BATHSE BA2 ....108 D5
Axe Cl WSM BS23 ....125 F1
Aycote Cl AVONM BS11 ....121 H1
Aylesbury Crs BMSTR BS3 ....72 C5
Aylesbury Rd BMSTR BS3 ....72 C5
Aylmer Crs HGRV/WHIT BS14 .....86 A3
Aylminton Wk AVONM BS11 .....29 H3
Ayr St BATHSE BA2 ....2 A5
Azalea Rd MTN/WRL BS22 ....117 H3
Azelin Av
  BMSTRD/HC/WWD BS13 ....84 C4

B

Backfields CBRISNE BS2 ....5 G1
Backfields La CBRISNE BS2 ....56 A3
Back La KEYN BS31 ....88 B3
  MANG/FISH BS16 ....51 C4
  PTSHD/EG BS20 ....42 C4
Back of Kingsdown Pde
  RDLND/MONT BS6 ....55 H3
Back Rd BMSTR BS3 ....72 B2
Back Stoke La
  HNLZ/SM/SNYPK/WT BS9 ....44 D2
Back St WSM BS23 ....6 E4
Backwell Bow NAIL BS48 ....68 A5
Backwell Common NAIL BS48 ....79 F4
Backwell Hill Rd NAIL BS48 ....80 C2
Backwell Wk NAIL BS48 * 68 B2
Backwell Wk
  BMSTRD/HC/WWD BS13 ....84 A1
Badenham Gv AVONM BS11 ......29 F5
Baden Rd EVILLE/WHL BS5 ....57 E4
  KGWD/HNM BS15 ....59 C4
Bader Cl YATE/CS BS37 ....13 H4
Badger Pl PTSHD/EG BS20 ....39 G3
Badgers Cl ALMDB BS32 ....11 F5
Badger Sett EVILLE/WHL BS5 ......58 B4
Badgers Holt HGRV/WHIT BS14 ..86 B3
The Badgers MTN/WRL BS22 ...118 B5
Badgers Wk
  BRSG/KWL/STAPK BS4 ....74 C4
Badgers Wy
  OMX/HUT/LCK BS24 ....122 C3
Badgeworth YATE/CS BS37 ....25 H4
Badminton Rd
  MANG/FISH BS16 ....49 H5
Badminton Ct YATE/CS BS37 * 13 C5
Badminton Gdns
  CBATH/BATHN BA1 ....101 H4
Badminton Rd CBRISNE BS2 ....56 B2
  FRCTL/WBN BS36 ....35 C2
  MANG/FISH BS16 ....49 E1
  YATE/CS BS37 ....27 F2
  YATE/CS BS37 ....13 F5
Baglyn Av KGWD/HNM BS15 .....69 G5
Bagnell Cl HGRV/WHIT BS14 ......86 D4
Bagnell Rd HGRV/WHIT BS14 .....86 D4
Bagworth Dr
  OLD/WMLY/WICK BS30 ....76 C3
Bailbrook Gv
  CBATH/BATHN BA1 ....103 F1
Bailbrook La
  CBATH/BATHN BA1 ....103 G1
Baildon Rd WSM BS23 ....125 E2
Bailey Cl MTN/WRL BS22 ....122 B3

Bailey Ct PTSHD/EG BS20 ....40 B2
Baileys Ct ALMDB BS32 ....21 H4
Baileys Court Rd ALMDB BS32 ....21 G4
Baileys Mead Rd
  MANG/FISH BS16 ....47 E3
Baker Cl CLVDN BS21 ....65 C4
Bakersfield
  OLD/WMLY/WICK BS30 ....76 D3
Bakers Gnd BRSTK/PCHW BS34 ..21 H5
Bakersfield 7 F3
Balaclava Rd MANG/FISH BS16 ...47 G5
Baldwin St CBRIS/FH BS1 ....5 F4
Balfour Rd BMSTR BS3 ....72 C3
Ballance St CBATH/BATHN BA1 ....3 F1
Ballast La AVONM BS11 ....28 D3
Balmain St
  BRSG/KWL/STAPK BS4 ....73 H2
Balmoral Cl BRSTK/PCHW BS34 ..21 H4
Balmoral Ct MANG/FISH BS16 ....49 C3
Balmoral Rd HORF/LLZ BS7 ....56 C2
  KEYN BS31 ....88 B5
  OLD/WMLY/WICK BS30 ....76 A4
Balmoral Wy MTN/WRL BS22 ...121 H1
Baltic Pl PTSHD/EG BS20 ....38 D5
Bamfield HGRV/WHIT BS14 ....85 C2
Bampton Cl
  BMSTRD/HC/WWD BS13 ....84 A1
  MANG/FISH BS16 ....50 A2
Bampton Cft MANG/FISH BS16 ..50 A2
Bampton Dr MANG/FISH BS16 ...34 A3
Bangor Gv
  BRSG/KWL/STAPK BS4 ....75 E1
Bangrove Wk AVONM BS11 ....29 E5
Banister Gv
  BRSG/KWL/STAPK BS4 ....85 E2
Bank Pl PTSHD/EG BS20 ....42 D4
Bank Rd AVONM BS11 ....16 D3
  KGWD/HNM BS15 ....58 D5
Banks Cl CLVDN BS21 ....64 D5
Bankside MANG/FISH BS16 ....49 F4
Bankside Rd
  BRSG/KWL/STAPK BS4 ....74 C3
Bannerdown Cl
  CBATH/BATHN BA1 ....91 G5
Bannerdown Dr
  CBATH/BATHN BA1 ....91 F5
Bannerdown Rd
  CBATH/BATHN BA1 ....104 B1
Bannerleigh La CFTN/FAIL BS8 ...54 C5
Bannerleigh Rd CFTN/FAIL BS8 ..54 C5
Bannerman Rd
  EVILLE/WHL BS5 ....56 D3
Banner Rd RDLND/MONT BS6 .....56 A2
Bantock Cl
  BRSG/KWL/STAPK BS4 ....85 F1
Bantry Rd
  BRSG/KWL/STAPK BS4 ....85 F1
Banwell Cl
  BMSTRD/HC/WWD BS13 ....84 B1
  KEYN BS31 ....98 B2
Banwell Rd BATHSE BA2 ....110 B2
  KEYN BS31 ....72 B3
  OMX/HUT/LCK BS24 ....127 E3
Banyard Rd PTSHD/EG BS20 ....41 G3
Baptist St EVILLE/WHL BS5 ....57 E1
Barberry Farm Rd
  YTN/CONG BS49 ....112 B2
Barbour Gdns
  BMSTRD/HC/WWD BS13 ....96 A1
Barbour Rd
  BMSTRD/HC/WWD BS13 ....96 A1
Barcroft Cl KGWD/HNM BS15 .....58 C3
Barkers Md YATE/CS BS37 ....14 B2
Barker Wk EVILLE/WHL BS5 ....56 C2
Barkleys HI MANG/FISH BS16 .....47 E3
Barley Cl FRCTL/WBN BS36 ....23 H2
Barley Cft
  HNLZ/SM/SNYPK/WT BS9 ....44 D3
Barley Cross MTN/WRL BS22 ....117 H3
Barnabas St CBRISNE BS2 ....56 A2
Barnard's Ct YTN/CONG BS49 ...112 C4
Barnard Wk KEYN BS31 ....88 A5
Barnes St EVILLE/WHL BS5 ....57 F1
Barnfield Wy
  CBATH/BATHN BA1 ....91 G5
Barnhill Rd YATE/CS BS37 ....26 D1
Barn Owl Wy
  BRSTK/PCHW BS34 ....21 H5
Barns Cl NAIL BS48 ....82 B5
  NAIL BS48 ....67 F4
Barns Gnd CLVDN BS21 ....65 E5
Barnstaple Rd
  BRSG/KWL/STAPK BS4 ....85 G1
Barnwell Cl HNBRY/STHM BS10 ..31 E1
Barnwood Cl NAIL BS48 ....67 F4
Barnwood Rd YATE/CS BS37 ....25 G3
Baron Cl
  OLD/WMLY/WICK BS30 ....89 H1
Barons Cl BMSTR BS3 ....72 A3
Barossa Pl CBRIS/FH BS1 * 5 F6
Barrack's La AVONM BS11 ....28 D5
Barratt St EVILLE/WHL BS5 ....56 D2
Barrington Cl
  KGWD/HNM BS15 ....59 F1
Barrington Ct
  KGWD/HNM BS15 ....59 F2
Barrow Cl CLVDN BS21 ....66 A2
Barrow Court La NAIL BS48 ....81 C3
Barrow Hi
  CLVDN BS21 ....61 F5
Barrow Hill Crs AVONM BS11 .....42 C1
Barrow Hill Rd AVONM BS11 ......42 C2
Barrow La
  BLAG/CWMG/WR BS40 ....93 G3
Barrowmead Dr AVONM BS11 ....40 A5
Barrow Rd BATHSE BA2 ....110 A1
  CBRISNE BS2 ....56 D3
  OMX/HUT/LCK BS24 ....126 B4
The Barrows MTN/WRL BS22 ....121 H4
Barrow St NAIL BS48 ....81 H4
Barrs Court Av
  OLD/WMLY/WICK BS30 ....76 D1
Barrs Court Rd
  OLD/WMLY/WICK BS30 ....76 D1
Barry Rd OLD/WMLY/WICK BS30 ..77 F5

OMX/HUT/LCK BS24 ....125 F5
Barry Rd 77 F4
Barter Cl MANG/FISH BS16 * 58 D3
Bartholomew Sq
  HORF/LLZ BS7 ....46 B1
Bartlett's Rd BMSTR BS3 ....72 D4
Bartlett St CBATH/BATHN BA1 .....3 F3
Bartletts Wy
  OMX/HUT/LCK BS24 ....127 E2
Bartley St BMSTR BS3 ....73 E2
Barton Blds
  CBATH/BATHN BA1 ....3 F3
Barton Cl
  Barton Ct EVILLE/WHL BS5 ....57 H5
  FRCTL/WBN BS36 ....23 E5
Barton Ct EVILLE/WHL BS5 ....57 E5
Barton Gn EVILLE/WHL BS5 * 56 D4
Barton Hill Rd EVILLE/WHL BS5 ..56 D4
Bartonia Gv
  BRSG/KWL/STAPK BS4 ....74 C5
Barton Mnr CBRISNE BS2 ....56 C5
Barton Rd CBRISNE BS2 ....5 K4
Barton V CBRISNE BS2 ....5 K4
Barwick AVONM BS11 * 43 E1
Barwood Cl KGWD/HNM BS15 ....59 F5
Batchfield La MANG/FISH BS16 ...37 G5
The Batch YTN/CONG BS49 ....112 B4
Bates Cl EVILLE/WHL BS5 ....56 D3
Bathampton La BATHSE BA2 .....103 H5
Bath Br BMSTR BS3 ....5 J7
Bath Blds RDLND/MONT BS6 ......56 A2
Bathford Hl
  CBATH/BATHN BA1 ....104 C2
Bath HI KEYN BS31 ....88 C4
Bath Rd BMSTR BS3 ....5 H6
  BRSG/KWL/STAPK BS4 ....73 H2
  KEYN BS31 ....88 D4
  THNB/SVB BS35 ....9 F1
Bath Road Brislington HI
  BRSG/KWL/STAPK BS4 ....74 D4
Bath St BMSTR BS3 ....72 B2
  CBATH/BATHN BA1 ....3 F5
  CBRIS/FH BS1 ....5 F5
  MANG/FISH BS16 ....49 E4
Bathurst Pde CBRIS/FH BS1 ....4 E7
Bathurst Rd MTN/WRL BS22 .....121 H2
Bathwell Rd
  BRSG/KWL/STAPK BS4 ....73 H3
Bathwick HI BATHSE BA2 ....3 K4
Bathwick Ri BATHSE BA2 ....3 K3
Bathwick St BATHSE BA2 ....3 H1
Batley Ct
  OLD/WMLY/WICK BS30 ....77 C2
Batstone Cl
  CBATH/BATHN BA1 ....102 D2
Battenburg Rd
  EVILLE/WHL BS5 ....58 A3
Batten's La YATE/CS BS37 ....58 E1
Batten's Ct EVILLE/WHL BS5 ....58 A1
Batten Rd EVILLE/WHL BS5 ....58 B3
Battersby Wy
  HNBRY/STHM BS10 ....30 C3
Battersea Rd EVILLE/WHL BS5 ....57 F4
Battery La PTSHD/EG BS20 ....39 H2
Battery Rd PTSHD/EG BS20 ....39 H2
Baugh Gdns MANG/FISH BS16 ...50 B1
Baxter Cl KGWD/HNM BS15 ....59 F3
Bay Gdns EVILLE/WHL BS5 ....57 E1
Bayham Rd
  BRSG/KWL/STAPK BS4 ....73 H3
Bayleys Dr KGWD/HNM BS15 .....58 C5
Baynton Meadow
  MANG/FISH BS16 ....50 A2
Baynton Rd BMSTR BS3 ....72 B2
Bay Rd CLVDN BS21 ....62 B4
Bayswater Av
  HNLZ/SM/SNYPK/WT BS9 ....44 D4
Bayswater Rd HORF/LLZ BS7 ......46 B1
Bay Tree Cl BRSTK/PCHW BS34 ...20 B3
Bay Tree Rd
  CBATH/BATHN BA1 ....103 E2
  CLVDN BS21 ....65 E3
Baytree Rd MTN/WRL BS22 ......121 H2
Bay Tree Vw MTN/WRL BS22 ....121 H2
Baytree Vw MTN/WRL BS22 .....121 H2
Bay Willow Dr
  RDLND/MONT BS6 ....64 C3
Beach End Rd WSM BS23 ....124 B4
Beachgrove Gdns
  MANG/FISH BS16 ....48 C4
Beachgrove Rd
  MANG/FISH BS16 ....48 C4
Beach Hi PTSHD/EG BS20 ....39 G2
Beach Ms CLVDN BS21 * 64 C1
Beach Rd MTN/WRL BS22 ....116 A5
  WSM BS23 ....124 C1
Beach Rd East PTSHD/EG BS20 ...39 H2
Beach Rd West
  PTSHD/EG BS20 ....39 H2
The Beach CLVDN BS21 ....64 C1
Beaconsfield La FRCTL/WBN BS36 ..22 D5
Beaconlea KGWD/HNM BS15 .....59 H5
Beacon Rd
  CBATH/BATHN BA1 ....102 D3
Beaconsfield Cl
  EVILLE/WHL BS5 ....56 D5
Beaconsfield Rd
  BRSG/KWL/STAPK BS4 ....74 A3
  CFTN/FAIL BS8 ....55 E1
  CLVDN BS21 ....65 E3
  EVILLE/WHL BS5 ....57 G3
  MTN/WRL BS22 ....121 C3
Beaconsfield St
  EVILLE/WHL BS5 ....56 D5
Beale Cl HGRV/WHIT BS14 * 85 F1
Beale Rd BMSTR BS3 ....72 C5
The Bean Acre AVONM BS11 ......28 D5
Bean St EVILLE/WHL BS5 ....57 E1
Bearbridge Rd
  BMSTRD/HC/WWD BS13 ....84 A5
Bear Yard Ms CFTN/FAIL BS8 * 4 C5
Beatrix Pl HORF/LLZ BS7 ....32 C5

Beauchamp Rd HORF/LLZ BS7 ....45 H4
Beauford Sq CBATH/BATHN BA1 ...3 F4
Beaufort Cl EVILLE/WHL BS5 ....57 F4
Beaufort Crs
  BRSTK/PCHW BS34 ....33 G1
Beaufort East
  CBATH/BATHN BA1 ....103 F3
Beaufort Ms
  CBATH/BATHN BA1 ....103 F3
  EVILLE/WHL BS8 * 54 D4
Beaufort Pl
  CBATH/BATHN BA1 ....103 F3
  MANG/FISH BS16 ....34 B4
Beaufort Rd CFTN/FAIL BS8 ....55 E2
  CFTN/FAIL BS8 ....55 C2
  FRCTL/WBN BS36 ....23 C2
  HORF/LLZ BS7 ....46 B2
  KGWD/HNM BS15 ....58 B1
  MANG/FISH BS16 ....49 E4
  WSM BS23 ....7 C4
  YATE/CS BS37 ....13 H5
Beaufort St EVILLE/WHL BS5 ....72 D4
  EVILLE/WHL BS5 ....56 C3
Beaufort Vls
  CBATH/BATHN BA1 * 103 E3
Beaufort West
  CBATH/BATHN BA1 ....103 F3
Beauley Rd BMSTR BS3 ....72 C2
Beaumont Cl
  OLD/WMLY/WICK BS30 ....76 D3
  WSM BS23 ....125 E2
Beaumont St EVILLE/WHL BS5 ....56 C3
Beaumont Ter EVILLE/WHL BS5 ..56 C3
Beau St CBATH/BATHN BA1 ....3 F5
Beaver Cl FRCTL/WBN BS36 ....23 F5
Beazer Cl MANG/FISH BS16 ....48 D5
Beck Cl MANG/FISH BS16 ....50 A2
Becket Dr MTN/WRL BS22 ....117 H4
Becket Rd MTN/WRL BS22 ....117 H4
Becket's La NAIL BS48 ....79 F1
Beckford Ct BATHSE BA2 * 3 K2
Beckford Gdns BATHSE BA2 ....3 K1
  HGRV/WHIT BS14 ....96 D1
Beckford Rd BATHSE BA2 ....3 K2
Beckhampton Rd BATHSE BA2 ......2 B7
Beckington Rd BRSG/KWL/STAPK BS4 ..73 G4
Beckington Wk BMSTR BS3 ....73 C4
Beckspool Rd MANG/FISH BS16 ..34 C5
Bedford Crs HORF/LLZ BS7 ....46 C3
Bedford Rd WSM BS23 ....124 D2
Bedford St CBATH/BATHN BA1 ..102 D4
Bedminster Br BMSTR BS3 ....73 F2
Bedminster Down Rd
  BMSTRD/HC/WWD BS13 ....72 B5
Bedminster Pde BMSTR BS3 ....73 E2
Bedminster Rd BMSTR BS3 ....72 C5
Bedwin Cl PTSHD/EG BS20 ....38 D4
Beech Av PTSHD/EG BS20 ....109 H3
Beech Cl
  HNLZ/SM/SNYPK/WT BS9 ....30 A5
Beech Gv BATHSE BA2 ....107 H3
Beechmont Dr
  OMX/HUT/LCK BS24 ....125 E5
Beechmont Gv
  HGRV/WHIT BS14 ....86 A1
Beech Rd HORF/LLZ BS7 ....46 A3
  YTN/CONG BS49 ....111 F5
Beechwood Av
  KGWD/HNM BS15 ....76 A1
  OMX/HUT/LCK BS24 ....126 D1
Beechwood Cl
  HGRV/WHIT BS14 ....86 B1
Beechwood Rd BATHSE BA2 ......111 F1
  MANG/FISH BS16 ....48 A4
  NAIL BS48 ....67 E4
  PTSHD/EG BS20 ....42 A4
  PTSHD/EG BS20 ....38 C4
Beehive Yd CBATH/BATHN BA1 .....3 H3
Beesmoor Rd
  FRCTL/WBN BS36 ....23 H3
Begbrook Dr MANG/FISH BS16 ...47 H2
Begbrook La MANG/FISH BS16 ...48 A1
Begbrook Pk MANG/FISH BS16 ...48 B1
Beggar Bush La CFTN/FAIL BS8 ...70 A2
Beggarswell Cl CBRISNE BS2 ....56 B3
Belfast Wk
  BRSG/KWL/STAPK BS4 ....85 F1
Belfields La MANG/FISH BS16 .....34 C4
Belfry OLD/WMLY/WICK BS30 ...59 H5
Belgrave Crs
  CBATH/BATHN BA1 ....102 D4
Belgrave Hi CFTN/FAIL BS8 ....55 E1
Belgrave Pl
  CBATH/BATHN BA1 ....102 D4
  CFTN/FAIL BS8 ....55 E4
Belgrave Rd
  CBATH/BATHN BA1 ....103 E3
  CFTN/FAIL BS8 ....55 E4
  MTN/WRL BS22 ....121 C3
Bellamy Av
  BMSTRD/HC/WWD BS13 ....84 D5
Bellamy Cl KGWD/HNM BS15 .....75 F1
Belland Dr HGRV/WHIT BS14 ......85 G5
Bella Vista Rd
  CBATH/BATHN BA1 ....102 C4
Bell Barn Rd
  HNLZ/SM/SNYPK/WT BS9 ....44 B2
Bell Cl HNBRY/STHM BS10 ....46 A1

Bellevue CFTN/FAIL BS8 ....4 A4
Bellevue Cl KGWD/HNM BS15 .....59 E4
Bellevue Crs CFTN/FAIL BS8 ....55 E4
Bellevue Pk
  BRSG/KWL/STAPK BS4 ....74 C4
Bellevue Rd
  BRSG/KWL/STAPK BS4 ....73 G2
  CLVDN BS21 ....64 D1
  EVILLE/WHL BS5 ....57 G3
Bellevue Rd KGWD/HNM BS15 ....59 F4
Bellevue Ter
  BRSG/KWL/STAPK BS4 ....73 G2
Bell Hill MANG/FISH BS16 ....47 E4
Bell Hill Rd EVILLE/WHL BS5 ....57 H5
Bellhouse Wk AVONM BS11 ....29 H4
Bellotts Rd BATHSE BA2 ....101 H4
Bell Rd FRCTL/WBN BS36 ....24 A3
Belluton Rd
  BRSG/KWL/STAPK BS4 ....73 H3
Belmont CBATH/BATHN BA1 * 3 F3
Belmont Dr BRSTK/PCHW BS34 ..21 C5
  CFTN/FAIL BS8 ....69 G3
Belmont Hi NAIL BS48 ....79 C2
Belmont Pk HORF/LLZ BS7 * 32 B4
Belmont Rd BATHSE BA2 ....111 C1
  BRSG/KWL/STAPK BS4 ....74 A3
  RDLND/MONT BS6 ....56 A1
Belmont St EVILLE/WHL BS5 ....56 D2
Belmore Gdns BATHSE BA2 ....107 C4
Belroyal Av
  BRSG/KWL/STAPK BS4 ....75 E3
Beisher Dr KGWD/HNM BS15 ......58 D3
Belstone Wk
  BRSG/KWL/STAPK BS4 ....84 D2
Belton Rd EVILLE/WHL BS5 ....56 D2
  PTSHD/EG BS20 ....39 E2
Belvedere CBATH/BATHN BA1 ......3 F2
Belvedere Crs MTN/WRL BS22 ...121 H2
Belvedere Rd
  RDLND/MONT BS6 ....45 E5
Belvoir Rd BATHSE BA2 * 2 A2
  RDLND/MONT BS6 ....56 A1
Bence Ct KGWD/HNM BS15 ....58 B5
Benford Cl MANG/FISH BS16 ....48 C2
Bennett La
  CBATH/BATHN BA1 ....102 D3
Bennett Rd EVILLE/WHL BS5 ....58 A1
Bennett's Ct YATE/CS BS37 ....26 B1
Bennett's Rd
  CBATH/BATHN BA1 ....103 F1
Bennett St CBATH/BATHN BA1 ......3 F3
Bennetts Wy CLVDN BS21 ....62 C5
Bensaunt Gv
  HNBRY/STHM BS10 ....31 H1
Bentley Cl HGRV/WHIT BS14 ....96 D1
Bentley Rd MTN/WRL BS22 ....118 A5
Benville Av
  HNLZ/SM/SNYPK/WT BS9 ....30 A5
Berenda Dr
  OLD/WMLY/WICK BS30 ....77 E5
Beresford Cl KEYN BS31 ....99 F2
Beresford Gdns
  CBATH/BATHN BA1 ....101 F1
Berkeley Av CFTN/FAIL BS8 ....4 C3
  HORF/LLZ BS7 ....45 F5
Berkeley Crs CFTN/FAIL BS8 ....4 C5
  WSM BS23 ....124 B4
Berkeley Gdns KEYN BS31 ....88 A5
Berkeley Gn MANG/FISH BS16 ....48 B3
Berkeley Green Rd
  EVILLE/WHL BS5 ....57 E1
Berkeley Pl
  CBATH/BATHN BA1 * 102 D4
Berkeley Rd MANG/FISH BS16 ....58 A1
  RDLND/MONT BS6 ....45 E4
Berkeleys Md ALMDB BS32 ....21 H4
Berkeley Sq CFTN/FAIL BS8 ....4 B3
Berkeley Wy MANG/FISH BS16 ...49 H1
Berkshire Rd HORF/LLZ BS7 ....45 F5
Berners Cl
  BRSG/KWL/STAPK BS4 * 85 E2
Berrow Wk BMSTR BS3 ....73 F4
Berry Hill Cl
  HNBRY/STHM BS10 ....32 D1
Berry La HORF/LLZ BS7 ....46 C2
Berwick Cl THNB/SVB BS35 ....17 H5
Berwick Dr HNBRY/STHM BS10 ...18 A5
Berwick La AVONM BS11 ....18 A5
Berwick Rd EVILLE/WHL BS5 ....56 D2
Beryl Gv HGRV/WHIT BS14 ....86 C1
Beryl Rd BMSTR BS3 ....72 C3
Besom La YATE/CS BS37 ....35 F4
Bethel Rd EVILLE/WHL BS5 ....57 F2
Betjeman Ct
  OLD/WMLY/WICK BS30 ....76 D1
Betts Gn MANG/FISH BS16 ....50 A1
Bevan Ct BRSTK/PCHW BS34 ....32 B3
Beverley Av MANG/FISH BS16 .....35 E5
Beverley Cl EVILLE/WHL BS5 ....58 B5
Beverley Gdns
  HNLZ/SM/SNYPK/WT BS9 ....44 B1
Beverstone Gdns HORF/LLZ BS7 ..32 D1
Beverston Gdns AVONM BS11 .....29 H5
Bevington Cl
  BRSTK/PCHW BS34 ....20 A1
Bevington Wk
  BRSTK/PCHW BS34 ....20 A1
Bewdley Rd BATHSE BA2 ....109 E3
Bexley Rd MANG/FISH BS16 ....50 A1
Bibstone KGWD/HNM BS15 ....59 G3
Bibury Av BRSTK/PCHW BS34 .....20 C2
Bibury Cl
  HNLZ/SM/SNYPK/WT BS9 ....45 H1
  NAIL BS48 ....67 E4
Bibury Crs
  HNLZ/SM/SNYPK/WT BS9 ....45 H1
  KGWD/HNM BS15 ....75 C4
Bickerton Cl
  HNBRY/STHM BS10 ....30 D2
Bickford Cl
  OLD/WMLY/WICK BS30 ....59 H5
Bickley Cl KGWD/HNM BS15 ....75 C4

Biddestone Rd *HORF/LLZ* BS7 **32** A4
Biddisham Cl *NAIL* BS48 **67** F5
Biddle St *YTN/CONG* BS49 **112** A4
Bideford Crs
BRSG/KWL/STAPK BS4 **85** G1
Bideford Rd *MTN/WRL* BS22 **122** C1
Bidwell Cl *HNBRY/STHM* BS10 **31** F2
Bifield Cl *HGRV/WHIT* BS14 **87** E4
Bifield Gdns *HGRV/WHIT* BS14 **86** D4
Bifield Rd *HGRV/WHIT* BS14 **87** E4
Bigwood La *CBRIS/FH* BS1 **4** C4
Bilberry Cl
HNLZ/SM/SNYPK/WT BS9 **30** A5
Bilbie Cl *HNBRY/STHM* BS10 **45** H2
Bilbie Rd *MTN/WRL* BS22 **118** A5
Bilbury La *CBATH/BATHN* BA1 **3** F5
Billand Cl
BMSTRD/HC/WWD BS13 **94** D1
Bindon Dr *HNBRY/STHM* BS10 **31** H1
Binhay Rd *YTN/CONG* BS49 **112** C4
Binley Gv *HGRV/WHIT* BS14 **86** C4
Binmead Gdns
BMSTRD/HC/WWD BS13 **84** C5
Birbeck Rd
HNLZ/SM/SNYPK/WT BS9 **44** C3
Birchall Rd *RDLND/MONT* BS6 **45** G4
Birch Av *CLVDN* BS21 **65** E1
Birch Cl *BRSTK/PCHW* BS34 **20** A3
OMX/HUT/LCK BS24 **127** E2
Birch Ct *KEYN* BS31 **87** H5
YATE/CS BS37 **13** H5
Birch Cft *HGRV/WHIT* BS14 **96** D1
Birchdale Rd *HGRV/WHIT* BS14 **85** H5
Birch Dene *NAIL* BS48 **67** H4
Birch Dr *MANG/FISH* BS16 **51** F3
The Birches *NAIL* BS48 * **67** H4
Birch Gv *PTSHD/EG* BS20 **39** G4
Birch Rd *BMSTR* BS3 **72** C2
KGWD/HNM BS15 **49** E5
YATE/CS BS37 **13** H5
Birchwood Av *WSM* BS23 **7** K4
Birchwood Ct
BRSG/KWL/STAPK BS4 **57** H5
Birchwood Rd
BRSG/KWL/STAPK BS4 **74** D2
Birdale Cl *HNBRY/STHM* BS10 **30** C2
Birdcombe Cl *NAIL* BS48 **67** F3
Birdlip Cl *NAIL* BS48 **79** G1
Birdwell La *LGASH* BS41 **70** C5
Birdwell Rd *LGASH* BS41 **70** C5
Birdwood *KGWD/HNM* BS15 **58** D5
Birkbeck Ct *WSM* BS23 **6** D5
Birkdale
OLD/WMLY/WICK BS30 **59** H5
YATE/CS BS37 **26** A2
Birkett Rd *WSM* BS23 **120** A2
Birkin St *CBRISNE* BS2 **5** K4
Birnbeck Rd *WSM* BS23 **6** A1
Biscay Dr *PTSHD/EG* BS20 **40** B3
Bisdee Rd
OMX/HUT/LCK BS24 **126** A3
Bishop Av *MTN/WRL* BS22 **117** H5
Bishop La *HORF/LLZ* BS7 * **46** A4
Bishop Manor Rd
HNBRY/STHM BS10 **45** H1
Bishop Ms *CBRISNE* BS2 * **56** A3
Bishop Rd *HORF/LLZ* BS7 **45** G4
MANG/FISH BS16 **50** A2
Bishops Cl
HNLZ/SM/SNYPK/WT BS9 **44** C5
Bishops Cove
BMSTRD/HC/WWD BS13 **84** A4
Bishops Knoll
HNLZ/SM/SNYPK/WT BS9 **44** A5
Bishops Md *YTN/CONG* BS49 **113** G3
Bishops Rd *YTN/CONG* BS49 **113** F3
Bishop St *CBRISNE* BS2 **56** A3
Bishop's Wd *ALMDB* BS32 **11** E1
Bishopsworth Rd
BMSTRD/HC/WWD BS13 **84** B2
Bishop Ter *CBRISNE* BS2 * **56** A3
Bishopthorpe Rd
HNBRY/STHM BS10 **45** H1
Bishport Av
BMSTRD/HC/WWD BS13 **95** H1
Bishport Cl
BMSTRD/HC/WWD BS13 **84** C5
Bisley *YATE/CS* BS37 **25** G3
Bissex Md *MANG/FISH* BS16 **49** H3
Bittern Cl *MTN/WRL* BS22 **122** C2
Bitterwell Cl *FRCTL/WBN* BS36 **36** B2
Blackacre *HGRV/WHIT* BS14 **97** F1
Blackberry Av
MANG/FISH BS16 **47** G3
Blackberry Dr
FRCTL/WBN BS36 **23** H4
MTN/WRL BS22 **122** D2
Blackberry Hl *MANG/FISH* BS16 **47** G3
Blackcurrant Dr *LGASH* BS41 **82** B1
Blackdown Ct
HGRV/WHIT BS14 **86** A4
Blackdown Rd *PTSHD/EG* BS20 **39** E3
Blackfriars Rd *NAIL* BS48 **78** C1
Blackhorse Hl *THNB/SVB* BS35 **19** F2
Blackhorse La
MANG/FISH BS16 **35** G5
Blackhorse Pl
MANG/FISH BS16 **49** G2
Blackhorse Rd
KGWD/HNM BS15 **58** D4
MANG/FISH BS16 **49** G2
Blackmoor *CLVDN* BS21 **64** C4
Blackmoor Rd *CFTN/FAIL* BS8 **53** E1
Blackmoors La *BMSTR* BS3 **71** H3
Blackmore Dr *BATHSE* BA2 **107** C2
Black Nore Point
PTSHD/EG BS20 **38** D3
Blackrock La *HGRV/WHIT* BS14 **97** G4
Blacksmith La
CBATH/BATHN BA1 **90** A3
Blackswarth Rd
EVILLE/WHL BS5 **57** F4
Blackthorn Cl
BMSTRD/HC/WWD BS13 **85** E4
Blackthorn Dr *ALMDB* BS32 **21** F3
Blackthorn Gdns
MTN/WRL BS22 **122** D2
Blackthorn Rd
BMSTRD/HC/WWD BS13 **85** E4
Blackthorn Sq *CLVDN* BS21 **64** D4
Blackthorn Wk
KGWD/HNM BS15 **59** E1
Blackthorn Wy *NAIL* BS48 **67** G4
Bladen Cl *PTSHD/EG* BS20 **40** A4
Bladud's Blds
CBATH/BATHN BA1 **3** G3
Blagdon Cl *BMSTR* BS3 **73** F4
OMX/HUT/LCK BS24 **125** E5
Blagdon Pk *BATHSE* BA2 **107** F3
Blagrove Cl
BMSTRD/HC/WWD BS13 **95** H1
Blagrove Crs
BMSTRD/HC/WWD BS13 **95** H1
Blaisdon *MTN/WRL* BS22 **122** A4
YATE/CS BS37 **26** A3
Blaisdon Cl *HNBRY/STHM* BS10 **30** D4
Blaisedell Vw
HNBRY/STHM BS10 **30** B2
Blaise Hamlet
HNBRY/STHM BS10 * **30** C3
Blaise Wk
HNLZ/SM/SNYPK/WT BS9 **44** A2
Blake End *MTN/WRL* BS22 **117** F4
Blakeney Gv *NAIL* BS48 **78** D1
Blakeney Mills *YATE/CS* BS37 **25** H1
Blakeney Rd
BRSTK/PCHW BS34 **20** A1
HORF/LLZ BS7 **46** C1
Blake Rd *HORF/LLZ* BS7 **46** D2
Blakes Rd *THNB/SVB* BS35 **8** C3
Blanchards *YATE/CS* BS37 **27** E2
Blandamour Wy
HNBRY/STHM BS10 **31** H3
Blandford Cl
HNLZ/SM/SNYPK/WT BS9 **45** F2
NAIL BS48 **67** E5
Blenheim Cl *MTN/WRL* BS22 **122** D1
Blenheim Dr
BRSTK/PCHW BS34 **32** D1
YATE/CS BS37 **13** G4
Blenheim Gdns
CBATH/BATHN BA1 **102** D2
Blenheim Rd
RDLND/MONT BS6 **45** F5
Blenheim St *EVILLE/WHL* BS5 **56** C2
Blenheim Wy *PTSHD/EG* BS20 **40** A4
Blenman Cl *MANG/FISH* BS16 **48** A1
Blethwin Cl *HNBRY/STHM* BS10 **30** D4
Blind La *CBATH/BATHN* BA1 **101** H2
YTN/CONG BS49 **113** E4
Bloomfield Av *BATHSE* BA2 **108** B3
Bloomfield Dr *BATHSE* BA2 **108** A5
Bloomfield Gv *BATHSE* BA2 **108** B4
Bloomfield Pk *BATHSE* BA2 **108** B4
Bloomfield Ri *BATHSE* BA2 **108** A5
Bloomfield Ri North
BATHSE BA2 * **108** A5
Bloomfield Rd *BATHSE* BA2 **108** A5
BRSG/KWL/STAPK BS4 **74** B2
Bloomfield Road Link
BRSG/KWL/STAPK BS4 **74** B2
Bloy St *EVILLE/WHL* BS5 **57** E2
Bluebell Cl *THNB/SVB* BS35 **9** E2
Bluebell Rd *MTN/WRL* BS22 **117** H2
The Bluebells *ALMDB* BS32 **21** G3
Blueberry Wy *MTN/WRL* BS22 **122** C2
Blue Falcon Rd
KGWD/HNM BS15 **59** E1
Blue Water Dr
OMX/HUT/LCK BS24 **127** G3
Blythe Gdns *MTN/WRL* BS22 * **117** H5
Boat Stall La *CBATH/BATHN* BA1 **3** G4
Bockenem Cl *THNB/SVB* BS35 **9** E5
Bodley Wy
OMX/HUT/LCK BS24 **122** B4
Bodmin Wk
BRSG/KWL/STAPK BS4 **85** G1
Bolton Rd *HORF/LLZ* BS7 **46** A5
Bond St *CBRISNE* BS2 **5** H1
Bonnington Wk *HORF/LLZ* BS7 **46** D1
Bonville Rd
BRSG/KWL/STAPK BS4 **74** D5
Boon Vls *AVONM* BS11 **43** E1
Booth Rd *BMSTR* BS3 **72** D2
Boot La *BMSTR* BS3 **73** E2
Bordesley Rd *HGRV/WHIT* BS14 **96** D1
Boreal Wy
OMX/HUT/LCK BS24 **122** C3
Borgie Pl *MTN/WRL* BS22 **117** F5
Borleyton Wk
BMSTRD/HC/WWD BS13 **84** A5
Borver Gv
BMSTRD/HC/WWD BS13 **84** C5
Boscombe Crs *MANG/FISH* BS16 **35** F5
Boston Rd *HORF/LLZ* BS7 **32** B5
Boswell St *EVILLE/WHL* BS5 **57** E1
Botham Cl *MTN/WRL* BS22 **117** H4
Botham Dr
BRSG/KWL/STAPK BS4 **74** D5
Bottom Cl *HGRV/WHIT* BS14 **85** H5
Boucher Pl *CBRISNE* BS2 * **56** C1
Boulevard *WSM* BS23 **6** E3
Boulters Rd
BMSTRD/HC/WWD BS13 **84** D5
Boulton's Rd *KGWD/HNM* BS15 **58** D3
Boundary Cl *WSM* BS23 **124** D3
Boundary Rd *AVONM* BS11 **28** D2
FRCTL/WBN BS36 **24** B3
OMX/HUT/LCK BS24 **122** D4
Bourchier Gdns
BMSTRD/HC/WWD BS13 **95** G1
Bourne Cl *FRCTL/WBN* BS36 **23** E3
KGWD/HNM BS15 **58** B3
Bourne Rd *KGWD/HNM* BS15 **58** A3
Bourneville Rd
EVILLE/WHL BS5 **57** F3
Bournville Rd *WSM* BS23 **125** E2
Boursland Cl *ALMDB* BS32 **11** F5
Bourton Av *BRSTK/PCHW* BS34 **21** E2
Bourton Cl *BRSTK/PCHW* BS34 **21** E2
Bourton Combe *NAIL* BS48 **81** E2
Bourton La *MTN/WRL* BS22 **118** C4
Bourton Md *LGASH* BS41 * **70** D5
NAIL BS48 **81** E1
Bourton Wk
BMSTRD/HC/WWD BS13 **84** B1
Boverton Rd
BRSTK/PCHW BS34 **32** D2
Bowden Cl
HNLZ/SM/SNYPK/WT BS9 **30** A5
Bowden Pl *MANG/FISH* BS16 **49** F1
Bowden Rd *EVILLE/WHL* BS5 **57** G2
Bowden Wy *CFTN/FAIL* BS8 **69** G3
Bowen Rd
OMX/HUT/LCK BS24 **127** E2
Bower Ashton Ter *BMSTR* BS3 **72** A2
Bowerleaze
HNLZ/SM/SNYPK/WT BS9 **43** H3
Bower Rd *BMSTR* BS3 **72** B3
Bower Wk *BMSTR* BS3 **73** F3
Bowling Hl *YATE/CS* BS37 **26** C1
Bowling Rd *YATE/CS* BS37 **26** D2
Bow Md
BRSG/KWL/STAPK BS4 * **74** C5
Bowring Cl
BMSTRD/HC/WWD BS13 **95** H1
Bowsland Wy *ALMDB* BS32 **11** F5
Bowstreet La *THNB/SVB* BS35 **19** E2
Boxhedge Farm La
FRCTL/WBN BS36 **36** C2
Box Rd *CBATH/BATHN* BA1 **104** D1
Boyce Cl *BATHSE* BA2 **107** E2
Boyce Dr *CBRISNE* BS2 **56** C1
Boyce's Av *CFTN/FAIL* BS8 **55** E4
Boyd Cl
OLD/WMLY/WICK BS30 **61** F4
Boyd Rd *KEYN* BS31 **99** E1
Brabazon Rd
BRSTK/PCHW BS34 **32** D3
Bracewell Gdns
HNBRY/STHM BS10 **31** G1
Bracey Dr *MANG/FISH* BS16 **48** C2
Brackenbury Dr
BRSTK/PCHW BS34 **21** G5
Brackendene *ALMDB* BS32 **21** E1
Brackenwood Gdns
PTSHD/EG BS20 **38** D3
Brackenwood Rd *CLVDN* BS21 **62** C4
Bracton Dr *HGRV/WHIT* BS14 **85** H5
Bradeston Gv *MANG/FISH* BS16 **48** A1
Bradford Cl *CLVDN* BS21 **64** C4
Bradford Pk *BATHSE* BA2 **108** D5
Bradford Rd *BATHSE* BA2 **110** D1
CBATH/BATHN BA1 **104** C3
Bradhurst St *EVILLE/WHL* BS5 **56** D5
Bradley Av *AVONM* BS11 **43** E2
FRCTL/WBN BS36 **23** E5
Bradley Crs *AVONM* BS11 **43** E2
Bradley Rd *BRSTK/PCHW* BS34 **20** B2
PTSHD/EG BS20 **41** G3
Bradley Stoke Wy *ALMDB* BS32 **21** G2
Bradstone Rd *FRCTL/WBN* BS36 **22** D5
Bradville Gdns *LGASH* BS41 **82** C1
Bradwell Gv
HNBRY/STHM BS10 **31** G5
Braemar Av *HORF/LLZ* BS7 **32** B4
Braemar Crs *HORF/LLZ* BS7 **32** B4
Bragg's La *CBRISNE* BS2 **5** K2
Braikenridge Cl *CLVDN* BS21 **64** C4
Braikenridge Rd
BRSG/KWL/STAPK BS4 **74** C2
Brainsfield
HNLZ/SM/SNYPK/WT BS9 **44** D2
Brake Cl *ALMDB* BS32 **21** G4
KGWD/HNM BS15 **59** F4
The Brake *FRCTL/WBN* BS36 **24** A5
YATE/CS BS37 **14** A2
Bramble Dr
HNLZ/SM/SNYPK/WT BS9 **44** A5
Bramble La
HNLZ/SM/SNYPK/WT BS9 **44** A5
Bramble Rd *MTN/WRL* BS22 **117** F5
The Brambles
BMSTRD/HC/WWD BS13 **84** D5
MTN/WRL BS22 **123** G1
Bramble Wy *BATHSE* BA2 **109** E5
Bramblewood
YTN/CONG BS49 **112** B2
Brambling Wk
MANG/FISH BS16 **47** H2
Bramley Cl
OMX/HUT/LCK BS24 **126** D2
PTSHD/EG BS20 **42** C4
YTN/CONG BS49 **112** B4
Bramley Copse *LGASH* BS41 **82** B1
Bramley Ct
OLD/WMLY/WICK BS30 **76** C2
Bramley Dr *NAIL* BS48 **79** H4
Bramley Sq *YTN/CONG* BS49 * **115** E3
The Bramleys *NAIL* BS48 **78** C1
PTSHD/EG BS20 **40** B3
Brampton Wy *PTSHD/EG* BS20 **40** A3
Branche Gv
BMSTRD/HC/WWD BS13 **96** A1
Brandash Rd *YATE/CS* BS37 **27** E1
Brandon Hill La *CFTN/FAIL* BS8 **4** B3
Brandon Steep *CBRIS/FH* BS1 **4** C4
Brandon St *CBRIS/FH* BS1 **4** C5
Brangwyn Gv *HORF/LLZ* BS7 **46** D2
Brangwyn Sq *MTN/WRL* BS22 **122** C1
Branksome Crs
BRSTK/PCHW BS34 **32** D2
Branksome Dr
BRSTK/PCHW BS34 **32** D2
FRCTL/WBN BS36 **23** E4
Branksome Rd
RDLND/MONT BS6 **45** F5
Bransby Wy
OMX/HUT/LCK BS24 **122** D3
Branscombe Rd
HNLZ/SM/SNYPK/WT BS9 **44** A4
Branscombe Wk
PTSHD/EG BS20 **38** D5
Branwhite Cl *HORF/LLZ* BS7 **46** D1
Brassmill La
CBATH/BATHN BA1 **101** F5
Bratton Rd
BRSG/KWL/STAPK BS4 **85** E2
Braunton Rd *BMSTR* BS3 **72** D3
Braydon Av *BRSTK/PCHW* BS34 **21** F2
Brayne Ct
OLD/WMLY/WICK BS30 **76** C3
Breaches Ga *ALMDB* BS32 **21** H4
The Breaches *PTSHD/EG* BS20 **42** B4
Breach La *NAIL* BS48 **78** A1
Breach Rd *BMSTR* BS3 **72** B3
Breachwood Vw *BATHSE* BA2 **107** H5
Brean Down Av
HNLZ/SM/SNYPK/WT BS9 **45** F3
WSM BS23 **124** C2
Brean Gdns *BMSTR* BS3 **73** F4
Brecknock Rd
BRSG/KWL/STAPK BS4 **73** H3
Brecon Cl
HNLZ/SM/SNYPK/WT BS9 **45** F2
Brecon Rd
HNLZ/SM/SNYPK/WT BS9 **45** E2
Brecon Vw
OMX/HUT/LCK BS24 **125** F5
Bredon *YATE/CS* BS37 **25** H3
Bredon Cl *KGWD/HNM* BS15 **59** F4
Bredon Nook Rd
HNBRY/STHM BS10 **45** G1
Bree Cl *MTN/WRL* BS22 **117** H4
Brendon Av *WSM* BS23 **7** H1
Brendon Cl
OLD/WMLY/WICK BS30 **77** F2
Brendon Rd *BMSTR* BS3 **73** E3
PTSHD/EG BS20 **39** E3
Brenner St *EVILLE/WHL* BS5 **56** D1
Brent Cl *OMX/HUT/LCK* BS24 **125** G4
Brent Rd *HORF/LLZ* BS7 **46** B3
Brentry Av *EVILLE/WHL* BS5 **56** D4
Brentry La *HNBRY/STHM* BS10 **31** E3
Brentry Rd *MANG/FISH* BS16 **47** G4
Brereton Wy
OLD/WMLY/WICK BS30 **77** E2
Brewerton Cl
HNBRY/STHM BS10 **31** G2
Brewhouse *CBRIS/FH* BS1 * **5** G4
Briar Cl *NAIL* BS48 **67** H4
Briar Ct *PTSHD/EG* BS20 **42** C4
Briarfield Av *KGWD/HNM* BS15 **75** H1
Briar Md *YTN/CONG* BS49 **112** A2
Briar Rd *OMX/HUT/LCK* BS24 **126** B3
Briars Ct *BATHSE* BA2 **107** F3
Briarside Rd
HNBRY/STHM BS10 **31** G2
The Briars *NAIL* BS48 **79** G2
Briar Wk *MANG/FISH* BS16 **48** C5
Briar Wy *MANG/FISH* BS16 **48** B4
Briarwood
HNLZ/SM/SNYPK/WT BS9 **44** D2
Briary Rd *PTSHD/EG* BS20 **39** G3
Briavels Gv *RDLND/MONT* BS6 **56** B1
Brick St *CBRISNE* BS2 **5** K2
Bridewell La *CBATH/BATHN* BA1 **3** F4
OMX/HUT/LCK BS24 **127** E5
Bridewell St *CBRIS/FH* BS1 **5** F2
Bridge Cl *HGRV/WHIT* BS14 **86** B5
Bridge Farm Cl
HGRV/WHIT BS14 * **96** D1
Bridge Farm Sq
YTN/CONG BS49 **114** D2
Bridge Farm Wk
MANG/FISH BS16 **49** H5
Bridgeleap Rd
MANG/FISH BS16 **35** F5
Bridge Rd *BATHSE* BA2 **107** H2
CFTN/FAIL BS8 **54** B5
EVILLE/WHL BS5 **46** D5
KGWD/HNM BS15 **49** F5
WSM BS23 **7** H6
YATE/CS BS37 **13** E5
Bridges Ct *MANG/FISH* BS16 **48** B4
Bridges Dr *MANG/FISH* BS16 **48** C2
Bridge St *CBRIS/FH* BS1 **5** F4
EVILLE/WHL BS5 **57** F1
Bridge Valley Rd
CFTN/FAIL BS8 **54** C3
Bridge Wk *HORF/LLZ* BS7 **32** C5
Bridge Wy *FRCTL/WBN* BS36 **23** H2
Bridgman Gv
BRSTK/PCHW BS34 **32** D2
Bridgwater Ct
OMX/HUT/LCK BS24 **125** F3
Bridgwater Rd *LGASH* BS41 **82** D5
NAIL BS48 **93** E2
Briercliffe Rd
HNLZ/SM/SNYPK/WT BS9 **44** B1
Brierly Furlong
BRSTK/PCHW BS34 **33** F2
Briery Leaze Rd
HGRV/WHIT BS14 **85** H4
Brighton Crs *BMSTR* BS3 **72** C4
Brighton Ms *CFTN/FAIL* BS8 **55** F3
Brighton Pk *EVILLE/WHL* BS5 **56** D3
Brighton Pl *KGWD/HNM* BS15 **58** D2
Brighton Rd
BRSTK/PCHW BS34 **20** B2
RDLND/MONT BS6 **55** G2
WSM BS23 **7** F7
Brighton St *CBRISNE* BS2 **56** A2
Brighton Ter *BMSTR* BS3 **72** C4
Bright St *EVILLE/WHL* BS5 **56** D4
KGWD/HNM BS15 **58** D3
Brigstocke Rd *CBRISNE* BS2 **56** A2
The Brimbles *HORF/LLZ* BS7 **32** D3
Brimbleworth La
MTN/WRL BS22 **118** B5
Brinkworthy Rd
MANG/FISH BS16 **47** F2
Brinmead Wk
BMSTRD/HC/WWD BS13 **95** E1
Brins Cl *BRSTK/PCHW* BS34 **33** H1
Brinsea Rd *YTN/CONG* BS49 **114** D2
Brinsham La *YATE/CS* BS37 **14** C1
Brinsmead Crs
PTSHD/EG BS20 **42** D4
Briscoes Av
BMSTRD/HC/WWD BS13 **84** D5
Bristol & Bath Railway Pth
BATHSE BA2 **100** D4
EVILLE/WHL BS5 **57** F2
KEYN BS31 **99** H2
MANG/FISH BS16 **48** A4
OLD/WMLY/WICK BS30 **60** A4
Bristol Br *CBRIS/FH* BS1 **5** G4
Bristol Hl
BRSG/KWL/STAPK BS4 **74** C4
Bristol Pkwy North
BRSTK/PCHW BS34 * **34** A1
Bristol Rd *BATHSE* BA2 **100** A4
FRCTL/WBN BS36 **23** F2
HGRV/WHIT BS14 **97** F1
KEYN BS31 **88** A3
MANG/FISH BS16 **34** B5
MTN/WRL BS22 **123** F1
NAIL BS48 **68** B2
PTSHD/EG BS20 **39** H4
THNB/SVB BS35 **8** C5
YTN/CONG BS49 **114** D1
Bristol Road Lower *WSM* BS23 **6** E1
Bristow Broadway
AVONM BS11 **28** C4
Britannia Cl *MANG/FISH* BS16 **35** F4
Britannia Crs
BRSTK/PCHW BS34 **21** F5
Britannia Rd
BRSTK/PCHW BS34 **19** H3
EVILLE/WHL BS5 **56** D2
KGWD/HNM BS15 **58** C3
Britannia Wy *CLVDN* BS21 **64** C4
British Rd *BMSTR* BS3 **72** D3
Brittan Pl *PTSHD/EG* BS20 **41** G5
Britten Ct
OLD/WMLY/WICK BS30 **76** C2
Britton Gdns *KGWD/HNM* BS15 **58** C2
Brixham Rd *BMSTR* BS3 **72** D4
Brixton Rd *EVILLE/WHL* BS5 **56** D3
Brixton Road Ms
EVILLE/WHL BS5 **56** D3
Broadbury Rd
BRSG/KWL/STAPK BS4 **85** F1
Broad Cft *ALMDB* BS32 **11** E5
Broadcroft Av
YTN/CONG BS49 **113** F2
Broadcroft Cl *YTN/CONG* BS49 **113** F2
Broadfield Av
KGWD/HNM BS15 **58** C3
Broadfield Rd
BRSG/KWL/STAPK BS4 **73** H5
Broadlands *CLVDN* BS21 **65** F2
Broadlands Av *KEYN* BS31 **88** A3
Broadlands Dr *AVONM* BS11 **29** G4
Broad La *FRCTL/WBN* BS36 **24** B5
YATE/CS BS37 **37** E1
YATE/CS BS37 **13** G3
Broadleas
BMSTRD/HC/WWD BS13 **84** C2
Broadleaze *AVONM* BS11 **42** D1
Broadleys Av
HNLZ/SM/SNYPK/WT BS9 **45** F1
Broadmead *CBRIS/FH* BS1 **5** G2
Broadmead La *KEYN* BS31 **88** D3
Broadmoor La
CBATH/BATHN BA1 **101** F1
Broadmoor Pk
CBATH/BATHN BA1 **101** G2
Broadmoor V
CBATH/BATHN BA1 **101** F1
Broadoak Hl *LGASH* BS41 **95** E2
Broad Oak Rd
BMSTRD/HC/WWD BS13 **84** A5
Broadoak Rd *WSM* BS23 **124** C3
Broad Oaks *CFTN/FAIL* BS8 **54** C5
Broadoak Wk *MANG/FISH* BS16 **48** B4
Broad Pln *CBRISNE* BS2 **5** J4
Broad Quay *CBATH/BATHN* BA1 **3** F6
CBRIS/FH BS1 **4** E4
Broad Rd *KGWD/HNM* BS15 **58** C2
Broad Stones *BOAV* BA15 **105** F5
Broadstone Wk
BMSTRD/HC/WWD BS13 **85** E4
Broad St *CBATH/BATHN* BA1 **3** G3
CBRIS/FH BS1 **5** F3
MANG/FISH BS16 **49** G4
YATE/CS BS37 **26** D1
YTN/CONG BS49 **114** D2
Broad Wk
BRSG/KWL/STAPK BS4 **73** G4
Broadway *BATHSE* BA2 **3** J6
KEYN BS31 **89** G5
OMX/HUT/LCK BS24 **127** G2
OMX/HUT/LCK BS24 **125** E5
YATE/CS BS37 **14** B5
Broadway Av
HNLZ/SM/SNYPK/WT BS9 **45** H2
Broadway Ct *BATHSE* BA2 * **3** H6
Broadway Rd
BMSTRD/HC/WWD BS13 **84** A4
HORF/LLZ BS7 **45** H5
Broadways Dr
MANG/FISH BS16 **47** H1
Broad Weir *CBRIS/FH* BS1 **5** H3
Brock End *PTSHD/EG* BS20 **38** C5
Brockhurst Gdns
KGWD/HNM BS15 **58** A3
Brockhurst Rd
KGWD/HNM BS15 **58** A3
Brockley Cl
BRSTK/PCHW BS34 **21** E3
NAIL BS48 **67** E5
OMX/HUT/LCK BS24 **125** E5
Brockley Crs
OMX/HUT/LCK BS24 **125** E5
Brockley La *NAIL* BS48 **79** E5
Brockley Rd *KEYN* BS31 **99** E1
Brockley Wk
BMSTRD/HC/WWD BS13 **84** B1
Brockley Wy
YTN/CONG BS49 **113** G1
Brockridge La
FRCTL/WBN BS36 **24** A3
Brocks La *LGASH* BS41 **70** C5
Brocks Rd
BMSTRD/HC/WWD BS13 **95** H1
Brock St *CBATH/BATHN* BA1 **2** E2
Brockway *NAIL* BS48 **67** G4
Brockworth *YATE/CS* BS37 **25** G4
Brockworth Crs
MANG/FISH BS16 **47** H2
Bromfield Wk
MANG/FISH BS16 **49** H1
Bromley Dr *MANG/FISH* BS16 **34** D5
Bromley Heath Av
MANG/FISH BS16 **34** D5
Bromley Heath Rd
MANG/FISH BS16 **48** D1
Bromley Rd *HORF/LLZ* BS7 **46** B3
Brompton Cl
KGWD/HNM BS15 **59** F3
Brompton Rd
OMX/HUT/LCK BS24 **125** F4
Broncksea Rd *HORF/LLZ* BS7 **32** B4
Bronte Cl *WSM* BS23 **125** F2
Bronte Wk *HORF/LLZ* BS7 **32** C5
Brook Cl *LGASH* BS41 **71** E5
Brookcote Dr
BRSTK/PCHW BS34 **21** F4

Brookdale Rd
BMSTRD/HC/WWD BS13........84 C3
Brookfield Av *HORF/LLZ BS7*...45 H5
Brookfield Cl *YATE/CS BS37*......27 E1
Brookfield La
RDLND/MONT BS6.............55 H1
Brookfield Pk
CBATH/BATHN BA1..........101 G2
Brookfield Rd
BRSTC/PCHW BS34...........20 D2
RDLND/MONT BS6.............55 H2
Brookfield Wk *CLVDN BS21*.....65 F2
OLD/WMLY/WICK BS30.........77 F3
Brook Ga *BMSTR BS3*............71 H5
Brook Hl *RDLND/MONT BS6*......56 A2
Brookland Rd
RDLND/MONT BS6.............45 H3
WSM BS23...................121 G4
Brook La *MANG/FISH BS16*......47 G2
Brook Rd *RDLND/MONT BS6*......56 B2
Brooklea
OLD/WMLY/WICK BS30.........77 E2
Brookleaze
HNLZ/SM/SNYPK/WT BS9......44 A3
Brookleaze Blds
CBATH/BATHN BA1...........103 E2
Brook Lintons
BRSG/KWL/STAPK BS4........74 C3
Brooklyn Rd
BMSTRD/HC/WWD BS13........84 C1
CBATH/BATHN BA1...........103 F2
Brookmead *THNB/SVB BS35*......9 E5
Brook Rd *BMSTR BS3*...........73 E2
KGWD/HNM BS15.............59 C5
MANG/FISH BS16.............48 A4
RDLND/MONT BS6.............56 B2
Brookside
BLAG/CWMG/WR BS40.........93 C5
PTSHD/EG BS20.............42 D5
Brookside Cl
CBATH/BATHN BA1............91 E4
Brookside Dr
FRCTL/WBN BS36.............23 H2
Brookside Rd
BRSG/KWL/STAPK BS4........74 D4
Brook St *EVILLE/WHL BS5*......57 E4
YATE/CS BS37...............26 C1
Brookthorpe *AVONM BS11*......29 C5
Brookthorpe Ct *YATE/CS BS37*...25 H2
Brookview Wk
BRSG/KWL/STAPK BS13........84 C2
Brook Wy *ALMDB BS32*..........21 E1
Broom Farm Cl *NAIL BS48*......79 F1
Broom Hl *MANG/FISH BS16*.....47 G3
Broomhill Rd
BRSG/KWL/STAPK BS4........75 E5
The Brooms *MANG/FISH BS16*...35 G3
Brotherswood Ct *ALMDB BS32*...3 H5
Brougham Hayes *BATHSE BA2*....2 B5
Brougham Pl
CBATH/BATHN BA1...........103 F2
Brow Hl *CBATH/BATHN BA1*.....91 E5
Browning Ct *HORF/LLZ BS7*....32 D4
Brownlow Rd *WSM BS23*.......124 D2
The Brow *BATHSE BA2*.........1 J3
Broxholme Wk *AVONM BS11*.....29 F5
Bruce Av *EVILLE/WHL BS5*......57 E2
Bruce Rd *EVILLE/WHL BS5*......57 E2
Brue Cl *WSM BS23*............125 E1
Brunel Cl
OLD/WMLY/WICK BS30.........60 A4
Brunel Lock Development
CBRIS/FH BS1..............72 A1
Brunel Lock Rd *CBRIS/FH BS1*...72 A1
Brunel Rd
BMSTRD/HC/WWD BS13........84 A1
NAIL BS48..................66 C5
Brunel Wy *BMSTR BS3*..........71 H5
CBRIS/FH BS1..............72 A1
THNB/SVB BS35..............8 C5
Brunswick Pl
CBATH/BATHN BA1 *..........3 F2
CBRIS/FH BS1 *.............72 A1
Brunswick Sq *CBRISNE BS2*......5 G1
Brunswick St
CBATH/BATHN BA1...........103 E3
CBRISNE BS2................56 A3
Bruton Av *BATHSE BA2*........108 C5
PTSHD/EG BS20.............39 E3
Bruton Cl *EVILLE/WHL BS5*.....55 H4
NAIL BS48..................79 F1
Bruton Pl *CFTN/FAIL BS8*......4 A3
Bryansons Cl *MANG/FISH BS16*...47 F2
Bryant Gdns *CLVDN BS21*......64 C4
Bryants Cl *MANG/FISH BS16*....34 C4
Bryant's Hl *EVILLE/WHL BS5*....58 B3
Brynland Av *HORF/LLZ BS7*.....46 A4
Buchanans Whf North
CBRIS/FH BS1 *.............5 F5
Buchanans Whf South
CBRIS/FH BS1 *.............5 F5
Buckingham Dr
BRSTC/PCHW BS34...........33 F1
Buckingham Gdns
MANG/FISH BS16.............49 E2
Buckingham Pl
MANG/FISH BS16.............49 E2
Buckingham Rd
BRSG/KWL/STAPK BS4........74 C1
OMX/HUT/LCK BS24..........125 G4
Buckingham St *BMSTR BS3*......72 D4
Buckingham V
CFTN/FAIL BS8..............55 E3
Buckland Gn *MTN/WRL BS22*...117 H3
Bucklands Batch *NAIL BS48*.....79 G1
Bucklands Dr *NAIL BS48*.......79 G1
Bucklands Gv *NAIL BS48*.......79 F1
Bucklands La *NAIL BS48*.......79 F1
Bucklands Vw *NAIL BS48*.......79 H1
Bude Av *EVILLE/WHL BS5*.......58 A3
Bude Cl *NAIL BS48*............67 H5
Bude Rd *BRSTC/PCHW BS34*.....32 D2
Buller Rd
BRSG/KWL/STAPK BS4........74 B4
Bull La *EVILLE/WHL BS5*.......57 H5
PTSHD/EG BS20.............42 C4
Bumpers Batch *BATHSE BA2*...111 E2
Bunting Ct *MTN/WRL BS22*....122 B2

Burbank Cl
OLD/WMLY/WICK BS30.........76 D3
Burchells Green Cl
KGWD/HNM BS15.............58 B3
Burchells Green Rd
KGWD/HNM BS15.............58 B2
Burcombe Cl *MANG/FISH BS36*...24 B3
Burcott Rd *AVONM BS11*.......16 C5
Burden Cl *ALMDB BS32*........21 C4
Burfoote Gdns
HGRV/WHIT BS14.............86 D5
Burfoot Rd *HGRV/WHIT BS14*...86 D5
Burford Av *BRSTC/PCHW BS34*...21 E2
Burford Cl *BATHSE BA2*.......107 G4
PTSHD/EG BS20.............39 H1
Burford Gv *AVONM BS11*.......43 F3
Burgage Cl *YATE/CS BS37*......25 D2
Burghill Rd *HNBRY/STHM BS10*...31 E4
Burgundy Ct *FRCTL/WBN BS16*...23 E5
Burghley Rd *RDLND/MONT BS6*...56 A5
Burgis Rd *HGRV/WHIT BS14*....86 C3
Burleigh Gdns
CBATH/BATHN BA1...........101 F4
Burley Av *MANG/FISH BS16*....49 F3
Burley Crest *MANG/FISH BS16*...49 F2
Burley Gv *MANG/FISH BS16*....49 F2
Burlington Rd *PTSHD/EG BS20*...40 A1
RDLND/MONT BS6.............55 F1
Burlington St
CBATH/BATHN BA1............2 E1
WSM BS23...................6 E5
Burnbush Cl *HGRV/WHIT BS14*...86 D3
Burnell Dr *CBRISNE BS2*.......56 B3
Burneside Cl
HNBRY/STHM BS10...........31 G3
Burnett Hl *KEYN BS31*.........88 B1
Burney Wy
OLD/WMLY/WICK BS30.........76 D3
Burnham Cl *KGWD/HNM BS15*...59 F2
Burnham Dr *KGWD/HNM BS15*...59 F2
OMX/HUT/LCK BS24..........125 E5
Burnham Rd *AVONM BS11*.......42 D2
BATHSE BA2................107 H1
Burnt House Rd *BATHSE BA2*...110 B2
Burrington Av
OMX/HUT/LCK BS24..........125 E5
Burrington Cl *NAIL BS48*......67 F5
Burrington Wk
BMSTRD/HC/WWD BS13........84 A1
Burrough Wy
FRCTL/WBN BS36.............23 E5
Burton Cl *CBRIS/FH BS1*.......5 G7
Burton Ct *CBRIS/FH BS1*.......4 A5
Burton St *CBATH/BATHN BA1*....2 E1
Burwalls Rd *CFTN/FAIL BS8*....54 C5
Bury Hill Vw *MANG/FISH BS16*...35 E2
Bury Rd *MANG/FISH BS16*......35 E2
The Bury *OMX/HUT/LCK BS24*...125 E5
Bush Av *BRSTC/PCHW BS34*.....21 E5
Bushy Pk
BRSG/KWL/STAPK BS4........73 G3
Butcombe Wk
HGRV/WHIT BS14.............86 A4
Butlers Cl *EVILLE/WHL BS5*....57 H4
Butlers Wk *EVILLE/WHL BS5*....57 H5
Buttercliffe Ri *LGASH BS41*...71 F3
Buttercup Crs *MTN/WRL BS22*...117 H4
Butterfield Cl *FRCTL/WBN BS36*...23 H4
HNBRY/STHM BS10...........46 A1
Butterfield Rd
HNBRY/STHM BS10...........46 A1
Buttermere Rd *WSM BS23*......125 F1
Butterworth Ct
BRSG/KWL/STAPK BS4........85 E2
Butt La *THNB/SVB BS35*........8 C5
Buxton Wk *HORF/LLZ BS7*......32 C5
Bye Md *MANG/FISH BS16*.......35 G5
Byfield *BATHSE BA2*..........111 F1
Byfields *CLVDN BS21*..........64 D3
Byron Cl *OMX/HUT/LCK BS24*...126 C2
Byron Pl *CFTN/FAIL BS8*.......4 B3
MANG/FISH BS16.............59 H4
Byron Rd *BATHSE BA2*........108 C3
WSM BS23...................125 F2
Byron St *CBRISNE BS2*.........56 B2

C

OLD/WMLY/WICK BS30.........77 E4
Caledonian Rd *BATHSE BA2*.....2 A5
CBRIS/FH BS1...............4 B6
California Rd
BRSTC/PCHW BS34...........20 C3
Callicroft Rd
BRSTC/PCHW BS34...........20 B3
Callington Rd
BRSG/KWL/STAPK BS4........74 B5
Callowhill Ct *CBRIS/FH BS1*....5 G2
Calton Gdns *BATHSE BA2*.......3 F7
Calton Rd *BATHSE BA2*........3 C7
Calton Wk *BATHSE BA2*.........3 F7
Camberley Dr
FRCTL/WBN BS36.............23 F2
Camberley Rd
BRSG/KWL/STAPK BS4........84 D1
Camberley Wk
MTN/WRL BS22..............122 B4
Camborne Rd *HORF/LLZ BS7*....46 C1
Cambrian Dr *YATE/CS BS37*.....14 A4
Cambridge Crs
HNLZ/SM/SNYPK/WT BS9......45 E1
Cambridge Gv *CLVDN BS21*.....62 B5
Cambridge Pk
RDLND/MONT BS6.............45 F5
Cambridge Rd *CLVDN BS21*.....62 B5
HORF/LLZ BS7...............46 B3
Cambridge St *BMSTR BS3*......73 G2
EVILLE/WHL BS5.............57 E4
Cambridge Ter *CBATH/BATHN BA1*...3 J7
Camden Rd
CBATH/BATHN BA1...........102 D3
Camden Rw *CBATH/BATHN BA1*...3 F1
Camden Ter
CBATH/BATHN BA1...........102 D3
CFTN/FAIL BS8..............55 E5
WSM BS23...................7 F4
Cameley Gn *BATHSE BA2*......107 E1
Camelford Rd *EVILLE/WHL BS5*...57 F2
Cameron Wk *HORF/LLZ BS7*.....47 E2
Cameroons Cl *KEYN BS31*......88 C4
Camerton Cl *KEYN BS31*.......99 F1
Camerton Rd *EVILLE/WHL BS5*...57 F2
Camomile Wk *PTSHD/EG BS20*...40 B3
Campbell Farm Dr
AVONM BS11................29 F4
Campbell St *CBRISNE BS2*......56 A2
Campian Wk
BRSG/KWL/STAPK BS4........85 E3
Campion Cl *MTN/WRL BS22*....122 A4
THNB/SVB BS35..............9 E2
Campion Dr *ALMDB BS32*.......11 F5
Camp Rd *CFTN/FAIL BS8*.......54 D4
Camp Rd North *WSM BS23*....120 A2
Camp Vw *FRCTL/WBN BS36*.....35 E1
Campus The
BRSG/KWL/STAPK BS4........84 D3
Camwal Rd *CBRISNE BS2*.......73 H1
Canada Coombe
OMX/HUT/LCK BS24..........126 C4
Canada Wy *CBRIS/FH BS1*......72 B1
Canal Br *BATHSE BA2* *..........3 J7
Canberra Crs
OMX/HUT/LCK BS24..........122 D5
Canberra Gv
BRSTC/PCHW BS34...........32 D1
Canford La
HNLZ/SM/SNYPK/WT BS9......44 C1
Canford Rd
HNLZ/SM/SNYPK/WT BS9......44 D1
Cannans Cl *FRCTL/WBN BS36*....23 E3
Cann La *OLD/WMLY/WICK BS30*...60 C5
Cannons Ga *CLVDN BS21*.......64 C5
Cannon St *CBRIS/FH BS1*.......5 F2
Canons Cl *BATHSE BA2*........107 G5
Canon's Rd *CBRIS/FH BS1*......4 E5
Canons Wk *KGWD/HNM BS15*...59 E1
Canons Wy *CBRIS/FH BS1*......4 D6
Canowie Rd *RDLND/MONT BS6*...55 H4
Cantell Gv *HGRV/WHIT BS14*....87 E4
Canterbury Cl *MTN/WRL BS22*...117 H4
YATE/CS BS37...............14 A4
Canterbury Rd *BATHSE BA2*....2 B6
Canterbury St *EVILLE/WHL BS5*...56 D5
Cantock's Cl *CFTN/FAIL BS8*....4 A2
Canvey Cl *HNBRY/STHM BS10*...46 A1
Canynge Rd *CFTN/FAIL BS8*.....54 D3
Canynge Sq *CFTN/FAIL BS8*.....54 D3
Canynge St *CBRIS/FH BS1*......5 G5
Capel Cl *KGWD/HNM BS15*......59 H5
Capel Rd *AVONM BS11*.........29 H4
Capenor Cl *PTSHD/EG BS20*....39 G4
Capgrave Cl
BRSG/KWL/STAPK BS4........75 F3
Capgrave Crs
BRSG/KWL/STAPK BS4........75 F3
Caraway Gdns *EVILLE/WHL BS5*...57 E1
Carberry Vw
OMX/HUT/LCK BS24..........122 D3
Cardigan Crs *MTN/WRL BS22*...121 H5
Cardigan Rd
HNLZ/SM/SNYPK/WT BS9......45 E2
Cardill Cl
BMSTRD/HC/WWD BS13........84 B1
Cardinal Cl *BATHSE BA2*......110 B2
Carey's Cl *CLVDN BS21*........65 F1
Careys Wy
OMX/HUT/LCK BS24..........122 B4
Carice Gdns *CLVDN BS21*.......64 C4
Carisbrooke Rd
BRSG/KWL/STAPK BS4........85 E1
Carlow Rd
BRSG/KWL/STAPK BS4........85 E1
Carlton Ct
HNLZ/SM/SNYPK/WT BS9 *....45 E1
Carlton Man North *WSM BS23* *...6 D5
Carlton Man South *WSM BS23* *...6 D5
Carlton Pk *EVILLE/WHL BS5*....57 E3
Carlton St *WSM BS23*..........6 D5
Carlyle Rd *EVILLE/WHL BS5*....57 E2
Carmarthen Ct *YATE/CS BS37*...14 B3
Carmarthen Gv
OLD/WMLY/WICK BS30.........77 E5
Carmarthen Rd
HNLZ/SM/SNYPK/WT BS9......45 E2

Carnarvon Rd
RDLND/MONT BS6.............55 G1
Caroline Blds *BATHSE BA2*.....3 J6
Caroline Cl *KEYN BS31*........87 H5
YATE/CS BS37...............14 D5
Caroline Pl *CBATH/BATHN BA1* *...3 F1
Carpenter Cl *WSM BS23*........7 K5
Carpenter's Shop La
MANG/FISH BS16.............88 B4
Carre Gdns *MTN/WRL BS22*....117 C4
Carrington Rd *BMSTR BS3*......72 C4
Carrs Cl *BATHSE BA2*.........107 F1
Carsons Rd *MANG/FISH BS16*...59 H1
Carson's Rd *MANG/FISH BS16*...49 H5
Carsons Road Link
MANG/FISH BS16.............59 H1
Carter Wk *ALMDB BS32*........21 F2
Cartledge Rd *EVILLE/WHL BS5*...57 E2
Cassell Rd *MANG/FISH BS16*....48 C3
Cassey Bottom La
EVILLE/WHL BS5.............58 A4
Casson Dr *MANG/FISH BS16*....33 G5
Castle Cl *HNBRY/STHM BS10*....30 B1
YATE/CS BS37...............14 D5
Castle Coombe *THNB/SVB BS35*...8 D2
Castle Ct *BRSG/KWL/STAPK BS4*...74 B2
Castle Farm La *LGASH BS41*....94 A2
Castle Farm Rd
KGWD/HNM BS15.............75 G4
Castle Gdns *BATHSE BA2*......108 B4
Castle Rd *CLVDN BS21*........62 B4
KGWD/HNM BS15.............58 D5
MANG/FISH BS16.............51 G2
MTN/WRL BS22..............117 F5
OLD/WMLY/WICK BS30.........77 F3
Castle St *CBRIS/FH BS1*.......5 H3
THNB/SVB BS35..............8 B2
Castle Vw
OMX/HUT/LCK BS24..........122 C3
Castle View Rd *CLVDN BS21*....62 B5
Castlewood Cl *CLVDN BS21*.....64 D1
Catbrain Hl *HNBRY/STHM BS10*...19 F4
Catbrain La *HNBRY/STHM BS10*...19 F4
Catemead *CLVDN BS21*.........64 C5
Cater Rd
BMSTRD/HC/WWD BS13........84 C3
Catharine Pl *CBATH/BATHN BA1*...2 E2
Catherine Mead St *BMSTR BS3*...72 D2
Catherine St *AVONM BS11*......42 C1
Catherine Wy
CBATH/BATHN BA1...........91 E4
Catley Gv *LGASH BS41*........70 D5
Cattistock Dr *EVILLE/WHL BS5*...58 A5
Cattle Market Rd *CBRIS/FH BS1*...5 J6
Cattybrook Rd
BMSTRD/HC/WWD BS13........50 B3
Cattybrook Rd North
MANG/FISH BS16.............50 B2
Cattybrook St *EVILLE/WHL BS5*...56 D3
Caulfield Rd *MTN/WRL BS22*...117 H4
Causeway *CLVDN BS21*.........66 C3
Causeway The
FRCTL/WBN BS36.............24 A3
YTN/CONG BS49.............114 D2
Causeway Vw *NAIL BS48*.......76 C1
Cavan Wk
BRSTC/PCHW BS34...........73 E5
Cave Cl *MANG/FISH BS16*......48 D2
Cave Dr *MANG/FISH BS16*......48 D2
Cave Gv *MANG/FISH BS16*......49 H1
Cavell Ct *CLVDN BS21*........64 C4
Cavendish Cl *KEYN BS31*......99 E2
Cavendish Crs
CBATH/BATHN BA1...........102 A1
Cavendish Gdns
HNLZ/SM/SNYPK/WT BS9......44 A4
Cavendish Pl
CBATH/BATHN BA1...........102 B4
Cavendish Rd
BRSTC/PCHW BS34...........20 B2
CBATH/BATHN BA1...........102 B4
HNLZ/SM/SNYPK/WT BS9......45 E3
Caverners Ct *MTN/WRL BS22*...122 B4
Caversham Dr *NAIL BS48*......67 H4
Cave St *CBRISNE BS2*.........56 A3
Cecil Av *EVILLE/WHL BS5*......57 H2
Cecil Rd *CFTN/FAIL BS8*.......54 D3
CLVDN BS21................62 A5
WSM BS23...................124 C3
Cedar Av *MTN/WRL BS22*......121 H2
Cedar Cl *BRSTC/PCHW BS34*....20 B3
LGASH BS41................70 C5
Cedar Ct *BATHSE BA2*.........88 A5
Cedar Gv *BATHSE BA2*........108 A4
HNLZ/SM/SNYPK/WT BS9......44 B3
Cedarhurst Rd *PTSHD/EG BS20*...38 C5
Cedar Pk
HNLZ/SM/SNYPK/WT BS9......44 B3
Cedar Rw *AVONM BS11* *.......43 F2
Cedar Wy *BATHSE BA2*.........2 D6
FRCTL/WBN BS36.............22 D5
MANG/FISH BS16.............51 F5
NAIL BS48..................67 H4
PTSHD/EG BS20.............39 F4
Cedern Av
OMX/HUT/LCK BS24..........127 E5
Cedric Cl *CBATH/BATHN BA1*...101 H5
Cedric Rd *CBATH/BATHN BA1*...101 H5
Celandine Cl *THNB/SVB BS35*...9 E2
Celestine Rd *YATE/CS BS37*....13 G4
Celia Ter *BRSG/KWL/STAPK BS4*...74 B4
Cemetery Rd
BRSG/KWL/STAPK BS4........73 H3
Cennick Av *KGWD/HNM BS15*...59 E3
Centaurus Rd
BRSTC/PCHW BS34...........19 G3
Central Av *KGWD/HNM BS15*...75 H1
Central Wy *CLVDN BS21*.......64 D4
Centre Dr *BNWL BS29*........127 H2
Ceres Cl
OLD/WMLY/WICK BS30.........76 C4
Cerimon Ga *BRSTC/PCHW BS34*...33 E1
Cerney Gdns *NAIL BS48*.......67 H4
Cerney La *HNLZ/SM/SNYPK/WT BS9*...43 E3

Cesson Cl *YATE/CS BS37*.......27 E1
Chadleigh Gv
BRSG/KWL/STAPK BS4........84 D2
The Chaffins *CLVDN BS21*......65 E3
Chaingate La *YATE/CS BS37*....12 D1
Chakeshill Cl
HNBRY/STHM BS10...........31 G2
Chakeshill Dr
HNBRY/STHM BS10...........31 G2
Chalcombe Cl
BRSTC/PCHW BS34...........21 E2
Chalcroft Wk
BMSTRD/HC/WWD BS13........83 H5
Chalfield Cl *KEYN BS31*.......98 B2
Chalford Rd *MTN/WRL BS22*...121 H5
Chalford Ct *YATE/CS BS37*.....25 C2
Chalk Farm Cl *PLTN/PENS BS39*...95 H5
Chalks Rd *EVILLE/WHL BS5*.....57 F3
Challender Av
HNBRY/STHM BS10...........30 D3
Challoner Ct *CBRIS/FH BS1*....4 E7
Challow Dr *MTN/WRL BS22*....121 G1
Champion Rd
KGWD/HNM BS15.............59 G1
Champneys Av
HNBRY/STHM BS10...........30 D3
Champs Sur Marne
ALMDB BS32................21 G2
Chancel Cl
HNLZ/SM/SNYPK/WT BS9......44 A1
NAIL BS48..................67 E5
Chancery St *EVILLE/WHL BS5*...57 E4
Chandag Rd *KEYN BS31*........88 D5
Chandler Cl
CBATH/BATHN BA1...........101 C3
Chandos Rd *KEYN BS31*........88 B2
RDLND/MONT BS6.............55 F2
Channel Hts
OMX/HUT/LCK BS24..........125 E5
Channell's Hl
HNLZ/SM/SNYPK/WT BS9......31 E5
Channel Rd *CLVDN BS21*.......62 B4
Channel View Crs
PTSHD/EG BS20.............39 F5
Channel View Rd
PTSHD/EG BS20.............39 F3
Ch</br>annon's Hl *MANG/FISH BS16*...47 H4
Chantry Cl *NAIL BS48*........66 C5
Chantry Dr *MTN/WRL BS22*....117 G4
Chantry Gv *AVONM BS11*......30 A3
Chantry La *MANG/FISH BS16*...51 H5
Chantry Mead Rd
BATHSE BA2................108 B4
Chantry Rd *CFTN/FAIL BS8*.....55 F5
THNB/SVB BS35..............8 C2
Chapel Barton *BMSTR BS3*.....72 C4
NAIL BS48..................67 F4
Chapel Cl *NAIL BS48*.........67 H4
Chapel Ct *CBATH/BATHN BA1* *...3 F5
Chapel Gdns
HNBRY/STHM BS10...........31 E4
Chapel Green La
RDLND/MONT BS6.............55 F1
NAIL BS48..................80 C1
Chapel La *AVONM BS11*........29 H3
EVILLE/WHL BS5.............57 G1
KGWD/HNM BS15.............75 H1
MANG/FISH BS16.............48 C5
OLD/WMLY/WICK BS30.........77 E3
WUE CL12..................9 H3
Chapel Orch *YATE/CS BS37*.....13 C5
Chapel Pill La *PTSHD/EG BS20*...43 E4
Chapel Rd
BMSTRD/HC/WWD BS13........84 B3
EVILLE/WHL BS5.............56 D2
KGWD/HNM BS15.............75 H1
Chapel Rw *CBATH/BATHN BA1*...104 D2
CBATH/BATHN BA1...........2 E4
PTSHD/EG BS20.............42 C4
Chapel St *CBRISNE BS2*........73 H1
THNB/SVB BS35..............8 B2
Chapel Wy
BRSG/KWL/STAPK BS4........57 C5
HNBRY/STHM BS10...........31 H5
Chaplin Rd *EVILLE/WHL BS5*....57 E1
Chapter St *CBRISNE BS2*.......56 B2
Chapter Wk *RDLND/MONT BS6*...55 F1
Charborough Rd
BRSTC/PCHW BS34...........32 B3
Chard Cl *NAIL BS48*..........79 C1
Chardstock Av
HNLZ/SM/SNYPK/WT BS9......30 A5
Charfield *KGWD/HNM BS15*....59 H5
Charfield Rd
HNLZ/SM/SNYPK/WT BS9......31 G4
Chargrove
OLD/WMLY/WICK BS30.........60 A5
YATE/CS BS37...............26 A1
Charis Av *HNBRY/STHM BS10*...45 G1
Charlcombe La
CBATH/BATHN BA1...........102 C2
Charlcombe Ri
CBATH/BATHN BA1...........102 C2
Charlcombe View Rd
CBATH/BATHN BA1...........102 D2
Charlcombe Wy
CBATH/BATHN BA1...........102 C2
Charlcome Ri *PTSHD/EG BS20*...38 B5
Charlecombe Rd
HNLZ/SM/SNYPK/WT BS9......44 D2
Charles Av *BRSTC/PCHW BS34*...33 G1
Charles Ct *CFTN/FAIL BS8*.....4 C2
Charles Pl *CFTN/FAIL BS8*.....54 C5
Charles St *BRSTC/PCHW BS34*...32 D3
Charles St *CBATH/BATHN BA1*...2 E4
CBRIS/FH BS1...............4 E2
Charles Wesley Ct
EVILLE/WHL BS5.............58 A5
Charlock Rd
MTN/WRL BS22..............122 A4
Charlotte St *CBATH/BATHN BA1*...2 E4
CBRIS/FH BS1...............4 C4
Charlotte St South
CBRIS/FH BS1...............4 C4

Charlton Av
BRSTK/PCHW BS34 ....32 B3
WSM BS23.........................124 C2
Charlton Gdns
HNBRY/STHM BS10 ....31 H1
Charlton La
HNBRY/STHM BS10 ....31 E2
Charlton Leaze
HNBRY/STHM BS10 ....19 E4
Charlton Mead Dr
HNBRY/STHM BS10 ....31 H1
Charlton Pk *KEYN BS31*........88 A4
Charlton Pl *HNBRY/STHM BS10*..31 H2
Charlton Rd
HNBRY/STHM BS10 ....31 F4
KEYN BS31.......................88 A4
KGWD/HNM BS15.............58 B2
WSM BS23.......................124 C2
Charlton St *EVILLE/WHL BS5*...56 D4
Charlton Vw *PTSHD/EG BS20*...39 G3
Charminster Rd
MANG/FISH BS16...............48 B5
Charmouth Rd
CBATH/BATHN BA1.........101 G5
Charnell Rd *MANG/FISH BS16*...49 E4
Charnhill Brow
MANG/FISH BS16...............49 F4
Charnhill Crs *MANG/FISH BS16*...49 F4
Charnhill Dr *MANG/FISH BS16*...49 F4
Charnhill Rdg *MANG/FISH BS16*...49 F4
Charnhill V *MANG/FISH BS16*...49 G4
Charnwood Rd *MANG/FISH BS16*...49 G4
Charnwood Rd
HGRV/WHIT BS14..............97 E1
Charterhouse Cl *NAIL BS48*....67 C3
Charterhouse Rd
EVILLE/WHL BS5................57 F3
Charter Rd *MTN/WRL BS22*....121 G3
Charter Wk *HGRV/WHIT BS14*...85 H5
Chasefield La *MANG/FISH BS16*...48 B4
Chase Rd *KGWD/HNM BS15*....58 D1
The Chase *MANG/FISH BS16*....47 E1
Chatcombe Pk *BATHSE BA2*....26 A3
Chatham Pk *BATHSE BA2*.....109 F1
Chatham Rw *CBATH/BATHN BA1*...3 G2
Chatsworth Pk *THNB/SVB BS35*...8 D2
Chatsworth Rd
BRSG/KWL/STAPK BS4........74 B2
MANG/FISH BS16...............48 B5
Chatterton Gn
HGRV/WHIT BS14..............85 G5
Chatterton Rd *YATE/CS BS37*...25 H1
Chatterton Sq *CBRIS/FH BS1*....5 H7
Chaucer Rd *BATHSE BA2*......108 C3
WSM BS23.......................125 F2
Chauncey Gv
BMSTRD/HC/WWD BS13....84 C4
Cheapside *CBRISNE BS2*.........56 B3
Cheapside St *BMSTR BS3*.........73 G2
Cheap St *CBATH/BATHN BA1*.....3 G4
Cheddar Gv
BMSTRD/HC/WWD BS13....84 B1
Chedworth *KGWD/HNM BS15*...49 E5
YATE/CS BS37...................26 C2
Chedworth Rd *HORF/LLZ BS7*...46 C2
Cheese La *CBRISNE BS2*.........5 K4
Chelford Gv *BRSTK/PCHW BS34*...20 D2
Chelmer Gv *KEYN BS31*.........88 C5
Chelmsford Wk
BRSG/KWL/STAPK BS4........75 E1
Chelsea Cl *KEYN BS31*..........88 D4
Chelsea Pk *EVILLE/WHL BS5*....57 E3
Chelsea Rd
CBATH/BATHN BA1.........101 H5
EVILLE/WHL BS5................56 D2
Chelston Rd
BRSG/KWL/STAPK BS4........85 E2
Chelswood Av
MTN/WRL BS22................121 H3
Cheltenham Crs
RDLND/MONT BS6 *...........55 H2
Cheltenham Rd
RDLND/MONT BS6.............55 H2
Cheltenham St *BATHSE BA2*......2 D6
Chelvey Est *NAIL BS48* *..........79 F5
Chelvey La *NAIL BS48*............79 H4
Chelvey Rd *NAIL BS48*...........79 H1
Chelvey Ri *NAIL BS48*............79 F5
Chelvy Cl
BMSTRD/HC/WWD BS13....96 A1
Chelwood Dr *BATHSE BA2*.....110 D1
Chelwood Rd *AVONM BS11*......42 D1
KEYN BS31.......................89 H5
Chepstow Pk *MANG/FISH BS16*...35 H4
Chepstow Rd
BRSG/KWL/STAPK BS4........85 E1
Chequers Cl
OLD/WMLY/WICK BS30.......77 F3
Cherington *KGWD/HNM BS15*...75 C1
YATE/CS BS37...................25 H4
Cherington Rd
HNBRY/STHM BS10 ....45 G1
NAIL BS48........................67 H5
Cheriton Pl
HNLZ/SM/SNYPK/WT BS9...45 F1
OLD/WMLY/WICK BS30.......77 F1
Cherry Cl *CLVDN BS21*...........65 E3
Cherry Cv *YTN/CONG BS49*....112 B3
Cherry Garden La
OLD/WMLY/WICK BS30.......77 F4
Cherry Garden Rd
OLD/WMLY/WICK BS30.......77 F4
Cherry Gdns
OLD/WMLY/WICK BS30.......77 F5
Cherry Gv *MANG/FISH BS16*....49 G2
YTN/CONG BS49...............112 B3
Cherry Hay *CLVDN BS21*.........64 D4
Cherry La *CBRIS/FH BS1*..........5 H2
Cherry Rd *LGASH BS41*...........70 C4
NAIL BS48........................67 G5
YATE/CS BS37...................26 C1
Cherry St *KEYN BS31*...........87 H5
Cherrytree Cl *MANG/FISH BS16*...50 A4
Cherrytree Crs
MANG/FISH BS16...............50 A4
Cherrytree Rd
MANG/FISH BS16...............58 C1
Cherry Wd
OLD/WMLY/WICK BS30.......77 E4

Cherrywood Ri
MTN/WRL BS22................122 C1
Cherrywood Rd
MTN/WRL BS22................122 C1
Chertsey Rd *RDLND/MONT BS6*...55 F2
Cherwell Cl *THNB/SVB BS35*.....8 D5
Cherwell Rd *KEYN BS31*.........88 D5
Chescombe Rd
YTN/CONG BS49...............112 B4
Chesham Rd North
MTN/WRL BS22................121 G3
Chesham Rd South
MTN/WRL BS22................121 G3
Chesham Wy *KGWD/HNM BS15*...58 D2
Cheshire Cl *YATE/CS BS37*.......14 A4
Chesle Cl *PTSHD/EG BS20*......38 C5
Cheslefield *PTSHD/EG BS20*....38 C5
Chesle Wy *PTSHD/EG BS20*.....38 C5
Chesley Hl
OLD/WMLY/WICK BS30.......60 D4
Chessel Cl *ALMDB BS32*.........11 E5
Chessel Ct *BMSTR BS3* *.........72 C4
Chessel St *BMSTR BS3*...........72 C3
Chessington Av
HGRV/WHIT BS14..............86 A4
Chesterfield Av
RDLND/MONT BS6.............56 A1
Chesterfield Rd
MANG/FISH BS16...............49 E3
RDLND/MONT BS6.............56 A1
Chestermaster Cl *ALMDB BS32*...10 C2
Chester Park Rd
MANG/FISH BS16...............58 B1
Chester Rd *EVILLE/WHL BS5*....57 G2
Chesters
OLD/WMLY/WICK BS30.......76 D2
Chester St *EVILLE/WHL BS5*....56 D1
Chesterton Dr *NAIL BS48*........67 H4
The Chestertons *BATHSE BA2*...32 C2
Chestnut Av *MTN/WRL BS22*...122 D2
Chestnut Cha *NAIL BS48*.........67 H4
Chestnut Cl *HGRV/WHIT BS14*...86 D4
YTN/CONG BS49...............114 D2
Chestnut Ct *MANG/FISH BS16*...49 C3
Chestnut Dr *THNB/SVB BS35*....8 D3
YATE/CS BS37...................26 C1
YTN/CONG BS49...............113 E2
Chestnut Gv *BATHSE BA2*.......107 H3
CLVDN BS21......................65 E1
Chestnut Rd *KGWD/HNM BS15*...49 F5
LGASH BS41.....................71 E4
MANG/FISH BS16...............48 D2
Chestnut Springs
YATE/CS BS37...................13 F2
Chestnut Wk
BMSTRD/HC/WWD BS13....84 B3
KEYN BS31.......................99 F1
Chestnut Wy *KGWD/HNM BS15*...49 F5
Chetwode Cl
HNBRY/STHM BS10 ....31 H2
Chevening Cl
BRSTK/PCHW BS34.............33 F1
Cheviot Dr *THNB/SVB BS35*......9 F4
Cheviot Wy
OLD/WMLY/WICK BS30.......77 F1
Cheyne Rd
HNLZ/SM/SNYPK/WT BS9...44 B2
Chichester Wy
OMX/HUT/LCK BS24..........122 D3
YATE/CS BS37...................13 H4
Chillington Ct
BRSTK/PCHW BS34.............20 A1
Chillwood Cl *YATE/CS BS37*.....12 C4
Chiltern Cl *HGRV/WHIT BS14*...86 A5
OLD/WMLY/WICK BS30.......77 F1
Chiltern Pk *THNB/SVB BS35*.....9 E4
Chilton Rd
BRSG/KWL/STAPK BS4........85 H1
CBATH/BATHN BA1...........103 E3
The Chimes *NAIL BS48*...........78 D1
The Chine *MANG/FISH BS16*....47 F3
Chine Vw *MANG/FISH BS16*.....35 F5
Chiphouse Rd
KGWD/HNM BS15.............59 E1
Chipperfield Dr
KGWD/HNM BS15.............59 F2
Chipping Cross *CLVDN BS21*....64 C4
The Chippings
MANG/FISH BS16...............47 F3
Chisbury St *EVILLE/WHL BS5*...47 E5
Chittening Rd *AVONM BS11*.....17 E3
Chock La
HNLZ/SM/SNYPK/WT BS9...45 E1
Christchurch Av
MANG/FISH BS16...............48 D3
Christchurch Cl *NAIL BS48*......67 F4
Christchurch La
MANG/FISH BS16...............48 D2
Christchurch Pth South
WSM BS23 *.......................7 F3
Christchurch Rd
CFTN/FAIL BS8..................55 E4
Christian Cl *MTN/WRL BS22*....117 H5
Christina Ter *CFTN/FAIL BS8* *...72 B1
Christmas St *CBRIS/FH BS1*......4 E3
Chubb Cl
OLD/WMLY/WICK BS30.......76 C1
Church Av *EVILLE/WHL BS5*.....56 D2
HNLZ/SM/SNYPK/WT BS9...44 C4
OLD/WMLY/WICK BS30.......60 A4
Church Cl *BATHSE BA2*...........104 A2
CBATH/BATHN BA1...........104 C2
CLVDN BS21......................64 A3
FRCTL/WBN BS36...............23 H2
PTSHD/EG BS20.................39 H3
YTN/CONG BS49...............112 C4
Church Farm Rd
MANG/FISH BS16...............49 H2
Church Hayes Cl *NAIL BS48*.....79 F1
Church Hayes Dr *NAIL BS48*....79 F1
Church Hl
BRSG/KWL/STAPK BS4........74 D4
Churchill Av *CLVDN BS21*.......64 C3
Churchill Cl *CLVDN BS21*........64 C3
OLD/WMLY/WICK BS30.......76 D1
Churchill Dr
HNLZ/SM/SNYPK/WT BS9...44 B1

Churchill Rd
BRSG/KWL/STAPK BS4........74 B2
WSM BS23.........................7 J5
Churchland Wy
OMX/HUT/LCK BS24..........123 E3
Church La *BATHSE BA2*..........109 F3
BMSTR BS3.......................72 D2
CBATH/BATHN BA1.............91 E5
CBRIS/FH BS1.....................5 H5
CFTN/FAIL BS8..................55 E4
CLVDN BS21......................66 C2
EVILLE/WHL BS5................57 F5
FRCTL/WBN BS36...............24 A4
FRCTL/WBN BS36...............22 C4
HGRV/WHIT BS14..............97 E1
HNBRY/STHM BS10 ....30 C3
LGASH BS41.....................71 F4
MANG/FISH BS16...............35 E3
NAIL BS48........................80 A4
NAIL BS48........................66 D5
OLD/WMLY/WICK BS30.......59 H2
OMX/HUT/LCK BS24..........126 A4
PTSHD/EG BS20.................41 G5
YTN/CONG BS49...............112 C4
Church Leaze *AVONM BS11*.....42 D2
Church Mdw *HGRV/WHIT BS14*...97 F1
Church Pde
BRSG/KWL/STAPK BS4........74 D4
Churchpath Rd
PTSHD/EG BS20.................42 C4
Church Pl *PTSHD/EG BS20*......42 C4
Church Ri
BLAG/CWMG/WR BS40........93 H5
Church Rd *ALMDB BS32*.........111 C1
BLAG/CWMG/WR BS40........93 H5
BMSTR BS3.......................73 D3
BMSTRD/HC/WWD BS13....84 B4
BRSTK/PCHW BS34.............32 C2
CBATH/BATHN BA1...........101 H3
CFTN/FAIL BS8..................53 C3
EVILLE/WHL BS5................57 F4
FRCTL/WBN BS36...............35 E1
HGRV/WHIT BS14..............86 A5
HNLZ/SM/SNYPK/WT BS9...44 D3
HORF/LLZ BS7...................46 A2
KGWD/HNM BS15.............59 E1
LGASH BS41.....................94 C2
MANG/FISH BS16...............58 D1
MTN/WRL BS22................122 A1
OLD/WMLY/WICK BS30.......89 H1
PLTN/PENS BS39...............96 D5
PTSHD/EG BS20.................42 A4
THNB/SVB BS35..................8 C2
THNB/SVB BS35................19 E1
YATE/CS BS37...................14 A5
YTN/CONG BS49...............112 C4
Church Rd North
PTSHD/EG BS20.................39 H3
Church Rd South
PTSHD/EG BS20.................39 H4
Churchside *MANG/FISH BS16*...48 B1
Church St *CBATH/BATHN BA1*...104 C2
CBRIS/FH BS1.....................5 H5
EVILLE/WHL BS5................56 D5
NAIL BS48........................80 B4
OLD/WMLY/WICK BS30.......68 A4
Church Vw *MTN/WRL BS22*.....122 A4
NAIL BS48........................81 F1
Churchward Cl
KGWD/HNM BS15.............75 C1
Churchward Rd
MTN/WRL BS22................118 A5
YATE/CS BS37...................13 F4
Churchways *HGRV/WHIT BS14*...86 B5
Churchways Av *HORF/LLZ BS7*...46 A2
Churchways Crs *HORF/LLZ BS7*...46 A2
Churclands Rd *BMSTR BS3*.....72 C4
Churston Cl *HGRV/WHIT BS14*...96 C1
The Circle *BATHSE BA2*..........107 G4
Circular Rd
HNLZ/SM/SNYPK/WT BS9...54 C1
Circus Ms *CBATH/BATHN BA1*....2 E2
Circus Pl *CBATH/BATHN BA1*....2 E2
The Circus *CBATH/BATHN BA1*...2 E2
City Rd *CBRISNE BS2*..............56 A3
City Vw *CBATH/BATHN BA1*....102 D4
The Clamp
OLD/WMLY/WICK BS30.......77 F3
Clanage Rd *BMSTR BS3*..........71 H2
Clapton La *PTSHD/EG BS20*.....39 H5
Clapton Wk
HNLZ/SM/SNYPK/WT BS9...43 H5
Clara Cross La *BATHSE BA2*.....110 C2
Clare Av *HORF/LLZ BS7*...........45 G5
Clare Gdns *BATHSE BA2*........110 D1
Claremont Av *HORF/LLZ BS7*...45 G5
Claremont Bldgs
CBATH/BATHN BA1...........102 D3
Claremont Gdns *CLVDN BS21*...65 E4
Claremont Rd
CBATH/BATHN BA1...........103 E3
HORF/LLZ BS7...................46 A4
Claremont St *EVILLE/WHL BS5*...56 C3
Claremont Ter
CBATH/BATHN BA1 *..........102 D3
Claremont Wk
CBATH/BATHN BA1...........102 D3
Clarence Av *MANG/FISH BS16*...49 E3
Clarence Gdns
MANG/FISH BS16...............49 E3
Clarence Grove Rd *WSM BS23*...124 D1
Clarence Pl
CBATH/BATHN BA1...........101 G5
CBRISNE BS2....................72 D1
Clarence Rd *CBRIS/FH BS1*.......5 J7
CBRISNE BS2....................56 B2
KGWD/HNM BS15.............58 B2
MANG/FISH BS16...............58 D1
Clarence Rd East *WSM BS23*...124 D1
Clarence Rd North
WSM BS23.......................124 C1
Clarence Rd South
WSM BS23.......................124 C1
Clarence St
CBATH/BATHN BA1...........102 D4
Clarence Ter *BATHSE BA2*......109 G3
Clarendon Rd *BATHSE BA2*......3 J7
RDLND/MONT BS6.............55 C1
WSM BS23.........................7 G3

Clarendon Vis *BATHSE BA2*.......3 J7
Clare Rd *EVILLE/WHL BS5*.......56 D1
KGWD/HNM BS15.............58 B2
RDLND/MONT BS6.............55 H2
Clare St *CBRIS/FH BS1*............4 E4
EVILLE/WHL BS5................57 E3
Clare Wk *THNB/SVB BS35*........8 C2
Clark Cl *NAIL BS48*................67 H2
Clark Dr *MANG/FISH BS16*......47 H2
Clarken Cl *NAIL BS48*............67 G3
Clarken Coombe *LGASH BS41*...70 D3
Clarke St *BMSTR BS3*.............73 E2
Clarkson Av *MTN/WRL BS22*...121 H2
Clarks St *EVILLE/WHL BS5*.......56 D1
Clarks Wy *BATHSE BA2*.........107 H5
Clatworthy Dr
HGRV/WHIT BS14..............85 H2
Claude Av *BATHSE BA2*..........107 H2
Claude Ter *BATHSE BA2*.........107 H2
Clavell Rd *HNBRY/STHM BS10* ...30 C5
Claverham Cl *YTN/CONG BS49*...112 D3
Claverham Pk
YTN/CONG BS49...............113 F2
Claverham Rd
MANG/FISH BS16...............48 A3
YTN/CONG BS49...............113 E3
Claverton Bldgs *BATHSE BA2* *...3 H7
Claverton Ct *BATHSE BA2*.......109 H5
Claverton Down Rd
BATHSE BA2.....................109 G5
Claverton Rd *KEYN BS31*........99 E3
Claverton Rd West *KEYN BS31*...99 E1
Claverton St *BATHSE BA2*.........3 G6
Clayfield *YATE/CS BS37*..........14 A2
Clayfield Rd
BRSG/KWL/STAPK BS4........74 D3
Clay Hl *EVILLE/WHL BS5*.........57 G1
Clay La *BRSTK/PCHW BS34*......21 E5
OLD/WMLY/WICK BS30.......77 G5
WUE GL9............................9 F3
Claymore Crescent
KGWD/HNM BS15.............58 B2
Claypiece Rd
BMSTRD/HC/WWD BS13....84 A5
Claypit Hl *YATE/CS BS37*.........26 D3
Clay Pit Rd *RDLND/MONT BS6*...45 E5
Claypool Rd *KGWD/HNM BS15*...59 F1
Clayton Cl *PTSHD/EG BS20*......40 A4
Clayton St *AVONM BS11*.........42 D4
EVILLE/WHL BS5................56 D5
Cleave Av *MANG/FISH BS16*....49 E1
Cleave Ct *MANG/FISH BS16*....49 E1
Cleevedale Rd *BATHSE BA2*......107 H5
Cleeve Dr *YTN/CONG BS49*.....113 C3
Cleeve Gdns *MANG/FISH BS16*...48 D1
Cleeve Gn *BATHSE BA2*..........107 E1
Cleeve Gv *KEYN BS31*............88 A4
Cleeve Hill *MANG/FISH BS16*...48 D1
Cleeve Hill Extension
MANG/FISH BS16...............48 D1
Cleeve Hill Rd
YTN/CONG BS49...............113 H4
Cleeve La
OLD/WMLY/WICK BS30.......61 H2
Cleeve Lawns *MANG/FISH BS16*...48 D1
Cleeve Lodge Rd
MANG/FISH BS16...............49 E1
Cleeve Park Rd
MANG/FISH BS16...............48 D1
Cleeve Pl *NAIL BS48*..............67 H5
Cleeve Rd
BRSG/KWL/STAPK BS4........74 A5
MANG/FISH BS16...............49 E2
YATE/CS BS37...................26 A1
Cleeves Ct
OLD/WMLY/WICK BS30.......76 C4
Cleevewood Pk
MANG/FISH BS16...............34 D5
Cleeve Wood Rd
MANG/FISH BS16 *.............34 D5
Clement St *CBRISNE BS2*..........5 J1
Clermont Cl *BRSTK/PCHW BS34*...20 D2
Clevedale *MANG/FISH BS16*....48 D1
Clevedon La *CLVDN BS21*........63 H5
Clevedon Rd *CFTN/FAIL BS8*....69 E1
CLVDN BS21......................66 B2
HORF/LLZ BS7...................45 H4
NAIL BS48........................81 F1
PTSHD/EG BS20.................40 B5
WSM BS23.........................6 D7
Clevedon Ter
RDLND/MONT BS6.............55 H3
THNB/SVB BS35..................9 F4
Cleveland Cl *BATHSE BA2*.......109 F1
Cleveland Pl East
CBATH/BATHN BA1..............3 H1
Cleveland Pl West
CBATH/BATHN BA1..............3 G1
Cleveland Rw *BATHSE BA2*.......109 F1
Cleve Rd *BRSTK/PCHW BS34*....32 C1
Clewson Ri *HGRV/WHIT BS14*...96 C1
Cliff Court Dr
MANG/FISH BS16...............48 B1
Clifford Gdns *AVONM BS11*.....43 E2
Clifford Rd *MANG/FISH BS16*...48 C4
Cliff Rd *MTN/WRL BS22*.........121 F1
Cliff House Rd *BMSTR BS3*......72 B2
Clifton Av *WSM BS23*.............6 E6
Clifton Cl *CFTN/FAIL BS8*........54 D4
Clifton Down *CFTN/FAIL BS8*....54 D3
Clifton Down Rd
CFTN/FAIL BS8..................54 D3
Clifton High Gv
HNLZ/SM/SNYPK/WT BS9...44 C3
Clifton Hl *CFTN/FAIL BS8*........54 D4
Clifton Pk *CFTN/FAIL BS8*.......54 D4
Clifton Park Rd *CFTN/FAIL BS8*...54 D3
Clifton Pl *EVILLE/WHL BS5*......56 D3
Clifton Rd *CFTN/FAIL BS8*.......54 D4
EVILLE/WHL BS5................56 D3
Clifton St *BMSTR BS3*............73 G2
Clifton Vale *CFTN/FAIL BS8*.....54 D4
Clifton Vale Cl *CFTN/FAIL BS8*...54 D4
Clifton Vw *BMSTR BS3*...........73 C2
Cliftonwood Crs *CFTN/FAIL BS8*...4 A5
Clifton Wood Rd *CFTN/FAIL BS8*...4 A4

Cliftonwood Ter
BATHSE BA2.....................55 E5
Clift Pl *CBRIS/FH BS1*............5 F6
Clift Rd *BMSTR BS3*...............72 B2
Clinton Rd *BMSTR BS3*...........72 D4
Clive Rd *HGRV/WHIT BS14*......86 B2
Cloisters Rd *FRCTL/WBN BS36*...23 E4
Clonmel Rd
BRSG/KWL/STAPK BS4........73 E5
Closemead *CLVDN BS21*.........64 D4
The Close *BRSTK/PCHW BS34*...21 E4
FRCTL/WBN BS36...............24 A4
HNBRY/STHM BS10 ....18 D5
MANG/FISH BS16...............48 D5
THNB/SVB BS35..................8 C4
Clothier Rd
BRSG/KWL/STAPK BS4........75 E4
Clouds Hill Av *EVILLE/WHL BS5*...57 F5
Clouds Hill Rd *EVILLE/WHL BS5*...57 H5
Clovelly Cl *EVILLE/WHL BS5*....57 H5
Clovelly Rd *EVILLE/WHL BS5*....57 H5
WSM BS23.......................122 D1
Clover Cl *CLVDN BS21*...........65 F2
Clover Ct *MTN/WRL BS22*.......122 A4
Cloverdale Dr
OLD/WMLY/WICK BS30.......76 D3
Clover Gnd
HNLZ/SM/SNYPK/WT BS9...31 F5
Cloverlea Rd
OLD/WMLY/WICK BS30.......77 F1
Clover Leaze *ALMDB BS32*.......21 F4
MTN/WRL BS22................117 H2
Clyde Av *KEYN BS31*.............99 E1
Clyde Gdns *BATHSE BA2*........107 C1
EVILLE/WHL BS5................58 B5
Clyde Gv *BRSTK/PCHW BS34*....32 B3
Clyde La *RDLND/MONT BS6*.....55 F1
Clyde Ms *RDLND/MONT BS6*....55 F1
Clyde Rd *BRSG/KWL/STAPK BS4*...73 H3
FRCTL/WBN BS36...............23 H2
RDLND/MONT BS6.............55 F1
Clyde Ter *BMSTR BS3*.............72 D5
BRSG/KWL/STAPK BS4........73 H3
Clynder Gv *CLVDN BS21*.........64 C2
Coalbridge Cl *MTN/WRL BS22*...122 C1
Coaley Rd *AVONM BS11*..........42 D3
Coalpit Rd *CBATH/BATHN BA1*...91 F5
Coalsack La *FRCTL/WBN BS36*...35 H2
Coalville Rd *FRCTL/WBN BS36*...23 F5
Coape Rd *HGRV/WHIT BS14*.....87 E4
Coates Gv *NAIL BS48*.............67 H4
Coates Wk
BRSG/KWL/STAPK BS4........85 E3
Cobblestone Ms *CFTN/FAIL BS8*...55 E4
Cobden St *EVILLE/WHL BS5*.....57 E4
Coberley *KGWD/HNM BS15*.....58 C5
Cobhorn Dr
BMSTRD/HC/WWD BS13....84 A5
Cobley Cft *CLVDN BS21*..........64 C5
Coburg Rd *RDLND/MONT BS6*...56 A2
Cobthorn Wy *YTN/CONG BS49*...115 E1
Cock Rd *KGWD/HNM BS15*.......59 E5
Codrington Pl *CFTN/FAIL BS8* *...55 E4
Codrington Rd *HORF/LLZ BS7*...45 H5
Cogan Rd *KGWD/HNM BS15*.....59 E5
Cogsall Rd *HGRV/WHIT BS14*....87 E3
Coker Rd *MTN/WRL BS22*........122 D1
Colbourne Rd *BATHSE BA2*......110 A2
Colchester Crs
BRSG/KWL/STAPK BS4........85 E2
Coldharbour La
MANG/FISH BS16...............33 G4
WSM BS23.......................124 C3
Coldharbour Rd
RDLND/MONT BS6.............45 F5
Coldpark Gdns
BMSTRD/HC/WWD BS13....83 H4
Coldpark Rd
BMSTRD/HC/WWD BS13....83 H4
Coldrick Cl *HGRV/WHIT BS14*...96 C1
Colebrook Rd
KGWD/HNM BS15.............58 C3
Coleford La
HNBRY/STHM BS10 ....31 H5
Colehouse La *CLVDN BS21*......64 C5
Colemead
BMSTRD/HC/WWD BS13....84 C4
Coleridge Rd *CLVDN BS21*.......64 C2
EVILLE/WHL BS5................47 F5
WSM BS23.......................125 F1
Coleridge Vale Rd East
CLVDN BS21......................64 D2
Coleridge Vale Rd North
CLVDN BS21......................64 C3
Coleridge Vale Rd South
CLVDN BS21......................64 C3
Coleridge Vale Rd West
CLVDN BS21......................64 C3
Cole Rd *CBRISNE BS2*.............56 D5
Colesborne Cl *YATE/CS BS37*...25 H2
Coleshill Dr
BMSTRD/HC/WWD BS13....84 C4
College Av *MANG/FISH BS16*....48 A3
College Ct *MANG/FISH BS16*....48 A3
College Flds *CFTN/FAIL BS8*.....54 D5
College Park Dr
BMSTRD/HC/WWD BS13....83 H4
College Rd *CBATH/BATHN BA1*...102 B3
CFTN/FAIL BS8..................54 D5
HNLZ/SM/SNYPK/WT BS9...45 E1
MANG/FISH BS16...............48 A3
College Sq *CBRIS/FH BS1*..........4 C5
College St *CBRIS/FH BS1*..........4 C4
College Vw
CBATH/BATHN BA1 *..........102 D3
College Wy *BRSTK/PCHW BS34*...32 D1
Collet Cl *MTN/WRL BS22*........118 B4
Collett Av *YATE/CS BS37*.........75 C1
Collett Wy *YATE/CS BS37*.........13 G4
Colliers Break *MANG/FISH BS16*...49 H3
Collingwood Av
KGWD/HNM BS15.............59 E2
Collingwood Cl *KEYN BS31*......99 F2
MTN/WRL BS22................117 F4
Collingwood Rd
RDLND/MONT BS6.............55 F2
Collin Rd *BRSG/KWL/STAPK BS4*...74 C2
Collins Av *BRSTK/PCHW BS34*...21 E4

Collinson Rd
    BMSTRD/HC/WWD BS13........84 C4
Collins St AVONM BS11............28 B5
Colliter Crs BMSTR BS3...........72 B4
Collum La MTN/WRL BS22.......117 E1
Coln Sq THNB/SVB BS35.............8 D4
Colombo Crs WSM BS23.........124 D3
Colston Av CBRIS/FH BS1...........4 C4
Colston Cl FRCTL/WBN BS36......35 E1
    MANG/FISH BS16..................48 D5
Colston Dl MANG/FISH BS16......47 G4
Colston Fort CBRISNE BS2 *......55 H3
Colston Hl MANG/FISH BS16......47 H4
Colston Pde CBRIS/FH BS1...........5 G6
Colston Rd EVILLE/WHL BS5......57 E2
Colston St CBRIS/FH BS1.............4 E5
    MANG/FISH BS16..................48 D5
Colston Yd CBRISNE BS2.............4 C2
Colthurst Dr KGWD/HNM BS15..76 A1
Colts Gn YATE/CS BS37..............27 C2
Colwyn Rd EVILLE/WHL BS5......57 E2
Combe Av PTSHD/EG BS20........39 G2
Combe Flds PTSHD/EG BS20......39 G2
Combe Gv CBATH/BATHN BA1..101 G5
Combe La BATHSE BA2............110 A3
Combe Pk CBATH/BATHN BA1..101 H4
Combermere THNB/SVB BS35......9 E4
Combe Rd BATHSE BA2...............7 F1
    PTSHD/EG BS20....................39 H3
Combe Road Cl BATHSE BA2....111 F1
Combeside BATHSE BA2...........108 D4
Combe Side NAIL BS48.............79 H2
Combfactory La
    HNLZ/SM/SNYPK/WT BS9.......56 D3
Comfortable Pl
    CBATH/BATHN BA1 ....2 B3
Commercial Rd CBRIS/FH BS1....4 E7
Commercial Wy
    MTN/WRL BS22...................123 E1
The Common (East)
    ALMDB BS32..........................21 E1
Commonfield Rd AVONM BS11..29 H4
Common Ga YATE/CS BS37 *......15 G3
Common La PTSHD/EG BS20......52 B2
Common Mead La
    MANG/FISH BS16..................34 A4
Commonmead La
    YATE/CS BS37........................27 H1
Common Rd FRCTL/WBN BS36..23 F3
    KGWD/HNM BS15..................75 G3
The Common
    BRSTK/PCHW BS34...............20 D1
    MANG/FISH BS16..................48 B1
Compton Dr
    HNLZ/SM/SNYPK/WT BS9.......44 A1
    OMX/HUT/LCK BS24..............122 B4
Compton Gn KEYN BS31............88 B5
Compton Md NAIL BS48 *............82 A5
Compton St EVILLE/WHL BS5....57 E4
Comyn Wk MANG/FISH BS16......48 A3
Concorde Dr CLVDN BS21...........64 B4
    HNBRY/STHM BS10................31 F3
Concorde Rd
    BRSTK/PCHW BS34...............20 A3
The Concourse
    BRSG/KWL/STAPK BS4..........74 C4
Condor Cl MTN/WRL BS22.......122 A3
Condover Rd
    BRSG/KWL/STAPK BS4..........75 E3
Conduit Pl CBRISNE BS2............56 C2
Conduit Rd CBRISNE BS2...........56 C2
Conference Av PTSHD/EG BS20..40 A3
Conference Cl PTSHD/EG BS20...40 A3
Congleton Rd EVILLE/WHL BS5..57 F3
Conham Hl KGWD/HNM BS15......75 F1
Conham Rd KGWD/HNM BS15....75 E1
Conifer Cl FRCTL/WBN BS36......23 C1
    MANG/FISH BS16..................48 D2
Coniston Av
    OMX/HUT/LCK BS24..............126 B1
Coniston Cl
    OLD/WMLY/WICK BS30..........60 B5
Coniston Crs WSM BS23..........125 E2
Coniston Rd
    BRSTK/PCHW BS34...............20 A2
Connaught Pl WSM BS23.............6 D2
Connaught Rd
    BRSG/KWL/STAPK BS4..........85 F1
Connection Rd BATHSE BA2....107 F1
Constable Cl KEYN BS31............88 C3
Constable Dr MTN/WRL BS22..117 G5
Constable Rd HORF/LLZ BS7....46 C2
Constantine Av
    BRSTK/PCHW BS34...............21 G5
Constitution Hl CFTN/FAIL BS8....4 A4
Convent Cl HNBRY/STHM BS10..30 B2
Convocation Av BATHSE BA2...109 H2
Conway Gn KEYN BS31..............98 B1
Conway Rd
    BRSG/KWL/STAPK BS4..........74 B2
Conygar Cl CLVDN BS21.............62 D5
Conygre Rd BRSTK/PCHW BS34..32 D2
Cooke Cl OLD/WMLY/WICK BS30..77 F2
Cooke's Dr THNB/SVB BS35........11 E1
Cooks Cl ALMDB BS32................11 E1
Cook's Folly Rd
    HNLZ/SM/SNYPK/WT BS9.......54 B1
Cooks Gdns NAIL BS48...............68 A4
Cooks La FRCTL/WBN BS36........66 A5
Cook's La CLVDN BS21...............65 H3
Cooksley Rd EVILLE/WHL BS5....57 E3
Cook St AVONM BS11.................28 B5
Cookworthy Cl
    EVILLE/WHL BS5....................56 D5
Coombe Av THNB/SVB BS35........8 C2
Coombe Bridge Av
    HNLZ/SM/SNYPK/WT BS9.......44 B2
Coombe Brook Cl
    KGWD/HNM BS15..................58 B2
Coombe Cl HNBRY/STHM BS10..30 B2
Coombe Dl
    HNLZ/SM/SNYPK/WT BS9.......44 A2
    NAIL BS48..............................92 B4
Coombe Gdns
    HNLZ/SM/SNYPK/WT BS9.......44 A2
Coombe Hay La BATHSE BA2...110 A2

Coombe La CFTN/FAIL BS8........52 A1
    HNLZ/SM/SNYPK/WT BS9.......44 B2
Coombe Rd EVILLE/WHL BS5....57 E1
    NAIL BS48................................6 E2
    WSM BS23................................6 E2
Coombe Rocke
    HNLZ/SM/SNYPK/WT BS9.......44 B2
Coombes Wy
    OLD/WMLY/WICK BS30..........77 G2
Coombe Wy
    HNBRY/STHM BS10................30 D4
Cooperage La BMSTR BS3...........4 A7
Cooperage Rd EVILLE/WHL BS5..57 E4
Co-Operation Rd
    EVILLE/WHL BS5....................57 E2
Cooper Rd
    HNLZ/SM/SNYPK/WT BS9.......44 D1
    THNB/SVB BS35......................8 C2
Coopers Dr YATE/CS BS37........14 B2
The Coots HGRV/WHIT BS14......86 D3
Copeland Dr HGRV/WHIT BS14..86 A4
Cope Pk ALMDB BS32................11 E2
Copford La LGASH BS41.............71 E5
Copley Ct KGWD/HNM BS15......76 B1
Copley Gdns HORF/LLZ BS7......46 C2
    MTN/WRL BS22....................122 C1
Copperfield Dr
    HNLZ/SM/SNYPK/WT BS9.....117 G4
The Coppice ALMDB BS32...........21 E3
    BMSTRD/HC/WWD BS13.........83 H5
Copse Cl OMX/HUT/LCK BS24..125 F5
Copseland BATHSE BA2...........109 G2
Copse Rd
    BRSG/KWL/STAPK BS4..........74 A3
    CLVDN BS21...........................64 C1
    KEYN BS31.............................89 F5
The Copse MTN/WRL BS22......123 C1
Copthorne Cl HGRV/WHIT BS14..86 A4
Coralberry Dr MTN/WRL BS22.122 C2
Corbet Cl AVONM BS11...............29 H3
Corbett Cl YATE/CS BS37...........14 B3
Cordwell Wk
    HNBRY/STHM BS10................45 H1
Corey Cl CBRISNE BS2...............56 B2
Corfe Cl NAIL BS48....................67 E5
Corfe Crs KEYN BS31................88 B4
Corfe Pl OLD/WMLY/WICK BS30..77 F5
Corfe Rd
    BRSG/KWL/STAPK BS4..........85 E2
Coriander Dr ALMDB BS32..........22 A3
Coriander Wk EVILLE/WHL BS5..57 E1
Corinum Cl MANG/FISH BS16......50 A2
Cork Pl CBATH/BATHN BA1 *.......2 A3
Cork St CBATH/BATHN BA1..........2 A2
Cork Ter CBATH/BATHN BA1 ....2 A2
Cormorant Cl MTN/WRL BS22..122 C2
Corner Cft CLVDN BS21..............64 C3
Cornfield Cl ALMDB BS32............21 E1
The Cornfields
    MTN/WRL BS22....................117 G5
Cornhill Dr HGRV/WHIT BS14.....85 H2
Cornish Gv HGRV/WHIT BS14.....86 D3
Cornish Rd HGRV/WHIT BS14.....86 D3
Cornish Wk HGRV/WHIT BS14....86 D3
Cornleaze
    BMSTRD/HC/WWD BS13.........84 B4
Corn St CBATH/BATHN BA1.........3 F5
    CBRIS/FH BS1........................5 F4
Cornwall Crs YATE/CS BS37......14 B4
Cornwallis Av CFTN/FAIL BS8....54 D5
Cornwallis Crs CFTN/FAIL BS8..54 D5
Cornwallis Gv CFTN/FAIL BS8....54 D5
Cornwall Rd HORF/LLZ BS7......45 H4
Coronation Av BATHSE BA2.....107 H4
    KEYN BS31.............................88 A5
    MANG/FISH BS16..................48 A4
Coronation Cl
    OLD/WMLY/WICK BS30..........76 D1
Coronation Pl CBRIS/FH BS1 *...5 F4
Coronation Rd BMSTR BS3.........72 B2
    CBATH/BATHN BA1 ....2 A2
    KGWD/HNM BS15..................59 F4
    MANG/FISH BS16..................48 A4
    MTN/WRL BS22....................122 B1
Corondale Rd MTN/WRL BS22..122 A3
The Corridor
    CBATH/BATHN BA1 *...............3 G5
Corsley Wk
    BRSG/KWL/STAPK BS4..........85 G1
Corston Dr BATHSE BA2...........106 A1
Corston La BATHSE BA2.............99 H4
Corston Wk AVONM BS11...........42 C1
Cossham Cl THNB/SVB BS35.......8 D2
Cossham Rd EVILLE/WHL BS5...57 F3
    MANG/FISH BS16....................51 C4
Cossham Wk EVILLE/WHL BS5...58 A2
Cossington Rd
    BRSG/KWL/STAPK BS4..........85 G1
Cossins Rd RDLND/MONT BS6...45 F5
Costland Dr
    BMSTRD/HC/WWD BS13.........84 A3
Cote Dr
    HNLZ/SM/SNYPK/WT BS9.......45 A3
Cote House La
    HNLZ/SM/SNYPK/WT BS9.......45 E3
Cote La
    HNLZ/SM/SNYPK/WT BS9.......45 E3
Cote Lea Pk
    HNLZ/SM/SNYPK/WT BS9.......45 E3
Cote Paddock
    HNLZ/SM/SNYPK/WT BS9.......44 D4
Cote Pk
    HNLZ/SM/SNYPK/WT BS9.......44 C2
Cote Rd
    HNLZ/SM/SNYPK/WT BS9.......45 E4
Cotham Brow
    RDLND/MONT BS6..................55 H1
Cotham Gdns
    RDLND/MONT BS6 *................55 F2
Cotham Gv RDLND/MONT BS6...55 H2
Cotham Hl RDLND/MONT BS6....55 G2
Cotham Lawn Rd
    RDLND/MONT BS6..................55 G3
Cotham Pk RDLND/MONT BS6...55 G2
Cotham Park Man
    RDLND/MONT BS6 *................55 G2
Cotham Pk North
    RDLND/MONT BS6..................55 G2

Cotham Pl RDLND/MONT BS6 *..55 G3
Cotham Rd RDLND/MONT BS6...55 G3
Cotham Rd South
    RDLND/MONT BS6..................55 H3
Cotham Side
    RDLND/MONT BS6..................55 H2
Cotham V RDLND/MONT BS6.....55 G2
Cotman Wk HORF/LLZ BS7.......46 D2
    MTN/WRL BS22....................122 C1
Cotrith Gv HNLZ/SM/SNYPK/WT BS9..30 C2
Cotswold Cl PTSHD/EG BS20.....39 H4
Cotswold Rd BATHSE BA2.......108 A3
    BMSTR BS3.............................73 E3
    YATE/CS BS37........................26 D2
Cotswold Vw BATHSE BA2.......107 G2
    KGWD/HNM BS15..................58 D1
Cotswold Wy
    CBATH/BATHN BA1 ....2 C2
Cottage Gdns EVILLE/WHL BS5..58 A4
Cottage Pl CBRISNE BS2..............4 E1
Cottington Ct
    KGWD/HNM BS15..................76 B1
Cottisford Rd EVILLE/WHL BS5..46 D4
Cottle Gdns HGRV/WHIT BS14...87 E3
Cottle Rd HGRV/WHIT BS14......87 E3
Cotton Mill La EVILLE/WHL BS5..73 H3
Cottonwood Dr
    OLD/WMLY/WICK BS30..........76 D5
Cottrell Av KGWD/HNM BS15....58 B1
Cottrell Rd EVILLE/WHL BS5......57 G1
Coulson Dr MTN/WRL BS22.....118 A5
Coulson's Cl HGRV/WHIT BS14..96 C1
Coulson's Rd HGRV/WHIT BS14..96 C1
Coulson Wk KGWD/HNM BS15...58 C1
Counterpool Rd
    KGWD/HNM BS15..................58 C4
Countership La
    CBATH/BATHN BA1 ....5 G4
Countership Gdns
    HGRV/WHIT BS14...................86 B3
Countess Wk MANG/FISH BS16..47 F2
County St
    BRSG/KWL/STAPK BS4..........73 H2
County Wy BRSTK/PCHW BS34..34 A1
Court Av BRSTK/PCHW BS34......21 H5
    VTN/CONG BS49..................112 B4
Court Cl HORF/LLZ BS7..............46 A2
    PTSHD/EG BS20....................39 H4
The Court Cl NAIL BS48.............80 B4
Courtenay Rd KEYN BS31..........98 B2
Courtenay Cresent
    BRSG/KWL/STAPK BS4..........85 E2
Court Farm Rd
    HGRV/WHIT BS14...................96 C1
    MANG/FISH BS16...................76 A5
Courtfield Gv MANG/FISH BS16..48 A4
Court Gdns
    CBATH/BATHN BA1 ....104 B1
    YATE/CS BS37........................26 A2
Courtlands ALMDB BS32.............21 E1
    KEYN BS31.............................88 B4
Courtlands La BMSTR BS3..........71 H2
Court La CBATH/BATHN BA1.....104 C2
    CLVDN BS21...........................65 C2
Courtney Rd KGWD/HNM BS15..59 G4
Courtney Wy KGWD/HNM BS15..59 G4
Court Pl MTN/WRL BS22..........122 C1
Court Rd FRCTL/WBN BS36........66 C5
    HORF/LLZ BS7........................46 B2
    KGWD/HNM BS15..................58 D4
    MTN/WRL BS22....................116 B3
Courtside Ms
    RDLND/MONT BS6..................55 G2
Court Vw
    OLD/WMLY/WICK BS30..........61 G5
Court View Cl ALMDB BS32........10 C2
Cousins Cl HNLZ/SM/SNYPK/WT BS9..30 B2
Cousins La EVILLE/WHL BS5......57 H4
Cousins Ms
    BRSG/KWL/STAPK BS4..........55 H5
Couzens Cl YATE/CS BS37.........14 D5
Couzens Pl BRSTK/PCHW BS34..21 H5
Coventry Wk
    BRSG/KWL/STAPK BS4..........57 H5
Cowdray Rd
    BRSG/KWL/STAPK BS4..........85 E2
Cowhorn Hl
    OLD/WMLY/WICK BS30..........77 F2
Cowler Wk
    BMSTRD/HC/WWD BS13.........84 A5
Cowling Dr HGRV/WHIT BS14....86 B4
Cowling Rd HGRV/WHIT BS14....86 B4
Cowper Rd RDLND/MONT BS6...55 F2
Cowper St EVILLE/WHL BS5......57 F2
Cox Ct OLD/WMLY/WICK BS30...76 C2
Coxley Dr CBATH/BATHN BA1..103 E2
Coxway CLVDN BS21..................65 E3
Crabtree Cl LGASH BS41............94 C3
Crabtree La LGASH BS41...........94 B3
Crabtree Pk CLVDN BS21 *.........64 C4
Crabtree Wk EVILLE/WHL BS5...58 A1
Cradock Cl
    OLD/WMLY/WICK BS30..........76 D2
Cranberry Wk
    HNLZ/SM/SNYPK/WT BS9.......30 A3
Cranbourne Cha WSM BS23........7 K1
Cranbourne Rd
    BRSTK/PCHW BS34...............20 D3
Cranbrook Rd
    RDLND/MONT BS6..................45 G5
Crandale Rd BATHSE BA2............2 A6
Crandell Cl HNBRY/STHM BS10..30 D1
Crane Cl KGWD/HNM BS15........59 H5
Cranford Cl MTN/WRL BS22.....122 A2
Cranham Cl KGWD/HNM BS15...59 F1
Cranham Dr
    BRSTK/PCHW BS34...............21 G3
Cranham Rd
    HNBRY/STHM BS10................31 G5
Cranhill Rd CBATH/BATHN BA1...2 B2
Cranleigh BATHSE BA2.............110 D2
Cranleigh Court Rd
    YATE/CS BS37........................13 H5
Cranleigh Gdns
    HNLZ/SM/SNYPK/WT BS9.......44 C4
Cranleigh Rd HGRV/WHIT BS14..86 A3
Cranmore Av KEYN BS31...........88 B3
Cranmore Crs
    HNBRY/STHM BS10................31 H4

Cranmore Pl BATHSE BA2.......110 B2
Cranside Av RDLND/MONT BS6..45 G5
Cransley Crs
    HNLZ/SM/SNYPK/WT BS9.......45 G1
Crantock Av
    BMSTRD/HC/WWD BS13.........84 C1
Crantock Dr ALMDB BS32..........10 D2
Crantock Rd YATE/CS BS37.......25 H1
Cranwell Gv HGRV/WHIT BS14..85 H4
Cranwell Rd
    OMX/HUT/LCK BS24..............127 F1
Crates Cl KGWD/HNM BS15 *....59 E3
Craven Cl
    OLD/WMLY/WICK BS30..........76 C1
Craven Wy
    OLD/WMLY/WICK BS30..........76 C1
Crawford Cl CLVDN BS21...........64 B4
Craydon Gv HGRV/WHIT BS14...86 C5
Craydon Rd HGRV/WHIT BS14...86 C4
Craydon Wk HGRV/WHIT BS14..86 C4
Crediton Crs
    BRSG/KWL/STAPK BS4..........73 G5
Crescent Gdns
    CBATH/BATHN BA1 ....2 D3
Crescent Rd MANG/FISH BS16...48 C2
The Crescent
    HNLZ/SM/SNYPK/WT BS9.......44 A2
    MANG/FISH BS16...................48 D5
    MTN/WRL BS22........................33 G4
    MTN/WRL BS22....................122 B1
    NAIL BS48..............................79 H3
    OLD/WMLY/WICK BS30..........61 F4
Crescent Vw BATHSE BA2...........2 E7
Cresswell Cl MTN/WRL BS22...122 D1
The Crest
    BRSG/KWL/STAPK BS4..........74 B4
Creswicke Av
    KGWD/HNM BS15..................75 H1
Creswicke Rd
    BRSG/KWL/STAPK BS4..........85 F2
Crewkerne Cl NAIL BS48............57 G4
Crew's Hole Rd
    EVILLE/WHL BS5....................57 G4
Cribbs Cswy
    HNBRY/STHM BS10................19 E5
Cricket Field Gn NAIL BS48 *.....67 E4
Cricket La HNBRY/STHM BS10...31 E5
Cricklade Ct NAIL BS48..............67 H5
Cricklade Rd HORF/LLZ BS7......46 A4
Cripps Rd BMSTR BS3................72 C4
Crispin La THNB/SVB BS35..........8 C3
Crispin Wy KGWD/HNM BS15....59 F1
Crockerne Dr PTSHD/EG BS20...42 C5
Croft Av MANG/FISH BS16..........47 E4
Croft Cl OLD/WMLY/WICK BS30..89 C1
Crofters Wk ALMDB BS32...........10 C1
Crofton Av HORF/LLZ BS7..........46 A2
Crofton Flds FRCTL/WBN BS36..23 E4
Croft Rd CBATH/BATHN BA1.....103 E5
Crofts End Rd EVILLE/WHL BS5..57 G2
The Croft CLVDN BS21...............65 F3
    MANG/FISH BS16...................49 F5
    NAIL BS48..............................79 H2
    OLD/WMLY/WICK BS30 *.........77 F3
    OMX/HUT/LCK BS24..............126 B3
Croft Vw
    HNLZ/SM/SNYPK/WT BS9.......45 G1
Crokeswood Wk AVONM BS11...29 C4
Crome Rd HORF/LLZ BS7...........46 D1
Cromer Rd EVILLE/WHL BS5......57 E1
    WSM BS23................................7 H6
Cromwell Ct KGWD/HNM BS15..76 B2
Cromwell Dr MTN/WRL BS22...117 H4
Cromwell Rd EVILLE/WHL BS5...58 A3
    RDLND/MONT BS6..................55 H1
Cromwells Hide
    MANG/FISH BS16....................47 G3
Cromwell St BMSTR BS3............72 D3
Crookes La MTN/WRL BS22.....116 B4
Croomes Hl MANG/FISH BS16....48 D2
Cropthorne Rd HORF/LLZ BS7...32 C4
Cropthorne Rd South
    HORF/LLZ BS7........................32 C5
Crosby Rw CFTN/FAIL BS8........55 E5
Crosscombe Dr
    BMSTRD/HC/WWD BS13.........95 C1
Crosscombe Wk
    BMSTRD/HC/WWD BS13.........95 C1
Cross Elms La
    HNLZ/SM/SNYPK/WT BS9.......44 C3
Crossfield Rd MANG/FISH BS16..49 E5
Cross Lanes PTSHD/EG BS20.....42 B4
Crossleaze Rd
    KGWD/HNM BS15..................75 H3
Crossley Cl FRCTL/WBN BS36....23 F3
Crossman Av FRCTL/WBN BS36..23 E3
Crossman Wk CLVDN BS21.........65 F2
Cross St KEYN BS31..................88 C2
    KGWD/HNM BS15..................58 C2
    WSM BS23................................6 E4
Cross Tree Gv ALMDB BS32........21 F2
Cross Wk HGRV/WHIT BS14......85 H3
Crossways La THNB/SVB BS35.....9 F2
Crossways Rd
    BRSG/KWL/STAPK BS4..........73 H5
    THNB/SVB BS35.......................9 F2
Crow La CBRIS/FH BS1................5 F4
    HNBRY/STHM BS10................30 D5
Crowley Wy AVONM BS11.........28 B4
Crowndale Rd
    BRSG/KWL/STAPK BS4..........73 H5
Crown Gdns
    OLD/WMLY/WICK BS30..........59 H4
Crown Hl CBATH/BATHN BA1...101 H5
    EVILLE/WHL BS5....................57 H3
Crown Wk KGWD/HNM BS15.....57 H2
Crownleaze MANG/FISH BS16....48 D5
Crown Rd CBATH/BATHN BA1..101 G3
    KGWD/HNM BS15..................58 D1
    OLD/WMLY/WICK BS30..........59 H4
Crown Wy
    OLD/WMLY/WICK BS30..........60 A4
Crows Gv ALMDB BS32..............11 F4
Crow's Nest HORF/LLZ BS7.......46 C2
Crowther Rd HORF/LLZ BS7......46 C4
Crowther St BMSTR BS3............72 C3
Croydon St EVILLE/WHL BS5......57 F2
The Crunnis ALMDB BS32...........21 G4
Crusty La PTSHD/EG BS20.........42 C3

Crystal Wy ALMDB BS32.............21 G2
Cuckoo La ALMDB BS32.............35 F2
Cuffington Av
    BRSG/KWL/STAPK BS4..........74 C2
Culverhill Rd YATE/CS BS37.......26 C1
Culvers Cl KEYN BS31...............88 B3
Culvers Rd KEYN BS31...............88 B3
Culver St CBRIS/FH BS1...............4 D4
The Culwert ALMDB BS32............21 G2
Culverwell Rd
    BMSTRD/HC/WWD BS13.........84 B5
Cumberland Basin
    CBRIS/FH BS1........................72 B1
Cumberland Basin Rd
    CFTN/FAIL BS8.......................72 A1
Cumberland Cl CBRIS/FH BS1...72 A1
Cumberland Gv
    RDLND/MONT BS6..................56 B1
Cumberland Pl CFTN/FAIL BS8..54 D5
Cumberland Rd CBRIS/FH BS1...72 B1
Cumberland Rw
    CBATH/BATHN BA1 ....2 E4
Cumberland St CBRISNE BS2......2 D5
Cumbria Cl THNB/SVB BS35.........9 F3
Cunningham Gdns
    MANG/FISH BS16...................48 B3
Cunnington Cl
    OLD/WMLY/WICK BS30..........76 D5
Curland Gv HGRV/WHIT BS14....86 A4
Curlew Cl MANG/FISH BS16 *.....47 G2
Curlew Gdns MTN/WRL BS22...122 C2
Curlew Pl PTSHD/EG BS20.........40 B2
Currells La
    BLAG/CWMG/WR BS40...........92 C3
Curtis La BRSTK/PCHW BS34.....34 C5
Custom Cl HGRV/WHIT BS14......85 H2
Cutler Rd
    BMSTRD/HC/WWD BS13.........84 A3
Cuttsheath Rd WUE GL12............9 H3
Cygnet Crs MTN/WRL BS22.....122 C2
Cygnet Gdns RDLND/MONT BS6..55 F1
Cynder Wy MANG/FISH BS16.....35 G4
Cynthia Rd BATHSE BA2...........107 H2
Cypress Gdns CFTN/FAIL BS8....54 C5
Cypress Cv
    HNLZ/SM/SNYPK/WT BS9.......45 G2
Cyrus Ct MANG/FISH BS16........49 H1

D

Dafford's Blds
    CBATH/BATHN BA1 ....103 E2
Dahlia Gdns BATHSE BA2.............3 G2
Dairy Cl VTN/CONG BS49.........112 A2
Daisy Bank BATHSE BA2...........109 E3
Daisy Rd EVILLE/WHL BS5..........57 E1
Dakin Cl BRSG/KWL/STAPK BS4..73 H4
Dakota Dr HGRV/WHIT BS14......85 H5
Dalby Av BMSTR BS3..................73 E3
Dale St EVILLE/WHL BS5.............57 E2
Daley Cl MTN/WRL BS22..........118 A5
Dalkeith Av KGWD/HNM BS15....58 C2
Dalrymple Rd CBRISNE BS2.......56 B1
Dalston Rd BMSTR BS3..............72 C2
Dalton Sq CBRISNE BS2..............56 B1
Dame Court Cl
    MTN/WRL BS22....................117 G4
Dampier Rd BMSTR BS3............72 B3
Danbury Crs
    HNBRY/STHM BS10................31 G4
Danbury Wk
    HNBRY/STHM BS10................31 G4
Dancey Md
    BMSTRD/HC/WWD BS13.........83 H3
Dandy's Meadow
    PTSHD/EG BS20....................40 A3
Danesbury KGWD/HNM BS15....76 A2
Dangerfield Av
    BMSTRD/HC/WWD BS13.........83 H3
Daniel Cl CLVDN BS21...............65 F2
Daniel Ms BATHSE BA2................3 J2
Daniel St BATHSE BA2.................3 J2
Dapps Hl KEYN BS31..................89 E5
Dark La BATHSE BA2...............104 A3
    NAIL BS48..............................80 A4
Darley Cl HNBRY/STHM BS10....30 B2
Darlington Pl BATHSE BA2...........3 J5
Darlington Rd BATHSE BA2..........3 J4
Darlington St BATHSE BA2............3 J3
Darmead OMX/HUT/LCK BS24..123 E2
Darnley Av HORF/LLZ BS7.........46 B2
Dart Cl THNB/SVB BS35...............9 E4
Dartmouth Av BATHSE BA2..........7 H4
Dartmouth Av BATHSE BA2.......107 H2
Dartmouth Cl MTN/WRL BS22..122 C1
Dart Rd CLVDN BS21..................65 E2
Daubeny Cl MANG/FISH BS16.....48 B3
Daventry Rd
    BRSG/KWL/STAPK BS4..........73 G5
Davey St CBRISNE BS2...............56 B2
Davey Ter CBRISNE BS2 *...........56 B2
David's Rd HGRV/WHIT BS14.....86 B3
David St CBRISNE BS2.................5 G3
Davies Dr
    BRSG/KWL/STAPK BS4..........75 E1
Davin Crs PTSHD/EG BS20........42 C5
Davis Ct THNB/SVB BS35 *..........8 C2
Davis La CLVDN BS21................64 D5
Davis St AVONM BS11................28 B5
Dawes Cl CLVDN BS21...............65 F3
Dawley Cl FRCTL/WBN BS36......23 E3
Dawlish Rd BMSTR BS3..............73 E4
Dawn Rd KGWD/HNM BS15........58 B4
Day Crs MANG/FISH BS16..........48 A4
Day's Rd CBRISNE BS2...............56 C5
Deacon Cl FRCTL/WBN BS36.....23 E3
Deadmill La MTN/WRL BS22.....122 D1
Deadmill La
    CBATH/BATHN BA1 ....103 F1
Dean Av THNB/SVB BS35.............8 D2
Dean Cl KGWD/HNM BS15.........75 F2
    MTN/WRL BS22....................118 A5
Dean Crs BMSTR BS3.................72 D3

Deanery Rd *CBRIS/FH* BS1 .... 4 C5
   KGWD/HNM BS15 .... 59 G3
Deanhill La
   CBATH/BATHN BA1 .... 101 E2
Dean La *BMSTR* BS3 .... 72 D2
Dean Rd *AVONM* BS11 .... 16 C5
   YATE/CS BS37 .... 13 C4
Dean's Dr *EVILLE/WHL* BS5 .... 58 A1
Deans Md *AVONM* BS11 .... 29 C5
The Deans *PTSHD/EG* BS20 .... 39 E4
Dean St *BMSTR* BS3 .... 72 D2
   CBRISNE BS2 ....
Debecca's La *PTSHD/EG* BS20 ...... 42 B4
De Clifford Rd *AVONM* BS11 .... 30 A1
Deep Coombe Rd *BMSTR* BS3 ...... 72 B4
Deep Pit Rd *EVILLE/WHL* BS5 .... 57 H2
Deep St *CBRIS/FH* BS1 .... 5 F2
Deerhurst *KGWD/HNM* BS15 .... 59 E1
   YATE/CS BS37 .... 25 G2
Deering Cl *AVONM* BS11 .... 29 H4
Deer Md *CLVDN* BS21 .... 64 B4
Deerswood *KGWD/HNM* BS15 ...... 59 E1
Delabere Av *MANG/FISH* BS16 ..... 48 B3
Delapre Rd *WSM* BS23 .... 124 D3
De La Warre Ct
   BRSG/KWL/STAPK BS4 .... 57 H5
Delius Gv
   BRSG/KWL/STAPK BS4 .... 85 E2
The Dell *ALMDB* BS32 .... 21 C3
   HNLZ/SM/SNYPK/WT BS9 .... 44 D3
   MTN/WRL BS22 .... 117 H4
   NAIL BS48 .... 67 E4
   OLD/WMLY/WICK BS30 .... 77 F1
Delvin Rd *HNBRY/STHM* BS10 ..... 31 G5
Denbigh St *CBRISNE* BS2 .... 56 A2
Dene Cl *KEYN* BS31 .... 98 A1
Dene Rd *HGRV/WHIT* BS14 .... 86 D5
Denleigh Cl *HGRV/WHIT* BS14 ...... 86 B5
Denmark Pl *HORF/LLZ* BS7 .... 56 C2
Denmark Rd *BATHSE* BA2 .... 2 A5
Denmark St *CBRIS/FH* BS1 .... 4 D4
Denning Ct *MTN/WRL* BS22 ...... 118 A4
Dennisworth *MANG/FISH* BS16 ... 51 F3
Dennor Rd *HGRV/WHIT* BS14 ...... 86 A2
Denny Vw *PTSHD/EG* BS20 .... 38 D3
Denny-view Rd *CFTN/FAIL* BS8 .. 138 C3
Denston Dr *PTSHD/EG* BS20 ...... 40 A4
Denston Wk
   BMSTR/HC/WWD BS13 .... 84 B2
Denton Patch
   MANG/FISH BS16 .... 49 H1
Dentwood Gv
   HNLZ/SM/SNYPK/WT BS9 .... 43 H1
Derby Rd *HORF/LLZ* BS7 .... 46 A5
Derby St *EVILLE/WHL* BS5 .... 57 F4
Derham Cl *YTN/CONG* BS49 .... 112 D3
Derham Pk *YTN/CONG* BS49 .... 112 D3
Derham Rd
   BMSTR/HC/WWD BS13 .... 84 B4
Dermot St *CBRISNE* BS2 * 56 C2
Derricke Rd *HGRV/WHIT* BS14 ... 87 E3
Derrick Rd *KGWD/HNM* BS15 ..... 58 D3
Derry Rd *BMSTR* BS3 .... 72 C4
Derwent Rd *EVILLE/WHL* BS5 ...... 57 H2
Derwent Gv *KEYN* BS31 .... 88 D4
Derwent Rd *EVILLE/WHL* BS5 ...... 57 H2
   WSM BS23 .... 125 F2
Devaney Cl
   BRSG/KWL/STAPK BS4 .... 75 E1
De Verose Ct *KGWD/HNM* BS15 .. 76 B2
Devon Cv *EVILLE/WHL* BS5 .... 57 E3
Devon Rd *EVILLE/WHL* BS5 .... 57 F2
Devonshire Blds *BATHSE* BA2 ... 108 C3
Devonshire Dr *PTSHD/EG* BS20 .. 38 D3
Devonshire Pl *BATHSE* BA2 ...... 108 C3
Devonshire Rd *BATHSE* BA2 ..... 103 H5
   RDLND/MONT BS6 ....
   WSM BS23 .... 124 D3
Dewfalls Dr *ALMDB* BS32 .... 21 F1
Dial Hill Rd *CLVDN* BS21 .... 64 D1
Dial La *BLAG/CWMG/WR* BS40 .... 93 E3
   MANG/FISH BS16 .... 48 D2
Diamond Batch
   OMX/HUT/LCK BS24 .... 123 E2
Diamond Rd *EVILLE/WHL* BS5 ..... 57 H4
Diamond St *BMSTR* BS3 .... 72 D3
Diana Gdns *ALMDB* BS32 .... 21 G2
Dibden Cl *MANG/FISH* BS16 .... 35 G5
Dibden La *MANG/FISH* BS16 ...... 49 G1
Dibden Rd *MANG/FISH* BS16 ...... 35 G5
Dickens Cl *HORF/LLZ* BS7 .... 32 C5
Dickenson Rd *WSM* BS23 .... 6 E7
Dickinson's Gv
   YTN/CONG BS49 .... 115 E3
Dickinsons Fld *BMSTR* BS3 .... 73 E4
Didsbury Cl *HNBRY/STHM* BS10 .. 30 D4
Dighton Ga *BRSTK/PCHW* BS34 .. 21 C5
Dighton St *CBRIS/FH* BS1 .... 5 F1
Dingle Cl
   HNLZ/SM/SNYPK/WT BS9 .... 44 A2
Dingle Rd
   HNLZ/SM/SNYPK/WT BS9 .... 44 A1
The Dingle *FRCTL/WBN* BS36 ...... 35 E2
   YATE/CS BS37 .... 14 B3
Dingle Vw
   HNLZ/SM/SNYPK/WT BS9 .... 44 A1
Dinglewood Cl
   HNLZ/SM/SNYPK/WT BS9 .... 44 B1
Dings Wk *CBRISNE* BS2 .... 56 C5
Dirac Rd *HORF/LLZ* BS7 .... 46 B4
Dixon Gdns
   CBATH/BATHN BA1 .... 102 C3
Dixon Rd
   BRSG/KWL/STAPK BS4 .... 85 E2
Dock Gate La *CFTN/FAIL* BS8 * ... 72 B1
Dodington La *YATE/CS* BS37 ...... 26 D4
Dodington Rd *YATE/CS* BS37 ..... 26 C5
Dodisham Wk
   MANG/FISH BS16 .... 47 H5
Dog La *HNBRY/STHM* BS10 .... 30 A1
Dolecroft La *MTN/WRL* BS22 ...... 118 B3
Dolemoor La *YTN/CONG* BS49 .. 114 A2
Dolman Cl *HNBRY/STHM* BS10 ... 30 D4
Dominion Rd *BATHSE* BA2 .... 101 H5
   MANG/FISH BS16 .... 47 H5
Donald Rd
   BMSTR/HC/WWD BS13 .... 84 A2
Doncaster Early Wy *HORF/LLZ* BS7. 32 A5

Doncaster Rd
   HNBRY/STHM BS10 .... 31 F4
Donegal Rd
   BRSG/KWL/STAPK BS4 .... 73 E5
Dongola Av *HORF/LLZ* BS7 .... 46 A4
Dongola Rd *HORF/LLZ* BS7 .... 46 A4
Doone Rd *HORF/LLZ* BS7 .... 32 B5
Dorcas Av *BRSTK/PCHW* BS34 ... 21 H5
Dorchester Cl *NAIL* BS48 .... 79 E1
Dorchester Rd *HORF/LLZ* BS7 ..... 46 C1
Dorchester St
   CBATH/BATHN BA1 .... 3 G6
Dorester Cl *HNBRY/STHM* BS10 .. 31 G1
Dorian Cl *HORF/LLZ* BS7 .... 46 A1
Dorian Rd *HORF/LLZ* BS7 .... 46 A1
Dorian Wy *HORF/LLZ* BS7 .... 32 A5
Dormeads Vw
   OMX/HUT/LCK BS24 .... 122 C4
Dormer Cl *FRCTL/WBN* BS36 ...... 24 B4
Dormer Rd *EVILLE/WHL* BS5 .... 56 D4
Dorset Cl *BATHSE* BA2 .... 2 B5
Dorset Gv *CBRISNE* BS2 .... 56 C1
Dorset Rd
   HNLZ/SM/SNYPK/WT BS9 .... 45 F2
   KGWD/HNM BS15 .... 58 D2
Dorset St *BATHSE* BA2 .... 2 B5
   BMSTR BS3 .... 72 C3
Dorset Wy *YATE/CS* BS37 .... 14 C4
Douglas Rd *HORF/LLZ* BS7 .... 46 B1
   KGWD/HNM BS15 .... 58 D3
   WSM BS23 .... 125 E1
Doulton Wy *HGRV/WHIT* BS14 ... 85 H4
Dovecote *YATE/CS* BS37 .... 26 A3
Dovedale *THNB/SVB* BS35 .... 9 E5
Dove La *CBRISNE* BS2 .... 56 B3
Dovercourt Rd *HORF/LLZ* BS7 ..... 46 C5
Dover Pl *CBATH/BATHN* BA1 * ... 102 D3
   CFTN/FAIL BS8 .... 4 A3
Dovers La *CBATH/BATHN* BA1 ... 104 D2
Dovers Pk *CBATH/BATHN* BA1 ... 104 D2
Dove St *CBRISNE* BS2 .... 55 H5
Dove St South *CBRISNE* BS2 * 5 F1
Dovetail Dr *WSM* BS23 .... 7 K5
Dovey Ct
   OLD/WMLY/WICK BS30 ..... 77 F1
Dowdeswell Cl
   HNBRY/STHM BS10 .... 30 D2
Dowding Cl *YATE/CS* BS37 .... 15 E5
Dowding Rd
   CBATH/BATHN BA1 .... 103 E3
Dowland Gv
   BRSG/KWL/STAPK BS4 .... 85 E3
Dowling Rd
   BMSTR/HC/WWD BS13 .... 96 A1
Down Av *BATHSE* BA2 .... 111 E1
Downend Cl *PTSHD/EG* BS20 ..... 38 D3
Downend Rd *HORF/LLZ* BS7 .... 46 B3
Downend Park Rd
   MANG/FISH BS16 .... 48 D3
Downend Rd *HORF/LLZ* BS7 .... 46 B3
   KGWD/HNM BS15 .... 58 D2
Downfield *KEYN* BS31 * 88 A4
Downfield Dr *FRCTL/WBN* BS36 .. 23 H2
Downfield Rd *CFTN/FAIL* BS8 ..... 55 E2
Down La *BATHSE* BA2 .... 104 A3
Downleaze
   HNLZ/SM/SNYPK/WT BS9 .... 44 C5
   MANG/FISH BS16 .... 34 D5
   PTSHD/EG BS20 .... 39 E3
Downman Rd *HORF/LLZ* BS7 ..... 46 C5
Downs Barton *BMSTR* BS36 ...... 34 D1
   PTSHD/EG BS20 .... 38 B5
Downs Cl *MTN/WRL* BS22 ...... 122 C2
Downs Cote Av
   HNLZ/SM/SNYPK/WT BS9 .... 44 D2
Downs Cote Dr
   HNLZ/SM/SNYPK/WT BS9 .... 44 D2
Downs Cote Gdns
   HNLZ/SM/SNYPK/WT BS9 .... 45 E2
Downs Cote Pk
   HNLZ/SM/SNYPK/WT BS9 .... 45 E2
Downs Cote Vw
   HNLZ/SM/SNYPK/WT BS9 .... 45 E2
Downside *PTSHD/EG* BS20 .... 39 G3
Downside Cl *BATHSE* BA2 .... 104 A3
   OLD/WMLY/WICK BS30 ..... 59 F5
Downside Pk *NAIL* BS48 * 92 A3
Downside Rd *CFTN/FAIL* BS8 ..... 55 E4
   NAIL BS48 .... 92 A4
   WSM BS23 .... 125 E2
Downs Pk East
   HNLZ/SM/SNYPK/WT BS9 .... 45 E3
Downs Pk West
   RDLND/MONT BS6 .... 45 E3
Downs Rd
   HNLZ/SM/SNYPK/WT BS9 .... 45 E2
   LGASH BS41 .... 94 C2
The Downs *PTSHD/EG* BS20 ...... 39 E4
Downton Rd
   BRSG/KWL/STAPK BS4 .... 73 E5
Dowry Pl *CFTN/FAIL* BS8 .... 72 A1
Dowry Rd *CFTN/FAIL* BS8 .... 55 E5
Dowry Sq *CFTN/FAIL* BS8 .... 55 E5
Dragon Ct *EVILLE/WHL* BS5 .... 57 G2
Dragon Rd *FRCTL/WBN* BS36 ..... 34 D1
Dragons Hill Cl *KEYN* BS31 .... 88 C4
Dragons Hill Ct *KEYN* BS31 .... 88 C4
Dragons Hill Gdns *KEYN* BS31 ... 88 C4
Dragonswell Rd
   HNBRY/STHM BS10 .... 31 E3
Dragon Wk *EVILLE/WHL* BS5 ...... 57 H2
Drainsfield Wy *BATHSE* BA2 ..... 107 H5
Drake Av *BATHSE* BA2 .... 108 C5
Drake Cl *KEYN* BS31 .... 98 B2
   MTN/WRL BS22 .... 117 G4
Drake Rd *BMSTR* BS3 .... 72 B3
Drakes Wy *PTSHD/EG* BS20 .... 39 E3
Dram La *EVILLE/WHL* BS5 .... 58 A5
Draycot Pl *CBRIS/FH* BS1 .... 4 E7
Draycott Rd *HORF/LLZ* BS7 .... 46 B4
Draydon Rd
   BRSG/KWL/STAPK BS4 .... 84 D2
Drayton Cl *HGRV/WHIT* BS14 ..... 86 A1
Drayton Rd
   HNLZ/SM/SNYPK/WT BS9 .... 30 A5
The Drive *HGRV/WHIT* BS14 .... 86 B4
   HNLZ/SM/SNYPK/WT BS9 .... 45 F3
   WSM BS23 .... 7 H2
Drove Rd *WSM* BS23 .... 7 C5
The Drove *PTSHD/EG* BS20 .... 41 F2

E

Eagle Cl *MTN/WRL* BS22 .... 122 A3
Eagle Crs *MANG/FISH* BS16 .... 51 G4
Eagle Dr *BRSTK/PCHW* BS34 ...... 20 A2
Eagle Pk *CBATH/BATHN* BA1 ...... 91 E4
Eagle Rd *BRSG/KWL/STAPK* BS4 .. 74 C4
   CBATH/BATHN BA1 .... 91 E4
The Eagles *YTN/CONG* BS49 .... 112 B3
Eagles Wd *ALMDB* BS32 .... 11 F4

Druetts Cl *HNBRY/STHM* BS10 ... 46 A2
Druid Cl
   HNLZ/SM/SNYPK/WT BS9 .... 44 C3
Druid Hl
   HNLZ/SM/SNYPK/WT BS9 .... 44 C3
Druid Rd
   HNLZ/SM/SNYPK/WT BS9 .... 44 B4
Druid Stoke Av
   HNLZ/SM/SNYPK/WT BS9 .... 44 A3
Druid Woods
   HNLZ/SM/SNYPK/WT BS9 .... 44 A3
Drummond Ct
   OLD/WMLY/WICK BS30 ..... 76 C2
Drummond Rd *CBRISNE* BS2 ..... 56 C2
   MANG/FISH BS16 .... 47 H5
Dr Whites Cl *CBRIS/FH* BS1 .... 5 G6
Dryleaze *KEYN* BS31 .... 88 B2
   YATE/CS BS37 .... 14 A2
Dryleaze Rd *MANG/FISH* BS16 ... 47 H2
Drysdale Cl *MTN/WRL* BS22 .... 121 H2
Dubbers La *EVILLE/WHL* BS5 ...... 57 G1
Dublin Crs
   HNLZ/SM/SNYPK/WT BS9 .... 45 F2
Duchess Rd *CFTN/FAIL* BS8 .... 55 E2
Duchess Wy *MANG/FISH* BS16 ... 47 F3
Ducie Rd *EVILLE/WHL* BS5 .... 56 D4
   MANG/FISH BS16 .... 49 E4
Duckmoor Rd *BMSTR* BS3 .... 72 B3
Dudley Cl *KEYN* BS31 .... 88 C5
Dudley Ct
   OLD/WMLY/WICK BS30 ..... 76 C2
Dudley Gv *HORF/LLZ* BS7 .... 32 B5
Dugar Wk *RDLND/MONT* BS6 ..... 45 G5
Duke St *BATHSE* BA2 .... 3 H5
Dulverton Rd *HORF/LLZ* BS7 ...... 45 H4
Dumaine Av
   BRSTK/PCHW BS34 .... 21 G5
Dumfries Pl *WSM* BS23 .... 124 D1
Duncan Gdns
   CBATH/BATHN BA1 .... 101 F1
Duncombe La
   KGWD/HNM BS15 .... 58 A1
Duncombe Rd
   KGWD/HNM BS15 .... 58 A1
Dundas Cl *HNBRY/STHM* BS10 ... 30 C3
Dundonald Rd
   RDLND/MONT BS6 .... 45 F5
Dundridge Gdns
   EVILLE/WHL BS5 .... 57 H5
Dundridge La *EVILLE/WHL* BS5 ... 57 H5
Dundry Cl *KGWD/HNM* BS15 ..... 58 D5
Dundry La
   BLAG/CWMG/WR BS40 ...... 93 H5
Dundry Vw
   BRSG/KWL/STAPK BS4 .... 73 H5
Dunkeld Av *MTN/WRL* BS22 .... 118 D4
Dunford Rd *BMSTR* BS3 .... 73 E3
Dungravon Rd
   OMX/HUT/LCK BS24 .... 122 C4
Dunkeld Av
   BRSTK/PCHW BS34 .... 32 B3
Dunkerry Rd *BMSTR* BS3 .... 73 E3
Dunkery Cl *NAIL* BS48 .... 67 F5
Dunkery Rd *WSM* BS23 .... 7 H2
Dunkirk Rd *MANG/FISH* BS16 ..... 47 H5
Dunlin Dr *PTSHD/EG* BS20 .... 40 A3
Dunmail Rd
   HNBRY/STHM BS10 .... 31 G3
Dunmore St *BMSTR* BS3 * 73 G2
Dunsford Pl *BATHSE* BA2 .... 3 K4
Dunster Crs
   OMX/HUT/LCK BS24 .... 125 F4
Dunster Gdns
   OLD/WMLY/WICK BS30 ..... 59 G5
Dunster Rd
   BRSG/KWL/STAPK BS4 .... 85 G1
   KEYN BS31 .... 88 B5
Dunsters Rd *YTN/CONG* BS49 .. 113 F2
Durban Rd *BRSTK/PCHW* BS34 ... 20 B2
Durban Wy *YTN/CONG* BS49 .... 112 B2
Durbin Park Rd *CLVDN* BS21 ..... 62 A5
Durbin Wk *EVILLE/WHL* BS5 .... 56 C3
Durdham Pk
   RDLND/MONT BS6 .... 45 F5
Durley Hl *KEYN* BS31 .... 87 G1
Durley La *KEYN* BS31 .... 88 A2
Durley Pk *BATHSE* BA2 .... 108 B5
Durnford Av *BMSTR* BS3 .... 72 B2
Durnford St *BMSTR* BS3 .... 72 B2
Dursley Cl *HORF/LLZ* BS7 .... 32 B5
Dursley Rd *AVONM* BS11 .... 43 E3
Durville Rd
   BMSTR/HC/WWD BS13 .... 84 C3
Durweston Wk
   HGRV/WHIT BS14 .... 86 B1
Dutton Cl *HGRV/WHIT* BS14 ...... 86 C4
Dutton Rd *HGRV/WHIT* BS14 ..... 86 C4
Dutton Wk *HGRV/WHIT* BS14 .... 86 C4
Dyers Cl
   BMSTR/HC/WWD BS13 .... 85 H3
Dyer's La *YATE/CS* BS37 .... 13 E4
Dylan Thomas Ct
   OLD/WMLY/WICK BS30 * 76 D1
Dyrham Cl
   HNLZ/SM/SNYPK/WT BS9 .... 45 H2
   KGWD/HNM BS15 .... 59 F3
   MANG/FISH BS16 .... 51 G4
   THNB/SVB BS35 .... 8 D1
Dyrham Pde
   BRSTK/PCHW BS34 .... 21 E2
Dyrham Rd *KGWD/HNM* BS15 ... 59 F3
Dyson Cl *YTN/CONG* BS49 ...... 112 B3

Earlesfield *NAIL* BS48 .... 66 D5
Earlham Gv *WSM* BS23 .... 7 H1
Earl Russell Wy
   EVILLE/WHL BS5 .... 56 D4
Earlsmead *MANG/FISH* BS16 ..... 47 H4
Earlstone Cl
   OLD/WMLY/WICK BS30 ..... 76 D3
Earlstone Crs
   OLD/WMLY/WICK BS30 ..... 76 D1
Earl St *CBRIS/FH* BS1 .... 5 F1
Easedale Cl *HNBRY/STHM* BS10 .. 31 H3
Eastbourne Av
   CBATH/BATHN BA1 * 103 E3
Eastbourne Rd
   EVILLE/WHL BS5 .... 56 D3
Eastbury Rd *MANG/FISH* BS16 ... 48 A4
Eastbury Rd *MANG/FISH* BS16 ... 40 A1
East Cl *BATHSE* BA2 .... 108 C3
Eastcombe Gdns *WSM* BS23 .... 7 H1
Eastcombe Rd *WSM* BS23 .... 7 H1
Eastcote Pk *HGRV/WHIT* BS14 .... 86 A4
East Cft
   HNLZ/SM/SNYPK/WT BS9 .... 45 C1
East Dundry La *LGASH* BS41 ..... 95 E2
East Dundry Rd
   HGRV/WHIT BS14 .... 96 C2
Easter Ct *YATE/CS* BS37 .... 25 E1
Eastfield
   HNLZ/SM/SNYPK/WT BS9 .... 45 F1
Eastfield Av
   CBATH/BATHN BA1 .... 101 G2
Eastfield Dr *YATE/CS* BS37 .... 14 A2
Eastfield Gdns *WSM* BS23 .... 7 G1
Eastfield Pk *WSM* BS23 .... 7 G1
Eastfield Rd
   HNLZ/SM/SNYPK/WT BS9 .... 45 F1
   OMX/HUT/LCK BS24 .... 126 B4
   RDLND/MONT BS6 .... 55 H1
Eastfield Ter
   HNLZ/SM/SNYPK/WT BS9 .... 45 F1
Eastgate Rd *EVILLE/WHL* BS5 ..... 46 B5
East Gv *RDLND/MONT* BS6 .... 56 B2
East Hill Eastfield Rd
   HNLZ/SM/SNYPK/WT BS9 * ... 45 F1
Eastlake Cl *HORF/LLZ* BS7 .... 46 D1
Eastland Av *THNB/SVB* BS35 .... 8 C2
Eastland Rd *THNB/SVB* BS35 ...... 8 C2
Eastlea *CLVDN* BS21 .... 64 B3
East Lea Rd
   CBATH/BATHN BA1 .... 101 F4
Eastleigh Cl *MANG/FISH* BS16 ... 49 E4
Eastleigh Rd
   HNBRY/STHM BS10 .... 46 C4
   MANG/FISH BS16 .... 49 E4
Eastlyn Rd
   BMSTR/HC/WWD BS13 .... 84 C1
Eastmead La
   HNLZ/SM/SNYPK/WT BS9 .... 44 C3
Eastnor Rd *HGRV/WHIT* BS14 ..... 96 D1
Easton Hill Rd *THNB/SVB* BS35 .... 9 F3
Easton Rd *EVILLE/WHL* BS5 .... 56 D4
   PTSHD/EG BS20 .... 42 C4
Easton Wy *EVILLE/WHL* BS5 .... 56 D4
Eastover Cl
   HNLZ/SM/SNYPK/WT BS9 .... 31 E5
Eastover Gv *BATHSE* BA2 .... 110 A1
East Pde
   HNLZ/SM/SNYPK/WT BS9 .... 44 A2
East Pk *EVILLE/WHL* BS5 .... 57 E1
East Park Dr *EVILLE/WHL* BS5 ..... 57 E1
East Priory Cl
   BMSTR/HC/WWD BS13 .... 84 A4
East Ridge Dr
   BMSTR/HC/WWD BS13 .... 84 A4
East Shrubbery
   RDLND/MONT BS6 .... 55 F5
East St *AVONM* BS11 .... 28 A4
East St *BMSTR* BS3 .... 72 D2
Ebdon Rd *MTN/WRL* BS22 ...... 117 G5
Ebenezer La
   HNLZ/SM/SNYPK/WT BS9 .... 44 D1
Ebenezer St *EVILLE/WHL* BS5 ..... 57 F4
Eckweek Gdns *BATHSE* BA2 ...... 111 F5
Eden Gv *HORF/LLZ* BS7 .... 32 C4
Eden Park Cl
   CBATH/BATHN BA1 .... 91 F5
Eden Park Dr
   CBATH/BATHN BA1 .... 91 F5
Eden Ter *CBATH/BATHN* BA1 * .. 102 D3
Eden Vls *CBATH/BATHN* BA1 * 3 F3
Edgar Blds *CBATH/BATHN* BA1 .... 3 F3
Edgecombe Av
   MTN/WRL BS22 .... 122 A1
Edgecumbe Rd
   RDLND/MONT BS6 .... 55 H1
Edgefield Cl *HGRV/WHIT* BS14 .... 96 A5
Edgefield Rd *HGRV/WHIT* BS14 ... 96 A5
Edgehill Rd *CLVDN* BS21 .... 62 B4
Edgeware Rd *BMSTR* BS3 .... 72 D2
   EVILLE/WHL BS5 .... 48 C4
Edgewood Cl
   HGRV/WHIT BS14 .... 86 A1
   OLD/WMLY/WICK BS30 ..... 59 G5
Edgeworth *YATE/CS* BS37 .... 25 G4
Edgeworth Rd *BATHSE* BA2 ..... 107 H5
Edinburgh Pl *WSM* BS23 .... 6 D2
Edinburgh Rd *KEYN* BS31 .... 98 C2
Edington Gv
   HNBRY/STHM BS10 .... 31 E3
Edmund Cl *MANG/FISH* BS16 ..... 48 D4
Edmund Ct *MANG/FISH* BS16 .... 51 F2
Edna Av *BRSG/KWL/STAPK* BS4 .. 74 D3

Edward Rd
   BRSG/KWL/STAPK BS4 .... 74 A2
   CLVDN BS21 .... 62 C5
   KGWD/HNM BS15 .... 59 E3
Edward Rd South *CLVDN* BS21 ... 62 C4
Edward Rd West *CLVDN* BS21 ..... 62 C4
Edward St *BATHSE* BA2 .... 3 J5
   CBATH/BATHN BA1 .... 101 H5
   EVILLE/WHL BS5 .... 57 E3
Edwin Short Cl
   OLD/WMLY/WICK BS30 ..... 89 H1
Effingham Rd
   RDLND/MONT BS6 ....
Egerton Brow *HORF/LLZ* BS7 ..... 45 H4
Egerton Rd *BATHSE* BA2 .... 108 B3
   HORF/LLZ BS7 .... 45 H5
Eggshill La *YATE/CS* BS37 .... 25 H1
Eighth Av *HORF/LLZ* BS7 .... 32 D5
Eirene Ter *PTSHD/EG* BS20 .... 42 D4
Eighth Av *KGWD/HNM* BS15 ...... 59 C3
Elberton Rd
   HNLZ/SM/SNYPK/WT BS9 .... 43 H1
Elborough Av
   YTN/CONG BS49 .... 112 B3
Elborough Gdns
   OMX/HUT/LCK BS24 .... 127 F3
Elbury Av *KGWD/HNM* BS15 ...... 58 C1
Elderberry Wk
   HNBRY/STHM BS10 .... 31 G3
Elderwood Dr
   OLD/WMLY/WICK BS30 ..... 76 D3
Elderwood Rd
   HGRV/WHIT BS14 .... 86 A2
Eldon Pl *CBATH/BATHN* BA1 ..... 103 E2
Eldon Ter *BMSTR* BS3 .... 73 E3
Eldon Wy
   BRSG/KWL/STAPK BS4 .... 74 B1
Eldred Cl
   HNLZ/SM/SNYPK/WT BS9 .... 44 A3
Eleanor Cl *BATHSE* BA2 .... 107 F2
Eleventh Av *HORF/LLZ* BS7 .... 32 D4
Elfin Rd *MANG/FISH* BS16 .... 48 A3
Elgar Cl *BRSG/KWL/STAPK* BS4 ... 85 E3
   CLVDN BS21 .... 65 E4
Elgin Av *HORF/LLZ* BS7 .... 32 B4
Elgin Pk *RDLND/MONT* BS6 .... 55 F1
Elgin Rd *MANG/FISH* BS16 .... 58 B1
Eliot Cl *HORF/LLZ* BS7 .... 32 C5
   WSM BS23 .... 125 F3
Elizabeth Cl
   OMX/HUT/LCK BS24 .... 126 A3
   THNB/SVB BS35 .... 9 E4
Elizabeth Crs
   BRSTK/PCHW BS34 .... 33 G1
Elizabeths Ms
   BRSG/KWL/STAPK BS4 .... 57 H5
Elizabeth Wy *MANG/FISH* BS16 .. 48 C2
Ella Cl *MANG/FISH* BS16 .... 48 C3
Ellacombe Rd
   OLD/WMLY/WICK BS30 ..... 76 B4
Ellan Hav Rd *ALMDB* BS32 .... 22 A4
Ellbridge Cl
   HNLZ/SM/SNYPK/WT BS9 .... 44 B3
Ellenborough Crs *WSM* BS23 ...... 6 E7
Ellenborough Gdns *WSM* BS23 * .. 6 E7
Ellenborough Pk North
   WSM BS23 .... 6 D6
Ellenborough Park Rd
   WSM BS23 .... 6 E6
Ellenborough Pk South
   WSM BS23 .... 6 D6
Ellesmere *THNB/SVB* BS35 .... 8 D4
Ellesmere Rd
   BRSG/KWL/STAPK BS4 .... 74 C5
   WSM BS23 .... 124 C4
Ellfield Cl
   BMSTR/HC/WWD BS13 .... 84 A3
Ellicks Cl *ALMDB* BS32 .... 11 G5
Ellicott Rd *HORF/LLZ* BS7 .... 46 B2
Ellinghurst Cl
   HNBRY/STHM BS10 .... 31 E5
Elliott Av *MANG/FISH* BS16 .... 34 C4
Elis Av
   BMSTR/HC/WWD BS13 .... 84 B1
Ellis Pk *MTN/WRL* BS22 .... 118 B5
Elliston Dr *BATHSE* BA2 .... 107 H5
Elliston La *RDLND/MONT* BS6 ..... 55 G1
Elliston Rd *RDLND/MONT* BS6 .... 55 G1
Ellsbridge Cl *KEYN* BS31 .... 89 E4
Ellsworth Rd
   HNBRY/STHM BS10 .... 30 D3
Elm Cl *AVONM* BS11 .... 29 F4
   BNWL BS29 .... 127 H2
   BRSTK/PCHW BS34 .... 21 F3
   NAIL BS48 .... 66 D5
   YATE/CS BS37 .... 25 H4
Elmcroft Crs *HORF/LLZ* BS7 .... 46 C4
Elmdale Crs *THNB/SVB* BS35 ...... 8 D3
Elmdale Gdns
   MANG/FISH BS16 .... 48 A4
Elmdale Rd *BMSTR* BS3 .... 8 B1
   CFTN/FAIL BS8 ....
Elmfield *KGWD/HNM* BS15 .... 59 E5
Elmfield Cl *KGWD/HNM* BS15 ..... 59 E5
Elmfield Rd
   HNLZ/SM/SNYPK/WT BS9 .... 31 E5
Elm Gv *BATHSE* BA2 .... 107 H5
   OMX/HUT/LCK BS24 .... 126 C2
Elmgrove Av *EVILLE/WHL* BS5 ..... 56 D5
Elmgrove Dr *YATE/CS* BS37 .... 14 B5
Elmgrove Pde
   RDLND/MONT BS6 ....
Elmgrove Rd *MANG/FISH* BS16 ... 47 G5
   RDLND/MONT BS6 .... 55 H2
Elmham Wy
   OMX/HUT/LCK BS24 .... 123 E2
Elm Hayes
   BMSTR/HC/WWD BS13 .... 84 A3
Elmhirst Gdns *YATE/CS* BS37 ..... 14 C5
Elmhurst Av *EVILLE/WHL* BS5 ..... 47 F5
Elmhurst Rd
   OMX/HUT/LCK BS24 .... 126 B4
Elmhyrst Rd *WSM* BS23 .... 7 H3
Elming Down Cl *ALMDB* BS32 .... 21 F4
Elm La *RDLND/MONT* BS6 .... 55 F1
Elmlea Av
   HNLZ/SM/SNYPK/WT BS9 .... 44 D3
Elmleigh Av *MANG/FISH* BS16 ... 49 H3

Elmleigh Cl MANG/FISH BS16 ......49 G3
Elmleigh Rd MANG/FISH BS16......49 G3
Elm Lodge Rd NAIL BS48............67 F4
Elmore KGWD/HNM BS15............48 F5
　YATE/CS BS37 ....25 H2
Elm Pk BRSTK/PCHW BS34..........20 B1
　HORF/LLZ BS7..........................46 C2
Elm Rd BRSTK/PCHW BS34..........32 C5
　Rd HORF/LLZ BS7......................46 A3
Elms Gv BRSTK/PCHW BS34.........20 D1
Elmsleigh Rd WSM BS23............124 C2
Elmsley La MTN/WRL BS22.........116 D2
The Elms CBATH/BATHN BA1.......103 G2
Elmtree Av CLVDN BS21..............66 B2
　MANG/FISH BS16.......................49 G1
Elmtree Cl KGWD/HNM BS15.......58 D2
Elmtree Dr
　BMSTRD/HC/WWD BS13............84 A4
Elm Tree Pk PTSHD/EG BS20 *.....41 F4
Elm Tree Rd CLVDN BS21.............64 D3
　OMX/HUT/LCK BS24..................126 C2
Elmvale Dr
　OMX/HUT/LCK BS24..................126 C4
Elm Wk PTSHD/EG BS20..............39 G4
　YTN/CONG BS49........................112 B4
Elm Wd YATE/CS BS37 ....26 A2
Elsbert Dr
　BMSTRD/HC/WWD BS13............83 H5
Elstree Rd EVILLE/WHL BS5..........57 G2
Elton La HORF/LLZ BS7................55 H1
Elton Rd CFTN/FAIL BS8..............4 C2
　CLVDN BS21..............................64 C2
　KGWD/HNM BS15.......................58 B2
　MTN/WRL BS22........................117 H4
　RDLND/MONT BS6.....................45 H5
Elton St CBRISNE BS2.................5 K1
Elvard Cl
　BMSTRD/HC/WWD BS13............84 B5
Elvard Rd
　BMSTRD/HC/WWD BS13............84 B4
Elvaston Rd BMSTR BS3...............73 F3
Elwell La
　BLAG/CWMG/WR BS40..............93 C3
Ely Gv
　HNLZ/SM/SNYPK/WT BS9..........43 H1
Embassy Rd EVILLE/WHL BS5........57 G2
Embassy Wk EVILLE/WHL BS5.......57 G2
Embercourt Dr NAIL BS48.............79 H1
Embleton Rd
　HNBRY/STHM BS10....................31 F3
Emersons Green La
　MANG/FISH BS16.......................49 H2
Emersons Wy MANG/FISH BS16....50 A1
Emerson Wy MANG/FISH BS16......49 H1
Emery Rd
　BRSG/KWL/STAPK BS4...............75 E4
Emet Gv MANG/FISH BS16...........49 H2
Emet La MANG/FISH BS16............49 H2
Emily Pl CFTN/FAIL BS8 *.............54 D4
Emlyn Rd EVILLE/WHL BS5...........118 A4
Emlyn Rd EVILLE/WHL BS5...........57 E1
Emma-Chris Wy
　BRSTK/PCHW BS34...................33 E3
Emmett Wd HGRV/WHIT BS14......97 E1
Empire Crs KGWD/HNM BS15.......58 D3
Emra Cl EVILLE/WHL BS5.............57 H2
Enfield Rd MANG/FISH BS16.........48 A5
Engine Common La
　YATE/CS BS37 ....13 C3
Engine La NAIL BS48...................78 C1
England's Crs FRCTL/WBN BS36....23 E5
Englishcombe La BATHSE BA2......107 H4
Englishcombe Pk
　BATHSE BA2.............................107 H3
Englishcombe Ri BATHSE BA2......107 F4
Englishcombe Rd
　BMSTRD/HC/WWD BS13............95 H1
Englishcombe Wy
　BATHSE BA2.............................108 A4
Ennerdale Cl WSM BS23.............125 F1
Ennerdale Rd
　HNBRY/STHM BS10....................31 H3
Entry Hl BATHSE BA2.................108 C5
Entry Hill BATHSE BA2................108 C5
Entry Hill Gdns BATHSE BA2........108 C5
Entry Hill Pk BATHSE BA2............108 C5
Entry Ri BATHSE BA2..................110 D1
Epney Cl BRSTK/PCHW BS34........20 B1
Epsom Cl MANG/FISH BS16.........35 F4
Epworth Rd
　HNBRY/STHM BS10....................31 E3
Erin Wk BRSG/KWL/STAPK BS4.....85 E1
Ermine Wy AVONM BS11...............42 C1
Ermleet Rd RDLND/MONT BS6......55 C1
Ernest Barker Cl
　EVILLE/WHL BS5 *.....................56 D4
Ernestville Rd
　MANG/FISH BS16.......................47 H5
Ervine Ter CBRISNE BS2..............56 B5
Esgar Ri MTN/WRL BS22.............117 F5
Eskdale THNB/SVB BS35...............9 E5
Eskdale Cl MTN/WRL BS22...........122 A3
Esmond Gv CLVDN BS21...............64 D1
Esplanade Rd PTSHD/EG BS20.....39 C1
Essery Rd EVILLE/WHL BS5..........57 E1
Esson Rd KGWD/HNM BS15.........58 B2
Estcourt Gdns
　MANG/FISH BS16.......................47 E5
Estelle Pk EVILLE/WHL BS5 *.......57 E1
Estoril YATE/CS BS37..................26 B1
Estune Wk LGASH BS41................70 D5
Etloe Rd RDLND/MONT BS6.........46 A5
Eton La BNWL BS29....................123 C4
Eton Rd BRSG/KWL/STAPK BS4.....74 C3
Ettlingen Wy CLVDN BS21............65 E3
Ettricke Dr MANG/FISH BS16........48 D1
Eugene St CBRISNE BS2...............4 E1
Evans Cl BRSG/KWL/STAPK BS4....75 E1
Evans Rd RDLND/MONT BS6.........55 F1
Eveleigh Av
　CBATH/BATHN BA1...................103 G2
Evelyn Rd CBATH/BATHN BA1......101 G4
　HNBRY/STHM BS10....................31 G5
Evelyn Ter
　CBATH/BATHN BA1 *.................102 D3
Evenlode Gdns AVONM BS11........43 F3
Evenlode Wy KEYN BS31...............98 B1
Evercreech Rd
　HGRV/WHIT BS14......................85 H5

Everest Av MANG/FISH BS16........47 G4
Everest Rd MANG/FISH BS16........47 G4
Eve Rd EVILLE/WHL BS5...............56 D5
Ewart Rd MTN/WRL BS22............121 H3
Ewell Rd HGRV/WHIT BS14..........86 A3
Excelsior St BATHSE BA2..............3 H6
Exeter Blds RDLND/MONT BS6......55 F1
Exeter Rd BMSTR BS3..................72 C2
　PTSHD/EG BS20........................40 A4
　WSM BS23...............................124 D1
Exford Cl WSM BS23..................125 E4
Exley Cl OLD/WMLY/WICK BS30....77 F1
Exmoor Rd BATHSE BA2.............108 C5
Exmoor St BMSTR BS3................72 C2
Exmouth Rd
　BRSG/KWL/STAPK BS4..............73 G5
Explore La CBRIS/FH BS1..............4 B3
Exton Cl HGRV/WHIT BS14...........86 A4
Eyer's La CBRISNE BS2..................5 J2
Eyers Rd OMX/HUT/LCK BS24.....122 C4

F

Faber Gv
　BMSTRD/HC/WWD BS13............84 D5
Fabian Dr BRSTK/PCHW BS34......21 G5
Factory Rd FRCTL/WBN BS36.......23 F5
Failand Crescent
　HNLZ/SM/SNYPK/WT BS9..........44 A3
Failand Wk
　HNLZ/SM/SNYPK/WT BS9..........44 A2
Fairacre Cl HORF/LLZ BS7............24 D3
　OMX/HUT/LCK BS24..................127 E2
Fairacres Cl KEYN BS31...............88 B5
Fairfax St CBRIS/FH BS1................5 G3
Fairfield Av
　CBATH/BATHN BA1...................102 D2
Fairfield Cl MTN/WRL BS22..........121 C2
　NAIL BS48................................80 B2
Fairfield Md NAIL BS48................80 B2
Fairfield Pk
　CBATH/BATHN BA1 *.................102 D2
Fairfield Park Rd
　CBATH/BATHN BA1...................102 D2
Fairfield Pl BMSTR BS3................72 C2
Fairfield Rd BMSTR BS3...............72 C2
　CBATH/BATHN BA1...................102 D3
　RDLND/MONT BS6.....................55 H5
Fairfield Ter
　CBATH/BATHN BA1 *.................102 D2
Fairfield Vw
　CBATH/BATHN BA1 *.................102 D2
Fairfield Wy NAIL BS48................80 B3
Fairfoot Rd
　BRSG/KWL/STAPK BS4..............73 H3
Fairford Cl KGWD/HNM BS15........59 F1
Fairford Crs
　BRSTK/PCHW BS34...................20 D2
Fairford Rd AVONM BS11..............42 C1
Fair Furlong
　BMSTRD/HC/WWD BS13............84 B5
Fairhaven YATE/CS BS37...............26 B1
Fairhaven Rd
　RDLND/MONT BS6.....................45 G4
Fair Lawn
　OLD/WMLY/WICK BS30.............76 D2
Fairlawn Av
　BRSTK/PCHW BS34...................32 C2
Fairlawn Rd RDLND/MONT BS6.....55 H5
Fairlyn Dr KGWD/HNM BS15.........49 F5
Fairoaks
　OLD/WMLY/WICK BS30.............76 D3
Fairview MTN/WRL BS22...............116 D5
Fair View Dr RDLND/MONT BS6....55 C1
Fairview Rd KGWD/HNM BS15......59 F3
Fairway BRSG/KWL/STAPK BS4....74 C5
Fairway Cl MTN/WRL BS22..........121 C1
　OLD/WMLY/WICK BS30.............76 D2
Fairways KEYN BS31...................99 F2
Falcon Cl BRSTK/PCHW BS34......20 A2
　HNLZ/SM/SNYPK/WT BS9..........30 D5
　PTSHD/EG BS20........................39 H4
Falcon Crs MTN/WRL BS22..........122 A3
Falcondale Rd
　HNLZ/SM/SNYPK/WT BS9..........44 D1
Falcondale Wk
　HNLZ/SM/SNYPK/WT BS9..........31 E5
Falcon Dr BRSTK/PCHW BS34......20 A2
Falconer Rd
　CBATH/BATHN BA1...................101 F1
Falcon Wk CBATH/BATHN BA1......20 A2
Falcon Wy THNB/SVB BS35...........9 F2
Fairfield Rd
　BRSG/KWL/STAPK BS4..............74 B3
Fairfield Wk HNBRY/STHM BS10....31 H3
Falkland Rd RDLND/MONT BS6.....56 B1
Fallodon Ct
　HNLZ/SM/SNYPK/WT BS9..........44 D1
Fallodon Wy
　HNLZ/SM/SNYPK/WT BS9..........45 F3
Fallowfield MTN/WRL BS22..........117 C4
　OLD/WMLY/WICK BS30.............77 F2
Falmouth Cl NAIL BS48................67 H5
Falmouth Rd HORF/LLZ BS7.........46 B1
Fane Cl HNBRY/STHM BS10.........31 C5
Fanshawe Rd
　HGRV/WHIT BS14......................85 H2
Farendell Rd MANG/FISH BS16.....35 H4
Far Handstones
　OLD/WMLY/WICK BS30.............76 D2
Farington Rd
　HNLZ/SM/SNYPK/WT BS9..........45 H1
Farlands MANG/FISH BS16...........51 H1
Farleigh Ri
　CBATH/BATHN BA1...................105 F2
Farleigh Rd CLVDN BS21..............64 A4
　KEYN BS31..............................88 A5
　NAIL BS48................................80 B3
Farleigh Wk
　BMSTRD/HC/WWD BS13............84 B1
Farler's End NAIL BS48................79 G1
Farley Cl BRSTK/PCHW BS34.......21 E5
Farm Cl HNBRY/STHM BS10.........31 H5
　MTN/WRL BS22........................118 A4
Farm Ct MANG/FISH BS16...........49 E1
Farmer Rd
　BMSTRD/HC/WWD BS13............83 H5

Farmhouse Cl NAIL BS48............67 F4
Farmhouse Ct NAIL BS48 *...........67 F4
Farm La THNB/SVB BS35.............18 D1
Farm Rd MANG/FISH BS16...........51 C3
　MTN/WRL BS22........................121 G2
　OMX/HUT/LCK BS24..................126 B4
Farmwell Cl
　BMSTRD/HC/WWD BS13............84 C4
Farnaby Cl
　BRSG/KWL/STAPK BS4..............84 D2
Farnborough Rd
　OMX/HUT/LCK BS24..................127 F1
Farndale EVILLE/WHL BS5............58 A5
Farndale Rd MTN/WRL BS22........122 A3
Farne Cl
　HNLZ/SM/SNYPK/WT BS9..........45 F3
Farrant Cl
　BRSG/KWL/STAPK BS4..............85 E3
Farrs La BATHSE BA2..................109 E5
Farr's La CBRIS/FH BS1..................4 E5
Farr St AVONM BS11......................4 B5
Faulkland Rd BATHSE BA2.............2 A7
Faversham Dr
　OMX/HUT/LCK BS24..................125 F5
Fawkes Cl KGWD/HNM BS15........59 H3
Featherstone Rd
　MANG/FISH BS16.......................47 G4
Feeder Rd CBRISNE BS2..............73 H1
Felix Rd EVILLE/WHL BS5.............56 D3
Felixstead Rd
　HNBRY/STHM BS10....................32 A4
Feltham Rd MANG/FISH BS16.......51 C3
Felton Gv
　BMSTRD/HC/WWD BS13............84 A1
Felton La
　BLAG/CWMG/WR BS40..............93 E5
Felton St
　BLAG/CWMG/WR BS40..............92 D5
Fennel Dr ALMDB BS32................22 A3
Fennell Gv HNBRY/STHM BS10.....31 E3
Fenners MTN/WRL BS22..............122 A3
Fenns La LGASH BS41.................70 A4
Fenshurst Gdns LGASH BS41.......82 C1
Fenswood Md LGASH BS41..........70 B5
Fenswood Rd LGASH BS41..........70 B5
Fenton Cl KEYN BS31..................99 E1
Fenton Rd HORF/LLZ BS7............45 H4
Fermaine Av
　BRSG/KWL/STAPK BS4..............75 E3
Fernbank Rd
　RDLND/MONT BS6.....................55 G1
Fernbrook Cl MANG/FISH BS16.....34 B4
Fern Cl HNBRY/STHM BS10.........31 F2
Ferndale Av
　OLD/WMLY/WICK BS30.............76 C3
Ferndale Rd
　CBATH/BATHN BA1...................103 F1
　HORF/LLZ BS7..........................32 C3
　PTSHD/EG BS20........................39 H2
Ferndene ALMDB BS32................11 E5
Ferndown YATE/CS BS37.............26 A1
Ferndown Cl AVONM BS11...........43 G1
Fern Gv ALMDB BS32...................21 F3
　NAIL BS48................................78 D1
Fernhill La AVONM BS11..............29 H4
Fernlea Rd MTN/WRL BS22..........121 H4
Fernlea Gdns PTSHD/EG BS20.....39 G2
Fernlea Rd MTN/WRL BS22..........121 H4
Fernleaze FRCTL/WBN BS36........24 A4
Fern Rd MANG/FISH BS16............48 D3
Ferndale NAIL BS48....................79 H2
Fernsteed Rd
　BMSTRD/HC/WWD BS13............84 A3
Fern St CBRISNE BS2..................56 B2
Fernville Est CLVDN BS21.............64 C3
Ferry Ct BATHSE BA2 *..................3 J5
Ferry La BATHSE BA2....................3 H5
Ferry Rd KGWD/HNM BS15..........76 A5
Ferry St CBRIS/FH BS1...................5 F5
Fiddes Rd RDLND/MONT BS6.......45 G4
Fielders Wood La ALMDB BS32.....21 G2
Fieldgrove La PTSHD/EG BS20.....40 C2
Field Farm Cl
　BRSTK/PCHW BS34...................33 H1
Fielding's Rd BATHSE BA2 *..........107 H1
Field La OLD/WMLY/WICK BS30....76 D3
Field Rd KGWD/HNM BS15...........58 D3
The Fields MTN/WRL BS22..........123 C1
Field View MANG/FISH BS16........48 C2
Fiennes Cl MANG/FISH BS16........49 E4
Fifth Av HORF/LLZ BS7.................32 C4
Fifth Wy AVONM BS11..................29 E1
Filby Dr BRSTK/PCHW BS34.........29 E2
Filton Av HORF/LLZ BS7...............46 A2
　HORF/LLZ BS7..........................32 C5
Filton Gv HORF/LLZ BS7..............46 B2
Filton La BRSTK/PCHW BS34........33 H3
Filton Rd BRSTK/PCHW BS34.......33 F3
　HORF/LLZ BS7..........................46 B1
Filwood Broadway
　BRSG/KWL/STAPK BS4..............85 F1
Filwood Cl MANG/FISH BS16........48 B5
Filwood Dr KGWD/HNM BS15.......59 F3
Filwood Rd MANG/FISH BS16.......48 A5
Finch Cl MTN/WRL BS22.............122 B3
　THNB/SVB BS35..........................8 D2
The Finches PTSHD/EG BS20.......40 B2
Finch Rd YATE/CS BS37................26 B2
Finisterre Pde PTSHD/EG BS20....40 B2
Finmere Gdns MTN/WRL BS22....117 H4
Fircliff Pk PTSHD/EG BS20...........39 H1
Fireclay Rd EVILLE/WHL BS5.........57 F5
Fire Engine La
　FRCTL/WBN BS36......................24 B3
Fire Station La AVONM BS11........28 A1
Firework Cl KGWD/HNM BS15......59 H3
Firfield St
　BRSG/KWL/STAPK BS4..............73 H2
Firgrove Crs YATE/CS BS37...........14 B5
Fir Leaze NAIL BS48...................66 C5
First Av BATHSE BA2..................108 B5
　BRSG/KWL/STAPK BS4..............74 B2
　HORF/LLZ BS7..........................32 D4
The Firs BATHSE BA2.................111 F1
First Wy AVONM BS11..................28 A5
Fir Tree Av
　OMX/HUT/LCK BS24..................126 B2
Fir Tree Cl BRSTK/PCHW BS34.....20 A3
Fir Tree La EVILLE/WHL BS5..........58 A5

Fisher Av KGWD/HNM BS15.........59 G2
Fisher Rd KGWD/HNM BS15.........59 G1
Fishers Md LGASH BS41...............70 B5
Fishponds Rd EVILLE/WHL BS5.....57 E1
Fishpond Hl HNBRY/STHM BS10...31 F1
Fitchett Wk
　HNBRY/STHM BS10....................30 D2
Fitzgerald Rd BMSTR BS3.............73 G3
Fitzharding Rd
　PTSHD/EG BS20........................43 E5
Fitzroy Circ PTSHD/EG BS20........40 B2
Fitzroy Rd MANG/FISH BS16........58 B1
Fitzroy St
　BRSG/KWL/STAPK BS4..............73 H2
Five Acre Dr MANG/FISH BS16.....47 H1
Flamingo Crs MTN/WRL BS22.....122 B3
Flax Bourton Rd
　CFTN/FAIL BS8..........................69 G3
Flaxman Cl HORF/LLZ BS7...........46 D2
Flaxpits La CFTN/FAIL BS8............22 C4
Florence Gv MTN/WRL BS22........121 G3
Florence Pk ALMDB BS32............10 D2
　RDLND/MONT BS6.....................45 F4
Florence Rd MANG/FISH BS16......51 C3
Flowerdown Br
　MTN/WRL BS22........................122 A4
Flowerdown Rd
　OMX/HUT/LCK BS24..................127 F2
Flowers Hl
　BRSG/KWL/STAPK BS4..............74 D5
Flowers Hill Cl
　BRSG/KWL/STAPK BS4..............74 D5
Flowerwell Rd
　BMSTRD/HC/WWD BS13............84 C4
Folleigh Cl LGASH BS41...............71 E4
Folleigh Dr LGASH BS41..............71 E4
Folleigh La LGASH BS41..............71 E4
Folliot Cl MANG/FISH BS16..........34 A5
Folly Bridge Cl YATE/CS BS37 *....13 H5
Folly Brook Rd
　MANG/FISH BS16.......................35 G3
Folly La CBRISNE BS2..................56 C5
　WSM BS23...............................124 D5
The Folly KEYN BS31..................99 G2
Fontana Cl
　OLD/WMLY/WICK BS30.............77 E3
Fonthill Rd CBATH/BATHN BA1.....102 B2
　HNBRY/STHM BS10....................31 H3
Fontmell Ct MANG/FISH BS16......35 F4
Fontwell Dr MANG/FISH BS16......35 F4
Footes La FRCTL/WBN BS36.........23 H3
Footshill Cl KGWD/HNM BS15......58 C5
Footshill Dr KGWD/HNM BS15.....58 C4
Footshill Rd KGWD/HNM BS15.....58 C4
Forde Cl
　OLD/WMLY/WICK BS30.............76 C1
Fordell Pl
　BRSG/KWL/STAPK BS4..............73 H5
Ford La EVILLE/WHL BS5.............49 H2
Ford St EVILLE/WHL BS5.............56 C5
Forefield Pl BATHSE BA2 *.............3 H7
Forefield Ri BATHSE BA2.............108 D3
Forefield Ter BATHSE BA2..............3 H7
Forest Av MANG/FISH BS16.........48 B5
Forest Dr HNBRY/STHM BS10......31 F2
　WSM BS23.................................7 K1
Forest Edge KGWD/HNM BS15.....75 H2
Forester Av BATHSE BA2...............3 H1
Forester Ct BATHSE BA2...............3 J1
Forester La BATHSE BA2...............3 J1
Forester Rd BATHSE BA2..............3 J2
　PTSHD/EG BS20........................39 H4
Forest Hills ALMDB BS32.............10 D2
Forest La CBATH/BATHN BA1......108 C5
Forest Rd KGWD/HNM BS15.........58 D3
Forest Wk MANG/FISH BS16........58 B1
Forge End PTSHD/EG BS20..........41 G5
Fortfield Rd HGRV/WHIT BS14......86 A4
Forth Av PTSHD/EG BS20............40 B2
Forum Blds
　CBATH/BATHN BA1 *...................3 F6
Fosse Barton NAIL BS48..............66 D4
Fosse Cl NAIL BS48...................66 D4
Fossedale Av HGRV/WHIT BS14....86 A3
Fosse Gdns BATHSE BA2............110 B2
Fosse La CBATH/BATHN BA1........91 F5
　NAIL BS48................................66 D4
Fosseway CLVDN BS21................64 D4
Fosse Wy NAIL BS48...................66 D4
The Fosseway CFTN/FAIL BS8......55 E5
Foster St EVILLE/WHL BS5...........57 H1
Foundry La EVILLE/WHL BS5........57 H1
Fountain Blds
　CBATH/BATHN BA1 *...................3 F3
Fountaine Ct EVILLE/WHL BS5......57 E1
Fountains Dr
　OLD/WMLY/WICK BS30.............59 F5
Four Acre Av MANG/FISH BS16....35 E5
Four Acre Crs MANG/FISH BS16...35 E4
Four Acre Rd MANG/FISH BS16....35 E4
Four Acres
　BMSTRD/HC/WWD BS13............83 H5
Four Acres Cl
　BMSTRD/HC/WWD BS13............84 A5
　NAIL BS48................................79 F1
Fourth Av HORF/LLZ BS7.............32 C5
Fourth Wy AVONM BS11...............28 A5
Fowey Cl NAIL BS48...................79 H1
Fowey Rd MTN/WRL BS22..........117 H4
Fox And Hounds La KEYN BS31....88 C4
Fox Av YATE/CS BS37..................13 H5
Foxborough Gdns
　ALMDB BS32.............................11 F5
Fox Cl
　BRSG/KWL/STAPK BS4..............75 E1
Foxcombe Rd
　CBATH/BATHN BA1...................101 C5
　HGRV/WHIT BS14......................86 A4
Foxcote KGWD/HNM BS15...........59 F4
Foxcote Rd BMSTR BS3...............72 B3
Fox Ct OLD/WMLY/WICK BS30....76 C3
Foxcroft Cl ALMDB BS32..............21 H4
Foxcroft Rd EVILLE/WHL BS5........57 F5
Fox Den Rd BRSTK/PCHW BS34....33 F2
Foxe Rd FRCTL/WBN BS36...........23 H2
Foxfield Av ALMDB BS32..............11 F4
Foxglove Cl MANG/FISH BS16......47 G4
　MTN/WRL BS22........................117 H3
　THNB/SVB BS35..........................9 E2

Foxhill BATHSE BA2...................108 D5
Fox Rd EVILLE/WHL BS5..............56 C2
Fraley Rd
　HNLZ/SM/SNYPK/WT BS9..........45 E1
Frampton Ct
　OLD/WMLY/WICK BS30.............76 C2
Frampton Crs
　MANG/FISH BS16.......................48 C4
Frampton End Rd
　FRCTL/WBN BS36......................24 A1
Francis Fox Rd WSM BS23............7 F5
Francis Pl
　OLD/WMLY/WICK BS30.............76 C1
Francis Rd BMSTR BS3................72 D4
　HNBRY/STHM BS10....................31 G5
Francis Wy
　OLD/WMLY/WICK BS30.............60 B4
Francombe Gv
　HNBRY/STHM BS10....................45 H4
Frankland Ct
　CBATH/BATHN BA1...................101 F3
Frankley Blds
　CBATH/BATHN BA1...................102 D3
Frankley Ter
　CBATH/BATHN BA1 *.................102 D3
Franklin's Wy YTN/CONG BS49....113 F2
Franklyn La CBRISNE BS2.............56 B2
Franklyn St CBRISNE BS2.............56 B2
Fraser Cl MTN/WRL BS22............117 G4
Fraser St BMSTR BS3..................73 E3
Frayne Rd BMSTR BS3................72 B2
Frederick Pl CFTN/FAIL BS8...........4 A2
Fredrick St
　BRSG/KWL/STAPK BS4..............73 H2
Freeland Blds EVILLE/WHL BS5....57 E1
Freeland Pl CFTN/FAIL BS8..........54 C5
Freelands CLVDN BS21................66 A1
Freemans La NAIL BS48..............92 C2
Freemantle Gdns
　EVILLE/WHL BS5.......................47 E5
Freemantle Rd
　EVILLE/WHL BS5.......................47 E5
Freestone Rd CBRISNE BS2.........56 C5
Free Tank CBRIS/FH BS1...............5 H5
Freeview Rd BATHSE BA2...........107 F1
Fremantle La
　RDLND/MONT BS6.....................55 H2
Fremantle Rd
　RDLND/MONT BS6.....................55 G2
Frenchay Campus
　MANG/FISH BS16 *....................33 G4
Frenchay Cl MANG/FISH BS16.....48 B1
Frenchay Hl MANG/FISH BS16.....48 B1
Frenchay Park Rd
　MANG/FISH BS16.......................47 H2
Frenchay Rd
　MANG/FISH BS16.......................48 B1
　WSM BS23...............................124 D2
French Cl NAIL BS48..................79 G1
Freshland Wy
　KGWD/HNM BS15......................58 B3
Freshmoor CLVDN BS21..............64 D2
Friar Av MTN/WRL BS22.............117 F5
Friary CBRIS/FH BS1.....................5 J3
Friary Cl CLVDN BS21.................62 A5
Friary Grange Pk
　FRCTL/WBN BS36......................23 E4
Friary Rd HORF/LLZ BS7..............46 A4
　PTSHD/EG BS20........................39 F3
Frobisher Av PTSHD/EG BS20......39 E3
Frobisher Cl MTN/WRL BS22.......117 F4
　PTSHD/EG BS20........................39 E3
Frobisher Rd BMSTR BS3.............72 B3
Frog La
　BLAG/CWMG/WR BS40..............92 D4
　CBRIS/FH BS1...........................4 C4
　FRCTL/WBN BS36......................24 C2
Frogmore St CBRIS/FH BS1...........4 D4
Frome Ct THNB/SVB BS35.............9 E5
Frome Gln FRCTL/WBN BS36.......35 C1
Frome Pl MANG/FISH BS16..........47 H2
Frome Rd BATHSE BA2...............110 C1
　YATE/CS BS37 ....27 C2
Frome Ter MANG/FISH BS16 *......47 G3
Frome Valley Rd
　MANG/FISH BS16.......................47 H2
Frome Valley Walkway
　FRCTL/WBN BS36......................35 E2
　MANG/FISH BS16.......................48 C1
　THNB/SVB BS35..........................12 C5
Frome Valley Wy
　YATE/CS BS37 ....27 C2
Frome Vw FRCTL/WBN BS36.......23 H5
Frome Wy FRCTL/WBN BS36.......23 H5
Froomshaw Rd
　MANG/FISH BS16.......................48 A1
Frost Hl YTN/CONG BS49............112 D4
Fry's Cl MANG/FISH BS16............47 H4
Frys Hl BRSG/KWL/STAPK BS4....74 C4
　KGWD/HNM BS15......................59 C1
Fry's Wy NAIL BS48...................66 D4
Fryth Wy NAIL BS48...................66 D4
Fulford Rd
　BMSTRD/HC/WWD BS13............84 C4
Fulford Wk
　BMSTRD/HC/WWD BS13............84 C4
Fullens Cl MTN/WRL BS22..........122 A4
Fuller Rd CBATH/BATHN BA1.......103 F2
Fullers Wy BATHSE BA2..............110 B2
Fulmar Cl THNB/SVB BS35.............9 E3
Fulmar Rd MTN/WRL BS22..........122 C3
Furber Ct EVILLE/WHL BS5...........58 B5
Furber Rdg EVILLE/WHL BS5........58 B5
Furber Rd EVILLE/WHL BS5..........58 B5
Furber V EVILLE/WHL BS5............58 B5
Furland Rd MTN/WRL BS22.........121 C1
The Furlong RDLND/MONT BS6....55 H2
Furnwood EVILLE/WHL BS5...........58 A5
Furze Cl MTN/WRL BS22.............117 C3
Furze Rd MANG/FISH BS16..........48 C5
　MTN/WRL BS22........................116 D3
Furzewood Rd
　KGWD/HNM BS15......................59 F3

Fylton Cft HGRV/WHIT BS14........97 E1

G

Gable Rd EVILLE/WHL BS5 *........56 C2
Gabriel Cl
  OLD/WMLY/WICK BS30........77 E1
Gadshill Dr BRSTK/PCHW BS34....21 G5
Gadshill Rd EVILLE/WHL BS5........47 E5
Gages Cl KGWD/HNM BS15........59 F4
Gages Rd KGWD/HNM BS15........59 F4
Gainsborough Dr
  MTN/WRL BS22........117 G5
Gainsborough Gdns
  CBATH/BATHN BA1........101 H4
Gainsborough Ms
  HNBRY/STHM BS10 *........31 F3
Gainsborough Rd KEYN BS31........88 C4
Gaingale Wy PTSHD/EG BS20........40 B3
The Galleries CBRIS/FH BS1 *........5 G2
Gallivan Cl BRSTK/PCHW BS34....20 D3
Galway Rd
  BRSG/KWL/STAPK BS4........73 H5
Gander Cl
  BMSTRD/HC/WWD BS13........84 C5
Gander Rd MTN/WRL BS22........122 B1
Garden Cl
  HNLZ/SM/SNYPK/WT BS9........44 A3
  MTN/WRL BS22........122 B1
Gardeners Wk LGASH BS41........71 E5
Gardens Rd CLVDN BS21........64 C1
The Gardens MANG/FISH BS16....33 H4
Gardner Av
  BMSTRD/HC/WWD BS13........84 C5
Gardner Rd PTSHD/EG BS20........39 H2
Garfield Rd EVILLE/WHL BS5........58 A3
Garner Ct MTN/WRL BS22........118 A4
Garnet St BMSTR BS3........72 C4
Garnett Pl ALMDB BS32........21 F3
Garonor Wy PTSHD/EG BS20........41 H3
Garrett Dr ALMDB BS32........21 F3
Garrick Rd BATHSE BA2........107 G2
Garsdale Cl MTN/WRL BS22........122 A3
Garsdale Rd MTN/WRL BS22........122 A3
Garstons CBATH/BATHN BA1........105 E2
Garstons Cl NAIL BS48........79 G3
The Garstons PTSHD/EG BS20....39 C4
Garth Rd
  BMSTRD/HC/WWD BS13........84 B1
Gasferry Rd CBRIS/FH BS1........4 B7
Gaskins HORF/LLZ BS7........46 C3
Gas La CBRISNE BS2........58 C4
Gaston Av KEYN BS31........88 C4
The Gastons AVONM BS11........29 C5
Gatcombe Dr
  BRSTK/PCHW BS34........33 G1
Gatcombe Rd
  BMSTRD/HC/WWD BS13........84 C4
Gatehouse Av
  BMSTRD/HC/WWD BS13........84 B4
Gatehouse Cl
  BMSTRD/HC/WWD BS13........84 B4
Gatehouse Ct
  BMSTRD/HC/WWD BS13........84 C4
Gatehouse Wy
  BMSTRD/HC/WWD BS13........84 B4
Gatesby Md BRSTK/PCHW BS34...21 G5
Gathorne Crs YATE/CS BS37........13 H5
Gathorne Rd BMSTR BS3........72 C2
Gatton Rd CBRISNE BS2........56 C2
Gaunts Cl PTSHD/EG BS20........38 D4
Gaunt's La CBRIS/FH BS1 *........4 D4
Gaunts Rd YATE/CS BS37........26 D2
Gay Elms Rd
  BMSTRD/HC/WWD BS13........84 B3
Gayner Rd HORF/LLZ BS7........46 C1
Gays Hill CBATH/BATHN BA1......102 D4
Gays Rd KGWD/HNM BS15........75 G2
Gay St CBATH/BATHN BA1........3 F3
Gaythorne Crs YATE/CS BS37......13 H5
Gazelle Rd
  OMX/HUT/LCK BS24........125 C3
Gazzard Cl FRCTL/WBN BS36......23 E3
Gee Moors KGWD/HNM BS15......59 F4
Geffie Cl CBRIS/FH BS1........4 A7
Geoffrey Cl
  BMSTRD/HC/WWD BS13........83 H3
George And Dragon La
  BMSTRD/HC/WWD BS13........85 E5
George Cl NAIL BS48........57 F3
George Jones Rd CBRISNE BS2......56 C4
George Jones Rd CBRISNE BS2......56 C4
Georges Pl BATHSE BA2 *........3 J4
George's Rd
  CBRIS/FH BS1........102 D3
Georges Sq CBRIS/FH BS1........5 G5
George St CBATH/BATHN BA1......3 J3
  EVILLE/WHL BS5........57 E5
  WSM BS23........7 F4
George Whitefield Ct
  CBRIS/FH BS1 *........5 F2
Georgian Vw CBATH/BATHN BA1..107 G4
Gerald Rd BMSTR BS3........72 B3
Gerard Rd WSM BS23........7 E2
Gerrard Blds BATHSE BA2........3 J3
Gerrard Cl
  BRSG/KWL/STAPK BS4........84 C5
Gerrish Av EVILLE/WHL BS5........57 E3
Gibbet La KGWD/HNM BS16........77 H3
Gibbet La HGRV/WHIT BS14........97 F3
Gibbsfold Rd
  BMSTRD/HC/WWD BS13........95 H1
Gibson Rd RDLND/MONT BS6......55 H2
Gifford Ct BRSTK/PCHW BS34 *....3 J4
Gifford Rd HNBRY/STHM BS10....30 D1
Giffords Pl
  BMSTRD/HC/WWD BS13........84 A5
Gilbeck Rd NAIL BS48........66 D4
Gilbert Rd EVILLE/WHL BS5........57 E4
  KGWD/HNM BS15........58 D2
Gilberyn Dr MTN/WRL BS22......117 H5
Gilda Cl HGRV/WHIT BS14........86 B3
Gilda Crs HGRV/WHIT BS14........86 A3
Gilda Sq West
  HGRV/WHIT BS14........86 A4
Gillard Cl KGWD/HNM BS15......58 B3
Gillard Rd KGWD/HNM BS15......58 B3
Gill Av MANG/FISH BS16........48 B2

Gillebank Cl HGRV/WHIT BS14.....86 C4
Gillingham Hl EVILLE/WHL BS5.....75 E1
Gillingham Ter
  CBATH/BATHN BA1........103 E3
Gillingstool THNB/SVB BS35........8 D4
Gill Ms MTN/WRL BS22........117 H4
Gillmore Rd MTN/WRL BS22.....122 A2
Gillray Cl HORF/LLZ BS7........46 C4
Gillson Cl OMX/HUT/LCK BS24...126 A4
Gilpin Cl KGWD/HNM BS15........59 F2
Gilroy Cl OLD/WMLY/WICK BS30..77 E3
Gilslake Av HNBRY/STHM BS10....31 F2
Gimblet Rd MTN/WRL BS22......118 A4
Gingells Gn EVILLE/WHL BS5 *....58 A3
Gipsy Patch La
  BRSTK/PCHW BS34........20 D4
The Glades EVILLE/WHL BS5........57 C1
Gladstone Dr MANG/FISH BS16....48 D5
Gladstone La FRCTL/WBN BS36...24 A3
Gladstone Rd BATHSE BA2........109 F5
  HGRV/WHIT BS14........86 A3
  KGWD/HNM BS15........58 D2
Gladstone St BMSTR BS3........72 C3
  EVILLE/WHL BS5........57 E5
Glaisdale Rd MANG/FISH BS16....48 A3
Glanville Gdns
  KGWD/HNM BS15........59 E4
Glass House La CBRISNE BS2.......74 A1
Glastonbury Cl NAIL BS48........68 A5
  OLD/WMLY/WICK BS30 *........76 C1
Glastonbury Wy
  MTN/WRL BS22........122 D1
Glebe Av PTSHD/EG BS20........40 A4
Glebe Cl LGASH BS41........71 E4
Glebe Fld ALMDB BS32........10 C2
Glebelands Rd
  BRSTK/PCHW BS34........32 C2
Glebe Rd BATHSE BA2........107 G3
  CLVDN BS21........64 B3
  EVILLE/WHL BS5........57 G3
  LGASH BS41........71 F5
  PTSHD/EG BS20........40 A4
  WSM BS23........7 F3
Gledemoor Dr
  FRCTL/WBN BS36........24 B3
Glena Av
  BRSG/KWL/STAPK BS4........74 A4
Glenarm Rd
  BRSG/KWL/STAPK BS4........74 D4
Glenarm Wk
  BRSG/KWL/STAPK BS4........74 D4
Glenavon Pk
  HNLZ/SM/SNYPK/WT BS9.......44 A4
Glen Brook
  HNLZ/SM/SNYPK/WT BS9.......44 B4
Glenburn Rd KGWD/HNM BS15...58 B2
Glencoyne Sq
  HNBRY/STHM BS10........31 C3
Glencroft Wy MTN/WRL BS22....117 F5
Glendale CFTN/FAIL BS8 *........54 D5
  MANG/FISH BS16........48 C5
Glendare St EVILLE/WHL BS5.......57 E5
Glendevon Rd
  HGRV/WHIT BS14........96 D1
Glen Dr
  HNLZ/SM/SNYPK/WT BS9.......44 B3
Gleneagles Cl MTN/WRL BS22....117 C5
  NAIL BS48........67 H5
Gleneagles Dr
  HNBRY/STHM BS10........30 B2
Gleneagles Rd
  OLD/WMLY/WICK BS30........59 H5
Glenfall YATE/CS BS37........25 H3
Glenfrome Rd CBRISNE BS2........46 D5
Glen La BRSG/KWL/STAPK BS4....74 C4
Glen Pk EVILLE/WHL BS5........57 E1
Glen Park Gdns
  EVILLE/WHL BS5........58 A3
Glenroy Av KGWD/HNM BS15......58 B2
Glenside Campus
  MANG/FISH BS16 *........47 C3
Glenside Cl MANG/FISH BS16.....48 C1
Glenside Pk MANG/FISH BS16....47 C3
The Glen KEYN BS31........88 B3
  KGWD/HNM BS15........75 C2
  MTN/WRL BS22........121 C1
Glentworth Rd CFTN/FAIL BS8....4 E5
  RDLND/MONT BS6........55 G1
Glenwood MANG/FISH BS16.......48 C5
Glenwood Dr
  OLD/WMLY/WICK BS30........77 E2
Glenwood Ri PTSHD/EG BS20.....38 D3
Glenwood Rd
  OLD/WMLY/WICK BS30........45 C1
Glevum Cl MANG/FISH BS16.......50 A1
Gloster Av EVILLE/WHL BS5........47 F5
Gloucester Cl
  BRSTK/PCHW BS34........21 F5
Gloucester La CBRISNE BS2 *......5 K2
Gloucester Rd ALMDB BS32......10 D3
  AVONM BS11........28 A4
  CBATH/BATHN BA1........101 H4
  HORF/LLZ BS7........55 H1
  MANG/FISH BS16........49 E5
  THNB/SVB BS35........8 D2
Gloucester Rd North
  HORF/LLZ BS7........32 B4
Gloucester Rw CFTN/FAIL BS8....54 D4
Gloucester St
  CBATH/BATHN BA1........2 E2
  CBRISNE BS2........5 H1
  CFTN/FAIL BS8........54 D4
  EVILLE/WHL BS5........47 F5
  WSM BS23........6 D4
Gloucester Ter
  THNB/SVB BS35 *........8 C3
Glyn V BMSTR BS3........73 E5
Goddard Wy
  HNBRY/STHM BS10........31 E4
Godfrey Ct
  OLD/WMLY/WICK BS30........76 C2
Godwin Dr NAIL BS48........66 D4
Goffenton Dr MANG/FISH BS16...48 B2
Goldcrest Rd YATE/CS BS37........26 B3
Goldcrest Wy PTSHD/EG BS20....40 B2

Golden Hl RDLND/MONT BS6.......45 G3
Goldfinch Wy MANG/FISH BS16...51 G4
Goldney Av CFTN/FAIL BS8........55 E5
  OLD/WMLY/WICK BS30........60 A4
Goldney Rd CFTN/FAIL BS8........55 E5
Goldsbury Wk AVONM BS11........29 C4
Golf Club La KEYN BS31........99 F2
Golf Course La
  FRCTL/WBN BS34........32 B2
Golf Course Rd WSM BS23........109 C1
Gooch Cl
  OLD/WMLY/WICK BS30........77 F3
Gooch Wy MTN/WRL BS22........118 A5
Goodard Dr MTN/WRL BS22......118 A5
Goodeve Pk
  HNLZ/SM/SNYPK/WT BS9........44 B5
Goodeve Rd
  HNLZ/SM/SNYPK/WT BS9........54 B1
Goodhind St EVILLE/WHL BS5.....56 D5
Goodneston Rd
  MANG/FISH BS16........48 A5
Goodrich Cl YATE/CS BS37........25 E1
Goodring Hl AVONM BS11........29 C4
Good Shepherd Cl
  HORF/LLZ BS7........45 G4
Goodwin Dr HGRV/WHIT BS14....85 G5
Goodwood Gdns
  MANG/FISH BS16........35 F4
Goold Cl BATHSE BA2........99 H4
Goolden St
  BRSG/KWL/STAPK BS4........73 H5
Goose Acre ALMDB BS32........21 H4
Goosegreen FRCTL/WBN BS36....23 H2
Goose Gn
  OLD/WMLY/WICK BS30........60 A2
  YATE/CS BS37........14 A4
Goose Green Wy YATE/CS BS37...13 G5
Gooseland Cl HGRV/WHIT BS14...96 C1
Goosey La MTN/WRL BS22........123 F1
Gordano Gdns PTSHD/EG BS20...42 B4
Gordano Rd PTSHD/EG BS20......41 F1
Gor Dano Vw PTSHD/EG BS20....39 C3
Gordon Av EVILLE/WHL BS5........57 C2
Gordon Cl EVILLE/WHL BS5........57 C2
Gordon Rd BATHSE BA2........3 J7
  CBRISNE BS2........56 B2
  EVILLE/WHL BS5........57 F2
  HGRV/WHIT BS14........86 A3
Core Rd BMSTR BS3........72 B3
Core's Marsh Rd BMSTR BS3......72 B4
Gorham Cl AVONM BS11........30 A3
Gorlands Rd YATE/CS BS37........27 E1
Gorlangton Cl
  HGRV/WHIT BS14........85 H2
Gorse Hl MANG/FISH BS16........49 G1
Gorse La CFTN/FAIL BS8........4 A4
Gosforth Cl HNBRY/STHM BS10...31 F4
Gosforth Rd
  HNBRY/STHM BS10........31 F4
Goslet Rd HGRV/WHIT BS14.......86 D4
Goss Barton NAIL BS48........67 E5
Goss Cl NAIL BS48........66 D5
Goss La NAIL BS48........66 D5
Goss Vw NAIL BS48........66 D5
Gotley Rd
  BRSG/KWL/STAPK BS4........74 C4
Gott Dr BRSG/KWL/STAPK BS4....74 C1
Goulston Rd
  BMSTRD/HC/WWD BS13........84 B4
Goulston Wk
  BMSTRD/HC/WWD BS13........84 B4
Coulter St EVILLE/WHL BS5........56 D5
Gourney Cl AVONM BS11........29 H3
Gover Rd KGWD/HNM BS15........75 H3
Grace Cl YATE/CS BS37........27 G2
  YTN/CONG BS49........112 D3
Grace Dr KGWD/HNM BS15........59 C2
Grace Park Rd
  BRSG/KWL/STAPK BS4........74 C5
Grace Rd MANG/FISH BS16........48 C2
  MTN/WRL BS22........118 A5
Gradwell Cl MTN/WRL BS22......118 A5
Graeme Cl MANG/FISH BS16......48 A4
Graham Rd BMSTR BS3 *........72 D3
  EVILLE/WHL BS5........56 D2
  MANG/FISH BS16........48 C5
  WSM BS23........6 E6
Grainger Ct AVONM BS11........43 E1
Graitney Cl YTN/CONG BS49......113 G3
Grampian Cl
  OLD/WMLY/WICK BS30........77 F2
Granby Hl CFTN/FAIL BS8........54 D5
Grand Pde BATHSE BA2........3 G4
Grange Av
  BRSTK/PCHW BS34........21 E4
  KGWD/HNM BS15........76 A1
Grange Cl ALMDB BS32........11 E5
  BRSTK/PCHW BS34........33 H1
  MTN/WRL BS22........124 D5
Grange Cl North
  HNLZ/SM/SNYPK/WT BS9........45 F2
Grange Ct KGWD/HNM BS15......76 A1
  HNLZ/SM/SNYPK/WT BS9........45 F2
Grange Court Rd
  HNLZ/SM/SNYPK/WT BS9........45 F2
Grange Dr MANG/FISH BS16.......48 C2
Grange Farm Rd
  YTN/CONG BS49........112 A2
Grange Pk
  HNLZ/SM/SNYPK/WT BS9........44 B1
  MANG/FISH BS16........34 C5
Grange Rd
  BMSTRD/HC/WWD BS13........84 B4
  CFTN/FAIL BS8........55 E4
  KEYN BS31........98 D1
  WSM BS23........124 D5
The Grange
  HNLZ/SM/SNYPK/WT BS9........44 B1
Grangeville Cl
  OLD/WMLY/WICK BS30........77 E3
Grangewood Cl
  MANG/FISH BS16........48 C2
Granny's La KGWD/HNM BS15....59 E5
Grantham La
  KGWD/HNM BS15........58 C2
Grantham Rd
  KGWD/HNM BS15........58 C2
Grantson Cl
  BRSG/KWL/STAPK BS4........74 D4

Granville Cl KGWD/HNM BS15....75 C3
Granville Rd
  CBATH/BATHN BA1........102 B1
Granville St EVILLE/WHL BS5......57 F5
Grasmere Cl
  HNBRY/STHM BS10........31 E5
Grasmere Dr WSM BS23........122 A3
Grassington Dr YATE/CS BS37.....26 C1
Grass Meers Dr
  HGRV/WHIT BS14........85 H5
Grassmere Gdns
  OLD/WMLY/WICK BS30........60 C5
Grassmere Rd
  YTN/CONG BS49........112 B3
Gratitude Rd EVILLE/WHL BS5.....57 E2
Gravel Hill Rd YATE/CS BS37......14 B3
Gravel Hill Road (North)
  YATE/CS BS37........14 C3
Gravel Wk CBATH/BATHN BA1.....2 E2
Graveney Cl
  BRSG/KWL/STAPK BS4........74 C5
Gray Cl HNBRY/STHM BS10........30 D3
Gray Rd HNBRY/STHM BS10........30 D2
Great Ann St CBRISNE BS2........5 K2
Great Bedford St
  CBATH/BATHN BA1........2 E1
Great Brockeridge
  HNLZ/SM/SNYPK/WT BS9........44 D2
Great Dowles
  OLD/WMLY/WICK BS30........76 C2
Great George St
  CBRIS/FH BS1 *........4 D4
  HGRV/WHIT BS14........85 H2
Great Hayles Rd
  HGRV/WHIT BS14........85 H2
Great Leaze
  OLD/WMLY/WICK BS30........76 D2
Great Meadow Rd
  ALMDB BS32........21 H3
Great Park Rd ALMDB BS32........11 E4
Great Pulteney St BATHSE BA2....3 H3
Great Stanhope St
  CBATH/BATHN BA1........2 D4
Great Stoke Wy
  BRSTK/PCHW BS34........33 F2
Great Western La
  EVILLE/WHL BS5........57 F5
Great Western Rd CLVDN BS21....64 D2
Great Wood Cl
  BMSTRD/HC/WWD BS13........84 D5
Greenacre MTN/WRL BS22........121 C1
Greenacre Rd
  HGRV/WHIT BS14........96 D1
Greenacres
  CBATH/BATHN BA1........101 C1
Greenacres Pk
  FRCTL/WBN BS36........24 B5
Greenbank Av East
  EVILLE/WHL BS5........57 E2
Greenbank Av West
  EVILLE/WHL BS5........57 E2
Greenbank Gdns
  CBATH/BATHN BA1........101 C3
Greenbank Rd BMSTR BS3........72 B2
  EVILLE/WHL BS5........57 E2
  KGWD/HNM BS15........76 A1
Greenbank Vw
  EVILLE/WHL BS5........57 E1
Green Cft EVILLE/WHL BS5 *......57 H3
Greendale Rd BMSTR BS3........73 E3
  RDLND/MONT BS6........45 F4
Green Dell Cl
  HNBRY/STHM BS10........30 B2
Greenditch Av
  BMSTRD/HC/WWD BS13........84 D4
Greendown EVILLE/WHL BS5......58 B4
Greendown Pl BATHSE BA2......111 E1
Green Dragon Rd
  FRCTL/WBN BS36........22 D5
Greenfield Av
  HNBRY/STHM BS10........31 H5
Greenfield Crs NAIL BS48........67 F3
Greenfield Pk
  PTSHD/EG BS20........39 C5
Greenfield Pl WSM BS23........6 B2
Greenfield Rd
  HNBRY/STHM BS10........31 H4
Greengage Cl
  MTN/WRL BS22........122 B3
Green Hayes YATE/CS BS37........27 E2
Greenhill Cl MTN/WRL BS22.....117 H5
  NAIL BS48........67 E4
Greenhill Gv BMSTR BS3........72 B4
Greenhill La AVONM BS11........29 H4
Greenland Rd
  MTN/WRL BS22........122 A2
Greenlands Wy
  HNBRY/STHM BS10........30 C1
Green La AVONM BS11........28 B5
  CFTN/FAIL BS8........69 H2
  FRCTL/WBN BS36........22 C3
  THNB/SVB BS35........18 A1
Greenleaze
  BRSG/KWL/STAPK BS4........74 A5
Greenleaze Av
  MANG/FISH BS16........34 D4
Greenmore Rd
  BRSG/KWL/STAPK BS4........74 A4
Greenore KGWD/HNM BS15......58 C4
Green Pk CBATH/BATHN BA1......2 D3
Green Park Ms
  CBATH/BATHN BA1........2 E5
Greenpark Rd
  HNBRY/STHM BS10........32 A4
Green Pastures Rd NAIL BS48.....68 A4
Greenridge Cl
  BMSTRD/HC/WWD BS13........83 H5
Green's HI MANG/FISH BS16......47 G5
Green Side MANG/FISH BS16......49 G2
Greenside Cl
  HNBRY/STHM BS10........30 B2
Greenslade Gdns NAIL BS48......67 E4
Greensplott Rd AVONM BS11......16 D3
Green St BMSTR BS3........73 C2
  CBATH/BATHN BA1........3 F4
The Green BRSTK/PCHW BS34.....33 C1
  KGWD/HNM BS15........59 E1
  NAIL BS48........79 G4

OMX/HUT/LCK BS24........126 D2
  PTSHD/EG BS20........42 D4
Greenview
  OLD/WMLY/WICK BS30........76 D4
Green Wk
  BRSG/KWL/STAPK BS4........73 H5
Greenway Bush La BMSTR BS3....72 B2
Greenway Ct BATHSE BA2........108 C3
Greenway Dr
  HNBRY/STHM BS10........31 H5
Greenway La BATHSE BA2......108 C4
Greenway Pk CLVDN BS21........65 F2
  HNBRY/STHM BS10........31 H5
Greenway Rd
  RDLND/MONT BS6........55 F1
Greenways KGWD/HNM BS15....59 C2
Greenways Rd YATE/CS BS37......13 H4
The Greenway
  MANG/FISH BS16........48 C5
Greenwood Cl HORF/LLZ BS7.....46 A1
Greenwood Rd
  BRSG/KWL/STAPK BS4........73 H4
  MTN/WRL BS22........122 B1
Gregory Ct
  OLD/WMLY/WICK BS30........59 C5
Gregory Md YTN/CONG BS49....112 A2
Grenville Av
  OMX/HUT/LCK BS24........126 D2
Grenville Cl EVILLE/WHL BS5......57 H3
Grenville Pl CBRIS/FH BS1 *........72 A1
Grenville Rd RDLND/MONT BS6...46 A5
Greve Ct
  OLD/WMLY/WICK BS30........76 C2
Greville Rd BMSTR BS3........72 C2
Greville St BMSTR BS3........72 C2
Greyhound Wk CBRIS/FH BS1 *....5 G2
Greylands Rd
  BMSTRD/HC/WWD BS13........84 A2
Greystoke Av
  HNBRY/STHM BS10........31 E5
Greystoke Gdns
  HNBRY/STHM BS10........31 E5
Greystones MANG/FISH BS16.....35 E4
Griffen Rd
  OMX/HUT/LCK BS24........122 B4
Griffin Cl MTN/WRL BS22........123 E1
Griffin Rd CLVDN BS21........64 D2
Griggfield Wk
  HGRV/WHIT BS14........85 C2
Grimsbury Rd
  KGWD/HNM BS15........59 C3
Grindell Rd EVILLE/WHL BS5......57 F4
Grinfield Av
  BMSTRD/HC/WWD BS13........84 D5
Grinfield Ct
  BMSTRD/HC/WWD BS13........84 D5
Grittleton Rd HORF/LLZ BS7.......32 A5
Grosvenor Bridge Rd
  CBATH/BATHN BA1........103 F3
Grosvenor Pk
  CBATH/BATHN BA1........103 E3
Grosvenor Pl
  CBATH/BATHN BA1........103 E3
Grosvenor Rd CBRISNE BS2........56 B3
Grosvenor Ter
  CBATH/BATHN BA1........103 F2
Grosvenor Vls
  CBATH/BATHN BA1 *........103 E3
Grove Av CBRIS/FH BS1........5 F6
  HNLZ/SM/SNYPK/WT BS9........44 A1
Grove Bank
  MANG/FISH BS16........34 C4
Grove Dr MTN/WRL BS22........121 H2
Grove La WSM BS23........6 D2
Grove Leaze AVONM BS11........42 D2
Grove Pk
  BRSG/KWL/STAPK BS4........74 C4
  RDLND/MONT BS6........55 G1
Grove Park Av
  BRSG/KWL/STAPK BS4........74 C4
Grove Park Rd
  BRSG/KWL/STAPK BS4........74 C4
Grove Park Ter
  MANG/FISH BS16........47 H4
Grove Rd BNWL BS29........127 H2
  HNLZ/SM/SNYPK/WT BS9........44 A1
  MANG/FISH BS16........47 G4
  MTN/WRL BS22........121 H2
  RDLND/MONT BS6........55 F1
  WSM BS23........6 D2
Grovesend Rd
  THNB/SVB BS35........8 C4
The Groves
  BMSTRD/HC/WWD BS13........85 E5
Grove St BATHSE BA2........3 G3
The Grove
  BRSTK/PCHW BS34........20 D3
  CBATH/BATHN BA1........101 H3
  CBRIS/FH BS1........4 E6
  NAIL BS48........68 B3
  OLD/WMLY/WICK BS30........76 D2
Grove Vw MANG/FISH BS16......47 G2
Guernsey Av
  BRSG/KWL/STAPK BS4........75 E2
Guest Av MANG/FISH BS16........49 H2
Guildford Rd
  BRSG/KWL/STAPK BS4........57 C5
Guildhall Market
  CBATH/BATHN BA1 *........3 G4
Guinea La
  CBATH/BATHN BA1........3 F2
  MANG/FISH BS16........48 A3
Guinea St CBRIS/FH BS1........5 F7
Guilford's Bank FRCTL/WBN BS36....65 E3
Gullimores Gdns
  BMSTRD/HC/WWD BS13........84 C5
Gullivers Pl YATE/CS BS37........26 C2
Gullons Cl
  BMSTRD/HC/WWD BS13........84 B3
Gullon Wk
  BMSTRD/HC/WWD BS13........84 A4
Gullybrook La
  EVILLE/WHL BS5 *........56 D5
The Gully FRCTL/WBN BS36........23 F3
Gunning Cl
  KGWD/HNM BS15........58 D5
Gunter's Wk EVILLE/WHL BS5.....58 A4
Guthrie Rd CFTN/FAIL BS8........54 D3
Gwilliam St BMSTR BS3........73 E3
Gwyn St CBRISNE BS2........56 A2

Gypsy La KEYN BS31 98 C4

H

Haberfield Hl PTSHD/EG BS20 52 D1
Hacket Hl THNB/SVB BS35 9 G4
Hacket La THNB/SVB BS35 9 F3
Hadley Ct
OLD/WMLY/WICK BS30 59 H5
Hadley Rd BATHSE BA2 109 E5
Hadrian Cl
HNLZ/SM/SNYPK/WT BS9 44 A4
Hadrians Wk MANG/FISH BS16 50 A2
Halbrow Crs MANG/FISH BS16 48 C3
Haldon Cl BMSTR BS3 73 E5
Hale Cl KGWD/HNM BS15 76 A2
Hales Horn Cl ALMDB BS32 21 F4
Halfacre Cl HGRV/WHIT BS14 96 D1
Halfacre La HGRV/WHIT BS14 97 E1
Halifax Rd YATE/CS BS37 13 H3
Hallam Rd CLVDN BS21 64 C2
Hallards Cl AVONM BS11 29 F5
Hallen Cl HNBRY/STHM BS10 30 B2
MANG/FISH BS16 50 A2
Hallen Dr
HNLZ/SM/SNYPK/WT BS9 44 A1
Hallen Rd HNBRY/STHM BS10 30 A1
Halletts Wy PTSHD/EG BS20 39 H3
Halliwell Rd PTSHD/EG BS20 38 B4
Halls Gdns BRSTK/PCHW BS34 34 A1
Halls Rd KGWD/HNM BS15 58 D3
Hall St BMSTR BS3 72 C4
Halsbury Rd RDLND/MONT BS6 45 F4
Halstock Av MANG/FISH BS16 47 H5
Halston Dr CBRISNE BS2 56 B3
Halswell Gdns
BMSTRD/HC/WWD BS13 84 C5
Halswell Rd CLVDN BS21 64 D4
Halt End HGRV/WHIT BS14 97 F1
Halwyn Cl
HNLZ/SM/SNYPK/WT BS9 44 B3
Hamble Cl THNB/SVB BS35 8 D4
Hambledon Rd
MTN/WRL BS22 118 B4
Hambrook La
BRSTK/PCHW BS34 33 H1
Ham Farm La MANG/FISH BS16 49 H2
Ham Gn PTSHD/EG BS20 42 D4
Hamilton Rd BMSTR BS3 72 C2
CBATH/BATHN BA1 102 B2
EVILLE/WHL BS5 56 C3
WSM BS23 120 B2
Ham La LGASH BS41 94 C1
MANG/FISH BS16 47 G2
NAIL BS48 67 H2
The Hamlet NAIL BS48 67 H3
Hammersmith Rd
EVILLE/WHL BS5 57 F3
Hammond Cl
BRSG/KWL/STAPK BS4 74 C5
Hammond Gdns
HNLZ/SM/SNYPK/WT BS9 44 C1
Hampden Cl YATE/CS BS37 13 H3
Hampden Rd
BRSG/KWL/STAPK BS4 74 A3
MTN/WRL BS22 122 A1
Hampshire Wy YATE/CS BS37 14 B3
Hampstead Rd
BRSG/KWL/STAPK BS4 74 B3
Hampton Cl
OLD/WMLY/WICK BS30 76 D1
Hampton Cnr AVONM BS11 * 43 E2
Hampton La RDLND/MONT BS6 55 F2
Hampton Pk
RDLND/MONT BS6 55 F2
Hampton Rd
RDLND/MONT BS6 55 F1
Hampton Rw BATHSE BA2 3 K1
Hampton St KGWD/HNM BS15 58 D2
Hampton Vw
CBATH/BATHN BA1 103 E3
Hams Rd KEYN BS31 88 C2
Ham Wood Cl
OMX/HUT/LCK BS24 125 G5
Hanbury Cl KGWD/HNM BS15 76 A1
Hanbury Rd CFTN/FAIL BS8 55 E3
Handel Av EVILLE/WHL BS5 57 F4
Handel Cossham Ct
KGWD/HNM BS15 58 C2
Handel Rd KEYN BS31 88 A4
Handford Wy
OLD/WMLY/WICK BS30 77 E2
Hanford Ct HGRV/WHIT BS14 86 C2
Hanham Rd KGWD/HNM BS15 58 D5
Hanham Wy NAIL BS48 66 C4
Hannah More Rd NAIL BS48 66 D5
Hanover Cl MTN/WRL BS22 117 H4
Hanover Ct CBRIS/FH BS1 * 5 H2
Hanover Pl
CBATH/BATHN BA1 * 103 E4
CBRIS/FH BS1 4 B7
Hanover St
CBATH/BATHN BA1 103 E3
EVILLE/WHL BS5 57 E4
Hanover Ter
CBATH/BATHN BA1 * 103 E3
Hansford Cl BATHSE BA2 110 C1
Hansford Sq BATHSE BA2 110 C1
Hanson's Wy CLVDN BS21 64 C3
Hans Price Cl WSM BS23 7 F3
Hantone Hl BATHSE BA2 104 A4
Happerton La
PTSHD/EG BS20 52 C1
Hapsburg Cl MTN/WRL BS22 117 H4
Harbour Crs PTSHD/EG BS20 40 A3
Harbour Rd PTSHD/EG BS20 39 H2
Harbour Wall
HNLZ/SM/SNYPK/WT BS9 43 H4
Harbour Wy CBRIS/FH BS1 4 C6
Harbury Rd
HNLZ/SM/SNYPK/WT BS9 45 G1
Harbutts BATHSE BA2 104 A3
Harcombe Hl FRCTL/WBN BS36 35 E1
Harcombe Rd
FRCTL/WBN BS36 22 D5
Harcourt Av EVILLE/WHL BS5 58 A5
Harcourt Cl KEYN BS31 * 99 F2
Harcourt Gdns
CBATH/BATHN BA1 101 G2
Harcourt Hl RDLND/MONT BS6 45 G5
Harcourt Rd RDLND/MONT BS6 45 F4
Hardenhuish Rd
BRSG/KWL/STAPK BS4 74 C1
Harden Rd HGRV/WHIT BS14 86 D4
Hardings Ter EVILLE/WHL BS5 * 57 H3
Hardington Dr KEYN BS31 98 B2
Hardwick Cl
BRSG/KWL/STAPK BS4 74 D3
OLD/WMLY/WICK BS30 77 G1
Hardwicke YATE/CS BS37 25 G3
Hardwick Rd PTSHD/EG BS20 42 C4
Hardy Av BMSTR BS3 72 B3
Hardy Ct
OLD/WMLY/WICK BS30 76 C1
Hardy Rd BMSTR BS3 72 B4
Hareclive Rd
BMSTRD/HC/WWD BS13 84 C4
Harefield Cl KGWD/HNM BS15 75 H4
Harescombe YATE/CS BS37 26 A3
Harewood Rd EVILLE/WHL BS5 58 A2
Harford Cl
HNLZ/SM/SNYPK/WT BS9 44 A1
Harford Dr MANG/FISH BS16 34 C4
Harington Pl
CBATH/BATHN BA1 3 F4
Harlech Wy
OLD/WMLY/WICK BS30 77 E4
Harleston St EVILLE/WHL BS5 5 K1
Harley La CLVDN BS21 63 G4
Harley Ms CFTN/FAIL BS8 54 D4
Harley Pl CFTN/FAIL BS8 * 54 D4
Harley St CBATH/BATHN BA1 2 E1
Harmer Cl HNBRY/STHM BS10 30 D2
Harmony Dr PTSHD/EG BS20 38 D4
Harnhill Cl
BMSTRD/HC/WWD BS13 84 C5
Harnwood Sq HORF/LLZ BS7 46 A4
Harolds Wy KGWD/HNM BS15 58 C5
Harptree Cl NAIL BS48 79 E1
Harptree Ct
OLD/WMLY/WICK BS30 76 D2
Harptree Gv BMSTR BS3 72 C4
Harrington Av
HGRV/WHIT BS14 86 D3
Harrington Cl
OLD/WMLY/WICK BS30 89 H1
Harrington Gv
HGRV/WHIT BS14 86 D3
Harrington Rd
HGRV/WHIT BS14 86 D3
Harrington Wk
HGRV/WHIT BS14 86 D3
Harris Barton
FRCTL/WBN BS36 23 G3
Harris Ct
OLD/WMLY/WICK BS30 76 C2
Harris Gv
BMSTRD/HC/WWD BS13 95 G1
Harris La CFTN/FAIL BS8 53 F3
Harrison Cl MANG/FISH BS16 49 H2
Harrowdene Rd
BRSG/KWL/STAPK BS4 74 A3
Harrow Rd
BRSG/KWL/STAPK BS4 74 C3
Harry Stoke Rd
BRSTK/PCHW BS34 33 G2
Hartcliffe Rd
BRSG/KWL/STAPK BS4 85 F1
Hartcliffe Wk
BRSG/KWL/STAPK BS4 85 G1
Hartcliffe Wy BMSTR BS3 72 D5
BMSTRD/HC/WWD BS13 84 D2
Hart Cl PTSHD/EG BS20 43 E4
Hartfield Av
RDLND/MONT BS6 55 G3
Hartgill Cl
BMSTRD/HC/WWD BS13 95 G1
Hartington Pk
RDLND/MONT BS6 55 F1
Hartley Cl YATE/CS BS37 27 E1
Harts Cft YATE/CS BS37 14 B3
Harvest Cl ALMDB BS32 21 F1
Harvest La
OMX/HUT/LCK BS24 123 E3
Harvest Wy MTN/WRL BS22 117 H3
Harvey Cl MTN/WRL BS22 117 H4
Harveys La EVILLE/WHL BS5 57 G3
Harwood Gdns
MTN/WRL BS22 117 F4
Haselbury Gv KEYN BS31 99 F2
Haskins Ct
OLD/WMLY/WICK BS30 76 D2
Hassell Dr CBRISNE BS2 56 C4
Hastings Cl BMSTR BS3 72 D5
Hastings Rd BMSTR BS3 72 D5
Hatchet La BRSTK/PCHW BS34 33 G1
Hatchet Rd ALMDB BS32 21 F4
BRSTK/PCHW BS34 33 G1
Hatchmere THNB/SVB BS35 9 E4
Hatfield Blds BATHSE BA2 3 J7
Hatfield Rd BATHSE BA2 108 B4
WSM BS23 7 K3
Hatherley YATE/CS BS37 26 A3
Hatherley Rd HORF/LLZ BS7 46 A4
Hathway Wk EVILLE/WHL BS5 56 C3
Hatters' La YATE/CS BS37 27 E1
The Haven KGWD/HNM BS15 59 E2
Haversham Cl
MTN/WRL BS22 122 A2
Haverstock Rd
BRSG/KWL/STAPK BS4 73 H3
Haviland Gv
CBATH/BATHN BA1 101 F1
Haviland Pk
CBATH/BATHN BA1 101 G2
Havory CBATH/BATHN BA1 103 E3
Hawarden Ter
CBATH/BATHN BA1 103 E3
Hawburn Cl
BRSG/KWL/STAPK BS4 74 C4
Haweswater Cl
OLD/WMLY/WICK BS30 60 B5
Hawke Rd MTN/WRL BS22 117 F4
Hawkesbury Rd
MANG/FISH BS16 47 G5
Hawkesley Dr
BRSTK/PCHW BS34 21 F4
Hawkesworth Rd
YATE/CS BS37 13 G4
Hawkfield Cl
BMSTRD/HC/WWD BS13 85 E4
Hawkfield Rd
BMSTRD/HC/WWD BS13 85 E4
Hawkfield Wy
HGRV/WHIT BS14 85 E4
Hawkins Cl
OLD/WMLY/WICK BS30 77 F2
Hawkins Crs ALMDB BS32 21 F2
Hawkins St CBRISNE BS2 5 J3
Hawkley Dr ALMDB BS32 11 F4
Hawkridge Dr
MANG/FISH BS16 51 G3
Hawksmoor Cl
HGRV/WHIT BS14 85 H3
Hawksmoor La
MANG/FISH BS16 33 G5
Hawksworth Dr
KGWD/HNM BS15 75 G2
MTN/WRL BS22 118 A5
Hawthorn Av
KGWD/HNM BS15 75 G1
Hawthorn Cl
BRSTK/PCHW BS34 20 A3
PTSHD/EG BS20 38 D3
Hawthorn Crs THNB/SVB BS35 8 D2
YTN/CONG BS49 112 A2
Hawthorne Cl
MANG/FISH BS16 51 G3
Hawthorne Ri
HNBRY/STHM BS10 * 31 G2
The Hawthornes
MANG/FISH BS16 49 F4
Hawthorne St
BRSG/KWL/STAPK BS4 73 H3
Hawthorn Gdns
MTN/WRL BS22 122 A1
Hawthorn Gv BATHSE BA2 110 D1
Hawthorn Hts
MTN/WRL BS22 117 E5
Hawthorn Hl MTN/WRL BS22 117 F5
Hawthorn Pk MTN/WRL BS22 117 F5
Hawthorns La KEYN BS31 88 B4
Hawthorn Wy
BRSTK/PCHW BS34 21 G5
NAIL BS48 67 G4
Haycombe HGRV/WHIT BS14 85 G3
Haycombe Dr BATHSE BA2 107 F2
Haycombe La BATHSE BA2 107 F4
Hay Ct PTSHD/EG BS20 42 A4
Haycroft Rd
BRSTK/PCHW BS34 32 C2
Hayden Cl BATHSE BA2 2 D7
Haydock Cl MANG/FISH BS16 35 F4
Haydon Gdns HORF/LLZ BS7 46 D3
Hayeley Dr ALMDB BS32 21 G4
Hayes Cl CBRISNE BS2 56 C4
Hayesfield Pk BATHSE BA2 2 E7
Hayes Pl BATHSE BA2 2 E7
Hay Hl CBATH/BATHN BA1 3 F2
Hay Leaze YATE/CS BS37 13 H3
The Haymarket CBRIS/FH BS1 5 F2
Haymarket Wk CBRIS/FH BS1 5 F1
Haynes La MANG/FISH BS16 48 D3
Haythorn Ct MANG/FISH BS16 49 F3
Haytor Pk
HNLZ/SM/SNYPK/WT BS9 44 B2
Hayward Cl CLVDN BS21 64 C4
Hayward Rd EVILLE/WHL BS5 57 E4
MANG/FISH BS16 48 D5
Haywood Cl
OMX/HUT/LCK BS24 125 F5
Haywood Gdns
OMX/HUT/LCK BS24 125 F5
Hazel Av RDLND/MONT BS6 55 F1
Hazelbury Dr
OLD/WMLY/WICK BS30 60 A5
Hazelbury Rd HGRV/WHIT BS14 86 B1
NAIL BS48 67 E5
Hazel Cote Rd
HGRV/WHIT BS14 86 A5
Hazel Crs THNB/SVB BS35 9 E3
Hazeldene Rd
BRSTK/PCHW BS34 20 C3
WSM BS23 7 J2
Hazel Gv BATHSE BA2 108 A3
Hazelgrove FRCTL/WBN BS36 23 E5
Hazel Gv HORF/LLZ BS7 32 C5
Hazell Cl CLVDN BS21 65 E4
Hazelton Rd HORF/LLZ BS7 45 H5
Hazel Wy BATHSE BA2 110 B2
Hazelwood Rd
HNLZ/SM/SNYPK/WT BS9 44 B5
Head Cft NAIL BS48 81 G1
Headford Av EVILLE/WHL BS5 58 B4
Headford Rd
BRSG/KWL/STAPK BS4 73 E5
Headington Cl
KGWD/HNM BS15 76 A2
Headley Ct
BMSTRD/HC/WWD BS13 84 C3
Headley La
BMSTRD/HC/WWD BS13 84 C3
Headley Park Av
BMSTRD/HC/WWD BS13 84 C2
Headley Park Rd
BMSTRD/HC/WWD BS13 84 B2
Headley Rd
BMSTRD/HC/WWD BS13 84 B3
Headley Wk
BMSTRD/HC/WWD BS13 84 C2
Heart Meers HGRV/WHIT BS14 86 A4
Heath Cl FRCTL/WBN BS36 23 E4
Heathcote Dr
FRCTL/WBN BS36 24 B3
Heathcote Rd
MANG/FISH BS16 58 B1
Heathcote Wk
MANG/FISH BS16 58 C1
Heath Ct MANG/FISH BS16 48 D1
Heather Av FRCTL/WBN BS36 23 H4
Heather Cl KGWD/HNM BS15 58 B3
Heatherdene
HGRV/WHIT BS14 85 G2
Heather Dr BATHSE BA2 110 B2
Heathfield Cl
CBATH/BATHN BA1 101 F1
KEYN BS31 87 H4
Heathfield Crs
HGRV/WHIT BS14 85 H5
Heathfield Rd NAIL BS48 67 F4
Heathfields MANG/FISH BS16 34 D5
Heathfield Wy NAIL BS48 67 F3
Heath Gdns FRCTL/WBN BS36 24 A4
MANG/FISH BS16 34 D5
Heathgate YTN/CONG BS49 112 B3
Heath House La
EVILLE/WHL BS5 46 D4
Heath Rdg LGASH BS41 70 D4
Heath Ri
OLD/WMLY/WICK BS30 77 E1
Heath Rd EVILLE/WHL BS5 46 D5
KGWD/HNM BS15 75 G2
MANG/FISH BS16 48 D1
NAIL BS48 67 F3
Heath St EVILLE/WHL BS5 57 E1
Heath Wk MANG/FISH BS16 48 D1
Heber St EVILLE/WHL BS5 57 E4
Hebron Rd BMSTR BS3 72 D3
Hedge Cl OMX/HUT/LCK BS24 123 E3
Hedgemead Vw
MANG/FISH BS16 47 F3
The Hedgerows ALMDB BS32 21 F1
Hedgers Cl BMSTR BS3 72 B4
Hedges Cl CLVDN BS21 64 B4
The Hedges MTN/WRL BS22 118 B5
Hedwick St EVILLE/WHL BS5 57 F4
Heggard Cl
BMSTRD/HC/WWD BS13 84 B4
Hellier Wk
BMSTRD/HC/WWD BS13 95 H1
Helston Rd NAIL BS48 67 H5
Helting Ct CBATH/BATHN BA1 3 F5
Hemmings Pde
EVILLE/WHL BS5 56 D4
Hemming Wy
OMX/HUT/LCK BS24 126 B3
Hemplow Cl HGRV/WHIT BS14 86 C2
Hempton La ALMDB BS32 10 C5
Henacre Rd AVONM BS11 29 F5
Henbury Gdns
HNBRY/STHM BS10 * 30 C3
Henbury Rd
HNBRY/STHM BS10 30 C3
HNLZ/SM/SNYPK/WT BS9 31 E5
KGWD/HNM BS15 75 G1
Henbury Road Henbury Hl
HNLZ/SM/SNYPK/WT BS9 30 D5
Hencliffe Rd HGRV/WHIT BS14 86 C3
Hencliffe Wy KGWD/HNM BS15 75 G3
Henderson Rd
KGWD/HNM BS15 75 G1
Hendre Rd BMSTR BS3 72 B4
Henfield Crs
OLD/WMLY/WICK BS30 77 E2
Henfield Rd FRCTL/WBN BS36 36 B2
Hengaston St BMSTR BS3 72 C4
Hengrove Av HGRV/WHIT BS14 86 A1
Hengrove La HGRV/WHIT BS14 86 A1
Hengrove Rd
BRSG/KWL/STAPK BS4 73 H4
Hengrove Wy
BMSTRD/HC/WWD BS13 84 C4
Henleaze Av
HNLZ/SM/SNYPK/WT BS9 45 E3
Henleaze Gdns
HNLZ/SM/SNYPK/WT BS9 45 E3
Henleaze Pk
HNLZ/SM/SNYPK/WT BS9 45 G3
Henleaze Park Dr
HNLZ/SM/SNYPK/WT BS9 45 G2
Henleaze Rd
HNLZ/SM/SNYPK/WT BS9 45 E3
Henleaze Ter
HNLZ/SM/SNYPK/WT BS9 45 F1
Henley Gv
HNLZ/SM/SNYPK/WT BS9 45 F3
Henley La YTN/CONG BS49 112 D4
Henley Ldg YTN/CONG BS49 112 D4
Henley Pk YTN/CONG BS49 112 C4
Hennessy Cl HGRV/WHIT BS14 96 B1
Henrietta Gdns BATHSE BA2 3 H2
Henrietta Ms BATHSE BA2 3 H3
Henrietta Pl BATHSE BA2 3 G3
Henrietta Rd BATHSE BA2 3 H2
Henrietta St BATHSE BA2 3 H3
CBRISNE BS2 55 G3
Henry St BMSTR BS3 73 G2
CBATH/BATHN BA1 3 G5
Henry Williamson Ct
OLD/WMLY/WICK BS30 76 D1
Henshaw Cl KGWD/HNM BS15 58 C1
Henshaw Rd KGWD/HNM BS15 58 C1
Henshaw Wk KGWD/HNM BS15 58 C1
Hensley Gdns BATHSE BA2 108 B3
Hensley Rd BATHSE BA2 108 B4
Hensman's Hl CFTN/FAIL BS8 55 E5
Hepburn Rd CBRIS/FH BS1 56 A3
Herald Cl
HNLZ/SM/SNYPK/WT BS9 44 B3
Herapath St EVILLE/WHL BS5 57 E5
Herbert Crs EVILLE/WHL BS5 47 F5
Herbert Rd BATHSE BA2 2 A7
CLVDN BS21 64 D1
Herbert St BMSTR BS3 72 D2
EVILLE/WHL BS5 57 E3
Hercules Cl BRSTK/PCHW BS34 21 F4
Hereford Rd CBRISNE BS2 56 C1
Hereford St BMSTR BS3 73 E3
Herkomer Cl HORF/LLZ BS7 46 D1
Herluin Wy WSM BS23 121 G5
Hermes Cl KEYN BS31 98 D2
Hermitage Cl AVONM BS11 43 E1
Hermitage Rd
CBATH/BATHN BA1 102 B3
MANG/FISH BS16 48 D3
Hern La NAIL BS48 82 B4
Heron Cl MTN/WRL BS22 122 B2
Heron Gdns PTSHD/EG BS20 40 A4
Heron Rd EVILLE/WHL BS5 56 D2
Heron Wk CLVDN BS21 63 F1
Heron Wy YATE/CS BS37 26 B3
Herridge Cl
BMSTRD/HC/WWD BS13 84 C5
Herridge Rd
BMSTRD/HC/WWD BS13 84 C5
Hersey Gdns
BMSTRD/HC/WWD BS13 94 D1
Hesding Cl KGWD/HNM BS15 75 H3
Hestercombe Cl
OMX/HUT/LCK BS24 122 B4
Hestercombe Rd
BMSTRD/HC/WWD BS13 84 C3
Hester Wd YATE/CS BS37 14 B3
Hewland Ct AVONM BS11 30 A3
Hewlands Ct AVONM BS11 * 30 A3
Heyford Av EVILLE/WHL BS5 46 D5
Heyron Wk
BMSTRD/HC/WWD BS13 84 C5
Heywood Rd PTSHD/EG BS20 42 C4
Heywood Ter PTSHD/EG BS20 42 C4
Hicking Ct KGWD/HNM BS15 58 D2
Hickory La ALMDB BS32 11 F2
Hicks Av MANG/FISH BS16 35 H5
Hicks' Barton EVILLE/WHL BS5 57 H3
Hicks Common Rd
FRCTL/WBN BS36 23 E4
Hicks Ct
OLD/WMLY/WICK BS30 * 76 C2
Hidcote Ms
OMX/HUT/LCK BS24 122 B4
Higham St
BRSG/KWL/STAPK BS4 73 G2
High Bannerdown
CBATH/BATHN BA1 91 G5
Highbury Pde WSM BS23 * 6 B1
Highbury Pl
CBATH/BATHN BA1 102 D3
Highbury Rd BMSTR BS3 72 D5
HORF/LLZ BS7 46 B1
WSM BS23 6 B1
Highbury Ter
CBATH/BATHN BA1 102 D3
Highbury Vls
CBATH/BATHN BA1 * 102 D3
CBRISNE BS2 4 C1
Highcroft
OLD/WMLY/WICK BS30 60 A5
Highdale Av CLVDN BS21 64 D2
Highdale Cl HGRV/WHIT BS14 86 A5
Highdale Rd CLVDN BS21 64 D2
High Elm KGWD/HNM BS15 59 E5
Highett Dr EVILLE/WHL BS5 56 C2
Highfield Av KGWD/HNM BS15 76 A1
Highfield Cl BATHSE BA2 107 G2
Highfield Dr PTSHD/EG BS20 38 C5
Highfield Gdns
OLD/WMLY/WICK BS30 77 F4
Highfield Gv HORF/LLZ BS7 45 H3
Highfield Rd KEYN BS31 98 A2
OMX/HUT/LCK BS24 125 F5
YATE/CS BS37 26 C1
Highfields Cl
BRSTK/PCHW BS34 33 H2
High Gv
HNLZ/SM/SNYPK/WT BS9 43 H1
Highgrove St
BRSG/KWL/STAPK BS4 73 H2
Highgrove Wk
OMX/HUT/LCK BS24 122 D3
High Kingsdown CBRISNE BS2 55 G3
Highland Cl MTN/WRL BS22 121 G1
Highland Crs CFTN/FAIL BS8 55 E1
Highland Pl CFTN/FAIL BS8 55 E1
Highland Rd BATHSE BA2 107 G2
Highlands La
OMX/HUT/LCK BS24 122 D3
Highland Sq CFTN/FAIL BS8 * 55 E1
Highlands Rd LGASH BS41 70 D4
PTSHD/EG BS20 39 F3
Highland Ter BATHSE BA2 2 A5
High La FRCTL/WBN BS36 22 C2
Highleaze Rd
OLD/WMLY/WICK BS30 77 F2
Highmead Gdns
BMSTRD/HC/WWD BS13 83 H5
Highmore Gdns HORF/LLZ BS7 47 E1
Highnam Cl BRSTK/PCHW BS34 20 D1
High Pk HGRV/WHIT BS14 74 A5
Highridge Crs
BMSTRD/HC/WWD BS13 84 A4
Highridge Gn
BMSTRD/HC/WWD BS13 83 H3
Highridge Pk
BMSTRD/HC/WWD BS13 84 A3
Highridge Rd BMSTR BS3 72 C4
BMSTRD/HC/WWD BS13 83 H4
LGASH BS41 94 B1
Highridge Wk
BMSTRD/HC/WWD BS13 83 H2
High St AVONM BS11 42 D1
BATHSE BA2 107 G1
BATHSE BA2 104 A3
BLAG/CWMG/WR BS40 93 G5
CBATH/BATHN BA1 104 A1
CBATH/BATHN BA1 101 G2
CBATH/BATHN BA1 3 G4
CBRIS/FH BS1 5 F3
CFTN/FAIL BS8 55 E1
EVILLE/WHL BS5 56 D2
FRCTL/WBN BS36 22 D4
HNLZ/SM/SNYPK/WT BS9 31 E5
KEYN BS31 99 F1
KEYN BS31 88 B3
KGWD/HNM BS15 75 H1
MANG/FISH BS16 48 C4
MTN/WRL BS22 122 B1
NAIL BS48 67 F4
OLD/WMLY/WICK BS30 89 H1
PTSHD/EG BS20 41 F5
PTSHD/EG BS20 39 H3
THNB/SVB BS35 8 C3
WSM BS23 6 D2
YATE/CS BS37 26 D1
YATE/CS BS37 12 B3
YTN/CONG BS49 112 B3
Highview BATHSE BA2 * 2 D7
High Vw PTSHD/EG BS20 39 E4
Highview Rd
KGWD/HNM BS15 59 E1
Highway YATE/CS BS37 14 B5
Highwood La
BRSTK/PCHW BS34 19 G3
Highworth Crs YATE/CS BS37 25 H2
Highworth Rd
BRSG/KWL/STAPK BS4 74 C1
Hildesheim Br WSM BS23 7 G5
Hildesheim Cl WSM BS23 7 H6

Hildesheim Ct WSM BS23....6 E5
Hill Av BATHSE BA2....110 D1
  BRSTP BS3....73 C3
Hillbrook Rd THNB/SVB BS35....9 E4
Hill Burn
  HNLZ/SM/SNYPK/WT BS9....45 G2
Hillburn Rd KGWD/HNM BS15....58 A3
Hill Cl MANG/FISH BS16....35 H5
Hill Crest
  BRSG/KWL/STAPK BS4....74 A5
Hillcrest THNB/SVB BS35....8 C3
Hillcrest Cl NAIL BS48....67 F5
Hillcrest Dr BATHSE BA2....107 C4
Hillcrest Rd NAIL BS48....67 F5
  PTSHD/EG BS20....38 C5
Hillcroft Cl KGWD/HNM BS15....76 B2
  MTN/WRL BS22....121 F1
Hilldale Rd NAIL BS48....80 A4
Hill Dr CFTN/FAIL BS8....69 H3
Hill End Dr HNBRY/STHM BS10....30 B2
Hillfields Av MANG/FISH BS16....48 C5
Hill Gay Cl PTSHD/EG BS20....38 C4
Hill Gv
  HNLZ/SM/SNYPK/WT BS9....45 G2
Hillgrove St CBRISNE BS2....55 H3
Hillgrove St North
  CBRISNE BS2....55 H3
Hill House Rd MANG/FISH BS16....49 F3
Hill Lawn
  BRSG/KWL/STAPK BS4....74 C3
Hill Moor CLVDN BS21....65 G3
Hill Pk YTN/CONG BS49....115 E1
Hill Rd CLVDN BS21....
  LGASH BS41....94 C2
  MTN/WRL BS22....122 B1
  WSM BS23....7 G2
Hill Rd East MTN/WRL BS22....122 C1
Hills Barton
  BMSTRD/HC/WWD BS13....72 B5
Hillsborough Rd
  BRSG/KWL/STAPK BS4....74 B2
Hillside Cl KEYN BS31....88 D4
Hillsdon Rd
  HNLZ/SM/SNYPK/WT BS9....30 D5
Hillside MANG/FISH BS16....49 F3
  PTSHD/EG BS20....41 F5
Hillside Av KGWD/HNM BS15....58 A3
Hillside Cl FRCTL/WBN BS36....24 A3
Hillside Gdns MTN/WRL BS22....121 G2
Hillside La FRCTL/WBN BS36....24 A3
Hillside Rd BATHSE BA2....108 A3
  CLVDN BS21....64 D2
  EVILLE/WHL BS5....58 A4
  LGASH BS41....71 E4
  NAIL BS48....79 H4
  PTSHD/EG BS20....38 B4
Hillside St
  BRSG/KWL/STAPK BS4....73 H2
Hillside West
  OMX/HUT/LCK BS24....126 C3
Hill St BMSTR BS3....73 C2
  CBRIS/FH BS1....4 E3
  EVILLE/WHL BS5....57 H3
  KGWD/HNM BS15....59 F3
The Hill ALMDB BS32....
Hill Top PTSHD/EG BS20....39 E4
Hilltop Gdns EVILLE/WHL BS5....58 A4
Hilltop Rd MANG/FISH BS16....58 D1
Hilltop Vw CFTN/FAIL BS8....58 A4
Hillview
  HNLZ/SM/SNYPK/WT BS9....45 G2
Hillview Av CLVDN BS21....64 D3
Hill View Cl
  OLD/WMLY/WICK BS30....77 F2
Hillview Gdns
  BLAG/CWMG/WR BS40....92 D4
Hillview Park Homes
  BLAG/CWMG/WR BS40 *....92 C3
  MTN/WRL BS22 *....122 A3
Hill View Rd
  BMSTRD/HC/WWD BS13....84 B2
  CBATH/BATHN BA1....103 E3
  MANG/FISH BS16....51 G3
  WSM BS23....7 K4
Hillyfield Rd
  BMSTRD/HC/WWD BS13....84 B3
Hinckley Cl MTN/WRL BS22....118 B5
Hinton Cl KEYN BS31....99 F1
Hinton Dr
  OLD/WMLY/WICK BS30....60 A5
Hinton La CFTN/FAIL BS8 *....54 C7
Hinton Rd EVILLE/WHL BS5....57 E2
  MANG/FISH BS16....48 A4
Hiscocks Dr BATHSE BA2....108 B3
Hither Bath Br
  BRSG/KWL/STAPK BS4....74 B5
Hither Gn CLVDN BS21....65 F3
Hither Md FRCTL/WBN BS36....23 H4
Hobart Rd WSM BS23....125 C5
Hobbiton Rd MTN/WRL BS22....117 H5
Hobbs La NAIL BS48....82 B5
  OLD/WMLY/WICK BS30....
Hobb's La CBRIS/FH BS1 *....4 D4
Hobhouse Cl
  HNLZ/SM/SNYPK/WT BS9....45 E1
Hodwell La LGASH BS41....71 F4
Hockeys La MANG/FISH BS16....47 H5
Hodders La MTN/WRL BS22....118 C2
Hoddon La MANG/FISH BS16....51 C3
Hodshill CBATH/BATHN BA2....110 D4
Hogarth Wk HORF/LLZ BS7....46 D1
Hogues Wk
  BMSTRD/HC/WWD BS13....84 C5
Holbeach Wy
  HGRV/WHIT BS14....96 D1
Holbrook Crs
  BMSTRD/HC/WWD BS13....85 E5
Holbrook La
  OLD/WMLY/WICK BS30....61 G4
Holcombe Cl BATHSE BA2....104 A3
Holcombe Gn
  CBATH/BATHN BA1....101 G2
Holcombe Gv KEYN BS31....88 A4
Holcombe La BATHSE BA2....104 A3
Holcombe Ter
  CBATH/BATHN BA1 *....101 G2
Holcombe V BATHSE BA2....104 A3
Holdenhurst Rd
  KGWD/HNM BS15....58 C2

Holders Wk LGASH BS41....70 C5
Holford Ct NAIL BS48....67 F5
Holford Ct HGRV/WHIT BS14....86 A4
Holland Rd
  CBATH/BATHN BA1....103 E5
  CLVDN BS21....64 B4
Holland St WSM BS23....7 J5
Hollidge Gdns BMSTR BS3....72 D2
Hollies La CBATH/BATHN BA1....91 F3
Hollis Av PTSHD/EG BS20....39 C5
Hollis Cl LGASH BS41....82 D1
Hollis Crs PTSHD/EG BS20....39 G5
Hollister's Dr
  BMSTRD/HC/WWD BS13....96 A1
Holloway BATHSE BA2....3 F7
Hollow La MTN/WRL BS22....117 C5
Holloway Rd CBRISNE BS2....86 A5
Hollowmead Cl
  YTN/CONG BS49....113 F3
Hollowmead
  YTN/CONG BS49....113 F3
Hollow Rd ALMDB BS32....10 C3
  KGWD/HNM BS15....59 E3
The Hollows FRCTL/WBN BS36....36 A3
The Hollow BATHSE BA2....107 F3
Hollway Cl HGRV/WHIT BS14....86 D4
Hollway Rd HGRV/WHIT BS14....86 D4
Hollybrook Trading Est
  EVILLE/WHL BS5....58 B1
Hollybush La
  HNLZ/SM/SNYPK/WT BS9....44 C3
Holly Cl EVILLE/WHL BS5....58 A1
  MANG/FISH BS16....51 C3
  MTN/WRL BS22....122 D2
  NAIL BS48....67 H3
Holly Crs KGWD/HNM BS15....59 E3
Holly Dr BATHSE BA2....110 B2
Holly Gn KGWD/HNM BS15....59 G2
Holly Gv MANG/FISH BS16....48 C5
Hollyguest Rd
  KGWD/HNM BS15....59 E5
Holly Hl YATE/CS BS37....12 C4
Holly Hill Rd KGWD/HNM BS15....59 F3
Holly La CLVDN BS21....62 D4
Hollyleigh Av
  BRSTK/PCHW BS34....32 B3
Holly Lodge Cl EVILLE/WHL BS5....58 A1
Holly Lodge Rd
  EVILLE/WHL BS5....57 H1
Hollyman Wk CLVDN BS21....65 F2
Hollymead La
  HNLZ/SM/SNYPK/WT BS9....44 C4
Holly Rdg PTSHD/EG BS20....39 E3
Hollywood La THNB/SVB BS35....18 D2
Hollywood Rd
  BRSG/KWL/STAPK BS4....74 C3
Holmdale Rd
  BRSTK/PCHW BS34....32 D2
Holmesdale Rd BMSTR BS3....73 F3
Holmes Gv
  HNLZ/SM/SNYPK/WT BS9....45 F3
Holmes Hill Rd
  EVILLE/WHL BS5....57 H3
Holmes St EVILLE/WHL BS5....56 D5
Holmoak Rd KEYN BS31....87 H5
Holm Rd OMX/HUT/LCK BS24....126 B4
Holms Rd WSM BS23....7 J6
Holmwood KGWD/HNM BS15....75 H1
Holmwood Cl FRCTL/WBN BS36....22 D4
Holmwood Gdns
  HNLZ/SM/SNYPK/WT BS9....31 E5
Holsom Cl HGRV/WHIT BS14....86 D3
Holsom Rd HGRV/WHIT BS14....87 E3
Holst Gdns
  BRSG/KWL/STAPK BS4....84 D2
Holton Rd HORF/LLZ BS7....46 C2
Holtsdown La
  CBATH/BATHN BA1....90 D1
Holyrood Cl BRSTK/PCHW BS34....33 F1
Holy Well Cl
  BRSG/KWL/STAPK BS4....57 G5
Homeapple Hl
  OLD/WMLY/WICK BS30....60 C4
Home Cl HNBRY/STHM BS10....32 A3
Home Farm Rd CFTN/FAIL BS8....53 C3
Home Farm Wy
  THNB/SVB BS35....19 E1
Homefield
  OMX/HUT/LCK BS24....126 C1
  THNB/SVB BS35....9 E4
  YATE/CS BS37....14 A4
  YTN/CONG BS49....114 D3
Homefield Cl KEYN BS31....99 F1
Home Field Cl
  MANG/FISH BS16....49 H2
Homefield Rd KEYN BS31....99 F1
  MANG/FISH BS16....51 F3
Home Gnd AVONM BS11....42 D1
Homeground CLVDN BS21....65 E5
Home Gnd
  HNLZ/SM/SNYPK/WT BS9....45 F1
Homeground MANG/FISH BS16....49 H1
Homelea Pk East
  CBATH/BATHN BA1....101 F5
Homelea Pk West
  CBATH/BATHN BA1....101 F5
Homeleaze Rd
  HNBRY/STHM BS10....31 H2
Home Md
  BRSG/KWL/STAPK BS4 *....85 F2
  OLD/WMLY/WICK BS30....76 D2
Homemead Dr
  BRSG/KWL/STAPK BS4....74 C5
Home Orch YATE/CS BS37....13 H5
Homestead PTSHD/EG BS20....38 C5
Homestead Cl
  FRCTL/WBN BS36....24 B3
Homestead Gdns
  MANG/FISH BS16....34 B4
The Homestead CLVDN BS21....64 C2
  KEYN BS31....98 A2
Honey Garston Cl
  BMSTRD/HC/WWD BS13....84 C5
Honey Garston Rd
  BMSTRD/HC/WWD BS13....84 C5
Honey Hill Rd
  KGWD/HNM BS15....59 F3
Honeylands PTSHD/EG BS20....39 G5
Honeymead HGRV/WHIT BS14....86 B3
Honeysuckle Cl ALMDB BS32....11 G5

Honey Suckle La
  MANG/FISH BS16....47 G4
Honeysuckle Pl
  OMX/HUT/LCK BS24....122 D2
Honeywick Cl BMSTR BS3....72 D4
Honeywicke Cl BMSTR BS3....72 D4
Honiton Rd CLVDN BS21....65 E4
  MANG/FISH BS16....48 A5
Hooper Rd HGRV/WHIT BS14....86 C4
Hoover's La YATE/CS BS37....12 A4
Hopechapel Hl CFTN/FAIL BS8....54 D5
Hope Rd BMSTR BS3....13 E5
  YATE/CS BS37....13 E5
Hope Sq CFTN/FAIL BS8....54 D5
Hopetoun Rd CBRISNE BS2....46 B5
Hopewell Gdns AVONM BS11....43 F1
Hopkin Cl THNB/SVB BS35....9 E5
Hopkins St WSM BS23....6 E5
Hopland Cl
  OLD/WMLY/WICK BS30....77 E3
Hopp's Rd KGWD/HNM BS15....58 D4
Horesham Cv
  BMSTRD/HC/WWD BS15....84 D4
Horfield Common
  HORF/LLZ BS7....46 A1
Horfield Rd CBRISNE BS2....4 E2
Horley Rd CBRISNE BS2....56 C2
Horsecastle Cl
  YTN/CONG BS49....112 A2
Horsecombe Brow
  BATHSE BA2....111 E1
Horsecombe Gv BATHSE BA2....111 E1
Horsecombe V BATHSE BA2....111 E1
Horsecroft Gdns
  OLD/WMLY/WICK BS30....59 C5
The Horsefair CBRIS/FH BS1....5 G2
Horsepool Rd
  BMSTRD/HC/WWD BS13....83 H5
Horse Race La CFTN/FAIL BS8....52 A4
Horseshoe Dr
  HNLZ/SM/SNYPK/WT BS9....44 A4
Horseshoe La YATE/CS BS37....26 D1
Horseshoe Wk BATHSE BA2....3 K6
Horse St YATE/CS BS37....27 E3
Horstmann Cl
  CBATH/BATHN BA1....101 C5
Hortham La ALMDB BS32....15 E1
Horton St CBRISNE BS2....5 K4
Horwood Cl
  OLD/WMLY/WICK BS30....76 D2
Horwood Rd NAIL BS48....79 H4
Hosey Wk
  BMSTRD/HC/WWD BS13....84 B4
Host St CBRIS/FH BS1....4 E3
Hottom Gdns HORF/LLZ BS7....46 C1
Hot Water La KGWD/HNM BS15....49 F5
Hotwell Rd CFTN/FAIL BS8....54 D5
Houlton St CBRISNE BS2....5 J1
Hounds Rd YATE/CS BS37....26 D2
Howard Av EVILLE/WHL BS5....57 C3
Howard Cl KEYN BS31....98 D1
Howard Rd BMSTR BS3....73 E4
  MANG/FISH BS16....48 D4
  RDLND/MONT BS6....45 F4
  THNB/SVB BS35....8 C2
Howard St EVILLE/WHL BS5....57 C2
Howard Wk
  OLD/WMLY/WICK BS30....60 B5
Howecroft Gdns
  HNLZ/SM/SNYPK/WT BS9....44 C4
Howells Md MANG/FISH BS16....49 H1
Howes Cl
  OLD/WMLY/WICK BS30....59 C5
Howett Rd EVILLE/WHL BS5....57 F1
How Hl BATHSE BA2....107 F1
Howitt Wy
  OMX/HUT/LCK BS24....122 C4
Howsmoor La
  MANG/FISH BS16....35 H5
Hoylake Dr
  OLD/WMLY/WICK BS30....59 H5
Huckford La FRCTL/WBN BS36....35 C5
Huckford Rd FRCTL/WBN BS36....23 E5
Huckley Wy ALMDB BS32....21 H4
Hudd's Hill Rd EVILLE/WHL BS5....57 H3
Hudd's Vale Rd
  EVILLE/WHL BS5....57 H3
Hudson Cl YATE/CS BS37....26 B2
Hughenden Rd CFTN/FAIL BS8....54 A3
  HORF/LLZ BS7....46 A3
Hughes Gdns HORF/LLZ BS7....32 C5
Hulbert Cl
  BRSG/KWL/STAPK BS4....75 F4
Hulse Rd BRSG/KWL/STAPK BS4....74 C5
Humberstan Wk AVONM BS11....29 E5
Humber Wy AVONM BS11....16 D5
Humphrys Barton
  BRSG/KWL/STAPK BS4....75 E1
Hungerford Cl
  BRSG/KWL/STAPK BS4....86 D1
Hungerford Crs
  BRSG/KWL/STAPK BS4....86 D1
Hungerford Gdns
  BRSG/KWL/STAPK BS4....86 D1
Hungerford Rd
  BRSG/KWL/STAPK BS4....74 D5
  CBATH/BATHN BA1....86 D1
Hungerford Wk
  BRSG/KWL/STAPK BS4....74 D5
Hung Rd AVONM BS11....43 E2
Hunters Cl KGWD/HNM BS15....75 F1
Hunters Rd KGWD/HNM BS15....59 F2
Hunters Rd East
  KGWD/HNM BS15....75 H1
Hunter's Wy
  BRSTK/PCHW BS34....32 D2
Huntingham Rd
  BMSTRD/HC/WWD BS13....83 H5
Huntley Gv NAIL BS48....67 H5
Hunts Ground Rd
  BRSTK/PCHW BS34....33 G3
Hunts La YTN/CONG BS49....113 E3
Hurle Crs CFTN/FAIL BS8....55 H3
Hurle Rd CFTN/FAIL BS8....55 H3
Hurlingham Rd HORF/LLZ BS7....56 B1
Hurn La KEYN BS31....88 C5

Hurn Rd CLVDN BS21....65 E3
Hursley Hl PLTN/PENS BS39....97 C5
Hursley La HGRV/WHIT BS14....97 H3
Hurston Rd
  BRSG/KWL/STAPK BS4....85 E1
Hurst Rd BRSG/KWL/STAPK BS4....85 E1
  WSM BS23....7 J6
Hurst Wk
  BRSG/KWL/STAPK BS4....85 F1
Hurstwood Rd
  MANG/FISH BS16....48 D3
Hutton Cl
  HNLZ/SM/SNYPK/WT BS9....44 B1
  KEYN BS31....98 B2
Hutton Hl OMX/HUT/LCK BS24....126 B4
Hutton Moor La
  MTN/WRL BS22....121 H4
  OMX/HUT/LCK BS24....125 H1
Hutton Moor Rd
  MTN/WRL BS22....121 G4
Hutton Pk
  OMX/HUT/LCK BS24 *....121 H5
Hyde Av THNB/SVB BS35....8 C1
Hyde Rd THNB/SVB BS35....64 C5
Hyland Gv
  HNLZ/SM/SNYPK/WT BS9....30 D5

I

Ida Rd EVILLE/WHL BS5....57 E3
Iddesleigh Rd
  RDLND/MONT BS6....45 F5
Idstone Rd MANG/FISH BS16....48 B4
Iford Cl KEYN BS31....99 F1
Ilchester Crs
  BMSTRD/HC/WWD BS13....72 C5
Ilchester Rd
  BMSTRD/HC/WWD BS13....84 C1
Iles Cl KGWD/HNM BS15....76 A2
Ilex Av CLVDN BS21....65 E2
Ilex Cl BMSTRD/HC/WWD BS13....84 A3
Ilminster Av
  BRSG/KWL/STAPK BS4....85 H1
Ilminster Cl CLVDN BS21....65 E4
  NAIL BS48....79 E1
Ilsyn Gv HGRV/WHIT BS14....86 C2
Imber Court Cl
  HGRV/WHIT BS14....86 A1
Imperial Pk
  BMSTRD/HC/WWD BS13 *....84 D3
Imperial Rd CFTN/FAIL BS8....55 F2
  HGRV/WHIT BS14....86 B1
Imperial Wk HGRV/WHIT BS14....74 A5
The Inclosures
  OMX/HUT/LCK BS24....122 C3
Ingleside Rd KGWD/HNM BS15....58 C2
Ingleton Dr MTN/WRL BS22....117 H4
Ingmire Rd EVILLE/WHL BS5....46 D5
Inkerman Cl HORF/LLZ BS7....46 A1
Innox Gdns
  BMSTRD/HC/WWD BS13....84 B4
Innox Gv BATHSE BA2....107 E5
Innox La CBATH/BATHN BA1....90 A4
Innox Rd BATHSE BA2....107 C2
Inns Court Av
  BRSG/KWL/STAPK BS4....85 E2
Inns Court Dr
  BRSG/KWL/STAPK BS4....85 E2
Inns Court Gn
  BRSG/KWL/STAPK BS4....85 E2
Instow Rd
  BRSG/KWL/STAPK BS4....85 F1
Instow Wk
  BRSG/KWL/STAPK BS4....85 F1
Inverness Rd BATHSE BA2....107 H1
Ipswich Dr
  BRSG/KWL/STAPK BS4....57 C5
Irby Rd BMSTR BS3....72 B3
Irena Rd MANG/FISH BS16....47 H5
Ireton Rd BMSTR BS3....72 C2
Iron Acton Wy YATE/CS BS37....25 H5
Ironchurch Rd AVONM BS11....16 B5
Ironmould La KEYN BS31....75 F5
Irving Cl CLVDN BS21....65 F2
Irving Rd MANG/FISH BS16....49 E4
I.s.f. Rd AVONM BS11....28 C2
Island Trade Pk AVONM BS11 *....28 C4
Isleys Ct
  OLD/WMLY/WICK BS30....76 C3
Islington Rd BMSTR BS3....72 C2
Ison Hill Rd
  HNBRY/STHM BS10....30 B2
Ivo Peters Rd BATHSE BA2....2 D5
Ivor Rd EVILLE/WHL BS5....57 E3
Ivor Ter PTSHD/EG BS20 *....39 G4
Ivy Av BATHSE BA2....107 H3
Ivy Bank Pk BATHSE BA2....108 C5
Ivy Ct PTSHD/EG BS20....38 D3
Ivy Gv BATHSE BA2....107 H3
Ivy La MANG/FISH BS16....48 A5
  OMX/HUT/LCK BS24....122 D5
Ivy Pl BATHSE BA2....107 H3
Ivy Wk BNWL BS29....127 H2
Ivywell Rd
  HNLZ/SM/SNYPK/WT BS9....44 C5
Iwood La
  BLAG/CWMG/WR BS40....115 C5

J

Jack Price Cl
  BMSTRD/HC/WWD BS13....95 H1
Jacob Pl CBRIS/FH BS1....5 F6
Jacobs Meadow
  PTSHD/EG BS20....40 B4
Jacob St CBRISNE BS2....5 H3
Jacob's Well Rd CFTN/FAIL BS8....4 A4
Jamaica St CBRISNE BS2....55 H3
James PI MANG/FISH BS16....49 E4
James PI CFTN/FAIL BS8 *....54 D4
James Rd MANG/FISH BS16....49 E4
James St CBRISNE BS2....56 C1
  EVILLE/WHL BS5....5 K1

James St West
  CBATH/BATHN BA1....2 D4
Jane St EVILLE/WHL BS5....56 C4
Jarretts Rd HNBRY/STHM BS10....31 H3
Jarvis St EVILLE/WHL BS5....56 D5
Jasmine Cl MTN/WRL BS22....122 D2
Jasmine Gv AVONM BS11....30 A3
Jasmine La YTN/CONG BS49....113 F1
Jasmine Wy
  OMX/HUT/LCK BS24....122 D2
Jasper St BMSTR BS3....72 C3
Jean Rd BRSG/KWL/STAPK BS4....74 D4
Jefferies Hill Bottom
  KGWD/HNM BS15....75 G1
Jeffery Ct
  OLD/WMLY/WICK BS30....59 H5
Jekyll Cl MANG/FISH BS16....47 C1
Jellicoe Av MANG/FISH BS16....33 C5
Jellicoe Ct MTN/WRL BS22....117 F4
Jena Ct KEYN BS31....99 E1
Jenner Ct YATE/CS BS37....27 F2
Jenny La HNBRY/STHM BS10....31 H3
Jersey Av
  BRSG/KWL/STAPK BS4....75 E2
Jesmond Rd CLVDN BS21....64 C2
  MTN/WRL BS22....118 B4
Jesse Hughes Ct
  CBATH/BATHN BA1....103 F2
Jessop Crs HNBRY/STHM BS10....31 E4
Jessop Under/pass BMSTR BS3....72 A2
Jews La BATHSE BA2....107 H1
Jinty La KGWD/HNM BS15....59 H1
Jobbins Cl YATE/CS BS37....26 C2
Jocelin Dr MTN/WRL BS22....117 C4
Jocelyn Rd HORF/LLZ BS7....46 B1
Jockey La EVILLE/WHL BS5....58 A4
John Carr's Ter CFTN/FAIL BS8....4 A4
Johnson Dr
  OLD/WMLY/WICK BS30....76 C1
Johnson Rd MANG/FISH BS16....50 A3
Johnsons La EVILLE/WHL BS5....57 F2
Johnsons Rd EVILLE/WHL BS5....57 F3
Johnstone St BATHSE BA2....3 H4
John St CBATH/BATHN BA1....3 F3
  CBRIS/FH BS1....5 F3
  CBRISNE BS2....56 C1
  KGWD/HNM BS15....58 C3
John Wesley Rd
  EVILLE/WHL BS5....58 B5
Jordan Wk ALMDB BS32....21 F2
Joyce Cl HORF/LLZ BS7....32 C5
Joy Hl CFTN/FAIL BS8 *....54 D5
Jubilee Crs MANG/FISH BS16....49 C2
Jubilee Gdns YATE/CS BS37....14 C5
  THNB/SVB BS35....9 E3
Jubilee PI CLVDN BS21....64 D4
  KGWD/HNM BS15....59 F4
Jubilee Rd
  BRSG/KWL/STAPK BS4....74 B5
  CBRISNE BS2....56 C2
  EVILLE/WHL BS5....49 E5
  WSM BS23....7 F4
Jubilee St CBRISNE BS2....5 H4
Jubilee Wy AVONM BS11....28 B3
  MTN/WRL BS22....118 B5
  THNB/SVB BS35....8 A5
  YATE/CS BS37....14 B2
Julian Cl
  HNLZ/SM/SNYPK/WT BS9....44 B5
Julian Rd CBATH/BATHN BA1....2 E1
  HNLZ/SM/SNYPK/WT BS9....44 C5
Julian Road Crescent La
  CBATH/BATHN BA1....2 D1
Julius Cl MANG/FISH BS16....50 A2
Julius Rd HORF/LLZ BS7....45 H5
Junction Av BATHSE BA2....2 C7
Junction Cut AVONM BS11....28 A4
Junction Rd BATHSE BA2....2 C7
  BRSG/KWL/STAPK BS4....74 B2
Junction Wy KGWD/HNM BS15....49 C5
Juniper Ct EVILLE/WHL BS5....57 E1
Juniper PI MTN/WRL BS22....117 C4
Juniper Wy ALMDB BS32....21 H3
Jupiter Rd BRSTK/PCHW BS34....19 H5
Justice Av KEYN BS31....99 F1
Justice Rd MANG/FISH BS16....47 H5
Jutland Rd AVONM BS11....28 B4

K

Karen Cl NAIL BS48....79 H3
Karen Dr NAIL BS48....79 H4
Kathdene Gdns HORF/LLZ BS7....46 B5
Kaynton Md
  CBATH/BATHN BA1....101 G5
Keats Ct HORF/LLZ BS7....32 C5
Keble Av
  BMSTRD/HC/WWD BS13....84 A4
Keeds La LGASH BS41....70 C5
Keedwell Hl LGASH BS41....70 C5
Keel Cl EVILLE/WHL BS5....57 H5
Keep Av OLD/WMLY/WICK BS30....64 B5
Keepers La HORF/LLZ BS7....45 F3
The Keep MTN/WRL BS22....117 H5
  OLD/WMLY/WICK BS30....77 H2
Keinton Wk
  HNBRY/STHM BS10....31 E3
Kelbra Crs FRCTL/WBN BS36....23 H4
Kellaway Av HORF/LLZ BS7....46 A2
  RDLND/MONT BS6....45 H3
Kellaway Crs
  HNLZ/SM/SNYPK/WT BS9....45 H2
Kellways NAIL BS48....79 C5
Kelso Pl CBATH/BATHN BA1 *....2 A3
Kelston Cl KEYN BS31....99 E1
  YATE/CS BS37....25 H3
Kelston Gdns
  HNBRY/STHM BS10....31 H5
Kelston Gv KGWD/HNM BS15....59 E5
Kelston Rd CBATH/BATHN BA1....100 D3
  HNBRY/STHM BS10....31 H5
  KEYN BS31....88 A5
  MTN/WRL BS22....118 A4
Kelston Vw BATHSE BA2....107 F2
Kelston Wk MANG/FISH BS16....48 C4
Kelting Gv CLVDN BS21....65 F3

Kemble Cl KGWD/HNM BS15 ...... 59 E5
 NAIL BS48.............................. 67 H5
Kemperleye Wy ALMDB BS22 ...... 21 F5
Kempe's Cl LGASH BS41............... 70 D4
Kempe Wy
 OMX/HUT/LCK BS24 .... 122 B4
Kempthorne La BATHSE BA2 .... 110 C1
Kempton Cl THNB/SVB BS35 .... 8 C1
Kencot Wk
 BMSTRD/HC/WWD BS13.......... 95 G1
Kendall Gdns MANG/FISH BS16.... 48 D4
Kendall Rd MANG/FISH BS16........ 48 D4
Kendon Av HORF/LLZ BS7............. 46 C1
Kendon Dr HNBRY/STHM BS10.... 45 H1
Kendon Wy
 HNBRY/STHM BS10................... 31 H5
Kenilworth Cl CLVDN BS21............ 26 B2
Kenilworth Cl KEYN BS31.............. 88 A5
Kenilworth Ct
 CBATH/BATHN BA1 *............. 102 D4
Kenilworth Dr
 OLD/WMLY/WICK BS30 .... 77 E5
Kenilworth Rd
 RDLND/MONT BS6 .... 55 G2
Kenmare Rd
 BRSG/KWL/STAPK BS4.............. 73 F5
Kenmore Crs HORF/LLZ BS7 .... 32 A4
Kenmore Dr HORF/LLZ BS7............ 32 A4
Kenmore Gv HORF/LLZ BS7 .... 32 A4
Kennard Ri KGWD/HNM BS15....... 58 C5
Kennard Rd KGWD/HNM BS15...... 58 C3
Kennaway Rd CLVDN BS21............ 64 D3
Kennel Cl WSM BS23.................... 125 F1
Kennedy Wy YATE/CS BS37........... 26 A1
Kennel Lodge Rd LGASH BS41...... 71 H2
Kenneth Rd
 BRSG/KWL/STAPK BS4.............. 74 C4
Kennet Pk BATHSE BA2................ 103 H5
Kennet Rd KEYN BS31.................. 88 C5
Kennet Wy THNB/SVB BS35 .... 9 E4
Kennington Av HORF/LLZ BS7 ...... 46 A4
 KGWD/HNM BS15.................... 58 D2
Kennington Rd
 CBATH/BATHN BA1 .... 101 G5
Kennion Rd EVILLE/WHL BS5........ 58 A4
Kennmoor Cl
 OLD/WMLY/WICK BS30 .... 59 G5
Kenn Moor Dr CLVDN BS21.......... 65 E4
Kenn Moor Rd
 YTN/CONG BS49...................... 112 B2
Kenn Rd CLVDN BS21................... 64 D4
 EVILLE/WHL BS5...................... 58 A4
Kensal Av BMSTR BS3.................. 73 F3
Kensal Rd BMSTR BS3.................. 73 F3
Kensington Cl THNB/SVB BS35...... 8 C2
Kensington Ct
 CBATH/BATHN BA1 .... 103 E3
Kensington Gdns
 CBATH/BATHN BA1 .... 103 E3
Kensington Pk
 EVILLE/WHL BS5...................... 56 C2
Kensington Park Rd
 BRSG/KWL/STAPK BS4.............. 74 B4
Kensington Pl
 CBATH/BATHN BA1 .... 103 E3
 CFTN/FAIL BS8......................... 55 E4
Kensington Rd
 EVILLE/WHL BS5...................... 58 A3
 RDLND/MONT BS6 .... 55 G2
 YATE/CS BS37.......................... 125 E1
Kent Av YATE/CS BS37.................. 14 B4
Kent Cl BRSTK/PCHW BS34........... 33 F1
Kenton Ms
 HNLZ/SM/SNYPK/WT BS9 .... 45 G3
Kent Rd HORF/LLZ BS7................. 46 A5
 YTN/CONG BS49...................... 114 D1
Kents Gn KGWD/HNM BS15......... 59 E3
Kent St BMSTR BS3...................... 72 D3
Kent Wy MTN/WRL BS22.............. 118 A4
Kenwood Cl KGWD/HNM BS15..... 59 F2
Keppel Cl KEYN BS31.................... 99 G2
Kerry Rd BRSG/KWL/STAPK BS4.... 73 F5
Kersteman Rd
 RDLND/MONT BS6 .... 45 H5
Kestrel Cl BRSTK/PCHW BS34....... 20 A2
 THNB/SVB BS35......................... 9 E2
Kestrel Dr MANG/FISH BS16......... 51 C4
 MTN/WRL BS22....................... 122 B2
Keswick Wk
 HNBRY/STHM BS10................... 31 G3
Ketch Rd BMSTR BS3................... 73 G3
Kew Rd WSM BS23.......................... 6 E1
Kewside MTN/WRL BS22............. 116 C4
Kewstoke Rd BATHSE BA2........... 108 D5
 HNLZ/SM/SNYPK/WT BS9 .... 44 C4
 MTN/WRL BS22....................... 116 C5
 WSM BS23.............................. 120 C1
Kew Wk
 BRSG/KWL/STAPK BS4.............. 86 B1
Keyes Pth MTN/WRL BS22........... 117 G4
Keynsham By-Pass KEYN BS31...... 88 B2
Keynsham Rd KEYN BS31.............. 97 F5
 OLD/WMLY/WICK BS30 .... 77 E5
Keys Av HORF/LLZ BS7................. 46 B1
Kielder Dr MTN/WRL BS22.......... 117 G5
Kilbirnie Rd HGRV/WHIT BS14...... 96 D1
Kildare Rd
 BRSG/KWL/STAPK BS4.............. 73 E5
Kilkenny La BATHSE BA2.............. 110 A2
Kilkenny Pl PTSHD/EG BS20......... 39 G2
Kilkenny St CBRISNE BS2................. 5 K4
Kilmersdon Rd
 BMSTRD/HC/WWD BS13.......... 84 C5
Kilminster Cl AVONM BS11............ 42 D1
Kiln Cl KGWD/HNM BS15............. 58 B2
Kilnhurst Cl
 OLD/WMLY/WICK BS30 .... 76 C4
Kilvert Cl
 BRSG/KWL/STAPK BS4.............. 74 C1
Kimberley Av MANG/FISH BS16.... 48 C3
Kimberley Cl MANG/FISH BS16..... 49 F1
Kimberley Crs
 MANG/FISH BS16..................... 48 C3
Kimberley Rd CLVDN BS21........... 64 C3
 KGWD/HNM BS15.................... 58 D2
 MANG/FISH BS16..................... 48 C3
Kinber Cl CBATH/BATHN BA1 ..... 101 F1

King Edward Cl
 HGRV/WHIT BS14....................... 85 H3
King Edward Rd BATHSE BA2......... 2 B7
Kingfisher Cl ALMDB BS32............ 11 G5
 THNB/SVB BS35......................... 9 E2
Kingfisher Dr MANG/FISH BS16.... 47 G2
Kingfisher Rd MTN/WRL BS22 .... 122 C3
 PTSHD/EG BS20........................ 40 C2
 YATE/CS BS37............................ 26 C2
King George's Rd
 BATHSE BA2........................... 107 H1
 BMSTRD/HC/WWD BS13.......... 84 A4
King John's Rd
 KGWD/HNM BS15.................... 58 B1
King Rd BRSG/KWL/STAPK BS4 .... 74 A5
King Road Av AVONM BS11........... 28 A3
Kingrove Crs YATE/CS BS37........... 27 E2
Kingrove La YATE/CS BS37............ 27 E3
Kings Av KGWD/HNM BS15.......... 75 G2
King's Av RDLND/MONT BS6......... 45 G4
Kingscote YATE/CS BS37............... 25 H4
Kingscote Pk EVILLE/WHL BS5...... 58 B5
Kingscourt Cl HGRV/WHIT BS14.... 85 H4
Kings Ct LGASH BS41.................... 70 B5
Kingsdown Av
 CBATH/BATHN BA1 .... 102 D2
Kingsdown Gv COR/BOX SN13... 105 G2
Kingsdown Pde
 RDLND/MONT BS6 .... 4 E1
Kingsdown Vw
 CBATH/BATHN BA1 .... 102 D2
Kings Dr BRSTK/PCHW BS34........ 34 A1
 KGWD/HNM BS15.................... 75 G2
King's Dr HORF/LLZ BS7............... 45 H4
Kingsfield BATHSE BA2.............. 107 H4
Kingsfield La KGWD/HNM BS15.... 59 E5
 OLD/WMLY/WICK BS30 .... 76 B2
King's Head La
 BMSTRD/HC/WWD BS13.......... 83 H2
Kingshill NAIL BS48.................... 66 D4
Kingshill Rd
 BRSG/KWL/STAPK BS4.............. 74 A5
Kingsholme Rd
 KGWD/HNM BS15.................... 58 D2
Kingsholm Rd
 HNBRY/STHM BS10................... 31 H5
Kingsland Rd CBRISNE BS2........... 56 C5
Kings La CLVDN BS21................... 62 B5
 RDLND/MONT BS6 .... 5 G1
Kingsleigh Ct KGWD/HNM BS15... 59 F4
Kingsleigh Gdns
 KGWD/HNM BS15.................... 59 F4
Kingsley Rd CLVDN BS21.............. 64 D3
 EVILLE/WHL BS5...................... 57 E2
 RDLND/MONT BS6 .... 55 H1
 WSM BS23.............................. 125 E3
Kingsmead NAIL BS48.................. 66 D4
Kingsmead North
 CBATH/BATHN BA1 .... 2 E5
Kingsmead Rd
 EVILLE/WHL BS5...................... 58 A2
Kingsmead Sq
 CBATH/BATHN BA1 *................ 3 F5
Kingsmead St
 CBATH/BATHN BA1 .... 3 F4
Kingsmead Wk
 EVILLE/WHL BS5...................... 58 A2
Kingsmead West
 CBATH/BATHN BA1 .... 2 E5
Kingsmill
 HNLZ/SM/SNYPK/WT BS9 .... 44 B3
King's Parade Av
 CFTN/FAIL BS8......................... 55 E2
King's Parade Ms
 CFTN/FAIL BS8......................... 55 E2
Kings Park Av CBRISNE BS2.......... 57 E5
King Sq CBRISNE BS2................... 55 H3
King Square Av CBRISNE BS2....... 55 H3
King's Rd
 BRSG/KWL/STAPK BS4.............. 74 B3
 CFTN/FAIL BS8......................... 55 E4
 CLVDN BS21............................ 62 B5
 PTSHD/EG BS20........................ 38 D4
Kings Sq
 OLD/WMLY/WICK BS30 .... 89 G1
Kingston Av CLVDN BS21............. 64 D5
 KEYN BS31.............................. 98 D2
Kingston Blds
 CBATH/BATHN BA1 *................ 3 G5
Kingston Cl MANG/FISH BS16...... 49 G1
Kingston La
 BLAG/CWMG/WR BS40............ 93 F4
Kingston Rd BMSTR BS3............... 72 D2
 CBATH/BATHN BA1 .... 3 G5
Kingston Wy NAIL BS48............... 78 D1
Kingstree St
 BRSG/KWL/STAPK BS4.............. 73 H2
King St AVONM BS11.................... 28 A4
 CBRIS/FH BS1............................. 4 E5
 EVILLE/WHL BS5...................... 57 E2
Kings Wk
 BMSTRD/HC/WWD BS13.......... 83 H2
Kingsway BATHSE BA2............... 107 H4
 BRSTK/PCHW BS34.................... 21 E4
 EVILLE/WHL BS5...................... 58 B4
 PTSHD/EG BS20........................ 38 D4
Kingsway Av KGWD/HNM BS15.... 58 B3
Kingsway Crs
 KGWD/HNM BS15.................... 58 B3
Kingswear Rd BMSTR BS3............ 73 E5
Kings Weston Av AVONM BS11..... 42 D1
Kings Weston La AVONM BS11 ..... 28 C1
Kingswood Hts
 KGWD/HNM BS15.................... 58 D2
Kington La THNB/SVB BS35.......... 8 A3
King William Av CBRIS/FH BS1 .... 4 E5
King William St BMSTR BS3.......... 72 C2
Kinsale Rd HGRV/WHIT BS14........ 86 B2
Kinsale Wk
 BRSG/KWL/STAPK BS4.............. 73 F5
Kinvara Rd
 BRSG/KWL/STAPK BS4.............. 85 F1
Kipling Av BATHSE BA2.............. 108 C3
Kipling Rd HORF/LLZ BS7............ 32 D4
 WSM BS23.............................. 125 F3
Kirkby Rd AVONM BS11................ 29 G4
Kirtlington Rd
 EVILLE/WHL BS5...................... 46 D5
Kite Hay Cl MANG/FISH BS16 *..... 47 G3

Kites Cl ALMDB BS32.................... 11 E5
Knapp Rd THNB/SVB BS35............. 9 E3
Knapps La EVILLE/WHL BS5.......... 57 G1
The Knapp YATE/CS BS37............. 14 A2
Knightcott Rd CFTN/FAIL BS8....... 53 F3
Knightsbridge Pk
 BMSTRD/HC/WWD BS13.......... 85 F5
Knights Cl
 HNLZ/SM/SNYPK/WT BS9 .... 45 F2
 MTN/WRL BS22....................... 117 H3
Knightstone Cswy WSM BS23......... 6 A2
Knightstone Ct
 EVILLE/WHL BS5...................... 57 F1
Knightstone Pk WSM BS23.......... 124 D1
Knightstone Pl
 KGWD/HNM BS15 *................. 75 G3
Knightstone Rd WSM BS23............. 6 A2
Knightstone Sq
 HGRV/WHIT BS14...................... 86 B4
Knightswood NAIL BS48 *............ 67 E3
Knightwood Rd
 BRSTK/PCHW BS34.................... 21 H5
Knole Cl ALMDB BS32.................. 10 B3
Knole La HNBRY/STHM BS10........ 31 E2
Knole Pk ALMDB BS32................. 10 B4
Knoll Hl
 HNLZ/SM/SNYPK/WT BS9 .... 44 B5
The Knoll PTSHD/EG BS20........... 39 H1
Knovill Cl AVONM BS11................ 29 H4
Knowle Rd
 BRSG/KWL/STAPK BS4.............. 73 G3
Knowles Rd CLVDN BS21.............. 64 C3
Knowsley Rd MANG/FISH BS16..... 47 G5
Kyght Cl KGWD/HNM BS15.......... 59 G3
Kylross Av HGRV/WHIT BS14........ 86 A4
Kynges Mill Cl
 MANG/FISH BS16..................... 48 A1

L

The Labbott KEYN BS31................ 88 B4
Laburnum Ct WSM BS23............. 121 G4
Laburnum Gv
 BMSTRD/HC/WWD BS13.......... 84 A3
 PTSHD/EG BS20........................ 39 G2
Laburnum Rd
 KGWD/HNM BS15.................... 75 H1
 WSM BS23................................. 7 K4
Laburnum Ter
 CBATH/BATHN BA1 .... 104 A1
Lacey Rd HGRV/WHIT BS14.......... 86 D3
Lacock Dr
 OLD/WMLY/WICK BS30 .... 76 C1
Ladd Cl KGWD/HNM BS15........... 59 F4
Ladden Ct THNB/SVB BS35............ 8 D4
Ladden Md YATE/CS BS37............. 13 H5
Ladies Miles CFTN/FAIL BS8......... 54 D2
Ladman Gv HGRV/WHIT BS14....... 86 D4
Ladman Rd HGRV/WHIT BS14....... 86 D4
Ladycroft CLVDN BS21................. 64 B4
Ladye Bay CLVDN BS21................ 62 D1
Ladye Wake MTN/WRL BS22...... 117 G4
Ladymead PTSHD/EG BS20.......... 40 B3
Ladysmith Rd
 RDLND/MONT BS6 .... 45 H4
Laggan Gdns
 CBATH/BATHN BA1 .... 102 B3
Lakemead Gv
 BMSTRD/HC/WWD BS13.......... 84 A3
Lake Rd HNBRY/STHM BS10......... 31 E3
 PTSHD/EG BS20........................ 39 G2
Lakeside MANG/FISH BS16.......... 49 E5
Lake View Rd EVILLE/WHL BS5..... 57 F5
Lakewood Crs
 HNBRY/STHM BS10................... 31 F5
Lakewood Rd
 HNBRY/STHM BS10................... 31 F5
Lambert Pl
 BRSG/KWL/STAPK BS4.............. 85 E3
Lamb Hl EVILLE/WHL BS5............ 57 G3
Lambley Rd EVILLE/WHL BS5........ 57 G3
Lamb La CBRISNE BS2.................. 5 L5
Lambourne Wy
 PTSHD/EG BS20........................ 40 B4
Lambourn Rd KEYN BS31............. 88 C5
Lambridge
 CBATH/BATHN BA1 .... 103 F3
Lambridge Blds
 CBATH/BATHN BA1 .... 103 F3
Lambridge Ms
 CBATH/BATHN BA1 .... 103 F3
Lambridge St
 CBATH/BATHN BA1 .... 103 F3
Lambrook Rd MANG/FISH BS16.... 48 A4
Lamb St CBRISNE BS2.................... 5 K2
Lamington Cl
 BMSTRD/HC/WWD BS13.......... 84 A3
Lamord Ga BRSTK/PCHW BS34.... 21 G5
Lampards Blds
 CBATH/BATHN BA1 .... 2 E1
Lampeter Rd
 HNLZ/SM/SNYPK/WT BS9 .... 44 D1
Lampton Av
 BMSTRD/HC/WWD BS13.......... 96 B1
Lampton Gv
 BMSTRD/HC/WWD BS13.......... 96 B1
Lampton Rd LGASH BS41............. 70 C5
Lanaway Rd MANG/FISH BS16..... 48 B1
Lancaster Rd HORF/LLZ BS7......... 46 B2
Lancaster Cl
 BRSTK/PCHW BS34.................... 33 F1
Lancaster Rd CBRISNE BS2........... 56 C1
 YATE/CS BS37............................ 14 B2
Lancaster St EVILLE/WHL BS5....... 57 E4
Lanceleot Rd MANG/FISH BS16..... 33 G5
Landemann Circ WSM BS23.......... 7 F1
Landemann Pth WSM BS23............ 7 F2
Landrail Wk MANG/FISH BS16...... 47 H2
Landseer Av HORF/LLZ BS7.......... 32 C4
Landseer Cl MTN/WRL BS22 *..... 122 C2
Landseer Rd BATHSE BA2........... 107 G1
The Land FRCTL/WBN BS36.......... 23 F3
Lanercost Rd
 HNBRY/STHM BS10................... 31 G3
Lanesborough Ri
 HGRV/WHIT BS14...................... 86 C2

Lanes End
 BRSG/KWL/STAPK BS4.............. 74 B5
Laneys Dro
 OMX/HUT/LCK BS24 .... 126 B1
Langdale Rd MANG/FISH BS16..... 47 H4
Langdon Rd BATHSE BA2........... 107 G3
Langfield Cl
 HNBRY/STHM BS10................... 30 C2
Langford Rd
 BMSTRD/HC/WWD BS13.......... 84 A1
 WSM BS23................................. 7 J5
Langford Wy KGWD/HNM BS15... 59 E4
Langham Rd
 BRSG/KWL/STAPK BS4.............. 74 A4
Langhill Av
 BRSG/KWL/STAPK BS4.............. 85 E2
Langley Crs BMSTR BS3............... 71 H5
Langton Court Rd
 BRSG/KWL/STAPK BS4.............. 74 C1
Langton Pk BMSTR BS3................ 73 D2
Langton Rd
 BRSG/KWL/STAPK BS4.............. 74 C1
Langton Wy
 BRSG/KWL/STAPK BS4.............. 57 C5
Lansdown YATE/CS BS37.............. 26 A2
Lansdown Cl KGWD/HNM BS15... 58 D1
Lansdown Crs
 CBATH/BATHN BA1 .... 102 C4
Lansdown Gdns
 MTN/WRL BS22....................... 118 A4
Lansdown Gv
 CBATH/BATHN BA1 .... 102 C4
Lansdown Grove Ct
 CBATH/BATHN BA1 .... 102 C4
Lansdown Hts
 CBATH/BATHN BA1 .... 102 C3
Lansdown La
 CBATH/BATHN BA1 .... 101 G1
Lansdown Pk
 CBATH/BATHN BA1 .... 102 B1
Lansdown Pl CFTN/FAIL BS8........ 55 E4
Lansdown Pl East
 CBATH/BATHN BA1 .... 102 C3
Lansdown Pl West
 CBATH/BATHN BA1 .... 102 B3
Lansdown Rd
 CBATH/BATHN BA1 .... 3 F1
 CFTN/FAIL BS8......................... 55 E4
 KEYN BS31.............................. 99 F1
 KGWD/HNM BS15.................... 58 D1
 MANG/FISH BS16..................... 51 G2
 RDLND/MONT BS6 .... 55 G2
Lansdown Ter
 CBATH/BATHN BA1 .... 3 F1
 RDLND/MONT BS6 .... 45 H3
Lansdown Vw BATHSE BA2......... 107 H2
 KGWD/HNM BS15.................... 59 E3
Lanthony Cl
 OMX/HUT/LCK BS24 .... 122 D3
Laphams Ct
 OLD/WMLY/WICK BS30 .... 76 C2
Lapwing Cl ALMDB BS32.............. 11 F5
 PTSHD/EG BS20........................ 40 B2
Lapwing Gdns
 MANG/FISH BS16..................... 47 G2
 MTN/WRL BS22....................... 122 C2
Larch Cl NAIL BS48...................... 67 H4
The Larches MTN/WRL BS22...... 117 H5
Larchgrove Crs
 MTN/WRL BS22....................... 122 C2
Larch Rd KGWD/HNM BS15......... 49 E5
Larch Wy BRSTK/PCHW BS34...... 20 A3
Larkfield FRCTL/WBN BS36.......... 24 B3
Larkhall Pl CBATH/BATHN BA1 ... 103 G2
Larkhall Ter
 CBATH/BATHN BA1 .... 103 F2
Larkhill Rd
 OMX/HUT/LCK BS24 .... 123 E5
Larkin Cl BRSG/KWL/STAPK BS4... 32 C4
Lark Pl CBATH/BATHN BA1 .... 2 A2
Lark Rd MTN/WRL BS22............. 122 C2
Lark's Rd MANG/FISH BS16......... 47 G3
Larksleaze Rd
 OLD/WMLY/WICK BS30 .... 76 B4
Larkspur Cl THNB/SVB BS35.......... 9 E2
Lasbury Gv
 BMSTRD/HC/WWD BS13.......... 84 D4
Latimer Cl
 BRSG/KWL/STAPK BS4.............. 74 D2
Latteridge Rd YATE/CS BS37......... 12 B3
Latton Rd HORF/LLZ BS7............. 32 B5
Launceston Av
 KGWD/HNM BS15.................... 75 G1
Launceston Rd
 KGWD/HNM BS15.................... 58 B2
Laura Pl BATHSE BA2.................... 3 H3
Laurel Dr NAIL BS48.................. 66 D4
Laurel Gdns YTN/CONG BS49.... 112 B2
The Laurels HNBRY/STHM BS10... 19 E4
 MTN/WRL BS22....................... 116 B4
Laurel St KGWD/HNM BS15......... 58 D5
Laurel Ter YTN/CONG BS49....... 112 B2
Laurie Crs
 HNLZ/SM/SNYPK/WT BS9 .... 45 H2
Laurie Lee Ct
 OLD/WMLY/WICK BS30 .... 76 D1
Lavender Cl MTN/WRL BS22...... 117 H5
 THNB/SVB BS35......................... 9 E3
Lavenham Rd YATE/CS BS37......... 13 F5
Lavers Cl KGWD/HNM BS15......... 59 G4
Lavington Cl CLVDN BS21............ 64 A4
Lavington Rd EVILLE/WHL BS5..... 58 B5
Lawford Av BRSTK/PCHW BS34.... 21 G4
Lawfords Ga CBRISNE BS2............ 5 K2
Lawford St CBRISNE BS2............... 5 K2
Lawn Rd MANG/FISH BS16........... 48 B3
The Lawns AVONM BS11 *........... 43 E1
 MTN/WRL BS22....................... 118 A5
 YTN/CONG BS49...................... 112 A2
Lawrence Av EVILLE/WHL BS5...... 56 D2

Lawrence Cl KGWD/HNM BS15 .... 59 G1
Lawrence Close Ms
 MANG/FISH BS16 *................. 122 B1
Lawrence Dr YATE/CS BS37.......... 13 F5
Lawrence Gv
 HNLZ/SM/SNYPK/WT BS9 .... 45 F3
Lawrence HI EVILLE/WHL BS5....... 56 D4
Lawrence Ms MTN/WRL BS22 .... 122 B1
Lawrence Weston Rd
 AVONM BS11............................ 29 H3
Law's Dr OMX/HUT/LCK BS24 .... 122 C4
Lawson Cl KEYN BS31.................. 98 D2
Laxey Rd HORF/LLZ BS7............... 46 B1
Laxton Cl THNB/SVB BS35.............. 9 E3
Leach Cl CLVDN BS21................... 65 E3
Leafy Wy OMX/HUT/LCK BS24 .. 127 E2
Lea Grove Rd CLVDN BS21.......... 64 C1
Leaholme Gdns
 HGRV/WHIT BS14...................... 96 D1
Leaman Cl YATE/CS BS37............. 26 C1
Leap V MANG/FISH BS16............. 50 B3
Leap Valley Crs
 MANG/FISH BS16..................... 35 G5
The Leaze YATE/CS BS37............ 13 H5
Leda Av HGRV/WHIT BS14........... 85 H2
Ledbury Rd MANG/FISH BS16..... 48 C2
Leechpool Wy YATE/CS BS37....... 14 A2
Lee Cl BRSTK/PCHW BS34........... 20 B3
Leedham Rd
 OMX/HUT/LCK BS24 .... 127 F1
Leeming Wy AVONM BS11............ 28 C5
Lees HI KGWD/HNM BS15............ 59 E3
Leeside PTSHD/EG BS20.............. 39 G3
Leewood Rd WSM BS23............. 120 D2
Leicester Sq MANG/FISH BS16..... 48 D5
Leicester St BMSTR BS3................ 73 E2
Leicester Wk
 BRSG/KWL/STAPK BS4.............. 75 E1
Leigh Cl CBATH/BATHN BA1 ...... 102 D2
Leigh La YATE/CS BS37................ 37 F4
Leigh Rd CFTN/FAIL BS8.............. 55 F3
Leigh St BMSTR BS3.................... 72 C3
Leighton Rd BMSTR BS3.............. 73 E5
 BRSG/KWL/STAPK BS4.............. 74 A4
 CBATH/BATHN BA1 .... 101 F1
Leigh View Rd PTSHD/EG BS20.... 39 H1
Leighwood Dr NAIL BS48............ 66 C5
Leinster Av
 BRSG/KWL/STAPK BS4.............. 85 E1
Leisure Rd KGWD/HNM BS15...... 76 B1
Lena Av EVILLE/WHL BS5............. 56 D2
Lena St EVILLE/WHL BS5.............. 56 D2
Lenover Gdns
 BMSTRD/HC/WWD BS13.......... 84 C5
Leonard La CBRIS/FH BS1.............. 4 E3
Leonard Rd EVILLE/WHL BS5....... 57 E4
Leonards Av EVILLE/WHL BS5...... 57 E2
Leopold Blds
 CBATH/BATHN BA1 *............. 102 D4
Leopold Rd RDLND/MONT BS6.... 56 A1
Lescren Wy AVONM BS11............. 28 D4
Lester Dr MTN/WRL BS22.......... 117 H5
Lewington Rd
 MANG/FISH BS16..................... 48 C4
Lewins Md CBRIS/FH BS1............... 4 E3
Lewin St EVILLE/WHL BS5............ 57 F4
Lewis Cl MANG/FISH BS16........... 49 H1
 OLD/WMLY/WICK BS30 .... 77 G1
Lewisham Gv WSM BS23................ 7 J4
Lewis Rd
 BMSTRD/HC/WWD BS13.......... 84 B1
Lewis St CBRISNE BS2................... 74 A1
Lewton La FRCTL/WBN BS36........ 23 E3
Leyland Wk
 BMSTRD/HC/WWD BS13.......... 84 A5
The Leys CLVDN BS21.................. 64 B4
Leyton Vls RDLND/MONT BS6..... 55 F1
Liberty Gdns CBRIS/FH BS1 *......... 4 C7
Lichfield Rd
 BRSG/KWL/STAPK BS4.............. 74 C1
Lilac Cl HNBRY/STHM BS10......... 31 G4
Lilac Wy MTN/WRL BS22........... 117 H5
Lillian St EVILLE/WHL BS5............ 57 E3
Lilliput Ct YATE/CS BS37.............. 26 C2
Lilliput Ct YATE/CS BS37.............. 26 C2
Lilstock Av HORF/LLZ BS7............ 46 B4
Lilton Wk
 BMSTRD/HC/WWD BS13.......... 72 B5
Lilymead Av
 BRSG/KWL/STAPK BS4.............. 74 B1
Lime Breach Wd NAIL BS48 *....... 67 E3
Lime Cl HNBRY/STHM BS10......... 31 G4
 OMX/HUT/LCK BS24 .... 127 E2
Lime Cft YATE/CS BS37................ 14 C3
Lime Gv BATHSE BA2.................... 3 J5
Lime Grove Gdns BATHSE BA2 ...... 3 J5
Lime Kiln Cl BRSTK/PCHW BS34... 33 E3
Lime Kiln Gdns ALMDB BS32....... 11 F4
Lime Kiln La CLVDN BS21............ 64 D2
Lime Kiln Rd CFTN/FAIL BS8......... 4 B4
Limekilns Cl KEYN BS31.............. 88 C4
Limerick Rd RDLND/MONT BS6.... 55 G1
Lime Rd BMSTR BS3..................... 73 E2
 KGWD/HNM BS15.................... 59 E5
Limestone Link BATHSE BA2....... 104 B2
 CBATH/BATHN BA1 .... 91 E5
Lime Tree Gv PTSHD/EG BS20..... 42 B3
Lime Trees Rd
 RDLND/MONT BS6 .... 45 H2
Lincoln Cl KEYN BS31.................. 97 G1
Lincoln St EVILLE/WHL BS5.......... 56 D4
Lincombe Av MANG/FISH BS16.... 48 C3
Lincombe Rd MANG/FISH BS16.... 48 C3
Linden Av WSM BS23................. 121 G3
Linden Cl FRCTL/WBN BS36......... 23 E4
 HNBRY/STHM BS10................... 31 G4
 KGWD/HNM BS15.................... 59 E3
Linden Dr ALMDB BS32................ 21 F2
Linden Gdns
 CBATH/BATHN BA1 .... 102 A4
Linden Rd CLVDN BS21................ 64 D1
 RDLND/MONT BS6 .... 55 G2
The Lindens MTN/WRL BS22...... 117 G4
Lindrea St BMSTR BS3.................. 72 C3
Lindsay Rd HORF/LLZ BS7............ 46 C4
Lindsey Cl PTSHD/EG BS20.......... 39 E3
Linemere Cl NAIL BS48................ 79 G1
Lines Wy HGRV/WHIT BS14.......... 97 F1
Lingfield Pk MANG/FISH BS16...... 35 H5

Link La BOAV BA15 105 C4
Link Rd BRSTK/PCHW BS34 32 B2
NAIL BS48 67 C4
PTSHD/EG BS20 39 G3
YATE/CS BS37 26 B1
Linkside CLVDN BS21 62 C4
Links Rd WSM BS23 124 B4
Linley Cl BATHSE BA2 107 F2
The Linleys
CBATH/BATHN BA1 101 H5
Linnell Cl HORF/LLZ BS7 46 D2
Linnet Cl BRSTK/PCHW BS34 20 A2
MTN/WRL BS22 122 B2
Lintern Crs
OLD/WMLY/WICK BS30 59 G5
Lintham Dr KGWD/HNM BS15 59 F5
Linton's Wk HGRV/WHIT BS14 85 H2
Lion Cl NAIL BS48 66 D4
Lisburn Rd
BRSG/KWL/STAPK BS4 73 F5
Lisle Rd MTN/WRL BS22 118 A4
Litfield Pl CFTN/FAIL BS8 * 54 D4
Litfield Rd CFTN/FAIL BS8 54 D3
Little Ann St CBRISNE BS2 5 K2
Little Birch Cft
HGRV/WHIT BS14 96 D1
Little Bishop St CBRISNE BS2 56 A3
Little Caroline Pl
CFTN/FAIL BS8 72 A1
Littledean YATE/CS BS37 26 A4
Little Dowles
OLD/WMLY/WICK BS30 76 D2
Little George St CBRISNE BS2 5 K1
WSM BS23 7 F4
Little Halt PTSHD/EG BS20 38 C4
Little Ham CLVDN BS21 64 C5
Little Hayes MANG/FISH BS16 48 B3
Little Headley Cl
BMSTRD/HC/WWD BS13 84 C2
Little King St CBRIS/FH BS1 5 F5
Little Md AVONM BS11 29 H4
Little Mead Cl
OMX/HUT/LCK BS24 126 B3
Little Meadow ALMDB BS32 21 H4
Little Meadow End NAIL BS48 79 F1
Little Orch WSM BS23 124 C5
Little Paradise BMSTR BS3 73 E2
Little Parr Cl
MANG/FISH BS16 47 E3
Little Paul St CBRISNE BS2 55 G3
Little Stanhope St
CBATH/BATHN BA1 * 2 D4
Little Stoke La
BRSTK/PCHW BS34 21 E3
Little Stoke Rd
HNLZ/SM/SNYPK/WT BS9 44 C4
Littleton La
BLAG/CWMG/WR BS40 94 B5
Littleton Rd BMSTR BS3 73 E4
Littleton St EVILLE/WHL BS5 57 E2
Little Withey Md
HNLZ/SM/SNYPK/WT BS9 44 D2
Littlewood Cl HGRV/WHIT BS14 97 E1
Littlewood La
YTN/CONG BS49 113 H1
Livingstone Rd BATHSE BA2 2 A6
Livingstone Ter BATHSE BA2 2 B7
Llewellyn Wy MTN/WRL BS22 118 A5
Lockemor Rd
BMSTRD/HC/WWD BS13 85 G5
Lockes Paddock
MTN/WRL BS22 118 B5
Lock Gdns
BMSTRD/HC/WWD BS13 83 H2
Locking Head Dro
OMX/HUT/LCK BS24 126 C1
Locking Moor Rd
MTN/WRL BS22 121 H3
Locking Rd MTN/WRL BS22 122 A3
WSM BS23 7 F4
Lockingwell Rd KEYN BS31 88 A4
Lockleaze Rd HORF/LLZ BS7 46 C2
Locksbrook Pl
CBATH/BATHN BA1 * 101 H5
Locksbrook Rd
CBATH/BATHN BA1 107 G1
MTN/WRL BS22 118 A3
Lockside PTSHD/EG BS20 40 A1
Lodge Cswy MANG/FISH BS16 47 H5
Lodge Cl YTN/CONG BS49 112 B3
Lodge Ct
HNLZ/SM/SNYPK/WT BS9 44 C4
Lodge Dr LGASH BS41 71 E4
OLD/WMLY/WICK BS30 77 F4
WSM BS23 121 F2
Lodge Gdns BATHSE BA2 110 B1
Lodge Hl KGWD/HNM BS15 58 C1
Lodge La NAIL BS48 67 H3
Lodge Pl CBRIS/FH BS1 4 D3
Lodge Rd KGWD/HNM BS15 58 C1
OLD/WMLY/WICK BS30 61 E3
YATE/CS BS37 13 E5
Lodgeside Av
KGWD/HNM BS15 58 C2
Lodgeside Gdns
KGWD/HNM BS15 58 C2
Lodge St CBRIS/FH BS1 4 D3
Lodge Wk MANG/FISH BS16 48 D2
Lodore Rd MANG/FISH BS16 47 H5
Lodway PTSHD/EG BS20 42 B4
Lodway Cl PTSHD/EG BS20 42 B3
Lodway Gdns PTSHD/EG BS20 42 C4
Lodway Rd
BRSG/KWL/STAPK BS4 74 B4
Logan Rd HORF/LLZ BS7 45 H5
Logus Ct
OLD/WMLY/WICK BS30 76 C2
Lombard St BMSTR BS3 73 E2
Lombardy Cl MTN/WRL BS22 122 B3
Lomond Rd HORF/LLZ BS7 32 B4
London Rd CBATH/BATHN BA1 3 G1
CBRISNE BS2 56 B2
OLD/WMLY/WICK BS30 60 A4
London Rd East
CBATH/BATHN BA1 104 B1
London Rd West
CBATH/BATHN BA1 103 F3
London Sq PTSHD/EG BS20 40 A1
London St KGWD/HNM BS15 58 D3
Long Acre CBATH/BATHN BA1 102 D4
Longacre CLVDN BS21 64 B5
Longacre Rd HGRV/WHIT BS14 96 D1
Long Acres Cl
HNLZ/SM/SNYPK/WT BS9 44 B1
Long Ashton Rd LGASH BS41 70 D5
Long Av CLVDN BS21 64 B3
Long Beach Rd
OLD/WMLY/WICK BS30 76 D4
Long Cl ALMDB BS32 21 G4
MANG/FISH BS16 48 C2
Long Cft YATE/CS BS37 13 H2
Long Cross AVONM BS11 29 E5
BLAG/CWMG/WR BS40 93 E5
Longden Rd MANG/FISH BS16 49 F2
Longdown Dr MTN/WRL BS22 118 A4
Long Eaton Dr
HGRV/WHIT BS14 86 A1
Longfellow Av BATHSE BA2 108 C3
Longfield Rd HORF/LLZ BS7 46 A5
Longford YATE/CS BS37 25 G2
Longford Av
HNBRY/STHM BS10 31 H5
Long Handstones
OLD/WMLY/WICK BS30 76 D2
Long Hay Cl BATHSE BA2 107 G2
Longleat Cl
HNLZ/SM/SNYPK/WT BS9 45 G3
Longleaze Gdns
OMX/HUT/LCK BS24 126 C3
Long Md YATE/CS BS37 14 A2
Longmead Av HORF/LLZ BS7 45 H3
Long Meadow
MANG/FISH BS16 47 F3
Longmeadow Rd KEYN BS31 87 H5
Longmead Rd
MANG/FISH BS16 35 H4
Longmoor Ct BMSTR BS3 72 B4
Longmoor Rd BMSTR BS3 72 B4
Longney Pl BRSTK/PCHW BS34 20 B1
Longreach Gv
HGRV/WHIT BS14 86 C2
Longridge Wy
OMX/HUT/LCK BS24 122 B4
Long Rd MANG/FISH BS16 49 G3
Long Rw CBRIS/FH BS1 * 5 G5
Longs Dr YATE/CS BS37 13 G4
Long-Thorn NAIL BS48 79 G3
Longthorne Pl BATHSE BA2 * 108 C5
Longton Grove Rd WSM BS23 6 E2
Long Valley Rd BATHSE BA2 107 E2
Longway Av HGRV/WHIT BS14 85 G5
Longwood
BRSG/KWL/STAPK BS4 75 F4
Longwood La CFTN/FAIL BS8 70 B2
Lonsdale Av WSM BS23 125 E2
Lorain Wk HNBRY/STHM BS10 30 D3
Lorton Cl HNBRY/STHM BS10 31 F4
Lorton Rd HNBRY/STHM BS10 31 F4
Lotts' Av NAIL BS48 80 A4
Loughman Cl
KGWD/HNM BS15 * 59 E3
Louisa St CBRISNE BS2 5 K4
Louise Av MANG/FISH BS16 49 G3
Love La YATE/CS BS37 26 C2
Lovelinch Gdns LGASH BS41 70 C5
Lovell Av
OLD/WMLY/WICK BS30 77 G2
Lovell's Hl KGWD/HNM BS15 75 G1
Loveridge Ct FRCTL/WBN BS36 23 H3
Loveringe Cl
HNBRY/STHM BS10 30 D1
Lowbourne HGRV/WHIT BS14 85 G3
Lower Ashley Rd
RDLND/MONT BS6 56 B2
Lower Borough Walls
CBATH/BATHN BA1 * 3 F5
Lower Bristol Rd BATHSE BA2 101 E5
Lower Burlington Rd
PTSHD/EG BS20 40 A1
Lower Camden Pl
CBATH/BATHN BA1 * 102 D4
Lower Castle St CBRIS/FH BS1 5 H2
Lower Chapel La
FRCTL/WBN BS36 24 A3
Lower Chapel Rd
KGWD/HNM BS15 75 H1
Lower Cheltenham Pl
RDLND/MONT BS6 56 B2
Lower Church La CBRIS/FH BS1 4 D3
Lower Church Rd WSM BS23 6 D2
Lower Clifton Hl CFTN/FAIL BS8 4 A4
Lower Cock Rd
KGWD/HNM BS15 59 F4
Lower College St CBRIS/FH BS1 4 C5
Lower Conham V
KGWD/HNM BS15 75 E1
Lower Court Rd ALMDB BS32 10 C2
Lower Down Rd
PTSHD/EG BS20 39 F3
Lower East Hayes
CBATH/BATHN BA1 * 103 E4
Lower Fallow Cl
HGRV/WHIT BS14 85 G5
Lower Gay St CBRISNE BS2 55 H3
Lower Grove Rd
MANG/FISH BS16 * 47 G4
Lower Guinea St CBRIS/FH BS1 5 F7
Lower Hanham Rd
KGWD/HNM BS15 58 C5
Lower Hedgemead Rd
CBATH/BATHN BA1 3 G1
Lower High St AVONM BS11 28 D5
Lower House Crs
BRSTK/PCHW BS34 32 D1
Lower Kingsdown Rd
COR/BOX SN13 105 G1
Lower Knole La
HNBRY/STHM BS10 31 E2
Lower Knowles Rd
CLVDN BS21 64 C3
Lower Lamb St CBRIS/FH BS1 4 C5
Lower Linden Rd CLVDN BS21 64 D2
Lower Maudlin St
CBRIS/FH BS1 5 F2
Lower Moor Rd YATE/CS BS37 14 A3
Lower Northend
CBATH/BATHN BA1 91 E4
Lower Norton La
MTN/WRL BS22 116 C4
Lower Oldfield Pk BATHSE BA2 2 C6
Lower Parade Ground Rd
OMX/HUT/LCK BS24 127 E1
Lower Park Rw CBRIS/FH BS1 4 E3
Lower Queen's Rd CLVDN BS21 64 D2
Lower Redland Rd
RDLND/MONT BS6 55 F1
Lower Sidney St BMSTR BS3 72 B2
Lower Station Approach Rd
CBRIS/FH BS1 5 J6
Lower Station Rd
MANG/FISH BS16 47 H4
Lower Stone Cl
FRCTL/WBN BS36 24 A2
Lowlis Cl HNBRY/STHM BS10 30 D2
Lowther Rd
HNBRY/STHM BS10 31 G3
Loxley Gdns BATHSE BA2 107 H3
Loxton Dr BATHSE BA2 107 G1
Loxton Rd WSM BS23 125 E3
Loxton Sq HGRV/WHIT BS14 85 H3
Lucas Cl BRSG/KWL/STAPK BS4 86 C1
Luccombe Hl
RDLND/MONT BS6 55 F1
Luckington Rd HORF/LLZ BS7 32 A5
Lucklands Rd
CBATH/BATHN BA1 101 H3
Luckley Av
BMSTRD/HC/WWD BS13 84 D4
Luckwell Rd BMSTR BS3 72 C3
Lucky La BMSTR BS3 73 E2
Ludlow Cl CBRISNE BS2 56 B2
KEYN BS31 88 A4
OLD/WMLY/WICK BS30 77 E4
Ludlow Ct
OLD/WMLY/WICK BS30 77 E4
Ludlow Rd HORF/LLZ BS7 46 C1
Ludwell Cl FRCTL/WBN BS36 22 D5
Lullington Rd
BRSG/KWL/STAPK BS4 74 A4
Lulsgate Rd
BMSTRD/HC/WWD BS13 84 B1
Lulworth Crs MANG/FISH BS16 35 F5
Lulworth Rd KEYN BS31 88 B5
Lunty Md NAIL BS48 79 H3
Lurgan Wk
BRSG/KWL/STAPK BS4 73 E5
Lutyens Cl MANG/FISH BS16 33 G5
Lux Furlong
HNLZ/SM/SNYPK/WT BS9 43 H1
Luxton St EVILLE/WHL BS5 56 D3
Lychgate Pk
OMX/HUT/LCK BS24 126 D2
Lydbrook Cl YATE/CS BS37 25 H2
Lyddington Rd HORF/LLZ BS7 32 A4
Lyddon Rd MTN/WRL BS22 118 A5
Lydford Wk BMSTR BS3 72 D4
Lydiard Cft KGWD/HNM BS15 75 H2
Lydney Rd HNBRY/STHM BS10 31 H5
MANG/FISH BS16 49 E4
Lydstep Ter BMSTR BS3 72 D2
Lyefield Rd MTN/WRL BS22 117 F4
The Lyes YTN/CONG BS49 114 D3
Lyme Gdns CBATH/BATHN BA1 101 F5
Lyme Rd CBATH/BATHN BA1 101 G5
Lymore Av BATHSE BA2 107 H2
Lymore Gdns BATHSE BA2 107 H2
Lymore Ter BATHSE BA2 107 H3
Lympsham Gn BATHSE BA2 110 B1
Lynbrook LGASH BS41 70 C5
Lynbrook La BATHSE BA2 108 C4
Lynch Cl MTN/WRL BS22 117 G5
Lynch Ct
OLD/WMLY/WICK BS30 * 76 C2
Lyncombe Hl BATHSE BA2 3 H7
Lyncombe V BATHSE BA2 108 D3
Lyncombe Vale Rd
BATHSE BA2 108 D4
Lyncombe Wk
MANG/FISH BS16 58 B1
Lyndale Av
HNLZ/SM/SNYPK/WT BS9 44 A3
Lyndale Rd EVILLE/WHL BS5 57 F3
YATE/CS BS37 25 H1
Lynde Cl
BMSTRD/HC/WWD BS13 84 C5
Lyndhurst Rd BATHSE BA2 107 H1
HNLZ/SM/SNYPK/WT BS9 44 D1
KEYN BS31 98 A1
WSM BS23 124 D2
Lyndhurst Ter
CBATH/BATHN BA1 102 D4
Lynfield Pk
CBATH/BATHN BA1 101 G2
Lynmouth Cl MTN/WRL BS22 122 D1
Lynmouth Rd CBRISNE BS2 56 C1
Lynn Rd MANG/FISH BS16 47 F3
Lynton Cl PTSHD/EG BS20 40 A4
Lynton Pl EVILLE/WHL BS5 57 E3
Lynton Rd BMSTR BS3 73 E5
Lynton Wy MANG/FISH BS16 34 B4
Lynx Crs OMX/HUT/LCK BS24 125 G4
Lyons Ct WSM BS23 7 G4
Lyons Court Rd
HGRV/WHIT BS14 86 C2
Lyppiatt Rd EVILLE/WHL BS5 57 F3
Lyppincourt Rd
HNBRY/STHM BS10 31 E2
Lysander Rd
HNBRY/STHM BS10 19 F4
Lysander Wk
BRSTK/PCHW BS34 21 G5
Lytchet Dr MANG/FISH BS16 35 F5
Lytes Cary Rd KEYN BS31 98 B2
Lytton Gdns BATHSE BA2 107 G3
Lytton Gv HORF/LLZ BS7 32 C5
KEYN BS31 88 D4
Lyveden Gdns
BMSTRD/HC/WWD BS13 84 C4
Lyvedon Wy LGASH BS41 71 E5

M

Mabberley Cl MANG/FISH BS16 50 A3
Macaulay Blds BATHSE BA2 109 F3
Macauley Rd HORF/LLZ BS7 32 C5
Macdonald Wk
KGWD/HNM BS15 58 D3
Macey's Rd
BMSTRD/HC/WWD BS13 96 A1
Macfarlane Cha WSM BS23 125 F1
Machin Cl HNBRY/STHM BS10 30 D2
Machin Gdns
HNBRY/STHM BS10 31 E2
Machin Rd HNBRY/STHM BS10 30 D2
The Macies
CBATH/BATHN BA1 101 G1
Mackie Av BRSTK/PCHW BS34 32 D3
Mackie Gv BRSTK/PCHW BS34 32 D3
Mackie Rd BRSTK/PCHW BS34 32 D3
Macleod Cl CLVDN BS21 64 A3
Macquarie Farm Cl
YTN/CONG BS49 112 A2
Macrae Ct KGWD/HNM BS15 * 59 E3
Macrae Rd PTSHD/EG BS20 43 E4
Madam La MTN/WRL BS22 122 C1
Madeira Rd CLVDN BS21 64 D2
WSM BS23 6 A1
Madeline Rd MANG/FISH BS16 57 H1
Madison Cl YATE/CS BS37 13 H5
Maesbury KGWD/HNM BS15 59 E5
Maesbury Rd KEYN BS31 98 B2
Maesknoll La PLTN/PENS BS39 96 D4
Maesknoll Rd
BRSG/KWL/STAPK BS4 73 H3
Magdalen Av BATHSE BA2 2 E7
Magdalene Pl CBRISNE BS2 56 B2
Magdalen Rd BATHSE BA2 2 E7
Magdalen Wy MTN/WRL BS22 117 H5
Magellan Cl MTN/WRL BS22 117 G4
Maggs Cl HNBRY/STHM BS10 31 G2
Maggs La EVILLE/WHL BS5 57 G1
HGRV/WHIT BS14 86 A5
Magnolia Av MTN/WRL BS22 122 D2
Magnolia Cl MTN/WRL BS22 122 A4
Magpie Bottom La
EVILLE/WHL BS5 58 B5
Magpie Cl MTN/WRL BS22 122 B3
Maidenhead Rd
BMSTRD/HC/WWD BS13 96 A1
Maiden Wy AVONM BS11 42 C1
Maidstone Gv
OMX/HUT/LCK BS24 125 F5
Maidstone St BMSTR BS3 73 G3
Main Rd MANG/FISH BS16 50 A4
NAIL BS48 81 E2
OMX/HUT/LCK BS24 126 A4
YTN/CONG BS49 113 H3
Main Vw FRCTL/WBN BS36 24 B3
Maisemore YATE/CS BS37 25 H4
Maisemore Av
BRSTK/PCHW BS34 20 D1
Makin Cl
OLD/WMLY/WICK BS30 77 F1
Malago Rd BMSTR BS3 72 D3
Malago Wk
BMSTRD/HC/WWD BS13 83 H5
Malden Md HGRV/WHIT BS14 85 H4
Maldowers La EVILLE/WHL BS5 58 A2
Mallard Cl ALMDB BS32 11 F5
EVILLE/WHL BS5 57 H2
YATE/CS BS37 26 C2
Mallow Cl CLVDN BS21 65 E2
THNB/SVB BS35 9 E2
The Mall CBATH/BATHN BA1 * 3 G6
CFTN/FAIL BS8 54 D4
Malmains Dr MANG/FISH BS16 34 B4
Malmesbury Cl
OLD/WMLY/WICK BS30 76 C1
RDLND/MONT BS6 45 G4
The Maltings MTN/WRL BS22 122 C1
RDLND/MONT BS6 * 56 B1
Maltlands MTN/WRL BS22 122 A3
Malvern Blds
CBATH/BATHN BA1 102 D2
Malvern Ct EVILLE/WHL BS5 57 H4
Malvern Dr
OLD/WMLY/WICK BS30 77 F1
THNB/SVB BS35 9 E4
Malvern Rd
BRSG/KWL/STAPK BS4 74 C3
EVILLE/WHL BS5 57 H4
WSM BS23 124 D1
Malvern Ter
CBATH/BATHN BA1 102 D3
Malvern Vls
CBATH/BATHN BA1 102 D3
Mancroft Av AVONM BS11 43 F1
Mangotsfield Rd
MANG/FISH BS16 49 F4
Manilla Crs WSM BS23 6 B1
Manilla Rd CFTN/FAIL BS8 55 E4
Manmoor La CLVDN BS21 65 G4
Manor Cl FRCTL/WBN BS36 24 A4
PTSHD/EG BS20 42 A4
PTSHD/EG BS20 39 E3
The Manor Cl CFTN/FAIL BS8 53 G3
Manor Ct NAIL BS48 79 H4
Manor Court Dr HORF/LLZ BS7 46 A1
Manor Dr CBATH/BATHN BA1 104 C2
Manor Farm Crs ALMDB BS32 21 F2
OMX/HUT/LCK BS24 125 G4
Manor Gdns MTN/WRL BS22 116 C4
OMX/HUT/LCK BS24 126 D2
Manor Gv BRSTK/PCHW BS34 10 D5
MANG/FISH BS16 49 G4
Manor La CFTN/FAIL BS8 53 F3
FRCTL/WBN BS36 23 F3
Manor Pk CBATH/BATHN BA1 101 G4
RDLND/MONT BS6 45 F5
Manor Pl BRSTK/PCHW BS34 34 A1
Manor Rd
BMSTRD/HC/WWD BS13 84 A3
CBATH/BATHN BA1 101 H3
CFTN/FAIL BS8 53 F5
HORF/LLZ BS7 46 A4
KEYN BS31 98 B1
MANG/FISH BS16 49 G4
MANG/FISH BS16 47 H3
WSM BS23 7 H1
Manor Va WSM BS23 7 J1
Manor Vls
CBATH/BATHN BA1 101 H3
Manor Wk THNB/SVB BS35 8 C1
Manor Wy CFTN/FAIL BS8 69 H2
YATE/CS BS37 15 E5
Mansel Cl KEYN BS31 98 D1
Mansfield Av WSM BS23 121 G3
Mansfield Cl WSM BS23 121 G3
Mansfield St BMSTR BS3 72 C4
Manston Cl HGRV/WHIT BS14 86 B2
Manvers St CBATH/BATHN BA1 3 G5
Manworthy Rd
BRSG/KWL/STAPK BS4 74 C3
Manx Rd HORF/LLZ BS7 46 B1
Maple Av MANG/FISH BS16 48 C5
THNB/SVB BS35 8 D3
Maple Cl BRSTK/PCHW BS34 21 E3
HGRV/WHIT BS14 86 C4
OLD/WMLY/WICK BS30 77 E2
WSM BS23 7 K3
Maple Gdns BATHSE BA2 108 B3
Maple Gv BATHSE BA2 108 B3
Mapleleaze
BRSG/KWL/STAPK BS4 74 C3
Maplemeade HORF/LLZ BS7 45 G4
Mapleridge La YATE/CS BS37 15 H1
Maple Rd
BRSG/KWL/STAPK BS4 74 C1
HORF/LLZ BS7 45 H3
The Maples NAIL BS48 66 D5
Maplestone Rd
HGRV/WHIT BS14 96 D1
Maple Wk KEYN BS31 88 A5
MANG/FISH BS16 51 G3
Mapstone Cl MANG/FISH BS16 34 B2
Marbeck Rd
HNBRY/STHM BS10 31 F4
Marchfields Wy WSM BS23 7 H7
Marconi Cl WSM BS23 121 G4
Marconi Rd PTSHD/EG BS20 38 D4
Mardale Cl HNBRY/STHM BS10 31 G3
Marden Rd KEYN BS31 88 D5
Mardon Rd
BRSG/KWL/STAPK BS4 57 F5
Mardyke Ferry Rd
CBRIS/FH BS1 4 A6
Margarets Blds
CBATH/BATHN BA1 * 2 E2
Margate St BMSTR BS3 73 F3
Marguerite Rd
BMSTRD/HC/WWD BS13 84 A1
Marigold Wk BMSTR BS3 72 B4
Marina Gdns MANG/FISH BS16 47 G5
Marindin Dr MTN/WRL BS22 118 A4
Marine Hl CLVDN BS21 64 C1
Marine Pde CLVDN BS21 64 C1
PTSHD/EG BS20 42 C3
WSM BS23 6 C7
Mariners Cl NAIL BS48 79 H3
Mariner's Cl MTN/WRL BS22 122 A2
Mariners Dr
HNLZ/SM/SNYPK/WT BS9 44 B4
NAIL BS48 79 H3
Mariner's Wy PTSHD/EG BS20 42 C3
Marion Rd KGWD/HNM BS15 75 G3
Marion Wk EVILLE/WHL BS5 58 A4
Marissal Cl HNBRY/STHM BS10 30 C2
Marissal Rd HNBRY/STHM BS10 30 C2
Mariston Wy
OLD/WMLY/WICK BS30 60 A5
Marjoram Pl ALMDB BS32 21 H3
Marjoram Wy PTSHD/EG BS20 40 B3
Market Av MTN/WRL BS22 118 B5
Market La WSM BS23 6 D2
Market Pl
BLAG/CWMG/WR BS40 93 G5
Market Sq MANG/FISH BS16 48 C5
Mark La CBRIS/FH BS1 4 D4
Marksbury Rd BMSTR BS3 72 D4
Marlborough Av
EVILLE/WHL BS5 * 47 G5
Marlborough Blds
CBATH/BATHN BA1 2 D2
Marlborough Dr
MANG/FISH BS16 34 B4
MTN/WRL BS22 118 A5
Marlborough Hl
RDLND/MONT BS6 4 E1
Marlborough Hill Pl
CBRISNE BS2 4 E1
Marlborough La
CBATH/BATHN BA1 2 C3
Marlborough St
CBATH/BATHN BA1 2 D1
CBRIS/FH BS1 4 E2
EVILLE/WHL BS5 47 G5
Marlepit Gv
BMSTRD/HC/WWD BS13 83 H3
Marle Pits NAIL BS48 79 H3
Marlfield Wk
BMSTRD/HC/WWD BS13 83 H2
Marling Rd EVILLE/WHL BS5 57 H3
Marlwood Dr
HNBRY/STHM BS10 31 E2
Marmaduke St BMSTR BS3 73 G3
Marmion Crs
HNBRY/STHM BS10 30 D2
Marne Cl HGRV/WHIT BS14 86 C4
Marsden Rd BATHSE BA2 107 G4
Marshall Wk
BRSG/KWL/STAPK BS4 * 85 E2
Marsham Wy
OLD/WMLY/WICK BS30 76 B1
Marsh Cl FRCTL/WBN BS36 35 E1
Marshfield Rd
MANG/FISH BS16 48 B4
Marshfield Wy
CBATH/BATHN BA1 102 D3
Marsh La BMSTR BS3 72 B4
EVILLE/WHL BS5 57 E4
PTSHD/EG BS20 41 G2
Marsh Rd BMSTR BS3 72 A3
YTN/CONG BS49 112 B4
Marsh St AVONM BS11 28 C5
CBRIS/FH BS1 4 E4
Marshwall La ALMDB BS32 10 B1
Marson Rd CLVDN BS21 64 D2
Marston Rd
BRSG/KWL/STAPK BS4 74 A4
Martcombe Rd
PTSHD/EG BS20 42 B5
Martha's Orch
BMSTRD/HC/WWD BS13 83 H2
Martin Cl BRSTK/PCHW BS34 20 A2
Martindale Ct MTN/WRL BS22 121 H3
Martindale Rd
MTN/WRL BS22 122 A3

Martingale Rd
  BRSG/KWL/STAPK BS4......74 C2
Martins Cl *KGWD/HNM* BS15 ....75 H1
Martins Gv *MTN/WRL* BS22......122 B1
Martin's Rd *BMSTR* BS3............75 H1
The Martins *PTSHD/EG* BS20......40 C2
Martin St *BMSTR* BS3................72 C3
Martlock Crs *BMSTR* BS3 ....72 D5
Martock Rd *BMSTR* BS3 ....72 D5
  KEYN BS31............................98 B1
Marwood Rd
  BRSG/KWL/STAPK BS4............85 F1
Marybush La *CBRISNE* BS2 ....5 H3
Mary Carpenter Pl
  CBRISNE BS2 * 56 B2
Marygold Leaze
  OLD/WMLY/WICK BS30 ....76 D2
Mary St *EVILLE/WHL* BS5..........57 F5
Mascot Rd *BMSTR* BS3 ....73 E5
Masefield Wy *HORF/LLZ* BS7......46 C1
Maskelyne Av
  HNBRY/STHM BS10 ....45 H1
Masons Vw *FRCTL/WBN* BS36....23 E5
Materman Rd
  HGRV/WHIT BS14..................86 D4
Matford Cl *FRCTL/WBN* BS36....23 E5
  HNBRY/STHM BS10................31 H1
Matthews Cl *HGRV/WHIT* BS14 ..87 E3
Matthew's Rd *EVILLE/WHL* BS5...57 E4
Maules La *MANG/FISH* BS16......55 H1
Maunsell Rd *AVONM* BS11 ....29 H5
Maurice Rd *RDLND/MONT* BS6....56 A1
Mautravers Cl *BATHSE* BA2........21 F3
Maxse Rd
  BRSG/KWL/STAPK BS4............74 A3
Maybec Gdns *EVILLE/WHL* BS5..58 A5
Maybourne
  BRSG/KWL/STAPK BS4............75 F4
Maybrick Rd *BATHSE* BA2..........2 A7
Mayfair Pk Rd
  RDLND/MONT BS6....................56 B1
Mayfair Av
  MANG/FISH BS16....................58 A1
  MTN/WRL BS22 * 122 D2
Mayfield Pk *MANG/FISH* BS16 ....58 A1
Mayfield Pk North
  MANG/FISH BS16....................58 A1
Mayfield Pk South
  MANG/FISH BS16....................58 A1
Mayfield Rd *BATHSE* BA2 ....2 A7
Mayfields *KEYN* BS31................88 B4
Mayflower Gdns *NAIL* BS48 ....67 H4
May La *CBATH/BATHN* BA1......101 G4
Maynard Cl
  BMSTRD/HC/WWD BS13........84 D4
  CLVDN BS21 ....65 F2
Maynard Rd
  BMSTRD/HC/WWD BS13........84 D4
Maypole Sq *KGWD/HNM* BS15 * ..75 H1
Mays Cl *FRCTL/WBN* BS56 ....24 B3
Maysfield Cl *PTSHD/EG* BS20....39 H5
Maysgreen La
  OMX/HUT/LCK BS24 ....119 C4
May's La *OMX/HUT/LCK* BS24 ..119 H5
May St *KGWD/HNM* BS15 ....58 C2
Maytree Av
  BMSTRD/HC/WWD BS13........84 C2
Maytree Cl
  BMSTRD/HC/WWD BS13........84 C2
May Tree Cl *NAIL* BS48 * 66 D5
Mayville Av *BRSTK/PCHW* BS34 ..32 C2
Maywood Crs *MANG/FISH* BS16 ..48 C4
Maywood Rd *MANG/FISH* BS16 ..48 C4
Maze St *EVILLE/WHL* BS5............56 D5
McCrae Rd
  OMX/HUT/LCK BS24 ....127 E1
McLaren Rd *AVONM* BS11 ....28 B4
Mead Cl *AVONM* BS11 * 43 E2
  BATHSE BA2 ....108 B4
Meadgate *MANG/FISH* BS16......55 H5
Meadlands *BATHSE* BA2............100 A5
Meadowbank *MTN/WRL* BS22 ..117 C5
Meadow Cl *MANG/FISH* BS16 ....49 F1
  NAIL BS48..............................80 A3
  NAIL BS48..............................67 F3
  PTSHD/EG BS20......................38 D3
Meadow Court Dr
  OLD/WMLY/WICK BS30 ....77 F3
Meadowcroft
  MANG/FISH BS16....................35 G5
Meadow Cft
  OMX/HUT/LCK BS24 ....125 G4
Meadow Dr *BATHSE* BA2............110 B2
  OMX/HUT/LCK BS24 ....126 D2
Meadow Gdns
  CBATH/BATHN BA1................101 F3
Meadow Gv *AVONM* BS11..........42 D1
Meadowland Rd
  HNBRY/STHM BS10................30 C1
Meadowlands
  MTN/WRL BS22 * 123 F1
Meadow La *BATHSE* BA2 ....103 G3
Meadow Md *FRCTL/WBN* BS36 ...23 F1
  YATE/CS BS37........................14 A2
Meadow Pk *CBATH/BATHN* BA1...91 G5
Meadow Pl *MTN/WRL* BS22......118 C5
Meadow Rd *CLVDN* BS21............64 C2
  YATE/CS BS37........................13 H5
Meadowside *THNB/SVB* BS35......9 E4
Meadowside Dr
  HGRV/WHIT BS14..................96 D1
The Meadows
  KGWD/HNM BS15..................76 A2
Meadow St *AVONM* BS11............28 A4
  WSM BS23................................6 D4
Meadowsweet Av
  BRSTK/PCHW BS34................32 D2
Meadow V *EVILLE/WHL* BS5 ....58 A2
Meadow Vw
  FRCTL/WBN BS36 ....24 A3
Meadow Wy *ALMDB* BS32 ....21 G3
Mead Rd *BMSTR* BS3................73 G2
  BRSTK/PCHW BS34 ....21 H4
  PTSHD/EG BS20......................39 G5
  YATE/CS BS37........................27 E2
The Meads *MANG/FISH* BS16......49 F1
Mead St *BMSTR* BS3..................73 G2

The Mead *BRSTK/PCHW* BS34 ....32 D1
  LCASH BS21 ....94 C2
Mead V *MTN/WRL* BS22............122 B3
Meadway
  HNLZ/SM/SNYPK/WT BS9 ......44 A2
Mead Wy *THNB/SVB* BS35 ....8 C5
Meadway Av *NAIL* BS48 ....67 E4
Meardon Rd *HGRV/WHIT* BS14....86 D3
Meardon Rd *BATHSE* BA2..........108 D5
Mede Cl *CBRIS/FH* BS1 ....5 G7
Medical Av *CFTN/FAIL* BS8..........4 D3
Medina Cl *THNB/SVB* BS35..........8 D5
Medway Cl *KEYN* BS31..............98 A1
Medway Dr *THNB/SVB* BS35........8 C4
Medway Dr *FRCTL/WBN* BS36......23 H3
  KEYN BS31 ....98 B1
Meere Bank *AVONM* BS11 ....28 C3
Meetinghouse La
  YTN/CONG BS49....................113 G2
Meg Thatchers Gn
  EVILLE/WHL BS5 ....58 B4
Melbourne Dr *YATE/CS* BS37......26 D1
Melbourne Rd *HORF/LLZ* BS7......45 H4
Melbourne Ter *CLVDN* BS21........64 C3
Melbury Rd
  BRSG/KWL/STAPK BS4............73 H4
Melcombe Rd *BATHSE* BA2..........2 A7
Melita Rd *RDLND/MONT* BS6......46 A5
Melient Av
  BMSTRD/HC/WWD BS13........95 H1
Mells Cl *KEYN* BS31..................98 B2
Melrose Av *CFTN/FAIL* BS8........55 F3
  YATE/CS BS37........................14 B5
Melrose Cl *YATE/CS* BS37..........14 C5
Melrose Gv *BATHSE* BA2..........107 G4
Melrose Pl *CFTN/FAIL* BS8..........55 F3
Melrose Ter
  CBATH/BATHN BA1................102 D2
Melton Crs *HORF/LLZ* BS7..........46 C1
Melville Rd *RDLND/MONT* BS6 ....55 F2
Melville Ter *BMSTR* BS3..............72 D3
Melvin Sq
  BRSG/KWL/STAPK BS4............73 F5
Memorial Cl *KGWD/HNM* BS15....75 G2
Memorial Rd
  KGWD/HNM BS15..................75 G2
Mendip Av *MTN/WRL* BS22......122 B2
  NAIL BS48..............................67 G5
Mendip Cl *KEYN* BS31................88 A4
  NAIL BS48..............................67 G5
Mendip Crs *MANG/FISH* BS16....49 C1
Mendip Gdns *BATHSE* BA2........110 B2
  YTN/CONG BS49 ....112 D4
Mendip Rd *BMSTR* BS3..............73 E3
  OMX/HUT/LCK BS24 ....127 F2
  PTSHD/EG BS20......................39 E3
  WSM BS23................................7 J4
  YTN/CONG BS49 ....112 B3
Mendip Vw
  OLD/WMLY/WICK BS30 ....61 G4
Mendip View Av
  MANG/FISH BS16....................48 A5
Menhyr Gv *HNBRY/STHM* BS10 ...31 F2
Merchants Quay *CBRIS/FH* BS1 ...4 E6
Merchants Rw *CBRIS/FH* BS1 * 4 C7
Merchant St *CBRIS/FH* BS1..........5 G2
Mercia Dr *CBRISNE* BS2..............56 C1
Mercier Cl *YATE/CS* BS37..........14 B5
Merfield Rd
  BRSG/KWL/STAPK BS4............74 A4
Meridian Pl *CFTN/FAIL* BS8..........4 A3
Meridian Rd *RDLND/MONT* BS6 ..55 G2
Meridian Ter *HORF/LLZ* BS7 * 45 H5
Meridian V *CFTN/FAIL* BS8 ....4 A3
Meriet Av
  BMSTRD/HC/WWD BS13........84 C5
Merioneth St *BMSTR* BS3............73 G3
Meriton St *CBRISNE* BS2............74 A1
Merlin Cl
  HNLZ/SM/SNYPK/WT BS9 ......30 D5
  MTN/WRL BS22 ....122 B3
Merlin Pk *PTSHD/EG* BS20 ....38 D4
Merlin Rdg *MANG/FISH* BS16......50 C4
Merlin Rd *BRSTK/PCHW* BS34 ....19 F3
Merlin Wy *YATE/CS* BS37............26 B3
Merrimans Rd *AVONM* BS11........28 D5
Merryweather Cl *ALMDB* BS32 ....22 D4
Merrywood Cl *BMSTR* BS3..........72 D2
Merrywood Rd *BMSTR* BS3..........72 D2
Merstham Rd *CBRISNE* BS2........56 C1
Merton Dr
  OMX/HUT/LCK BS24 ....122 D3
Merton Rd *HORF/LLZ* BS7 ....46 A3
Mervyn Rd *HORF/LLZ* BS7..........46 A4
Metford Gv *RDLND/MONT* BS6 ....45 F5
Metford Pl *RDLND/MONT* BS6......45 C5
Metford Rd *RDLND/MONT* BS6....45 F5
Methwyn Cl *MTN/WRL* BS22......121 H4
The Mews *CBATH/BATHN* BA1....101 F4
Mezellion Pl
  CBATH/BATHN BA1................102 D3
Middle Av *CBRIS/FH* BS1 * 4 E5
Middle La *CBATH/BATHN* BA1....103 E3
Middlepiece La *KEYN* BS31........98 C5
Middle Rd *KGWD/HNM* BS15......49 F5
Middleton Rd *AVONM* BS11........29 F5
Middle Yeo Gn *NAIL* BS48 * 67 E3
Midford Rd *BATHSE* BA2............111 G4
Midford La *BATHSE* BA2............110 D4
Midhaven Ri *MTN/WRL* BS22......117 H4
Midland Bridge Rd
  CBATH/BATHN BA1..................2 D5
Midland Rd *BATHSE* BA2............2 E4
  CBRISNE BS2............................5 K3
  EVILLE/WHL BS5 ....48 D4
Midland St *CBRISNE* BS2 ....5 K4
Midland Ter *MANG/FISH* BS16....47 H5
Midland Wy *THNB/SVB* BS35 ......8 C4
Midsummer Blds
  CBATH/BATHN BA1................102 D3
Milburn Rd *WSM* BS23 ....7 G1
Milbury Gdns *MTN/WRL* BS22 ..121 G1
Mildred St *EVILLE/WHL* BS5........58 C3
Mile End *CBATH/BATHN* BA1 * ..103 E3
Miles Ct *BATHSE* BA2 ....3 H6
  OLD/WMLY/WICK BS30 ....76 C2
Miles Rd *CFTN/FAIL* BS8............55 E2

Miles's Blds *CBATH/BATHN* BA1 ....3 F3
Miles St *BATHSE* BA2 ....3 H6
Milestone Ct *MTN/WRL* BS22 ...123 C1
Milk Wy *HGRV/WHIT* BS14........85 H2
Milford Av
  OLD/WMLY/WICK BS30 ....61 F4
Milford St *BMSTR* BS3................72 D2
Milk St *CBATH/BATHN* BA1 ....3 F5
Millard Cl *HNBRY/STHM* BS10....31 G3
Mill Av *CBRIS/FH* BS1..................5 F5
Millbank Cl
  BRSG/KWL/STAPK BS4............74 D3
Millbrook Av
  BRSG/KWL/STAPK BS4............75 E3
Millbrook Cl
  OLD/WMLY/WICK BS30 ....60 A5
Millbrook Pl *BATHSE* BA2 ....3 H7
Millbrook Rd *YATE/CS* BS37 ......13 F5
Mill Cl *FRCTL/WBN* BS36 ....24 A3
Mill Cl *BATHSE* BA2....................37 F1
Millcross *CLVDN* BS21 ....64 C4
Millennium Pl
  FRCTL/WBN BS36 ....24 B3
Miller Cl *WSM* BS23....................7 G5
Millers Cl *PTSHD/EG* BS20..........42 C4
Millers Dr
  OLD/WMLY/WICK BS30 ....77 F1
Millers Ri *MTN/WRL* BS22 ....117 H4
Milk Wy *BATHSE* BA2................103 H5
Millfield *THNB/SVB* BS35 ....8 D2
Millfield Dr
  OLD/WMLY/WICK BS30 ....60 A5
Millground Rd
  BMSTRD/HC/WWD BS13........85 H5
Miller Rd *YTN/CONG* BS49 ....113 G3
Milliman Cl
  BMSTRD/HC/WWD BS13........84 D4
Mill La *BATHSE* BA2..................107 G1
  BATHSE BA2..........................104 A2
  BMSTR BS3..............................73 E2
  FRCTL/WBN BS36 ....35 F1
  OLD/WMLY/WICK BS30 ....77 F1
  YATE/CS BS37........................27 H4
  YTN/CONG BS49 ....114 D2
Mill Leg *YTN/CONG* BS49 ....115 E2
Mill Pond Cl *OLD/WMLY/WICK* BS30..107 H2
Millpill Cl
  HNLZ/SM/SNYPK/WT BS9 ......44 B3
Mill Rd *FRCTL/WBN* BS36............35 H1
Millward Gv *MANG/FISH* BS16....48 C4
Milner Gn
  OLD/WMLY/WICK BS30 ....76 D1
Milner Rd *HORF/LLZ* BS7............46 B3
Milsom St *CBATH/BATHN* BA1 ......3 F4
  EVILLE/WHL BS5 ....56 C3
Milton Av *BATHSE* BA2..............108 C3
  WSM BS23................................7 J3
Milton Brow *MTN/WRL* BS22....121 G1
  YATE/CS BS37........................13 H5
Milton Cl *NAIL* BS48..................67 F3
Milton Hl *MTN/WRL* BS22........121 H2
Milton La *MTN/WRL* BS22 ....121 G1
Milton Pk *EVILLE/WHL* BS5........57 E4
Milton Park Rd
  MTN/WRL BS22 ....121 H2
Milton Ri *MTN/WRL* BS22 ....121 G2
Milton Rd *MTN/WRL* BS22 ....121 H2
  MTN/WRL BS22......................122 A2
  WSM BS23................................7 H3
  YATE/CS BS37........................13 H5
Milton St
  BMSTRD/HC/WWD BS13........85 E5
Milverton Gdns *CBRISNE* BS2 ....56 B1
Milward Rd *KEYN* BS31..............88 B3
Mina Rd *CBRISNE* BS2................56 C1
Minehead Rd
  BRSG/KWL/STAPK BS4............73 C5
Minerva Ct *LGASH* BS41 ....70 C4
Minerva Gdns *BATHSE* BA2......107 H3
Minor's La *HNBRY/STHM* BS10 ...17 G2
Minsmere Rd *KEYN* BS31 ....98 B1
Minster Wy *BATHSE* BA2..........103 F4
Minton Cl *HGRV/WHIT* BS14......86 A4
Minto Rd *CBRISNE* BS2................56 C1
Mission Rd *YATE/CS* BS37..........13 E3
Mitchell Cl *CBRIS/FH* BS1............5 G5
Mitchell La *CBRIS/FH* BS1............5 G5
Mitchell Wk
  OLD/WMLY/WICK BS30 ....60 B5
Mivart St *EVILLE/WHL* BS5........56 D1
Mizzymead Cl *NAIL* BS48 ....67 E5
Mizzymead Ri *NAIL* BS48............67 E5
Mizzymead Rd *NAIL* BS48..........67 F4
Modecombe Gv
  HNBRY/STHM BS10................30 D2
Mogg St *CBRISNE* BS2................56 C1
Molesworth Cl
  BMSTRD/HC/WWD BS13........84 B5
Molesworth Dr
  BMSTRD/HC/WWD BS13........84 B5
Monarch's Wy
  BLAG/CWMG/WR BS40 ....94 A5
  BRSG/KWL/STAPK BS4............75 E2
  CFTN/FAIL BS8........................55 E3
  EVILLE/WHL BS5 ....57 H5
  KEYN BS31..............................88 C2
  KGWD/HNM BS15..................75 G4
  LGASH BS41 ....70 D4
  NAIL BS48..............................80 D3
  OLD/WMLY/WICK BS30 ....61 G5
  YATE/CS BS37........................15 G4
Monk Rd *HORF/LLZ* BS7............45 H4
Monks Av *KGWD/HNM* BS15......58 B3
Monksdale Rd *BATHSE* BA2......108 A5
Monks Hl *MTN/WRL* BS22 ....116 C5
Monk's Park Av *HORF/LLZ* BS7....32 A4
Monks Park Wy
  HNBRY/STHM BS10................32 A5
Monkton Av
  OMX/HUT/LCK BS24 ....125 F4
Monkton Rd *KGWD/HNM* BS15....75 G2
Monmouth Cl *PTSHD/EG* BS20 ..38 D4
Monmouth Rd
  CBATH/BATHN BA1..................2 A1
Monmouth Rd *HORF/LLZ* BS7....45 H4
  KEYN BS31..............................88 A4
  PTSHD/EG BS20......................40 A3
Monmouth St *BMSTR* BS3..........73 G3
  CBATH/BATHN BA1..................3 F4

Monsdale Cl
  HNBRY/STHM BS10................31 E3
Monsdale Dr
  HNBRY/STHM BS10................31 E2
Montacute Circ
  OMX/HUT/LCK BS24 ....122 C3
Montague Cl
  BRSTK/PCHW BS34................21 G5
Montague Hl
  RDLND/MONT BS6..................55 H3
Montague Hl South
  CBRISNE BS2............................5 F1
Montague Rd *KEYN* BS31 ....99 E2
Montepelier *WSM* BS23................7 F1
Montgomery St *BMSTR* BS3........73 G2
Montpelier East *WSM* BS23..........7 G1
Montreal Av *HORF/LLZ* BS7........32 B5
Montrose Av
  RDLND/MONT BS6..................55 G2
Montrose Pk
  BRSG/KWL/STAPK BS4............74 C4
Montroy Cl
  HNLZ/SM/SNYPK/WT BS9 ......45 G2
Moon St *CBRIS/FH* BS1................5 G1
Moor Croft Dr
  OLD/WMLY/WICK BS30 ....76 C2
Moor Croft Rd
  OMX/HUT/LCK BS24 ....126 B3
Mordell Cl *YATE/CS* BS37..........25 H1
Moorend Farm Av
  AVONM BS11..........................17 E5
Moorend Gdns *AVONM* BS11......43 F1
Moorend Rd *MANG/FISH* BS16 ..34 D2
Moor End Spout *NAIL* BS48........67 E4
Moorfield Rd *NAIL* BS48............79 C2
Moorfields Cl *BATHSE* BA2........108 A5
Moorfields Dr *BATHSE* BA2........108 A4
Moorfields Rd *BATHSE* BA2......108 A5
  NAIL BS48..............................67 H3
Moor Gr *PTSHD/EG* BS20 ....40 B4
Moor Gv *AVONM* BS11................29 F5
Moorhill St *EVILLE/WHL* BS5......56 D2
Moorhouse La *AVONM* BS11 ......17 F5
  HNBRY/STHM BS10................30 D1
The Moorings *PTSHD/EG* BS20 ..42 C4
Moorland Rd *BATHSE* BA2 ....2 A6
  MTN/WRL BS22 ....124 C2
  YATE/CS BS37........................25 H1
Moorlands Cl *NAIL* BS48 ....67 E4
Moorlands Rd
  MANG/FISH BS16....................58 A1
Moor La *CLVDN* BS21 ....64 D3
  MTN/WRL BS22 ....64 C2
  RDLND/MONT BS6..................55 F1
  OMX/HUT/LCK BS24 ....125 H1
Moorlay Crs
  BLAG/CWMG/WR BS40 ....93 C4
Moor Pk *CLVDN* BS21 ....65 E3
Moorpark Av *YATE/CS* BS37 ......25 G1
Moorside Gv *YTN/CONG* BS49 ..112 B2
Moravian Ct *KGWD/HNM* BS15 ..58 D3
Moravian Rd *KGWD/HNM* BS15 ..58 D3
Morden Wk *HGRV/WHIT* BS14....86 C2
Moreton Cl *HGRV/WHIT* BS14 ....85 H5
Morford St *CBATH/BATHN* BA1 ....3 F2
Morgan Cl *KEYN* BS31................99 E2
  OMX/HUT/LCK BS24 ....123 E3
Morgans Hill Cl *NAIL* BS48........79 E1
Morgan St *CBRISNE* BS2............56 B2
Morley Av *MANG/FISH* BS16......49 G4
Morley Cl *BRSTK/PCHW* BS34......20 D5
  MANG/FISH BS16....................48 D5
Morley Rd *BMSTR* BS3................72 D2
Morley Sq *HORF/LLZ* BS7..........46 A5
Morley St *CBRISNE* BS2..............56 B2
Morley Ter *BATHSE* BA2 * 107 H1
  KGWD/HNM BS15..................58 D2
Mornington Rd *CFTN/FAIL* BS8 ...55 E1
Morpeth Rd
  BRSG/KWL/STAPK BS4............85 E1
Morris Cl *CBATH/BATHN* BA1......104 C1
Morris Rd *HORF/LLZ* BS7 ....46 C3
Morse Rd *EVILLE/WHL* BS5........57 E4
Morston Ct *MTN/WRL* BS22......121 H4
Mortimer Cl
  CBATH/BATHN BA1................101 G2
Mortimer Rd
  BRSTK/PCHW BS34................32 D4
  CFTN/FAIL BS8........................55 E1
Morton St *EVILLE/WHL* BS5........56 D4
Morton Wy *THNB/SVB* BS35 ....9 E1
Moseley Gv *WSM* BS23..............124 D4
Mountain Ash
  CBATH/BATHN BA1................102 A3
Mountain Wd
  CBATH/BATHN BA1................104 D2
Mountbatten Cl
  MTN/WRL BS22 ....117 F4
  YATE/CS BS37........................13 H4
Mount Beacon
  CBATH/BATHN BA1................102 D3
Mount Beacon Rw
  CBATH/BATHN BA1 * 102 C3
Mount Cl *FRCTL/WBN* BS36........23 C2
Mount Crs *FRCTL/WBN* BS36 ....58 D5
Mount Gdns *KGWD/HNM* BS15 ..58 D5
Mount Gv *BATHSE* BA2 ....107 G4
Mount Hill Rd
  KGWD/HNM BS15..................58 C5
Mount Pleasant
  PTSHD/EG BS20......................42 D4
Mount Pleasant Ter
  BMSTR BS3..............................73 G2
Mount Rd *BATHSE* BA2............107 G4
  CBATH/BATHN BA1................101 H4
The Mount *KGWD/HNM* BS15......58 D5
Mount Vw *BATHSE* BA2............107 G3
  CBATH/BATHN BA1................102 C3
Mow Barton
  BMSTRD/HC/WWD BS13........83 H3
  YATE/CS BS37........................13 H5
Mowbray Rd *HGRV/WHIT* BS14...86 B2
Mowcroft Rd
  BMSTRD/HC/WWD BS13........84 D5
Moxham Dr
  BMSTRD/HC/WWD BS13........84 D5

Mud La *YTN/CONG* BS49 ....113 E1
Muirfield
  OLD/WMLY/WICK BS30 ....59 G5
Mulberry Av *PTSHD/EG* BS20......40 A3
Mulberry Cl *KGWD/HNM* BS15 ..58 D5
  MTN/WRL BS22 ....122 D2
  NAIL BS48..............................79 H3
  PTSHD/EG BS20......................40 A3
Mulberry Dr *KGWD/HNM* BS15 ..59 F2
Mulberry Gdns
  MANG/FISH BS16....................48 D5
Mulberry Rd *YTN/CONG* BS49 ..115 E3
Mulberry Wk
  HNLZ/SM/SNYPK/WT BS9 ......44 C3
Muller Av *HORF/LLZ* BS7 ....46 B5
Muller Rd *EVILLE/WHL* BS5 ....47 E5
  HORF/LLZ BS7........................46 D5
Mulready Cl *HORF/LLZ* BS7........47 E2
Murdoch Sq *HORF/LLZ* BS7........32 B5
Murford Av
  BMSTRD/HC/WWD BS13........84 C4
Murford Wk
  BMSTRD/HC/WWD BS13........84 C5
Murray St *BMSTR* BS3................72 D2
Musgrove Cl *AVONM* BS11 ....30 A3
Myrtleberry Md
  MTN/WRL BS22 ....117 H5
Myrtle Dr *AVONM* BS11..............43 E3
Myrtle Gdns *YTN/CONG* BS49 ..112 B3
Myrtle Hl *PTSHD/EG* BS20..........40 A3
Myrtle Rd *CBRISNE* BS2..............4 D1
Myrtle St *BMSTR* BS3................72 C2
Myrtle Tree Crs
  MTN/WRL BS22 ....116 B2

N

Nags Head Hl *EVILLE/WHL* BS5 ...58 A5
Nailsea Cl
  BMSTRD/HC/WWD BS13........84 B2
Nailsea Ct *NAIL* BS48 ....78 C4
Nailsea Moor La *NAIL* BS48........78 A2
Nailsea Pk *NAIL* BS48................67 F4
Nailsea Park Cl *NAIL* BS48..........67 G4
Nailsea Wall *CLVDN* BS21..........65 H5
Nailsworth Av *YATE/CS* BS37......26 A1
Naishcombe Hl
  OLD/WMLY/WICK BS30 ....61 G4
Naish La *NAIL* BS48 ....93 E1
Napier Miles Rd *AVONM* BS11 ....29 G5
Napier Rd *AVONM* BS11............29 H5
  CBATH/BATHN BA1................101 F1
  RDLND/MONT BS6..................55 F1
Napier Sq *AVONM* BS11............28 A4
Napier St *EVILLE/WHL* BS5..........56 D5
Narroways Rd *CBRISNE* BS2......56 D1
Narrow La *MANG/FISH* BS16......49 G4
Narrow Plh *CBRISNE* BS2 ....5 G5
Narrow Quay *CBRIS/FH* BS1........4 C5
Naseby Wk *EVILLE/WHL* BS5......57 H2
Nash Cl *KEYN* BS31....................99 F1
Nash Dr *HORF/LLZ* BS7..............47 E1
Naunton Wy *MTN/WRL* BS22....122 A3
Neads Dr
  OLD/WMLY/WICK BS30 ....77 F1
Neale Wy *AVONM* BS11 * 28 C4
Neath Rd *EVILLE/WHL* BS5..........57 E3
Nelson Ct *MTN/WRL* BS16 * 117 H4
Nelson Pde *BMSTR* BS3..............73 E2
Nelson Pl East
  CBATH/BATHN BA1..................3 G1
Nelson Pl West
  CBATH/BATHN BA1..................2 D4
Nelson Rd *MANG/FISH* BS16......48 D3
Nelson St *BMSTR* BS3................72 B4
  CBRIS/FH BS1..........................5 F3
Nelson Ter *CBATH/BATHN* BA1 ....3 G1
Nelson Vls *CBATH/BATHN* BA1....2 C4
Neston Wk
  BRSG/KWL/STAPK BS4............85 G1
Netham Rd *EVILLE/WHL* BS5 ......57 E3
Netherton Wood La *NAIL* BS48 ..78 A4
Netherways *CLVDN* BS21............64 B4
Nettlestone Cl
  HNBRY/STHM BS10................30 C1
Nevalan Dr *EVILLE/WHL* BS5......57 F3
Neva Rd *WSM* BS23......................6 F4
Neville Rd *KGWD/HNM* BS15......59 E1
Nevil Rd *HORF/LLZ* BS7..............46 B4
Newbolt Cl *WSM* BS23..............125 F2
New Bond St *CBATH/BATHN* BA1...3 G4
New Bond Street Pl
  CBATH/BATHN BA1 * 3 F4
Newbourne Rd
  MTN/WRL BS22 ....121 H4
Newbrick Rd
  BRSTK/PCHW BS34................22 A5
New Br *CBATH/BATHN* BA1......101 E4
Newbridge Cl
  BRSG/KWL/STAPK BS4............57 F5
Newbridge Gdns
  CBATH/BATHN BA1................101 E4
Newbridge Hl
  CBATH/BATHN BA1................101 F4
Newbridge Rd
  BRSG/KWL/STAPK BS4............57 F5
  CBATH/BATHN BA1................101 E3
New Bristol Rd
  MTN/WRL BS22 ....122 C2
New Brunswick Av
  EVILLE/WHL BS5 ....58 B4
New Blds *MANG/FISH* BS16......47 H4
Newbury Rd *HORF/LLZ* BS7........46 C1
New Charlotte St *BMSTR* BS3......73 F3
New Charlton Wy
  BRSTK/PCHW BS34................19 E4
New Cheltenham Rd
  KGWD/HNM BS15..................58 D2
New Church Rd *WSM* BS23........124 D5
Newcombe Dr
  HNLZ/SM/SNYPK/WT BS9 ......44 A2
Newcombe Rd
  HNLZ/SM/SNYPK/WT BS9 ......44 D1
Newditch La
  BLAG/CWMG/WR BS40 ....92 D3
Newent Av *EVILLE/WHL* BS5......58 B5

New Fosseway Rd
HGRV/WHIT BS14 86 A3
Newfoundland Rd
CBRISNE BS2 56 B3
Newfoundland St CBRIS/FH BS1 5 J1
Newfoundland Wy
CBRISNE BS2 5 K1
PTSHD/EG BS20 40 A1
Newgate CBRIS/FH BS1 5 G3
Newhaven Pl PTSHD/EG BS20 38 C4
Newhaven Rd PTSHD/EG BS20 38 B5
New John St BMSTR BS3 * 72 D3
New Kings Ct HORF/LLZ BS7 45 G4
New Kingsley Rd CBRISNE BS2 * 5 J4
New King St CBATH/BATHN BA1 2 E4
Newland Dr
BMSTRD/HC/WWD BS13 84 B5
Newland Rd
BMSTRD/HC/WWD BS13 84 B5
WSM BS23 7 G7
Newlands Av FRCTL/WBN BS36 24 A3
Newlands Gn CLVDN BS21 64 D4
Newlands Hl PTSHD/EG BS20 39 G4
Newlands Rd KEYN BS31 88 A5
The Newlands
MANG/FISH BS16 48 B1
Newland Wk
BMSTRD/HC/WWD BS13 95 F1
New Leaze ALMDB BS32 11 E4
Newlyn Av
HNLZ/SM/SNYPK/WT BS9 44 B3
Newlyn Wk
BRSG/KWL/STAPK BS4 74 A5
Newlyn Wy YATE/CS BS37 14 B5
Newman Cl YATE/CS BS37 37 F1
New Mdw HGRV/WHIT BS14 85 H3
Newnham Cl HGRV/WHIT BS14 86 C2
Newnham Pl
BRSTK/PCHW BS34 20 B1
New Orchard St
CBATH/BATHN BA1 3 G5
Newport Cl CLVDN BS21 64 C3
PTSHD/EG BS20 38 D4
Newport Rd PTSHD/EG BS20 42 C3
Newport St BMSTR BS3 73 F3
Newquay Rd
BRSG/KWL/STAPK BS4 85 G1
New Queen St BMSTR BS3 73 F2
KGWD/HNM BS15 58 B2
New Rd BNWL BS29 127 H2
BRSTK/PCHW BS34 32 B2
CBATH/BATHN BA1 104 D2
CLVDN BS21 64 D3
PTSHD/EG BS20 42 C4
Newry Wk
BRSG/KWL/STAPK BS4 73 F5
Newsome Av PTSHD/EG BS20 42 C4
New Stadium Rd
EVILLE/WHL BS5 56 D1
New Station Rd
MANG/FISH BS16 48 A4
New Station Wy
MANG/FISH BS16 48 A4
New St CBATH/BATHN BA1 2 E4
CBRISNE BS2 5 J2
New Thomas St CBRISNE BS2 5 J3
Newton Cl KGWD/HNM BS15 59 G2
Newton Gn NAIL BS48 78 D1
Newton Rd BATHSE BA2 107 E1
OLD/WMLY/WICK BS30 76 D1
WSM BS23 124 D1
Newton's Rd MTN/WRL BS22 117 F4
Newton St EVILLE/WHL BS5 56 C3
New Wk KGWD/HNM BS15 75 G1
New Walls
BRSG/KWL/STAPK BS4 73 G2
Niblett Cl KGWD/HNM BS15 59 F5
Niblett's Hl EVILLE/WHL BS5 58 A5
Nibley La YATE/CS BS37 12 D4
Nibley Rd AVONM BS11 43 E3
Nicholas La EVILLE/WHL BS5 58 A5
Nicholas Rd EVILLE/WHL BS5 56 D2
Nicholas St BMSTR BS3 73 F2
Nicholettes
OLD/WMLY/WICK BS30 77 G1
Nicholls La FRCTL/WBN BS36 23 E3
Nichol's Rd PTSHD/EG BS20 38 D2
Nigel Pk AVONM BS11 43 E1
Nightingale Cl
BRSG/KWL/STAPK BS4 57 G5
FRCTL/WBN BS36 23 G4
MTN/WRL BS22 122 B2
THNB/SVB BS35 9 E2
Nightingale Gdns NAIL BS48 66 D4
Nightingale La
FRCTL/WBN BS36 23 F2
Nightingale Ri PTSHD/EG BS20 38 D5
Nile St CBATH/BATHN BA1 2 D4
Nine Tree Hl RDLND/MONT BS6 55 H2
Ninth Av HORF/LLZ BS7 32 D4
Nithsdale Rd WSM BS23 124 D2
Noble Av
OLD/WMLY/WICK BS30 77 F2
Nomis Pk YTN/CONG BS49 115 E4
Nore Gdns PTSHD/EG BS20 39 G2
Nore Park Dr PTSHD/EG BS20 38 D3
Nore Rd PTSHD/EG BS20 38 C4
Norfolk Av CBRISNE BS2 5 H1
RDLND/MONT BS6 56 A1
Norfolk Blds CBATH/BATHN BA1 2 D4
Norfolk Crs CBATH/BATHN BA1 2 D4
Norfolk Gv KEYN BS31 87 H5
Norfolk Pl BMSTR BS3 72 D3
Norfolk Rd PTSHD/EG BS20 40 A4
WSM BS23 125 E1
Norland Rd CFTN/FAIL BS8 54 D3
Norley Rd HORF/LLZ BS7 46 B1
Normanby Rd EVILLE/WHL BS5 56 D2
Norman Gv KGWD/HNM BS15 58 D1
Norman Rd CBRISNE BS2 56 C1
KEYN BS31 99 E1
OLD/WMLY/WICK BS30 59 H3
The Normans BATHSE BA2 104 A3
Normans Wy PTSHD/EG BS20 41 H5
Normanton Rd CFTN/FAIL BS8 55 E1
Norrisville Rd
RDLND/MONT BS6 56 A2
Northampton St
CBATH/BATHN BA1 2 E1
Northcote Rd CFTN/FAIL BS8 54 D2
EVILLE/WHL BS5 57 G3
MANG/FISH BS16 49 F2
Northcote St EVILLE/WHL BS5 56 D2
North Cft
OLD/WMLY/WICK BS30 77 G2
North Devon Rd
MANG/FISH BS16 48 A3
North Dro NAIL BS48 66 C4
North East Rd THNB/SVB BS35 8 D2
North End YTN/CONG BS49 112 A1
Northend Av KGWD/HNM BS15 58 D1
Northend Rd KGWD/HNM BS15 59 E1
Northern Wy CLVDN BS21 65 F2
Northfield YATE/CS BS37 25 H2
Northfield Av KGWD/HNM BS15 76 A1
Northfield Rd EVILLE/WHL BS5 58 B4
PTSHD/EG BS20 38 B5
Northfields
CBATH/BATHN BA1 102 C3
Northfields Cl
CBATH/BATHN BA1 102 C3
Northgate St CBATH/BATHN BA1 3 G4
North Green St CFTN/FAIL BS8 54 D5
North Gv PTSHD/EG BS20 42 C4
North Hills Cl
OMX/HUT/LCK BS24 125 G4
North La BATHSE BA2 109 G2
NAIL BS48 66 C5
Northleach Wk AVONM BS11 43 F3
North Leaze LGASH BS41 71 E4
Northleigh Av MTN/WRL BS22 121 H2
Northmead La YATE/CS BS37 12 B1
Northover Rd
HNLZ/SM/SNYPK/WT BS9 30 D4
North Parade Blds
CBATH/BATHN BA1 * 3 G5
North Parade Rd BATHSE BA2 3 H5
North Pk KGWD/HNM BS15 59 E2
North Rd BATHSE BA2 111 F1
BMSTR BS3 72 B2
BRSTK/PCHW BS34 33 G1
CFTN/FAIL BS8 54 B5
FRCTL/WBN BS36 23 F3
RDLND/MONT BS6 55 H1
THNB/SVB BS35 8 D2
YATE/CS BS37 13 F4
North Side Rd NAIL BS48 92 A4
North St BMSTR BS3 72 B2
CBRIS/FH BS1 5 G1
MANG/FISH BS16 48 D3
NAIL BS48 66 C5
OLD/WMLY/WICK BS30 77 F2
WSM BS23 6 D3
Northumberland Blds
CBATH/BATHN BA1 * 3 F4
Northumberland Pl
CBATH/BATHN BA1 3 G4
Northumberland Rd
RDLND/MONT BS6 55 G1
Northumbria Dr
HNLZ/SM/SNYPK/WT BS9 45 F3
North Vw MANG/FISH BS16 48 D4
RDLND/MONT BS6 45 E4
North View Cl BATHSE BA2 107 G2
Northville Rd HORF/LLZ BS7 32 C4
North Wy BATHSE BA2 107 F2
Northway BRSTK/PCHW BS34 32 D1
Northwick Rd HORF/LLZ BS7 32 B5
LGASH BS41 96 A5
Northwoods Wk
HNBRY/STHM BS10 31 H2
Norton Cl KGWD/HNM BS15 59 F4
Norton La HGRV/WHIT BS14 97 F3
MTN/WRL BS22 116 D4
PLTN/PENS BS39 96 B5
Norton Rd
BRSG/KWL/STAPK BS4 73 H4
Nortons Wood La CLVDN BS21 63 F5
Norwich Dr
BRSG/KWL/STAPK BS4 57 G5
Norwood Av BATHSE BA2 109 H3
Norwood Gv PTSHD/EG BS20 38 D3
Notgrove Cl MTN/WRL BS22 121 G1
Nottingham Rd HORF/LLZ BS7 46 A5
Nottingham St BMSTR BS3 73 F3
Nova Scotia Pl CBRIS/FH BS1 * 72 B1
Nova Wy AVONM BS11 28 B4
Novers Crs
BRSG/KWL/STAPK BS4 84 D1
Novers Hl BMSTR BS3 72 D5
BRSG/KWL/STAPK BS4 84 D1
Novers La
BRSG/KWL/STAPK BS4 84 D2
Novers Park Cl
BRSG/KWL/STAPK BS4 73 E5
Novers Park Dr
BRSG/KWL/STAPK BS4 84 D1
Novers Park Rd
BRSG/KWL/STAPK BS4 85 E1
Novers Rd
BRSG/KWL/STAPK BS4 84 D1
Nowhere La NAIL BS48 * 67 H5
Nugent Hl RDLND/MONT BS6 55 H2
Nunney Cl KEYN BS31 98 B2
Nursery Gdns
HNBRY/STHM BS10 31 E2
The Nursery BMSTR BS3 72 C3
Nutfield Gv BRSTK/PCHW BS34 32 D3
Nutgrove Av BMSTR BS3 73 F3
Nuthatch Dr MANG/FISH BS16 47 H2
Nuthatch Gdns
MANG/FISH BS16 48 A2
Nutwell Rd MTN/WRL BS22 122 B1
Nutwell Sq MTN/WRL BS22 122 B1
Nympsfield KGWD/HNM BS15 59 E1

O

Oak Av BATHSE BA2 107 H4
Oak Cl BRSTK/PCHW BS34 21 F3
YATE/CS BS37 13 H4
Oak Ct MTN/WRL BS22 118 B5
Oakdale Av MANG/FISH BS16 34 D5
Oakdale Cl MANG/FISH BS16 35 E5
Oakdale Ct MANG/FISH BS16 48 D1
Oakdale Gdns MTN/WRL BS22 122 C1
Oakdale Rd HGRV/WHIT BS14 85 H1
MANG/FISH BS16 35 E5
Oakdene Av EVILLE/WHL BS5 47 F5
Oak Dr PTSHD/EG BS20 39 F4
Oakenhill Rd
BRSG/KWL/STAPK BS4 74 D4
Oakenhill Wk
BRSG/KWL/STAPK BS4 74 D4
Oakfield Cl CBATH/BATHN BA1 2 A1
Oakfield Ct CFTN/FAIL BS8 * 55 F3
Oakfield Gv CFTN/FAIL BS8 4 A1
Oakfield Pl CFTN/FAIL BS8 4 A1
PTSHD/EG BS20 * 39 H5
Oakfield Rd CFTN/FAIL BS8 55 E3
KEYN BS31 98 A1
KGWD/HNM BS15 58 D4
Oakford Av WSM BS23 7 H3
Oakford La
CBATH/BATHN BA1 91 F1
Oak Gv PTSHD/EG BS20 42 C4
Oakhanger Dr AVONM BS11 29 H4
Oakhill Av
OLD/WMLY/WICK BS30 77 F4
Oakhill Cl NAIL BS48 68 A5
Oakhill La HNBRY/STHM BS10 30 A1
Oakhill Rd BATHSE BA2 108 C5
Oakhurst Rd
HNLZ/SM/SNYPK/WT BS9 44 D3
Oakland Rd EVILLE/WHL BS5 57 G3
RDLND/MONT BS6 55 F2
Oaklands Cl MANG/FISH BS16 49 H3
Oaklands Dr ALMDB BS32 10 C3
MANG/FISH BS16 34 A5
OLD/WMLY/WICK BS30 77 F4
Oaklands Rd MANG/FISH BS16 49 G3
Oak La EVILLE/WHL BS5 57 H1
Oakleaze Rd THNB/SVB BS35 8 D3
Oakleigh Av EVILLE/WHL BS5 57 F3
Oakleigh Cl NAIL BS48 80 A4
Oakleigh Gdns
OLD/WMLY/WICK BS30 77 F4
Oakley BATHSE BA2 109 H2
CLVDN BS21 64 B5
Oakley Rd HORF/LLZ BS7 46 B1
Oakmeade Pk
BRSG/KWL/STAPK BS4 74 A4
Oakridge Cl KGWD/HNM BS15 59 G4
Oak Rd HORF/LLZ BS7 46 A3
Oaksey Gv NAIL BS48 67 H4
The Oaks
BLAG/CWMG/WR BS40 93 G5
NAIL BS48 67 H4
Oak St BATHSE BA2 2 E6
Oaktree Av MANG/FISH BS16 51 G3
Oak Tree Cl KGWD/HNM BS15 75 H4
Oaktree Ct AVONM BS11 43 E1
Oaktree Crs ALMDB BS32 10 D5
Oaktree Gdns
BMSTRD/HC/WWD BS13 83 H4
Oaktree Pl MTN/WRL BS22 118 B5
Oakwood Av
HNLZ/SM/SNYPK/WT BS9 45 F2
Oakwood Gdns
FRCTL/WBN BS36 24 C3
Oakwood Rd
HNLZ/SM/SNYPK/WT BS9 45 F2
Oatfield NAIL BS48 92 A3
Oatlands Av HGRV/WHIT BS14 85 H3
Oberon Av EVILLE/WHL BS5 57 G1
Odins Rd BATHSE BA2 110 B1
Okebourne Cl
HNBRY/STHM BS10 31 F1
Okebourne Rd
HNBRY/STHM BS10 31 F2
Oldacre Rd HGRV/WHIT BS14 96 D2
Old Ashley Hl
RDLND/MONT BS6 56 B1
Old Aust Rd ALMDB BS32 11 E1
Old Banwell Rd
OMX/HUT/LCK BS24 127 E2
Old Barrow Hl AVONM BS11 42 D1
Old Bond St CBATH/BATHN BA1 3 F4
Old Bread St CBRISNE BS2 5 J4
Oldbridge Rd HGRV/WHIT BS14 97 F1
Old Bristol Rd MTN/WRL BS22 122 D1
Oldbury Cha
OLD/WMLY/WICK BS30 76 D4
Oldbury Court Dr
MANG/FISH BS16 48 A2
Oldbury Court Rd
MANG/FISH BS16 48 A3
Old Chapel La NAIL BS48 78 A2
Old Chelsea La CFTN/FAIL BS8 69 H3
Old Church Cl
OLD/WMLY/WICK BS30 * 60 B4
Old Church Rd CLVDN BS21 64 A3
NAIL BS48 79 E1
WSM BS23 124 C4
Old Farm La EVILLE/WHL BS5 58 B5
Old Ferry Rd BATHSE BA2 107 G1
Oldfield La BATHSE BA2 108 A3
Oldfield Pl CFTN/FAIL BS8 72 A1
Oldfield Rd BATHSE BA2 2 C7
CFTN/FAIL BS8 72 B1
Old Fosse Rd BATHSE BA2 110 A1
Old Frome Rd BATHSE BA2 110 C2
Old Gloucester Rd
FRCTL/WBN BS36 22 B3
MANG/FISH BS16 34 B5
Old Hl BLAG/CWMG/WR BS40 93 E5
Old Junction Rd WSM BS23 125 G1
Old King St CBATH/BATHN BA1 3 F3
Old King Street Ct
CBRIS/FH BS1 * 5 G2
Oldlands Av FRCTL/WBN BS36 24 A4
Old La CLVDN BS21 66 D2
MANG/FISH BS16 50 A2
Old Market St CBRISNE BS2 5 J3
Oldmead Wk
BMSTRD/HC/WWD BS13 83 H2
Old Midford Rd BATHSE BA2 111 E3
Old Mill Cl YATE/CS BS37 37 F1
Old Mill Rd PTSHD/EG BS20 39 H3
Old Mill Wy MTN/WRL BS22 122 C3
OMX/HUT/LCK BS24 122 C3
Oldmixon Crs
OMX/HUT/LCK BS24 125 F3
Old Mixon Rd
OMX/HUT/LCK BS24 125 H4
Oldmixon Rd
OMX/HUT/LCK BS24 125 F5
Old Newbridge Hl
CBATH/BATHN BA1 101 F4
Old Orch CBATH/BATHN BA1 3 G2
Old Orchard St
CBATH/BATHN BA1 3 G5
Old Pk CBRISNE BS2 4 D2
Old Park Hl CBRISNE BS2 4 D3
Old Park Rd AVONM BS11 42 D1
CLVDN BS21 62 B5
Old Pooles Yd
BRSG/KWL/STAPK BS4 74 D4
Old Post Office La WSM BS23 * 6 D2
Old Priory Rd PTSHD/EG BS20 42 B4
Old Quarry BATHSE BA2 108 A5
Old Quarry Ri AVONM BS11 43 E1
Old Quarry Rd AVONM BS11 42 D1
Old School Hl BATHSE BA2 110 D3
Old Sneed Av
HNLZ/SM/SNYPK/WT BS9 44 B4
Old Sneed Pk
HNLZ/SM/SNYPK/WT BS9 44 B4
Old Sneed Rd
HNLZ/SM/SNYPK/WT BS9 44 B4
Old St CLVDN BS21 65 E2
Old Vicarage Pl
CFTN/FAIL BS8 * 55 E2
Oldville Av CLVDN BS21 64 D3
Old Wells Rd BATHSE BA2 108 C4
Old Weston Rd NAIL BS48 81 G2
YTN/CONG BS49 114 A1
Olveston Rd HORF/LLZ BS7 46 A3
Olympus Cl BRSTK/PCHW BS34 21 F4
Olympus Rd
BRSTK/PCHW BS34 19 H3
Onega Ter CBATH/BATHN BA1 2 C3
Oolite Gv BATHSE BA2 110 B1
Oolite Rd BATHSE BA2 110 B1
Oram Ct OLD/WMLY/WICK BS30 76 C2
Orange Gv CBATH/BATHN BA1 3 G4
Orange St CBRISNE BS2 5 J1
Orchard Av CBRIS/FH BS1 * 4 D4
THNB/SVB BS35 8 D3
Orchard Bvd
OLD/WMLY/WICK BS30 77 E2
Orchard Cl
BLAG/CWMG/WR BS40 92 D4
FRCTL/WBN BS36 23 E4
HNLZ/SM/SNYPK/WT BS9 44 D3
KEYN BS31 87 H3
KGWD/HNM BS15 59 E3
MTN/WRL BS22 116 C5
NAIL BS48 81 F1
PTSHD/EG BS20 39 H3
YATE/CS BS37 14 B5
YTN/CONG BS49 114 D2
Orchard Ct YTN/CONG BS49 113 F2
Orchard Crs AVONM BS11 42 D1
Orchard Dr
BMSTRD/HC/WWD BS13 84 B3
Orchard Gdns
KGWD/HNM BS15 59 F3
Orchard Ga ALMDB BS32 11 E5
Orchard Gra THNB/SVB BS35 8 C2
Orchard La CBRIS/FH BS1 4 D4
Orchard Lea PTSHD/EG BS20 42 D4
Orchard Pl WSM BS23 6 E4
Orchard Rd CLVDN BS21 64 D4
EVILLE/WHL BS5 57 H3
FRCTL/WBN BS36 24 B3
HORF/LLZ BS7 46 A4
KGWD/HNM BS15 59 E3
LGASH BS41 70 C4
MANG/FISH BS16 51 F3
NAIL BS48 66 D5
OMX/HUT/LCK BS24 126 A4
Orchard Sq EVILLE/WHL BS5 57 F4
The Orchards
KGWD/HNM BS15 59 F3
PTSHD/EG BS20 * 42 C4
Orchard St CBRIS/FH BS1 4 D4
WSM BS23 6 E3
Orchard Ter BATHSE BA2 107 G1
The Orchard BATHSE BA2 100 A4
BRSTK/PCHW BS34 21 H5
OMX/HUT/LCK BS24 126 C1
PTSHD/EG BS20 42 C4
Orchard V KGWD/HNM BS15 59 F4
Orchid Dr BATHSE BA2 110 A1
Oriel Gdns CBATH/BATHN BA1 103 F2
Oriel Gv BATHSE BA2 107 G3
Orion Dr BRSTK/PCHW BS34 21 F4
Orland Wy
OLD/WMLY/WICK BS30 76 D3
Orlebar Gdns AVONM BS11 29 H3
Orme Dr CLVDN BS21 62 B5
Ormerod Rd
HNLZ/SM/SNYPK/WT BS9 44 C4
Ormonds Cl ALMDB BS32 11 G5
Ormsley Cl BRSTK/PCHW BS34 21 G2
Orpen Gdns HORF/LLZ BS7 46 D3
Orpen Pk ALMDB BS32 10 D4
Orpheus Av BRSTK/PCHW BS34 21 G4
Orwell Dr KEYN BS31 88 C5
Orwell St BMSTR BS3 73 F3
Osborne Av HORF/LLZ BS7 46 B5
WSM BS23 7 H4
Osborne Cl BRSTK/PCHW BS34 33 F1
Osborne Rd BMSTR BS3 72 D2
CBATH/BATHN BA1 107 G1
CFTN/FAIL BS8 55 E2
WSM BS23 7 H4
Osborne Ter BMSTR BS3 72 C4
Osborne Vls CBRISNE BS2 4 C1
Osmond Rd
OMX/HUT/LCK BS24 122 C4
Osprey Gdns MTN/WRL BS22 122 C2
Osprey Pk THNB/SVB BS35 9 E1
Osprey Rd EVILLE/WHL BS5 57 E4
Ostlings La
CBATH/BATHN BA1 104 C2
Ottawa Rd WSM BS23 125 E3
Otterford Cl HGRV/WHIT BS14 86 A4
Otter Rd CLVDN BS21 64 D4
Ottery Cl AVONM BS11 29 G4
Ottrells Md ALMDB BS32 11 E4
The Oval BATHSE BA2 107 H4
Overhill PTSHD/EG BS20 42 C5
Over La ALMDB BS32 10 A5
Overndale Rd
MANG/FISH BS16 48 C3
Overnhill Ct MANG/FISH BS16 48 C3
Overnhill Rd MANG/FISH BS16 48 C3
Overton Rd RDLND/MONT BS6 55 H1
Owen Dr CFTN/FAIL BS8 69 G2
Owen Gv
HNLZ/SM/SNYPK/WT BS9 45 F3
Owen St EVILLE/WHL BS5 57 E3
Owls Head Rd
KGWD/HNM BS15 59 E5
Oxbarton BRSTK/PCHW BS34 21 H5
Oxenham Ct EVILLE/WHL BS5 57 F3
Oxen Leaze ALMDB BS32 11 F5
Oxford Pl CFTN/FAIL BS8 54 D5
EVILLE/WHL BS5 56 D2
WSM BS23 * 6 D4
Oxford Rw CBATH/BATHN BA1 3 F2
Oxford Sq
OMX/HUT/LCK BS24 123 E5
Oxford St BMSTR BS3 73 G2
RDLND/MONT BS6 55 G3
WSM BS23 6 D5
Oxhouse Gdns
HNBRY/STHM BS10 30 C2
Oxhouse La CFTN/FAIL BS8 69 G1
Oxleaze
BMSTRD/HC/WWD BS13 85 E5
Oxleaze La LGASH BS41 94 D2
Ozleworth KGWD/HNM BS15 59 G3

P

Pack Horse La BATHSE BA2 110 D3
Paddock Cl ALMDB BS32 11 F5
MANG/FISH BS16 49 H2
Paddock Gdn HGRV/WHIT BS14 85 G5
Paddock Gdns
HGRV/WHIT BS14 85 G5
Paddock Park Homes
MTN/WRL BS22 * 123 E1
The Paddocks BATHSE BA2 111 F1
MANG/FISH BS16 35 G4
THNB/SVB BS35 9 E3
WSM BS23 124 C4
The Paddock CLVDN BS21 64 D4
PTSHD/EG BS20 39 H4
Paddock Woods
BATHSE BA2 109 G5
Padfield Cl BATHSE BA2 107 G2
Padleigh Hl BATHSE BA2 107 F5
Padstow Rd
BRSG/KWL/STAPK BS4 85 F1
Page Rd MANG/FISH BS16 48 D4
Pages Md AVONM BS11 28 C5
Painswick Av
BRSTK/PCHW BS34 20 D2
Painswick Dr YATE/CS BS37 26 A1
Palace Yard Ms
CBATH/BATHN BA1 2 E4
Palmdale Cl
OLD/WMLY/WICK BS30 76 D3
Palmer Rw WSM BS23 6 E3
Palmers Cl
OLD/WMLY/WICK BS30 59 G5
Palmers Leaze ALMDB BS32 22 A3
Palmerston Rd
RDLND/MONT BS6 45 F4
Palmerston St BMSTR BS3 72 C3
Palmer St WSM BS23 6 E3
Palmyra Rd BMSTR BS3 72 C4
Parade Ct EVILLE/WHL BS5 57 H2
The Parade AVONM BS11 43 E2
BMSTRD/HC/WWD BS13 * 84 B3
BRSTK/PCHW BS34 * 20 A3
HGRV/WHIT BS14 * 85 H1
YATE/CS BS37 26 C1
Paragon Blds
CBATH/BATHN BA1 3 G2
Paragon Rd WSM BS23 6 A1
The Paragon CBATH/BATHN BA1 3 G2
CFTN/FAIL BS8 54 D5
Parfitt's Hl EVILLE/WHL BS5 57 H5
Parish Brook Rd NAIL BS48 66 C5
Park Av ALMDB BS32 10 C5
BATHSE BA2 2 E7
BMSTR BS3 73 F3
EVILLE/WHL BS5 57 G3
FRCTL/WBN BS36 23 E4
YTN/CONG BS49 112 B2
Park Cl KEYN BS31 88 A4
KGWD/HNM BS15 59 E4
OLD/WMLY/WICK BS30 77 E1
Park Ct WSM BS23 124 D1
Park Crs EVILLE/WHL BS5 57 F3
MANG/FISH BS16 34 C4
OLD/WMLY/WICK BS30 77 E1
Park End BNWL BS29 127 H2
Parkers Av
OLD/WMLY/WICK BS30 61 G4
Parkers Barton
EVILLE/WHL BS5 56 D5
Parkers Cl HNBRY/STHM BS10 32 A1
Parker St BMSTR BS3 72 C3
Parkes Rd
OMX/HUT/LCK BS24 127 F1
Park Farm Ct
OLD/WMLY/WICK BS30 * 76 C2
Parkfield Av EVILLE/WHL BS5 57 F4
Parkfield Rd MANG/FISH BS16 51 E1
Park Gdns CBATH/BATHN BA1 2 A1
Park Gv
HNLZ/SM/SNYPK/WT BS9 45 G2
Park Hl AVONM BS11 43 E2
Parkhurst Av MANG/FISH BS16 48 B4
Parkhurst Rd WSM BS23 7 K4
Parklands KGWD/HNM BS15 59 E3
Parklands Av MTN/WRL BS22 117 G4
Parklands Rd BMSTR BS3 71 H2
Parkland Wy THNB/SVB BS35 8 C1
Park La CBATH/BATHN BA1 2 B2
FRCTL/WBN BS36 23 G5
Park Leaze BRSTK/PCHW BS34 20 A1
Park Pl CBATH/BATHN BA1 2 D1
CFTN/FAIL BS8 4 A2
EVILLE/WHL BS5 47 G5
WSM BS23 6 C2
Park Rd AVONM BS11 43 E2
BMSTR BS3 4 B7
CBATH/BATHN BA1 101 G5

CLVDN BS21 ....64 D1
HORF/LLZ BS7 ....32 C4
KEYN BS31 ....88 B4
KGWD/HNM BS15 ....58 D2
MANG/FISH BS16 ....49 E3
MANG/FISH BS16 ....47 F3
OLD/WMLY/WICK BS30 ......77 E1
THNB/SVB BS35 * 8 C2
YTN/CONG BS49 ....115 E3
Park Rw CBRIS/FH BS1 ......4 C3
FRCTL/WBN BS36 ....23 C2
Parkside Av FRCTL/WBN BS36 ..46 D4
Parkside Gdns EVILLE/WHL BS5..46 D4
Parkstone Av HORF/LLZ BS7 ..46 D2
Park St BRSG/KWL/STAPK BS4 ..73 H2
CBATH/BATHN BA1 ....102 B4
CBRIS/FH BS1 ....4 C3
EVILLE/WHL BS5 ....57 H5
YATE/CS BS37 ....12 B3
Park Street Av CBRIS/FH BS1 * ..4 C3
Park Street Ms
CBATH/BATHN BA1 ....2 D1
The Park ALMDB BS32 ....11 E4
KEYN BS31 ....88 B3
KGWD/HNM BS15 ....58 D4
MANG/FISH BS16 ....54 B4
OLD/WMLY/WICK BS30 ......77 E5
YTN/CONG BS49 ....112 B2
Park Vw MANG/FISH BS15 ...59 E4
THNB/SVB BS35 * 8 D2
Park View Av THNB/SVB BS35 ..8 D2
Parkwall Crs
OLD/WMLY/WICK BS30 ......76 C2
Parkwall Rd
OLD/WMLY/WICK BS30 ......76 D2
Parkway BRSTK/PCHW BS34 ..34 A4
Park Wy MTN/WRL BS22 ....123 E2
OLD/WMLY/WICK BS30 ......77 E1
Park Wood Cl MTN/WRL BS4..85 C5
Parnall Crs YATE/CS BS37 ....13 C5
Parnall Rd MANG/FISH BS16 ..48 A5
Parnell Rd CLDN BS21 ....65 E2
MANG/FISH BS16 ....47 C1
Parry Cl BATHSE BA2 ....107 C3
Parry's Cl
HNLZ/SM/SNYPK/WT BS9 ....44 C3
Parrys Gv
HNLZ/SM/SNYPK/WT BS9 ....44 C3
Parry's La
HNLZ/SM/SNYPK/WT BS9 ....44 C3
Parslow Barton
EVILLE/WHL BS5 ....58 A4
Parsonage La PTSHD/EG BS20 ..39 H4
Parsonage La
CBATH/BATHN BA1 ....3 F4
Parsonage Rd LGASH BS41 ....71 F4
Parsons Av BRSTK/PCHW BS34 ..21 F5
Parsons Gn CLVDN BS21 ......64 C5
MTN/WRL BS22 ....117 H5
Parsons Md NAIL BS48 ....81 E2
Parsons Paddock
HGRV/WHIT BS14 ....85 H2
Parson St BRSG/KWL/STAPK BS4 ..72 C5
Parsons Wk
OLD/WMLY/WICK BS30 ......60 B4
Partis Wy CBATH/BATHN BA1 ..101 F4
Partition St CBRIS/FH BS1 * ...4 D5
Partridge Cl MTN/WRL BS22 ..122 C2
YATE/CS BS37 ....14 B3
Partridge Dr MANG/FISH BS16 ..48 C2
Partridge Rd MANG/FISH BS16 ..51 C4
Passage Leaze AVONM BS11 ...42 D2
Passage Rd HNBRY/STHM BS10 ..30 D1
HNBRY/STHM BS10 ....19 E5
Passage Road Brentry Hl
HNBRY/STHM BS10 ....31 E2
Passage St CBRIS/FH BS1 .....5 H4
Pastures Av MTN/WRL BS22 ..118 D5
The Pasture ALMDB BS32 .....21 F1
Patch Ct MANG/FISH BS16 ....35 C5
Patch Cft CLVDN BS21 ....64 C5
Paulman Gdns LGASH BS41 ...82 C1
Paul's Cswy YTN/CONG BS49 ..114 D2
Paul St CBRISNE BS2 ....56 A2
Paulton Dr HORF/LLZ BS7 ....45 C4
Paulow Av BMSTR BS3 ....73 F3
Paulow Rd BMSTR BS3 ....73 F3
Pavey Cl
BMSTRD/HC/WWD BS13 .....84 D5
Pavey Rd
BMSTRD/HC/WWD BS13 .....84 D5
The Pavilions
BRSG/KWL/STAPK BS4 ......74 B5
Pawlett Rd
BMSTRD/HC/WWD BS13 .....95 H1
Pawlett Wk
BMSTRD/HC/WWD BS13 .....95 H1
Paxton AMNG/FISH BS16 .....33 C5
Paybridge Rd
BMSTRD/HC/WWD BS13 .....84 A5
Payne Dr EVILLE/WHL BS5 ....56 D4
Payne Rd OMX/HUT/LCK BS24 ..126 A4
Peache Rd MANG/FISH BS16 ..49 E2
Peacocks La KGWD/HNM BS15 ..58 C4
Pearces Hl MANG/FISH BS16 ..48 B1
Pearl St BMSTR BS3 ....72 C3
Pearsall Rd
OLD/WMLY/WICK BS30 ......76 B4
Pearse Cl MTN/WRL BS22 ....118 A3
Peart Cl
BMSTRD/HC/WWD BS13 .....83 H4
Peart Dr
BMSTRD/HC/WWD BS13 .....83 H5
Pear Tree Av LGASH BS41 ....82 B1
Peartree Cl
BMSTRD/HC/WWD BS13 .....84 C5
Pear Tree Hey YATE/CS BS37 ..14 A2
Peartree La EVILLE/WHL BS5 ..58 B5
KGWD/HNM BS15 ....59 E5
Pear Tree Rd ALMDB BS32 ....11 E5
Pedder Rd CLVDN BS21 ......64 D4
Peel St EVILLE/WHL BS5 ......56 B3
Pegasus Rd BRSTK/PCHW BS34 ..19 H3
Peg Hil YATE/CS BS37 ....14 B3
Pelican Cl MTN/WRL BS22 ...122 B3
Pemberton Ct
MANG/FISH BS16 ....48 B3
Pembery Rd BMSTR BS3 ......72 C5
Pembroke Av AVONM BS11....43 E3

Pembroke Gv CFTN/FAIL BS8 ..55 E4
Pembroke Pl CFTN/FAIL BS8 ..72 B1
Pembroke Rd AVONM BS11 ....43 E2
BMSTR BS3 ....72 D2
CFTN/FAIL BS8 ....55 E2
KGWD/HNM BS15 ....59 C2
PTSHD/EG BS20 ....38 B5
Pembroke St CBRISNE BS2 .....5 H1
Pembroke V CFTN/FAIL BS8 ..125 F5
Penard Wy KGWD/HNM BS15 ..59 F4
Penarth Dr
OMX/HUT/LCK BS24 ....127 E5
Pendennis Av MANG/FISH BS16 ..48 D4
Pendennis Pk
BRSG/KWL/STAPK BS4 ......74 C3
Pendennis Rd
MANG/FISH BS16 ....48 D3
Pendlesham Gdns WSM BS23 ..121 F2
Pendock Cl
OLD/WMLY/WICK BS30 ......77 F5
Pendock Ct MANG/FISH BS16 ..49 H1
Pendock Rd FRCTL/WBN BS36 ..23 E5
MANG/FISH BS16 ....48 B2
Penfield Rd CBRISNE BS2 .....56 C1
Penlea Ct AVONM BS11 ......43 F4
Pennard Pl PTSHD/EG BS20 ...40 B1
Pennard Ct HGRV/WHIT BS14 ..86 A4
Pennard Gn BATHSE BA2 ....107 F1
Penn Dr MANG/FISH BS16 ....34 C4
Penn Gdns CBATH/BATHN BA1 ..101 F4
Penngrove
OLD/WMLY/WICK BS30 ......76 D3
Penn Hill Rd
CBATH/BATHN BA1 ....101 F5
Pennine Gdns WSM BS23 ......7 J1
Pennine Rd
OLD/WMLY/WICK BS30 ......77 F2
Penniea
BMSTRD/HC/WWD BS13 .....84 C2
Penn Lea Rd
CBATH/BATHN BA1 ....101 F5
The Penns CLVDN BS21 ......65 E3
Penn St CBRIS/FH BS1 ....5 H2
Pennycress MTN/WRL BS22 ..122 A4
Pennyquick BATHSE BA2 ....106 B1
Pennyroyal Gv
MANG/FISH BS16 ....47 G3
Pennywell Rd
EVILLE/WHL BS5 ....56 C2
Pen Park Rd
HNBRY/STHM BS10 ....31 C2
Penpole Av AVONM BS11 .....43 E2
Penpole Cl AVONM BS11 .....42 D1
Penpole La AVONM BS11 .....43 E1
Penpole Pk AVONM BS11 .....43 E1
Penpole Pl AVONM BS11 .....43 E1
Penpole Pl AVONM BS11 .....43 E2
Penrice Cl MTN/WRL BS22 ...121 H1
Penrith Gdns
HNBRY/STHM BS10 ....31 H4
Penrose HGRV/WHIT BS14 ....85 G3
Pensfield Pk
HNBRY/STHM BS10 ....31 H1
Pensford Ct HGRV/WHIT BS14 ..86 C4
Penthouse Hl
CBATH/BATHN BA1 ....91 E5
Pentire Av
BMSTRD/HC/WWD BS13 .....84 B2
Pentland Av THNB/SVB BS35 ...9 F4
Pepys Cl KEYN BS31 ....88 C5
Pera PI CBATH/BATHN BA1 ...102 D4
Percival Rd CFTN/FAIL BS8 ...54 D4
Percy PI CBATH/BATHN BA1 ..103 E3
Peregrine Cl MTN/WRL BS22 ..122 C2
Perfect Vw
CBATH/BATHN BA1 ....102 D3
The Perrings NAIL BS48 ......67 G5
Perrott Rd KGWD/HNM BS15 ..59 G3
Perry Cl FRCTL/WBN BS36 ....24 B1
Perrycroft Av
BMSTRD/HC/WWD BS13 .....84 B3
Perrycroft Rd
BMSTRD/HC/WWD BS13 .....84 B3
Perrymans Cl MANG/FISH BS16 ..48 A2
Perrymead BATHSE BA2 .....109 E4
MTN/WRL BS22 ....118 A3
Perry Rd CBRIS/FH BS1 ....4 E3
LGASH BS41 ....70 C5
Perrys Lea ALMDB BS32 ......11 F5
Perry St EVILLE/WHL BS5 ....56 D3
Pesley Cl
BMSTRD/HC/WWD BS13 .....84 A5
Petercole Dr
BMSTRD/HC/WWD BS13 .....84 A4
Peterson Sq
BMSTRD/HC/WWD BS13 .....95 H1
Peter's Ter EVILLE/WHL BS5 ..57 E3
Petersway Gdns
EVILLE/WHL BS5 ....58 A5
Petherbridge Wy
HORF/LLZ BS7 ....46 C3
Petherton Cl KGWD/HNM BS15 ..59 E4
Petherton Gdns
HGRV/WHIT BS14 ....86 A1
Petherton Rd
HGRV/WHIT BS14 ....86 A1
Pettigrove Gdns
KGWD/HNM BS15 ....59 E4
Pettigrove Rd
KGWD/HNM BS15 ....59 E5
Pevensey Wk
BRSG/KWL/STAPK BS4 ......85 E2
Peverell Cl HNBRY/STHM BS10 ..30 D2
Peverell Dr HNBRY/STHM BS10 ..30 D2
Philadelphia Ct CBRIS/FH BS1 * ..5 H2
Philippa Cl HGRV/WHIT BS14 ..85 H2
Philip St BMSTR BS3 ....74 A1
CBRISNE BS2 ....56 B3
Phillips Rd WSM BS23 ....7 K7
Phippen St CBRIS/FH BS1 ....5 G6
Phipps Barton
KGWD/HNM BS15 ....58 B3
Phipps St BMSTR BS3 ....72 C2
Phoenix Gv RDLND/MONT BS6 ..45 F4
Phoenix Wy PTSHD/EG BS20 ..40 B2
Piccadilly Pl
CBATH/BATHN BA1 ....103 E3
Pickwick Rd
CBATH/BATHN BA1 ....102 D2
Picton La RDLND/MONT BS6 ..56 A2
Picton Ms RDLND/MONT BS6 ..56 A2

Picton St RDLND/MONT BS6 ...56 A2
Pier Cl PTSHD/EG BS20 ......40 A1
Pierrepont Pl
CBATH/BATHN BA1 ....3 G5
Pierrepont St
CBATH/BATHN BA1 ....3 G4
Pier Rd PTSHD/EG BS20 .....39 H1
Pigeon House Dr
BMSTRD/HC/WWD BS13 .....85 E5
Pigott Av
BMSTRD/HC/WWD BS13 .....84 B5
Pilemarsh EVILLE/WHL BS5 ...57 F4
Pilgrims Wy AVONM BS11 * ...42 C1
MANG/FISH BS16 ....34 D5
MTN/WRL BS22 ....122 B1
Pilgrims Whf
BRSG/KWL/STAPK BS4 ......57 G4
Pilkington Cl
BRSTK/PCHW BS34 ....33 E3
Pillingers Gdns
RDLND/MONT BS6 ....55 F1
Pillingers Rd
KGWD/HNM BS15 ....58 C4
Pill Rd CFTN/FAIL BS8 ....53 F2
PTSHD/EG BS20 ....42 D5
Pill Wy CLVDN BS21 ....64 B3
Pimms La MTN/WRL BS22 ...116 C5
Pimm's La MTN/WRL BS22 ..121 C1
Pimpernel Md ALMDB BS32 ..21 C3
Pince Cl MTN/WRL BS22 ....122 A1
Pinecroft HGRV/WHIT BS14 ..85 G2
Pine Cv HORF/LLZ BS7 ......32 B4
Pine Grove Pl HORF/LLZ BS7 ..55 H1
Pine Rdg HNBRY/STHM BS10 ..122 A1
Pine Ridge Cl
HNLZ/SM/SNYPK/WT BS9 * ..44 A4
Pine Rd HNBRY/STHM BS10 ..31 F2
Pines Rd
OLD/WMLY/WICK BS30 ......77 F5
The Pines KGWD/HNM BS15 ..59 G1
Pinetree Rd
OMX/HUT/LCK BS24 ....127 F2
Pinewood KGWD/HNM BS15 ..59 F2
Pinewood Cl
HNLZ/SM/SNYPK/WT BS9 ....45 F1
Pinhay Rd
BMSTRD/HC/WWD BS13 .....84 C3
Pinkers Md MANG/FISH BS16 ..50 A2
Pinnell Gv MANG/FISH BS16 ..50 A1
Pinnell Gv MANG/FISH BS16 ..50 A1
Pioneer Pk
BRSG/KWL/STAPK BS4 ......74 B1
Pipe La CBRIS/FH BS1 ....4 D4
Piper Rd YATE/CS BS37 .....14 A4
Pippin Ct
OLD/WMLY/WICK BS30 ......76 C2
The Pippins PTSHD/EG BS20 ..40 B3
Pitch and Pay La
HNLZ/SM/SNYPK/WT BS9 ....44 C5
Pitch And Pay Pk
HNLZ/SM/SNYPK/WT BS9 ....44 C5
Pitchcombe Gdns
HNLZ/SM/SNYPK/WT BS9 ....44 B1
Pitchcombe YATE/CS BS37 ....25 C3
Pitchcombe Gdns
HNLZ/SM/SNYPK/WT BS9 ....44 B1
Pithay Ct CBRIS/FH BS1 ......5 F3
The Pithay CBRIS/FH BS1 .....5 F3
Pit La NAIL BS48 ....79 H5
Pitlochry Cl HORF/LLZ BS7 ...32 B4
Pitman Ct CBATH/BATHN BA1 ..103 F2
Pitman Rd WSM BS23 ....6 E7
Pitt Rd HORF/LLZ BS7 ....46 A3
Pittville Cl THNB/SVB BS35 ....9 G7
Pittville Pl RDLND/MONT BS6 * ..55 F2
Pixash La KEYN BS31 ....89 E4
Pizey Av CLVDN BS21 ......64 B3
Pizey Cl CLVDN BS21 ....64 B3
Players Cl MANG/FISH BS16 ..34 B1
Playford Gdns AVONM BS11 ..29 E5
Pleasant Rd MANG/FISH BS16 ..48 D3
Pleshey Cl MTN/WRL BS22 ..122 A1
Ploughed Paddock NAIL BS48 ..67 E5
Plover Cl MTN/WRL BS22 ...122 A1
YATE/CS BS37 ....13 C5
Plumers Cl CLVDN BS21 .....65 E4
Plummer's HI EVILLE/WHL BS5 ..57 C3
Plumpton Ct MANG/FISH BS16 ..35 H4
Plumtree Rd MTN/WRL BS22 ..122 B3
Plunder St YTN/CONG BS49 ..113 H4
Podgers Dr
CBATH/BATHN BA1 ....101 C2
The Podium
CBATH/BATHN BA1 * 3 G4
Poets' Cl EVILLE/WHL BS5 ....57 F3
Polden Cl NAIL BS48 ....67 F5
Polden Rd PTSHD/EG BS20 ...39 E3
WSM BS23 ....7 H2
Pollard Rd
OMX/HUT/LCK BS24 ....122 C5
Polly Barnes Cl
KGWD/HNM BS15 ....75 C1
Polly Barnes Hi
KGWD/HNM BS15 ....75 C1
Polygon Rd CFTN/FAIL BS8 ..54 D5
The Polygon CFTN/FAIL BS8 ..54 D5
Pomfrett Gdns
HGRV/WHIT BS14 ....86 D4
Pomphrey Hi MANG/FISH BS16 ..49 H3
Ponsford Rd
BRSG/KWL/STAPK BS4 ......74 A5
Ponting Cl EVILLE/WHL BS5 ..58 A2
Poole Court Dr YATE/CS BS37 ..14 A5
Poolemead Rd BATHSE BA2 ..107 C2
Poole St AVONM BS11 ....28 B5
Pooles Whf CFTN/FAIL BS8 ..72 B1
Pooles Wharf Ct
CFTN/FAIL BS8 ....72 B1
Pool Rd MANG/FISH BS16 ....49 E5
Pope's Wk BATHSE BA2 ....109 E3
Poplar Av
HNLZ/SM/SNYPK/WT BS9 ....44 B2
Poplar Cl BATHSE BA2 .....108 A3
OLD/WMLY/WICK BS30 ......60 A5
Poplar Flds
OLD/WMLY/WICK BS30 * 60 B5
Poplar Pl MANG/FISH BS16 ...48 A5
Poplar Rd BATHSE BA2 .....110 B2
BMSTRD/HC/WWD BS13 .....84 A2

EVILLE/WHL BS5 ....57 H2
KGWD/HNM BS15 ....75 F1
OLD/WMLY/WICK BS30 ......60 B5
The Poplars MTN/WRL BS22 ..127 C2
PTSHD/EG BS20 ....42 B4
Poplar Rd MANG/FISH BS15 ..59 F3
Poplar Wk
OMX/HUT/LCK BS24 ....126 B1
Poplar Wy East AVONM BS11 ..17 E5
Poplar Wy West AVONM BS11 ..16 D4
Pople Wk HORF/LLZ BS7 .....46 D5
Poppy Cl MTN/WRL BS22 ...117 H3
Porlock Cl CLVDN BS21 ......65 E4
MTN/WRL BS22 ....125 E4
Porlock Gdns NAIL BS48 ....67 F5
Porlock Rd BATHSE BA2 ....108 D5
BMSTR BS3 ....73 E3
Portal Rd OMX/HUT/LCK BS24 ..127 G2
Portbury Common
PTSHD/EG BS20 ....40 A4
Portbury Gv AVONM BS11 ....42 D2
Portbury Wy PTSHD/EG BS20 ..41 F3
Porthisead Rd
MTN/WRL BS22 ....118 A4
Portland Cl NAIL BS48 ......67 E5
Portland Ct BMSTR BS3 ......72 A2
Portland Dr PTSHD/EG BS20 ..40 A4
Portland Pl CBATH/BATHN BA1 ..2 E1
CBRISNE BS2 * 5 H1
MANG/FISH BS16 ....48 D5
Portland Sq CBRISNE BS2 .....5 H1
Portland St CFTN/FAIL BS8 ..54 D4
MANG/FISH BS16 ....48 D5
Portland Ter CBATH/BATHN BA1 ..2 E1
Portmeirion Cl
HGRV/WHIT BS14 ....85 H4
Port Side Ct EVILLE/WHL BS5 * ..57 H5
Port Vw PTSHD/EG BS20 .....42 C3
Portview Rd AVONM BS11 ....28 B5
Portwall La CBRIS/FH BS1 ....5 G6
Portwall La East CBRIS/FH BS1 * ..5 H6
Portway AVONM BS11 ....42 C2
CFTN/FAIL BS8 ....53 H5
HNLZ/SM/SNYPK/WT BS9 ....43 H3
Portway La YATE/CS BS37 ....15 E5
Post Office La NAIL BS48 .....81 E2
Post Office Rd
OMX/HUT/LCK BS24 ....127 E1
Potters Wood Cl
KGWD/HNM BS15 ....58 D4
Pottery Cl WSM BS23 ....7 J7
Pound Dr MANG/FISH BS16 ..47 H3
Pound La MANG/FISH BS16 ..47 H4
The Pound ALMDB BS32 .....11 F3
Pound Md
BLAG/CWMG/WR BS40 .....92 D4
Pound Rd KGWD/HNM BS15 ..59 F1
The Pound ALMDB BS32 .....11 F3
Pountney Dr EVILLE/WHL BS5 ..56 D3
Powells Acres CLVDN BS21 ...65 E2
Powis Cl MTN/WRL BS22 ....121 H1
Powlett Ct BATHSE BA2 ......3 J2
Powlett Rd BATHSE BA2 .....3 J1
Pow's Rd KGWD/HNM BS15 ..58 D5
Poyntz Ct
OLD/WMLY/WICK BS30 ......76 C3
Poyntz Rd
BRSG/KWL/STAPK BS4 ......85 G1
Preacher Cl EVILLE/WHL BS5 ..58 B5
Preanes Gn MTN/WRL BS22 ..122 C1
Preddy's La EVILLE/WHL BS5 ..58 A5
Prescot Cl MTN/WRL BS22 ...121 G2
Prescott YATE/CS BS37 ......25 H2
Press Moor Dr
OLD/WMLY/WICK BS30 ......76 C2
Prestbury YATE/CS BS37 ....25 H2
Preston Wk
BRSG/KWL/STAPK BS4 ......73 H5
Prestwick Cl
BRSG/KWL/STAPK BS4 ......74 C5
Pretoria Rd
BRSTK/PCHW BS34 ....20 B2
Prewett St CBRIS/FH BS1 ....5 G7
Priddy Cl BATHSE BA2 .....107 G2
Priddy Ct HGRV/WHIT BS14 ..86 A4
Priddy Dr HGRV/WHIT BS14 ..86 A4
Priests Wy MTN/WRL BS22 ..122 A1
Priestwood Cl
HNBRY/STHM BS10 * 31 E2
Primrose Cl ALMDB BS32 ....21 G3
KGWD/HNM BS15 ....58 B2
Primrose Dr THNB/SVB BS35 ...9 E2
Primrose Hl
CBATH/BATHN BA1 ....102 A3
Primrose La KGWD/HNM BS15 ..58 C3
Princes Blds
CBATH/BATHN BA1 * 3 F3
CFTN/FAIL BS8 ....54 D5
Princes Ct
OLD/WMLY/WICK BS30 ......76 C2
Princes' La CFTN/FAIL BS8 ...54 D5
Princes' Pl HORF/LLZ BS7 ....46 A5
Prince's St CLVDN BS21 .....64 D2
Princess Cl KEYN BS31 ......88 B4
Princess Gdns
MANG/FISH BS16 ....47 F2
Princess Rw CBRISNE BS2 ....5 F1
Princess Royal Gdns
EVILLE/WHL BS5 ....57 E3
Princess St BMSTR BS3 ......73 F2
CBRISNE BS2 ....56 B3
Prince's St CBATH/BATHN BA1 ..3 F4
Princess Victoria St
CFTN/FAIL BS8 ....54 D5
Prince Street Rbt CBRIS/FH BS1 ..5 F6
Prince St CBRIS/FH BS1 .....5 F6
Prior Park Blds BATHSE BA2 ..3 J7
Prior Park Gdns BATHSE BA2 ..3 J7
Prior Park Rd BATHSE BA2 ...3 J7
Priors Lea YATE/CS BS37 ....26 A1
Priory Av
HNLZ/SM/SNYPK/WT BS9 ....45 E1
Priory Cl BATHSE BA2 ......109 E4
Priory Court Rd
HNLZ/SM/SNYPK/WT BS9 ....45 E1

Priory Dene
HNLZ/SM/SNYPK/WT BS9 ....45 E1
Priory Gdns AVONM BS11 ....42 D2
HORF/LLZ BS7 ....32 B5
KEYN BS31 ....88 B2
PTSHD/EG BS20 ....41 F5
WSM BS23 ....7 K4
Priory Ms WSM BS23 ....7 K4
Priory Rd AVONM BS11 ......42 D2
BRSG/KWL/STAPK BS4 ......74 A4
CFTN/FAIL BS8 ....4 E1
KEYN BS31 ....88 B2
PTSHD/EG BS20 ....41 F5
WSM BS23 ....7 K4
Priston Cl MTN/WRL BS22 ...118 A3
Pritchard St CBRISNE BS2 ....5 H1
Privet Dr
BMSTRD/HC/WWD BS13 .....84 D4
Probyn Cl MANG/FISH BS16 ..48 A1
Pro-Cathedral La CFTN/FAIL BS8 ..4 D3
Proctor Cl
BRSG/KWL/STAPK BS4 ......74 C5
The Promenade
HORF/LLZ BS7 * 55 H1
Prospect Av KGWD/HNM BS15 ..58 B1
Prospect Cl FRCTL/WBN BS36 ..23 H5
Prospect Crs KGWD/HNM BS15 ..59 F1
Prospect Gdns
CBATH/BATHN BA1 ....91 E4
Prospect La FRCTL/WBN BS36 ..23 H5
Prospect Pl BATHSE BA2 * 3 J5
EVILLE/WHL BS5 ....57 E5
WSM BS23 ....6 E2
Prospect Rd BATHSE BA2 ....109 F3
Prospect Ter BMSTR BS3 ....72 C5
Providence La LGASH BS41 ...70 C4
Providence Pl CBRISNE BS2 * ..5 J4
Prowse Cl THNB/SVB BS35 ....8 D3
Prudham St EVILLE/WHL BS5 ..57 C2
Puffin Cl MTN/WRL BS22 ....122 C3
Pullin Ct
OLD/WMLY/WICK BS30 ......77 G1
Pulteney Av BATHSE BA2 .....3 J5
Pulteney Br BATHSE BA2 .....3 J5
Pulteney Gdns BATHSE BA2 ...3 J5
Pulteney Gv BATHSE BA2 .....3 J5
Pulteney Ms BATHSE BA2 ....3 H3
Pulteney Rd BATHSE BA2 ....3 H3
Pulteney St BATHSE BA2 .....3 J5
Pulteney Ter BATHSE BA2 ....3 J5
Pump House La
BRSG/KWL/STAPK BS4 ......75 E1
Pump La CBATH/BATHN BA1 ..104 C3
CBRIS/FH BS1 ....5 H6
Pump Sq PTSHD/EG BS20 ...42 D5
Purcell Wk
BRSG/KWL/STAPK BS4 ......85 E2
Purdown Rd HORF/LLZ BS7 ..46 B2
Purdue Cl MTN/WRL BS22 ...118 A5
Purlewent Dr
CBATH/BATHN BA1 ....101 H5
Pursey Dr ALMDB BS32 .....21 G4
Purton Cl KGWD/HNM BS15 ..59 F5
Purton Rd HORF/LLZ BS7 ....55 H1
Puttinghorpe Dr
MTN/WRL BS22 ....121 H1
Puxley Cl HGRV/WHIT BS14 ..86 D3
Puxton Rd
OMX/HUT/LCK BS24 ....119 H5
Pye Cft ALMDB BS32 ....11 G4
Pyecroft Av
HNLZ/SM/SNYPK/WT BS9 ....45 F1
Pylle Hill Crs BMSTR BS3 ....73 G2
Pyne Point CLVDN BS21 .....64 C2
Pyne Rd AVONM BS11 ......43 F3
Pynne Cl HGRV/WHIT BS14 ..87 E4
Pynne Rd HGRV/WHIT BS14 ..87 E4
Pyracantha Wk
HGRV/WHIT BS14 ....85 H3

Q

The Quadrangle YATE/CS BS37 ..37 G1
Quadrant East
MANG/FISH BS16 ....48 C5
The Quadrant R
DLND/MONT BS6 ....45 F5
Quadrant West
MANG/FISH BS16 ....48 C5
Quaker La THNB/SVB BS35 ...9 J7
Quaker's Cl MANG/FISH BS16 ..34 D5
Quaker's Rd MANG/FISH BS16 ..34 D5
Quantock Cl
OLD/WMLY/WICK BS30 ......77 F1
Quantock Rd BMSTR BS3 ....73 E3
PTSHD/EG BS20 ....39 E3
WSM BS23 ....124 C2
Quantocks BATHSE BA2 ....108 D5
The Quarries ALMDB BS32 ...10 D2
Quarrington Rd HORF/LLZ BS7 ..46 B3
Quarry Barton
MANG/FISH BS16 ....34 C1
Quarry Cl BATHSE BA2 ......110 D1
Quarry La AVONM BS11 .....30 A4
FRCTL/WBN BS36 ....35 E3
Quarrymans Ct BATHSE BA2 ..111 F1
Quarry Ri OMX/HUT/LCK BS24 ..125 E5
Quarry Rd BATHSE BA2 .....109 G1
KGWD/HNM BS15 ....58 D5
MANG/FISH BS16 ....48 B1
YATE/CS BS37 ....26 C1
Quarry Rock Gdns
BATHSE BA2 ....109 G3
Quarry Steps CFTN/FAIL BS8 ..55 E1
Quarry Wy MANG/FISH BS16 ..47 G3
MANG/FISH BS16 ....35 H3
NAIL BS48 ....67 E4
Quay Head CBRIS/FH BS1 * ..5 G3
Quays Av PTSHD/EG BS20 ...40 A3
Quayside CBATH/BATHN BA1 ..55 H5
Quayside La EVILLE/WHL BS5 ..57 H5
Quay St CBRIS/FH BS1 ......5 F3
Quedgeley YATE/CS BS37 ....25 G4
Queen Ann Rd EVILLE/WHL BS5 ..57 E3
Queen Charlton La
HGRV/WHIT BS14 ....97 G1
Queen Quay CBRIS/FH BS1 * ..5 F5
Queen's Av CFTN/FAIL BS8 ...4 E2

Queenscote *PTSHD/EG* BS20........................39 G3
Queensdale Crs
 BRSG/KWL/STAPK BS4.......................73 H5
Queens Down Gdns
 BRSC/KWL/STAPK BS4........................73 H5
Queens Dr *KGWD/HNM* BS15.............75 G2
Queen's Dr *BATHSE* BA2.......................108 D5
 HORF/LLZ BS7...................................45 G4
Queens Ga
 HNLZ/SM/SNYPK/WT BS9..............44 B3
Queenshill Rd
 BRSC/KWL/STAPK BS4.......................73 H5
Queensholm Av
 MANG/FISH BS16...............................35 E4
Queensholm Cl
 MANG/FISH BS16...............................35 E4
Queensholm Crs
 MANG/FISH BS16...............................34 D4
Queensholm Dr
 MANG/FISH BS16...............................35 E5
Queen's Pde
 CBATH/BATHN BA1 ....2 E4
 CBRIS/FH BS1 ....4 B5
Queen's Parade Pl
 CBATH/BATHN BA1 ....2 E3
Queen Sq *CBRIS/FH* BS1......................4 J6
Queen Sq *CBRIS/FH* BS1......................4 C5
Queen Square Av
 CBRIS/FH BS1 *..................................5 F5
Queens Rd
 BRSC/KWL/STAPK BS4.......................74 D5
 NAIL BS48...88 A5
 NAIL BS48...79 F1
 PTSHD/EG BS20..................................38 B5
Queens Wk *THNB/SVB* BS35................8 C1
Queensway *BRSTK/PCHW* BS34.........21 G4
Queens Wy *PTSHD/EG* BS20................38 C4
Queen's Wy *MTN/WRL* BS22...............117 H4
Queen Victoria Rd
 RDLND/MONT BS6...............................45 E4
Queen Victoria St *CBRISNE* BS2.........56 C5
Queenwood Av
 CBATH/BATHN BA1............................102 D3
Quickthorn Cl
 HGRV/WHIT BS14..............................85 H5
Quiet St *CBATH/BATHN* BA1 *.............2 E4
Quilter Gv
 BRSG/KWL/STAPK BS4 *....................85 E2

R

Raby Ms *BATHSE* BA2.............................3 J3
Raby Pl *BATHSE* BA2...............................3 J3
Rackfield Pl *BATHSE* BA2......................107 G1
Rackham Cl *HORF/LLZ* BS7...................46 D2
Rackhay *CBRIS/FH* BS1 *.......................5 F4
Radley Rd *MANG/FISH* BS16.................48 B4
Radnor Rd
 HNLZ/SM/SNYPK/WT BS9.................45 F3
Raeburn Rd *EVILLE/WHL* BS5................58 B4
Ragland La
 CBATH/BATHN BA1............................102 C3
 CBATH/BATHN BA1............................102 D3
Raglan La
 BLAG/CWMG/WR BS40.....................93 F5
Raglan Pl *HORF/LLZ* BS7......................45 H5
 THNB/SVB BS35..................................8 C4
Raglan Rd *HORF/LLZ* BS7.....................45 H5
Raglan St
 CBATH/BATHN BA1............................102 C3
Raglan Ter
 CBATH/BATHN BA1............................102 D2
Raglan Vls
 CBATH/BATHN BA1............................102 D3
Railton Jones Cl
 BRSTK/PCHW BS34............................33 G2
Railway Pl *CBATH/BATHN* BA1.............3 H6
Railway Ter *MANG/FISH* BS16..............48 C4
Railway Vw *MANG/FISH* BS16 *...........34 D2
Raleigh Cl *KEYN* BS31...........................98 D2
Raleigh Ri *PTSHD/EG* BS20..................39 F2
Raleigh Rd *BMSTR* BS3.........................72 B2
Ralph Allen Dr *BATHSE* BA2.................109 A3
Ram Hl *FRCTL/WBN* BS36....................36 B1
Ramsay Cl *MTN/WRL* BS22...................117 H4
Ramscombe La
 CBATH/BATHN BA1............................91 E5
Ramsey Rd *HORF/LLZ* BS7 *................46 D2
Ranchways *PTSHD/EG* BS20.................38 D4
Randall Cl *KGWD/HNM* BS15................59 F1
Randall Rd *CFTN/FAIL* BS8....................55 E5
Randolph Av
 BMSTRD/HC/WWD BS13.....................84 C4
 YATE/CS BS37.....................................13 H5
Randolph Cl
 BMSTRD/HC/WWD BS13.....................84 C4
Rangers Wk *KGWD/HNM* BS15............75 H2
Rannoch Rd
 BRSTK/PCHW BS34............................32 B3
Ranscombe Av
 MTN/WRL BS22.................................122 A1
Ransford *CLVDN* BS21............................64 B4
Ratcliffe Dr *BRSTK/PCHW* BS34...........21 H3
Rathbone Cl *FRCTL/WBN* BS36............24 A5
Raven Cl *MTN/WRL* BS22....................122 B2
Ravendale Dr
 OLD/WMLY/WICK BS30......................77 H3

Ravenglass Crs
 HNBRY/STHM BS10.............................31 G3
Ravenhead Dr
 HGRV/WHIT BS14...............................86 A1
Ravenhill Av *BMSTR* BS3......................73 G4
Ravenhill Rd *BMSTR* BS3.....................73 G3
Ravenswood Rd
 RDLND/MONT BS6...............................55 G2
Rawens Wd
 OLD/WMLY/WICK BS30......................77 E3
Rawlins Av *MTN/WRL* BS22..................117 H3
Ravens Cross Rd *LGASH* BS41..............70 C5
Rayleigh Rd
 HNLZ/SM/SNYPK/WT BS9.................44 B1
Raymend Rd *BMSTR* BS3......................73 F3
Raymend Wk *BMSTR* BS3.....................73 F4
Raymill *BRSG/KWL/STAPK* BS4 *.........75 F4
Raymore Rd *LGASH* BS41......................70 C5
Raynes Rd *BMSTR* BS3.........................72 B3
Reading Ct *KGWD/HNM* BS15..............58 B3
Rector's Wy *WSM* BS23.........................7 G7
Rectory Ct *NAIL* BS48............................67 H4
 YATE/CS BS37.....................................14 B4
Rectory Dr *YTN/CONG* BS49................112 C4
Rectory La *BRSTK/PCHW* BS34............32 C2
Rectory Rd *FRCTL/WBN* BS36...............23 J5
 PTSHD/EG BS20..................................42 B5
Rectory Wy *YTN/CONG* BS49..............112 C4
Redcar Ct *MANG/FISH* BS16.................35 F5
Redcatch Rd *BMSTR* BS3......................73 G4
Redcliff Backs *CBRIS/FH* BS1...............5 G5
Redcliffe Ct *PTSHD/EG* BS20...............38 C5
Redcliffe Pde East
 CBRIS/FH BS1 ....5 F6
Redcliffe Pde West
 CBRIS/FH BS1 ....5 F6
Redcliffe Whf *CBRIS/FH* BS1 *.............5 F6
Redcliff Hl *CBRIS/FH* BS1....................5 G7
Redcliff Mead La *CBRIS/FH* BS1..........5 H7
Redcliff St *CBRIS/FH* BS1 *...................5 G5
Redcross Ms *CBRISNE* BS2 *................5 J3
Redcross St *CBRISNE* BS2....................5 J3
The Reddings
 KGWD/HNM BS15..............................59 F1
Redfield Hl
 OLD/WMLY/WICK BS30......................77 G2
Redford Crs
 BMSTRD/HC/WWD BS13.....................94 D1
Redford La *BRSTK/PCHW* BS34.............51 H4
Redford Wk
 BMSTRD/HC/WWD BS13.....................95 E1
Redhill Cl *MANG/FISH* BS16.................47 G5
Redhill Dr *MANG/FISH* BS16................47 G5
Red House La *ALMDB* BS32...................10 D5
Redland Av *PTSHD/EG* BS20................41 H2
Redland Court Rd
 RDLND/MONT BS6...............................45 G5
Redland Green Rd
 RDLND/MONT BS6...............................55 F1
Redland Gv *RDLND/MONT* BS6.............55 F1
Redland Hl *RDLND/MONT* BS6..............55 E1
Redland Pk *BATHSE* BA2.....................107 G1
 RDLND/MONT BS6...............................55 F2
Redland Rd *RDLND/MONT* BS6.............55 G1
Redland Ter *RDLND/MONT* BS6............55 E1
Redpoll Dr *PTSHD/EG* BS20.................40 C2
Redshelf Wk
 HNBRY/STHM BS10.............................31 G2
Redwick Cl *HNBRY/STHM* BS10............30 A3
Redwing Dr *MTN/WRL* BS22................122 B2
Redwing Gdns
 MANG/FISH BS16...............................47 G2
 OLD/WMLY/WICK BS30......................76 D3
Redwood Cl *NAIL* BS48.........................67 H4
Redwood La *MANG/FISH* BS16 *..........81 H2
Reed Cl *HNBRY/STHM* BS10.................45 H2
Reed Ct
 OLD/WMLY/WICK BS30......................76 C3
Reedley Rd
 HNLZ/SM/SNYPK/WT BS9.................44 C5
Reedling Cl *MANG/FISH* BS16 *...........47 G2
Reed Wy *MTN/WRL* BS22....................118 B5
Regency Dr
 BRSG/KWL/STAPK BS4.......................74 B4
Regent Rd *BMSTR* BS3.........................73 G2
Regents Cl *THNB/SVB* BS35..................8 C1
Regents St *CFTN/FAIL* BS8...................55 E5
Regent St *KGWD/HNM* BS15................58 C3
 WSM BS23...6 D4
The Regina *CBATH/BATHN* BA1 *.........3 F2
Remenham Dr
 HNLZ/SM/SNYPK/WT BS9.................45 F3
Remenham Pk
 HNLZ/SM/SNYPK/WT BS9.................45 F3
Rendcomb Cl *MTN/WRL* BS22.............121 G1
Repton Rd
 BRSG/KWL/STAPK BS4.......................74 B3
Retort Rd *AVONM* BS11........................28 C2
Reubens Ct *MTN/WRL* BS22.................117 G5
Reynolds Cl *KEYN* BS31........................88 D4
Reynolds Wk *HORF/LLZ* BS7................46 C1
Rhode Cl *KEYN* BS31.............................98 B2
Rhodyate Hl *YTN/CONG* BS49..............113 F5
Rhodyate La *YTN/CONG* BS49..............113 G4
Rhyne Ter *WSM* BS23...........................124 C4
Rhyne Vw *NAIL* BS48............................67 E3
Ribblesdale *THNB/SVB* BS35...............8 D4
Richards Cl *MTN/WRL* BS22.................118 A4
Richeson Cl
 HNBRY/STHM BS10.............................30 D3
Richeson Wk
 HNBRY/STHM BS10.............................30 D3
Richmond Av
 BRSTK/PCHW BS34............................21 G5
 RDLND/MONT BS6...............................56 B1
Richmond Cl *KEYN* BS31......................98 A3
 PTSHD/EG BS20..................................40 A3
Richmond Dr *CFTN/FAIL* BS8...............55 E1
Richmond Gn *NAIL* BS48......................67 G5
Richmond Hts
 CBATH/BATHN BA1............................102 C3
Richmond Hl
 CBATH/BATHN BA1.............................2 A5
 CFTN/FAIL BS8....................................4 A2
Richmond Hill Av *CFTN/FAIL* BS8.......4 A3

Richmond La
 CBATH/BATHN BA1............................102 C3
 CFTN/FAIL BS8....................................55 E4
Richmond Ms *CFTN/FAIL* BS8..............55 E4
Richmond Park Rd
 CFTN/FAIL BS8....................................55 E4
Richmond Pl
 CBATH/BATHN BA1............................102 C3
Richmond Rd
 CBATH/BATHN BA1............................102 C2
 EVILLE/WHL BS5.................................57 G3
 MANG/FISH BS16................................48 C3
 RDLND/MONT BS6...............................56 A1
Richmond St *BMSTR* BS3.....................73 G2
 WSM BS23...6 D4
Richmond Ter *AVONM* BS11.................28 A4
 CFTN/FAIL BS8....................................55 E4
Ricketts La *MTN/WRL* BS22................122 D1
Rickford Rd *NAIL* BS48.........................67 G5
The Ride *KGWD/HNM* BS15..................59 G1
Ridge Cl *PTSHD/EG* BS20.....................39 E4
Ridge Green Cl *BATHSE* BA2...............110 B2
Ridgehill
 HNLZ/SM/SNYPK/WT BS9.................45 G2
The Ridge *AVONM* BS11........................43 E1
 FRCTL/WBN BS36................................24 A3
 PTSHD/EG BS20..................................112 B5
Ridgeview *LGASH* BS41........................71 E4
Ridgeway *FRCTL/WBN* BS36................24 A3
 NAIL BS48...58 B5
 YATE/CS BS37.....................................14 C5
Ridgeway Av *WSM* BS23 *....................7 F7
Ridgeway Ct
 HNLZ/SM/SNYPK/WT BS9.................30 D4
Ridgeway Gdns
 HGRV/WHIT BS14...............................86 B4
Ridgeway La
 HGRV/WHIT BS14...............................86 A5
Ridgeway Pde
 EVILLE/WHL BS5.................................47 G5
Ridgeway Rd *LGASH* BS41...................70 D5
 MANG/FISH BS16................................49 E3
The Ridgeway
 HNBRY/STHM BS10.............................31 E4
 MTN/WRL BS22.................................121 G1
Riding Barn Hl
 OLD/WMLY/WICK BS30......................60 D5
Ridingleaze *AVONM* BS11.....................29 C4
Ridings Cl *FRCTL/WBN* BS36...............27 E1
Ridings Rd *FRCTL/WBN* BS36..............24 A4
The Ridings
 BMSTRD/HC/WWD BS13.....................83 H5
 FRCTL/WBN BS36................................24 A4
Ridley Av *KGWD/HNM* BS15................49 H5
Ringspit La *PLTN/PENS* BS39................97 H4
Ringswell Gdns
 CBATH/BATHN BA1............................103 F3
Ringwood Crs
 HNBRY/STHM BS10.............................31 H4
Ringwood Gv *WSM* BS23....................121 F2
Ringwood Rd *BATHSE* BA2...................107 H1
Ripley Rd *EVILLE/WHL* BS5..................58 A2
Ripon Ct *MANG/FISH* BS16..................35 F4
Ripon Rd
 BRSG/KWL/STAPK BS4.......................74 B2
Rippleside *PTSHD/EG* BS20...................39 G3
Rippleside Rd *CLVDN* BS21...................62 C5
The Ripple *CLVDN* BS21.........................67 E2
Risdale Rd *BMSTR* BS3.........................71 H5
Rivendell *MTN/WRL* BS22...................117 H4
Riverland Dr
 BMSTRD/HC/WWD BS13.....................84 A4
Riverleaze
 HNLZ/SM/SNYPK/WT BS9.................43 H3
 PTSHD/EG BS20..................................38 D2
River Md *CLVDN* BS21..........................64 D5
River Rd *YATE/CS* BS37........................26 C1
Riverside Cl *AVONM* BS11....................43 F3
 CLVDN BS21..64 B4
 MTN/WRL BS22.................................118 B5
Riverside Ct *BATHSE* BA2......................2 E5
 BRSG/KWL/STAPK BS4 *....................57 H5
Riverside Gdns
 BATHSE BA2..2 E5
Riverside Ms
 BRSG/KWL/STAPK BS4.......................57 G4
Riverside Rd *BATHSE* BA2.....................2 E5
Riverside Steps
 BRSG/KWL/STAPK BS4 *....................57 G4
Riverside Wy *KGWD/HNM* BS15..........75 H3
Rivers Rd *BATH/BATHN* BA1................102 D4
Rivers St *CBATH/BATHN* BA1................2 E2
Rivers Street Ms
 CBATH/BATHN BA1 *...........................2 E2
Rivers Street Pl
 CBATH/BATHN BA1 *...........................3 F2
River St *CBRISNE* BS2............................5 J2
River Ter *KEYN* BS31 *..........................88 C4
River Vw *MANG/FISH* BS16..................47 G3
River Wk *MTN/WRL* BS22....................123 G1
Riverway *NAIL* BS48..............................67 E3
Riverwood Rd
 MANG/FISH BS16................................34 C4
Riviera Crs *BRSTK/PCHW* BS34............49 E4
Riviera Wy *BRSTK/PCHW* BS34...........34 A1
Roath Rd *PTSHD/EG* BS20...................39 F1
Robbins Cl *ALMDB* BS32......................21 H4
Robbins Rd *MANG/FISH* BS16.............49 H2
Robel Av *FRCTL/WBN* BS36.................23 F2
Robert Ct *MANG/FISH* BS16................48 A3
Robertson Dr
 BRSG/KWL/STAPK BS4.......................57 H5
Robertson Rd *EVILLE/WHL* BS5...........57 F1
Robert St *EVILLE/WHL* BS5..................56 D4
Robin Cl *HNBRY/STHM* BS10................30 B3
Robin Dr *OMX/HUT/LCK* BS24.............126 B4
Robinia Wk *HGRV/WHIT* BS14.............85 G2
Robin La *CLVDN* BS21..........................62 B5
Robinson Cl *NAIL* BS48........................67 H4
Robinson Dr *EVILLE/WHL* BS5.............56 D4
Robinson Wy *NAIL* BS48.......................79 H4
Robin Wy *YATE/CS* BS37.......................26 D1
Rochester Cl
 OMX/HUT/LCK BS24..........................125 F5
Rochester Rd
 BRSG/KWL/STAPK BS4.......................74 D1
Rochfort Pl *BATHSE* BA2......................3 H1
Rock Av *NAIL* BS48...............................66 D4
Rock Cl *BRSG/KWL/STAPK* BS4...........74 D4

Rock Hall La *BATHSE* BA2.....................111 F1
Rockingham Gdns
 AVONM BS11.......................................29 G5
Rockingham Gv *WSM* BS23..................121 F2
Rockland Gv *MANG/FISH* BS16............47 F2
Rockland Rd
 MANG/FISH BS16................................48 C1
Rock La *BATHSE* BA2............................111 F1
 BRSTK/PCHW BS34............................21 H5
Rockleaze
 HNLZ/SM/SNYPK/WT BS9.................54 C1
Rockleaze Av
 HNLZ/SM/SNYPK/WT BS9.................44 C5
Rockleaze Rd
 HNLZ/SM/SNYPK/WT BS9.................54 C1
Rockliffe Av *BATHSE* BA2.......................3 K1
Rockliffe Rd *BATHSE* BA2.......................3 J1
Rock Rd *KEYN* BS31..............................88 D4
 OLD/WMLY/WICK BS30......................61 H3
 YTN/CONG BS49.................................112 C4
Rockside Av *MANG/FISH* BS16.............35 F5
Rockside Dr
 HNLZ/SM/SNYPK/WT BS9.................45 F2
Rockside Gdns
 FRCTL/WBN BS36................................24 A2
 MANG/FISH BS16................................35 F5
Rock La
 BLAG/CWMG/WR BS40......................93 G5
Rockstowes Wy
 HNBRY/STHM BS10.............................31 H2
Rock St *THNB/SVB* BS35........................8 C4
The Rock
 BRSG/KWL/STAPK BS4.......................54 B3
Rockwell Av *AVONM* BS11....................29 H4
Rodborough *YATE/CS* BS37...................25 G3
Rodbourne Rd
 HNBRY/STHM BS10.............................45 H1
Rodford Wy *HGRV/WHIT* BS14............35 H1
Rodfords Md *HGRV/WHIT* BS14............85 G2
Rodfford Wy *YATE/CS* BS37.................25 G3
Rodmead Wk
 BMSTRD/HC/WWD BS13.....................84 B5
Rodmoor Rd *PTSHD/EG* BS20...............39 F2
Rodney Av *BRSTK/PCHW* BS34.............58 A3
Rodney Crs *BRSTK/PCHW* BS34............32 C1
Rodney Rd *KEYN* BS31..........................99 E2
 KGWD/HNM BS15...............................58 A2
 NAIL BS48...58 A2
Rodney Wk *KGWD/HNM* BS15.............58 A2
Rodway Hl *MANG/FISH* BS16...............49 G4
Rodway Rd *BRSTK/PCHW* BS34...........32 B3
 MANG/FISH BS16................................49 G3
Rodway Vw *KGWD/HNM* BS15.............49 H5
Roebuck Cl *MTN/WRL* BS22................117 H4
Roegate Dr
 BRSG/KWL/STAPK BS4.......................57 G5
Rogers Cl
 OLD/WMLY/WICK BS30......................77 E1
Rogers Ct *YATE/CS* BS37......................27 E1
Rogers Wk
 OLD/WMLY/WICK BS30......................60 B4
Rokeby Av *RDLND/MONT* BS6..............55 C2
Roman Farm Ct *AVONM* BS11 *...........30 A3
Roman Farm Rd
 BRSG/KWL/STAPK BS4.......................84 A5
Roman Rd *BATHSE* BA2........................110 A2
 BMSTRD/HC/WWD BS13.....................84 B3
Roman Wk
 BRSG/KWL/STAPK BS4.......................74 B3
 BRSTK/PCHW BS34............................34 B4
Romney Av *HORF/LLZ* BS7..................44 A4
Ronald Rd *MANG/FISH* BS16...............47 H2
Ronayne Wk *MANG/FISH* BS16............48 C2
Rookery Cl *MTN/WRL* BS22.................117 F5
Rookery Rd
 BRSG/KWL/STAPK BS4.......................73 G5
Rookery Wy *HGRV/WHIT* BS14.............85 G5
Rooksbridge Wk
 BATHSE BA2..107 G2
Rope Wk *NAIL* BS48..............................79 H4
Rosebay Md *MANG/FISH* BS16.............87 G4
Rosebery Pk *EVILLE/WHL* BS5 *...........57 F3
Rosebery Rd *BATHSE* BA2.....................107 H1
Rosebery Rd *BATHSE* BA2.....................57 E4
 EVILLE/WHL BS5.................................57 F3
Rosebery Av *CBRISNE* BS2...................56 C2
Rosebery Ter *CFTN/FAIL* BS8...............4 A4
Rose Cl *FRCTL/WBN* BS36....................35 E1
Rosedale Av *WSM* BS23........................7 H3
Rosedale Rd *MANG/FISH* BS16............48 B5
Rose Gdns *MTN/WRL* BS22..................118 A4
Rose Green Rd
 EVILLE/WHL BS5.................................57 F1
Rose Hill *BATH/BATHN* BA1................103 E2
Roseland Cl
 CBATH/BATHN BA1............................103 F1
Rose La *FRCTL/WBN* BS36...................24 B3
Roselarge Gdns
 HNBRY/STHM BS10.............................31 E3
Rosemary Cl *ALMDB* BS32...................21 H3
Rosemary Crs
 PTSHD/EG BS20..................................40 B3
Rosemary La *EVILLE/WHL* BS5 *..........57 E1
Rose Md *HORF/LLZ* BS7.......................46 A2
Rosemont Ter *CFTN/FAIL* BS8 *...........4 A4
Rosemont La *BATHSE* BA2....................108 D5
Rosemount Rd *NAIL* BS48.....................81 G1
Rose Oak Dr
 FRCTL/WBN BS36................................24 B3
Rose Oak Gdns
 FRCTL/WBN BS36................................24 B3
Rose Oak La *FRCTL/WBN* BS36...........24 B3
Rose Rd *EVILLE/WHL* BS5....................57 F2
Rosery Cl
 HNLZ/SM/SNYPK/WT BS9.................31 E5
The Rosery *MANG/FISH* BS16..............48 C5
Roseville Av
 OLD/WMLY/WICK BS30......................76 D4
Rose Wk *MANG/FISH* BS16..................48 C5
Rosewarn Cl *BATHSE* BA2....................107 F5
Rosewell Ct *CBATH/BATHN* BA1 *........2 D3
Rosling Rd *HORF/LLZ* BS7...................46 A2
Roslyn Av *MTN/WRL* BS22...................121 G1
Roslyn Rd *RDLND/MONT* BS6..............55 C1
Rossall Av *BRSTK/PCHW* BS34.............21 H4
Rossall Rd
 BRSG/KWL/STAPK BS4.......................74 C3
Ross Cl *YATE/CS* BS37...........................14 D5
Rossendale Cl *MTN/WRL* BS22.............117 G5

Rossiter Gra
 BMSTR/HC/WWD BS13.......................84 A5
Rossiter's La *EVILLE/WHL* BS5.............58 A5
Rosslyn Cl *CBATH/BATHN* BA1.............101 G5
Rosslyn Rd
 CBATH/BATHN BA1............................101 G5
Rosslyn Wy *THNB/SVB* BS35................8 C1
Roundhill Gv *BATHSE* BA2....................107 G4
Roundhill Pk *BATHSE* BA2....................107 F5
Roundmoor Cl *KEYN* BS31...................99 E1
Roundmoor Gdns
 HGRV/WHIT BS14...............................86 C2
Roundways *FRCTL/WBN* BS36.............35 E4
Rousham Rd *EVILLE/WHL* BS5.............46 C5
Rowacres *BATHSE* BA2.........................107 G4
 HGRV/WHIT BS14...............................85 G3
Rowan Cl *MANG/FISH* BS16.................58 A1
 NAIL BS48...67 H4
Rowan Pl *OMX/HUT/LCK* BS24............123 E2
The Rowans *PTSHD/EG* BS20...............39 F4
Rowan Wy *KGWD/HNM* BS15...............75 G3
Rowberrow *HGRV/WHIT* BS14.............85 G2
Rowberrow Wy *NAIL* BS48....................67 F5
Rowland Av *MANG/FISH* BS16..............47 E4
Rowlands Cl
 CBATH/BATHN BA1............................104 C2
Rowlandson Gdns
 HORF/LLZ BS7....................................46 D2
Rowley St *BMSTR* BS3..........................72 E3
Rownham Cl *BMSTR* BS3......................71 H2
Rownham Hl *CFTN/FAIL* BS8................54 B5
Rownham Md *CFTN/FAIL* BS8...............72 B1
The Rows *MTN/WRL* BS22....................122 B1
Royal Albert Rd
 RDLND/MONT BS6...............................45 E4
Royal Av *CBATH/BATHN* BA1.................2 D3
Royal Cl *HNBRY/STHM* BS10.................30 B2
Royal Crs *CBATH/BATHN* BA1................2 C2
 WSM BS23...6 C2
Royal Fort Rd *CFTN/FAIL* BS8...............4 D2
Royal Pde *WSM* BS23...........................6 C3
Royal Pk *CFTN/FAIL* BS8......................55 E4
Royal Portbury Dock Rd
 PTSHD/EG BS20..................................41 G2
Royal Rd *MANG/FISH* BS16..................49 G2
Royal Sands *WSM* BS23.......................124 C2
Royal Victoria Pk
 HNBRY/STHM BS10.............................31 F3
Royal York Crs *CFTN/FAIL* BS8............54 D5
Royal York Ms
 CBATH/BATHN BA1 *...........................3 F3
Royal York Vls *CFTN/FAIL* BS8.............55 E5
Royate Hl *EVILLE/WHL* BS5.................57 F1
Roycroft Rd
 BRSG/KWL/STAPK BS4.......................32 D3
Roy King Gdns
 OLD/WMLY/WICK BS30......................77 F1
Royston Wk
 HNBRY/STHM BS10.............................31 H3
Rozel Rd *HORF/LLZ* BS7......................46 A2
Rubens Cl *KEYN* BS31...........................88 D4
Ruby St *BMSTR* BS3..............................72 C3
Ruddymead *CLVDN* BS21......................64 D3
Rudford Cl
 BRSTK/PCHW BS34............................20 D1
Rudge Cl *KGWD/HNM* BS15.................59 F1
Rudgewood Cl
 BMSTRD/HC/WWD BS13.....................85 E5
Rudgleigh Av *PTSHD/EG* BS20.............42 C4
Rudgleigh Rd *PTSHD/EG* BS20............42 C4
Rudhall Gv
 HNBRY/STHM BS10.............................46 A1
Rudmore Pk
 CBATH/BATHN BA1............................101 F5
Rudthorpe Rd *HORF/LLZ* BS7..............46 A3
Ruffet Rd *FRCTL/WBN* BS36................35 H1
Rugby Rd
 BRSG/KWL/STAPK BS4.......................74 C3
Runnymead Av
 BRSG/KWL/STAPK BS4.......................74 C5
Runnymede
 KGWD/HNM BS15...............................59 E2
Runswick Rd
 BRSG/KWL/STAPK BS4.......................74 B3
Rupert St *CBRIS/FH* BS1.......................5 F4
 EVILLE/WHL BS5.................................57 E4
Rush Cl *ALMDB* BS32...........................11 F5
Rush Hl *BATHSE* BA2............................107 C5
Rushmoor *CLVDN* BS21........................64 A4
Rushmoor Gv *NAIL* BS48......................79 G4
Rushmoor La *NAIL* BS48......................79 G4
Rushton Dr *FRCTL/WBN* BS36.............24 B3
Rushy *OLD/WMLY/WICK* BS30............76 D2
Rushy Wy *MANG/FISH* BS16................35 G4
Ruskin Gv *HORF/LLZ* BS7....................32 C5
Russell Av *KGWD/HNM* BS15...............58 D4
Russell Gv *RDLND/MONT* BS6.............45 G3
Russell Rd *CLVDN* BS21.......................64 C2
 MANG/FISH BS16................................58 B1
 OMX/HUT/LCK BS24..........................123 F5
 RDLND/MONT BS6...............................45 F4
Russell St *CBATH/BATHN* BA1...............3 F2
Russell Town Av
 EVILLE/WHL BS5.................................56 D3
The Russets *PTSHD/EG* BS20...............40 B4
Russett Cl *NAIL* BS48............................80 A5
Russett Gv *NAIL* BS48..........................78 D1
Russ St *CBRISNE* BS2...........................5 J5
Rutherford Cl
 OLD/WMLY/WICK BS30......................76 D3
Ruthven Rd
 BRSG/KWL/STAPK BS4.......................85 F1
Rutland Av
 OLD/WMLY/WICK BS30......................76 D4
Rutland Cl *MTN/WRL* BS22..................121 H3
Rutland Rd *HORF/LLZ* BS7...................46 A5
Rydal Av *OMX/HUT/LCK* BS24.............126 C2
Rydal Rd *WSM* BS23.............................125 E2
Ryde Rd
 BRSG/KWL/STAPK BS4.......................74 A4
Rye Cl *BMSTRD/HC/WWD* BS13...........83 H5
Ryecroft Av *MTN/WRL* BS22................122 B2
Ryecroft Ri *LGASH* BS41......................71 E5
Ryecroft Rd *FRCTL/WBN* BS36............24 A2
Ryedown La
 OLD/WMLY/WICK BS30......................77 F5
Ryland Pl *CBRISNE* BS2 *.....................57 F2
Rylestone Cl *FRCTL/WBN* BS36...........23 F2
Rylestone Gv
 HNLZ/SM/SNYPK/WT BS9.................44 D3

Rysdale Rd
HNLZ/SM/SNYPK/WT BS9........44 D2

S

Sabin Cl BATHSE BA2 ....107 G4
Sabrina Wy
HNLZ/SM/SNYPK/WT BS9........44 A4
Sadbury Cl MTN/WRL BS22....118 A4
Sadlier Cl AVONM BS11..........29 F5
Saffron Cl EVILLE/WHL BS5 *.....57 E3
Saffron Ct CBATH/BATHN BA1..102 D4
The Saffrons MTN/WRL BS22...118 A4
Sage Cl PTSHD/EG BS20..........38 C4
Sages Md ALMDB BS32..........21 G2
St Agnes Av
BRSG/KWL/STAPK BS4..........73 C4
St Agnes Cl
BRSG/KWL/STAPK BS4..........73 C4
NAIL BS48..............................67 H5
St Agnes Gdns
BRSG/KWL/STAPK BS4 *........73 C4
St Agnes Wk
BRSG/KWL/STAPK BS4..........73 C4
St Aidan's Cl EVILLE/WHL BS5...58 B5
St Aidan's Rd EVILLE/WHL BS5..58 A5
St Alban's Rd
RDLND/MONT BS6................45 F4
St Aldams Dr MANG/FISH BS16..51 F3
St Aldwyn's Cl HORF/LLZ BS7...32 B5
St Andrews
OLD/WMLY/WICK BS30..........59 H5
YATE/CS BS37....................26 B1
St Andrews Cl
MTN/WRL BS22 *.................117 C5
NAIL BS48..........................67 H5
St Andrew's Cl
YTN/CONG BS49...................114 D2
St Andrews Dr CLVDN BS21.....64 A3
St Andrews Rd NAIL BS48........80 A4
St Andrews Rd AVONM BS11......28 B4
RDLND/MONT BS6................56 A1
St Andrews Ter
CBATH/BATHN BA1 *...............3 F5
St Anne's Av KEYN BS31..........88 A3
St Annes Cl EVILLE/WHL BS5 *..57 H5
St Anne's Cl
OLD/WMLY/WICK BS30..........77 E2
St Annes Dr
OLD/WMLY/WICK BS30..........77 F4
St Anne's Dr
FRCTL/WBN BS36...................24 A5
OLD/WMLY/WICK BS30..........61 F4
St Anne's Park Rd
BRSG/KWL/STAPK BS4..........74 D1
St Anne's Rd
BRSG/KWL/STAPK BS4..........57 F5
St Anne's Ter
BRSG/KWL/STAPK BS4..........74 D1
St Anns Pl CBATH/BATHN BA1...2 D4
St Anns Wy BATHSE BA2..........3 K4
St Aubin's Av
BRSG/KWL/STAPK BS4..........75 E3
St Aubyn's Av WSM BS23......124 C4
St Augustine's Cl
PTSHD/EG BS20....................38 C4
St Augustines Pde
CBRIS/FH BS1........................4 E4
St Augustine's Pl
CBRIS/FH BS1 *.....................4 E4
St Augustines Yd
CBRIS/FH BS1 *.....................4 D4
St Austell Cl NAIL BS48...........79 H1
St Austell Rd MTN/WRL BS22..121 G3
St Barnabas Cl
OLD/WMLY/WICK BS30..........60 A4
St Bartholomew's Rd
HORF/LLZ BS7.......................46 B5
St Bede's Rd KGWD/HNM BS15..58 C1
St Bernard's Rd AVONM BS11....43 E2
St Bridges Cl MTN/WRL BS22..116 B2
St Catherine's Cl BATHSE BA2..109 F1
St Catherines Ct BMSTR BS3 *...73 E3
St Catherines Hospital
CBATH/BATHN BA1 *...............3 G5
St Catherine's Md
PTSHD/EG BS20....................42 D5
St Catherines Pl BMSTR BS3 *...73 E2
St Christophers Cl
BATHSE BA2.......................103 F5
St Clements Ct KEYN BS31......88 B5
St Clements Rd KEYN BS31......88 B4
St David Ms CBRIS/FH BS1 *......4 C5
St David's Av
OLD/WMLY/WICK BS30..........77 E1
St David's Cl MTN/WRL BS22...121 G1
St David's Crs
BRSG/KWL/STAPK BS4..........74 D1
St David's Rd THNB/SVB BS35....8 C3
St Dunstans Cl KEYN BS31.......88 A5
St Dunstan's Rd BMSTR BS3....72 D4
St Edward's Rd CFTN/FAIL BS8 *...4 A1
St Edyth's Rd
HNLZ/SM/SNYPK/WT BS9......43 H2
St Fagans Ct
OLD/WMLY/WICK BS30..........77 E4
St Francis Dr FRCTL/WBN BS36...23 F1
OLD/WMLY/WICK BS30..........61 F4
St Francis Rd BMSTR BS3........72 B2
KEYN BS31..........................87 H5
St Gabriel's Rd EVILLE/WHL BS5...56 C2
St Georges Av
HNLZ/SM/SNYPK/WT BS9......57 H5
St Georges Blds
EVILLE/WHL BS5 *................57 H5
St Georges Hi BATHSE BA2......2 C5
St George's Hi BATHSE BA2....103 G4
PTSHD/EG BS20....................42 A5
St Georges House
EVILLE/WHL BS5 *................57 G5
St Georges Pl
CBATH/BATHN BA1 *...............2 D3
St George's Rd CBRIS/FH BS1...4 B5
KEYN BS31..........................88 A4

PTSHD/EG BS20...................41 G1
St Gregory's Rd HORF/LLZ BS7...32 B5
St Gregory's Wk
HORF/LLZ BS7.......................32 C5
St Helena Rd
RDLND/MONT BS6................45 F4
St Helens Dr
OLD/WMLY/WICK BS30..........77 F4
St Helen's Wk EVILLE/WHL BS5..58 A2
St Helier Av
BRSG/KWL/STAPK BS4..........75 E1
St Hilary Cl
HNLZ/SM/SNYPK/WT BS9......44 B3
St Ivel Wy
OLD/WMLY/WICK BS30..........60 A5
St Ives Cl NAIL BS48..............67 H5
St Ives Rd WSM BS23.............125 F1
St James Cl ALMDB BS32........11 E4
St James PI MANG/FISH BS16....49 C3
St James's Pde
CBATH/BATHN BA1 *...............3 F5
St James's Pl
CBATH/BATHN BA1 *...............2 D1
St James's Sq
CBATH/BATHN BA1 *...............2 D1
St James's St
CBATH/BATHN BA1 *...............2 E1
MANG/FISH BS16...................49 G3
St James St WSM BS23............6 D4
St John's Br CLVDN BS21..........64 D2
St John's Br CBRIS/FH BS1 *......4 E2
St John's Cl WSM BS23............6 C1
St John's Ct KEYN BS31...........88 B3
St John's Crs BMSTR BS3........73 F4
St John's Hospital
CBATH/BATHN BA1 *...............3 F5
St John's La BMSTR BS3..........73 D3
St Johns Ms CFTN/FAIL BS8 *...55 F5
St John's Pl CBATH/BATHN BA1...3 F4
St John's Rd BATHSE BA2..........3 G2
BMSTR BS3.........................73 D3
CBATH/BATHN BA1................101 H5
CFTN/FAIL BS8......................55 E2
CLVDN BS21.........................64 C2
NAIL BS48...........................80 A4
St John's St BMSTR BS3..........72 D3
St John St THNB/SVB BS35........8 C3
St Johns Wy YATE/CS BS37......27 F1
St Joseph's Rd
HNBRY/STHM BS10................31 F2
St Jude's Ter MTN/WRL BS22...121 H2
St Keyna Rd KEYN BS31..........88 B4
St Kilda's Rd BATHSE BA2..........2 A7
St Ladoc Rd KEYN BS31..........87 G4
St Laud Cl
HNLZ/SM/SNYPK/WT BS9......44 A3
St Lawrence Ct AVONM BS11....29 E5
St Leonard's Rd
EVILLE/WHL BS5....................57 E1
HORF/LLZ BS7.......................46 A2
St Lucia Cl HORF/LLZ BS7.......32 A5
St Lucia Crs HORF/LLZ BS7.....32 A5
St Lukes Rd MANG/FISH BS16...49 H1
St Luke's Gdns
BRSG/KWL/STAPK BS4..........74 D4
St Luke's Ms
BRSG/KWL/STAPK BS4..........74 D4
St Luke's Rd BATHSE BA2......108 C4
BMSTR BS3.........................73 F2
St Luke St EVILLE/WHL BS5.....56 D4
St Margarets Cl NAIL BS48......79 H4
St Margaret's Dr
HNLZ/SM/SNYPK/WT BS9......45 G3
St Margaret's La NAIL BS48.....79 H4
St Margaret's Ter WSM BS23.....6 C3
St Marks Cl KEYN BS31...........88 B3
St Marks Gdns BATHSE BA2......3 H6
St Marks Rd BATHSE BA2..........3 G7
MTN/WRL BS22....................117 C5
St Mark's Rd EVILLE/WHL BS5...56 D2
St Mark's Ter EVILLE/WHL BS5 *..56 D2
St Martins Cl
BRSG/KWL/STAPK BS4 *........74 A5
St Martins Ct
MTN/WRL BS22 *.................117 F5
St Martin's Gdns
BRSG/KWL/STAPK BS4..........74 A4
St Martin's Rd
BRSG/KWL/STAPK BS4..........74 A4
St Martin's Wk
BRSG/KWL/STAPK BS4..........74 A5
St Marys Blds BATHSE BA2.......2 E6
St Marys Cl BATHSE BA2..........3 K3
St Mary's Cl BATHSE BA2..........3 J2
OMX/HUT/LCK BS24..............126 A4
St Mary's Ct
OMX/HUT/LCK BS24..............125 F5
St Mary's Pk NAIL BS48...........78 D1
St Mary's Pk NAIL BS48...........78 D1
St Mary's Rd AVONM BS11.......42 D1
CFTN/FAIL BS8......................54 B5
OMX/HUT/LCK BS24..............126 A4
PTSHD/EG BS20....................42 D5
St Mary St THNB/SVB BS35........8 C4
St Mary's Wk AVONM BS11.......42 D2
St Mary's Wy YATE/CS BS37.....14 B5
St Matthew's Av
RDLND/MONT BS6................55 H2
St Matthew's Cl WSM BS23........6 D1
St Matthews PI BATHSE BA2 *....3 J6
St Matthew's Rd
RDLND/MONT BS6................55 H2
St Matthias Pk CBRISNE BS2......5 J2
St Michael's Av CLVDN BS21.....64 D4
St Michaels Rd PTSHD/EG BS20..40 B2
Sand Farm La MTN/WRL BS22..116 B2
Sandford Cl CLVDN BS21.........64 B4
Sandford Rd CFTN/FAIL BS8.....72 B1
FRCTL/WBN BS36..................23 H4
WSM BS23..........................125 F2
Sandgate Rd
BRSG/KWL/STAPK BS4..........74 C3
Sand Hi BRSG/KWL/STAPK BS4...74 C3
Sandholme Cl MANG/FISH BS16..35 E5
Sandholme Rd
BRSG/KWL/STAPK BS4..........74 C3
Sandhurst YATE/CS BS37.........25 H2
Sandhurst Cl
BRSTK/PCHW BS34................20 D1

St Nicholas Pk
EVILLE/WHL BS5 *................56 D2
St Nicholas Rd
HGRV/WHIT BS14..................86 B5
WSM BS23..........................124 C4
St Nicholas' Rd CBRISNE BS2...56 B2
St Nicholas St CBRIS/FH BS1 *...5 F4
St Oswald's Rd
RDLND/MONT BS6................45 F5
St Patricks Ct BMSTR BS3 *.......3 K4
St Paul's Rd BMSTR BS3.........73 F2
CFTN/FAIL BS8.....................55 E4
WSM BS23..........................124 D1
St Paul St CBRISNE BS2............5 H1
St Peter's Av WSM BS23............6 C1
St Peter's Crs
BRSG/KWL/STAPK BS4..........74 C3
BRSTK/PCHW BS34................33 E3
WSM BS23..........................125 E1
St Peters Ri HGRV/WHIT BS14....85 G3
St Peters Rd PTSHD/EG BS20...39 H4
St Peters Ter BATHSE BA2.........2 B4
St Peter's Wk
HNLZ/SM/SNYPK/WT BS9......45 F3
St Philips Cswy
BRSG/KWL/STAPK BS4..........74 B2
CBRISNE BS2.......................56 D5
St Philips Rd CBRISNE BS2.......5 K3
St Phillips Rd CBRISNE BS2.....56 C4
St Pierre Dr
OLD/WMLY/WICK BS30..........59 H5
St Ronan's Av
RDLND/MONT BS6................55 G2
St Saviour's Av
FRCTL/WBN BS36..................23 H4
St Saviour's Rd
CBATH/BATHN BA1...............103 F3
St Saviours Ter
CBATH/BATHN BA1...............103 E3
St Saviours Wy
CBATH/BATHN BA1...............103 F3
St Stephen's Av CBRIS/FH BS1...4 E4
St Stephens Cl
HNBRY/STHM BS10 *.............31 C3
MANG/FISH BS16 *................49 E5
St Stephen's Cl
CBATH/BATHN BA1...............102 C4
St Stephens Ct
CBATH/BATHN BA1...............102 C4
St Stephens Pl
CBATH/BATHN BA1 *............102 C4
St Stephen's Rd
CBATH/BATHN BA1...............102 C4
MANG/FISH BS16...................48 D5
St Stephen's St CBRIS/FH BS1 *..4 E3
St Thomas Pl CBRIS/FH BS1 *.....5 G5
St Thomas St CBRIS/FH BS1 *....5 G5
St Vincent's Hl
RDLND/MONT BS6................55 E1
St Vincent's Rd CFTN/FAIL BS8...55 E5
St Wy BRSTK/PCHW BS34.......34 A1
St Werburgh's Pk CBRISNE BS2...56 C1
St Werburgh's Rd
CBRISNE BS2........................56 B1
St Whytes Rd
BRSG/KWL/STAPK BS4..........85 E1
St Winifreds Dr BATHSE BA2...109 G5
St Wulfstans Av
HNBRY/STHM BS10................31 E4
Salcombe Gdns
OLD/WMLY/WICK BS30..........122 D1
Salcombe Rd
BRSG/KWL/STAPK BS4..........85 H1
Salem Rd FRCTL/WBN BS36.....23 F3
Salisbury Av KGWD/HNM BS15..58 B3
Salisbury Dr MANG/FISH BS16 *..49 E2
Salisbury Gdns
MANG/FISH BS16...................49 E3
Salisbury Rd
BRSG/KWL/STAPK BS4..........74 C1
CBATH/BATHN BA1...............103 E2
MANG/FISH BS16...................49 E2
MTN/WRL BS22....................121 H2
RDLND/MONT BS6................55 H1
Salisbury St EVILLE/WHL BS5...56 D5
Salisbury Ter WSM BS23..........6 D3
Sallybarn Cl
OLD/WMLY/WICK BS30..........76 B4
Sally Hl PTSHD/EG BS20.........40 A1
Sallysmead Cl
BMSTRD/HC/WWD BS13.........84 C5
Salws Wy FRCTL/WBN BS36.....23 F3
Salmons Wy MANG/FISH BS16..35 G5
Salthouse Rd CLVDN BS21......64 B3
Salthrop Rd HORF/LLZ BS7.....46 A5
Saltings Cl CLVDN BS21..........64 B3
Saltmarsh Dr AVONM BS11.......42 A4
Saltwell Av HGRV/WHIT BS14....86 B4
Sambourne La
PTSHD/EG BS20....................42 C3
Samian Wy BRSTK/PCHW BS34..21 C5
Sampsons Rd
BMSTRD/HC/WWD BS13.........85 E5
Samuel St EVILLE/WHL BS5......57 E3
Samuel White Rd
KGWD/HNM BS15..................75 H3
Samuel Wright Cl
OLD/WMLY/WICK BS30..........77 G1
Sandbach Rd
BRSG/KWL/STAPK BS4..........74 C2
Sandbed Rd CBRISNE BS2.......56 C1
Sandburrows Rd
BMSTRD/HC/WWD BS13.........83 H5
Sandburrows Wk
BMSTRD/HC/WWD BS13.........84 A5
Sandcroft HGRV/WHIT BS14....85 G5
Sandcroft Av WSM BS23.........124 C4
Sanderling Pl PTSHD/EG BS20...40 B2

Sandhurst Rd
BRSG/KWL/STAPK BS4..........74 B3
Sandling Av HORF/LLZ BS7......46 C1
Sandown Cl MANG/FISH BS16...35 F4
Sandown Rd
BRSG/KWL/STAPK BS4..........74 C2
BRSTK/PCHW BS34................33 E2
Sandpiper Dr MTN/WRL BS22..122 C2
Sandringham Av
MANG/FISH BS16...................35 E5
Sandringham Pk
MANG/FISH BS16...................35 E5
Sandringham Rd
BRSG/KWL/STAPK BS4..........74 C3
BRSTK/PCHW BS34................33 F5
WSM BS23..........................125 E1
Sand Rd MTN/WRL BS22.........116 C3
Sandringham Ms CBATH/BATHN BA1...3 G3
Sandstone Ri FRCTL/WBN BS36..34 D1
Sandwich Rd
BRSG/KWL/STAPK BS4..........74 C3
Sandy Cl ALMDB BS32............21 G4
Sandy La CFTN/FAIL BS8..........53 E5
CLVDN BS21.........................47 E5
Sandydeaze
HNLZ/SM/SNYPK/WT BS9......44 C1
Sandy Ldg YATE/CS BS37........26 A2
Sandy Park Rd
BRSG/KWL/STAPK BS4..........74 B2
Saracen St CBATH/BATHN BA1 *...3 G3
Sarah St EVILLE/WHL BS5........56 D4
Sargent St BMSTR BS3...........73 F2
Sarum Cl MANG/FISH BS16......50 A2
Sarum Crs HNBRY/STHM BS10..31 G4
Sassoon Ct
OLD/WMLY/WICK BS30..........76 C1
Satchfield Cl
HNBRY/STHM BS10................30 D3
Satchfield Crs
HNBRY/STHM BS10................30 D3
Sates Wy
HNLZ/SM/SNYPK/WT BS9......45 C2
Saunders Rd MANG/FISH BS16..49 E4
Saunton Wk
BRSG/KWL/STAPK BS4..........85 F1
Savages Wood Rd
ALMDB BS32.........................21 F2
Savernake Rd MTN/WRL BS22..117 G5
Saville Crs MTN/WRL BS22......121 H3
Saville Gate Cl
HNLZ/SM/SNYPK/WT BS9......44 C5
Saville Ms RDLND/MONT BS6 *..55 H3
Saville Pl CFTN/FAIL BS8..........55 E5
Saville Rd
HNLZ/SM/SNYPK/WT BS9......44 C5
MTN/WRL BS22....................121 H3
Saville Rw CBATH/BATHN BA1 *...3 F2
Savoy Rd
BRSG/KWL/STAPK BS4..........74 C2
Saw Cl CBATH/BATHN BA1 *.......3 G4
Saw Mill La THNB/SVB BS35......8 C3
Sawyers Cl NAIL BS48............67 H4
Sawyers Ct CLVDN BS21.........65 E2
Saxby Cl CLVDN BS21.............64 B4
Saxon Ct MTN/WRL BS22.......118 C5
Saxon Rd CBRISNE BS2..........56 C1
MTN/WRL BS22....................121 H3
Saxon Wy ALMDB BS32...........21 E1
Say Wk
OLD/WMLY/WICK BS30..........60 B4
Scafell Cl WSM BS23................7 K1
Scandrett Cl
HNBRY/STHM BS10................30 C2
Scantleberry Cl
MANG/FISH BS16...................34 D5
The Scaurs MTN/WRL BS22....122 C1
School Cl BRSTK/PCHW BS34...21 E2
EVILLE/WHL BS5...................57 F1
HGRV/WHIT BS14..................85 C5
School Ct BRSTK/PCHW BS34...34 A1
School La CBATH/BATHN BA1...91 E5
NAIL BS48..........................82 A4
School Rd
BRSG/KWL/STAPK BS4..........73 H3
FRCTL/WBN BS36..................23 F2
KGWD/HNM BS15..................58 C3
OLD/WMLY/WICK BS30..........76 D2
School Vw NAIL BS48.............68 A5
School Wk EVILLE/WHL BS5 *...57 E1
YATE/CS BS37......................14 A5
The Scop ALMDB BS32...........10 C2
Scotch Horn Cl NAIL BS48......67 G4
Scotch Horn Wy NAIL BS48......67 G4
Scot Elm Dr
OMX/HUT/LCK BS24..............123 F2
Scotland La HGRV/WHIT BS14...87 E3
Scots Pine Av NAIL BS48.........67 G4
Scott Ct OLD/WMLY/WICK BS30..76 C1
Scott Lawrence Cl
HNBRY/STHM BS10................31 H3
Scott Rd WSM BS23...............125 F2
Scott Wk
OLD/WMLY/WICK BS30..........60 B4
Scott Wy YATE/CS BS37...........26 B2
Seabrook Rd MTN/WRL BS22..122 A2
Seagry Cl HNBRY/STHM BS10...32 A4
Sea Mills La
HNLZ/SM/SNYPK/WT BS9......44 A4
Searle Court Av
BRSG/KWL/STAPK BS4..........74 D1
Searle Crs WSM BS23...............7 K7
Seaton Rd EVILLE/WHL BS5.....57 E2
Seavale Rd CLVDN BS21.........64 C1
Seaview Rd PTSHD/EG BS20....38 C4
Seawalls Rd
HNLZ/SM/SNYPK/WT BS9......54 B1
Second Av BATHSE BA2..........108 A3
Second Wy AVONM BS11.........28 D4
Seddon Rd CBRISNE BS2.........56 C1
Sedgefield Gdns
MANG/FISH BS16...................35 F4
Sedgemoor Cl NAIL BS48........79 F1
Sedgemoor Rd BATHSE BA2....110 D1
WSM BS23............................7 H1
Sedgemoor Ter BATHSE BA2 *.108 D5
Sefton Park Rd HORF/LLZ BS7..46 B5
Sefton Sq
OMX/HUT/LCK BS24..............122 D3
Selborne Rd HORF/LLZ BS7.....46 B3

Selbourne Cl
CBATH/BATHN BA1...............101 E2
Selborne Rd WSM BS23.........124 D2
Selbrooke Crs
MANG/FISH BS16...................48 C2
Selby Rd EVILLE/WHL BS5.......57 H2
Selden Rd HGRV/WHIT BS14....86 B4
Selkirk Rd KGWD/HNM BS15....58 C1
Selley Wk
BMSTRD/HC/WWD BS13.........84 B4
Sellwood Cl MTN/WRL BS22...121 H4
Selworthy KGWD/HNM BS15....59 E4
Selworthy Cl KEYN BS31.........88 A4
Selworthy Rd
BRSG/KWL/STAPK BS4..........74 A5
WSM BS23..........................125 E2
Selworthy Ter BATHSE BA2 *...108 D5
Seneca Pl EVILLE/WHL BS5......57 F4
Seneca St EVILLE/WHL BS5......57 F4
Serbert Cl PTSHD/EG BS20.......40 A3
Serbert Rd PTSHD/EG BS20......40 A3
Serbert Wy PTSHD/EG BS20......40 A3
Sercombe Pk CLVDN BS21......65 E4
Seven Acres La
CBATH/BATHN BA1................91 E4
The Seven Acres
OMX/HUT/LCK BS24..............122 C4
Seven Dials CBATH/BATHN BA1 *...3 F4
Seventh Av HORF/LLZ BS7......32 D4
Seven View Rd THNB/SVB BS35..8 D2
Seven Av WSM BS23..............124 D1
Severn Dr THNB/SVB BS35........8 D2
Severnmeade PTSHD/EG BS20..38 D3
Severn Rd AVONM BS11..........42 D2
HNBRY/STHM BS10................17 G3
PTSHD/EG BS20....................42 C3
PTSHD/EG BS20....................39 G2
WSM BS23..........................124 D1
Severn Wy BRSTK/PCHW BS34..20 E1
THNB/SVB BS35......................9 E4
Sevier St CBRISNE BS2...........56 C1
Seville Ct PTSHD/EG BS20.......40 A1
Seville Rd PTSHD/EG BS20.......40 A1
Seymour Av HORF/LLZ BS7......46 A4
Seymour Cl CLVDN BS21.........65 E2
MTN/WRL BS22....................117 G4
Seymour Rd
CBATH/BATHN BA1 *...............3 H1
EVILLE/WHL BS5...................56 C2
KGWD/HNM BS15..................58 D5
Seyton Wk BRSTK/PCHW BS34..21 C5
Shackel Hendy Ms
MANG/FISH BS16...................49 H3
Shackleton Av YATE/CS BS37....26 B4
Shadow Wk
OMX/HUT/LCK BS24..............127 F5
Shadwell Rd HORF/LLZ BS7.....46 A4
Shaftesbury Av
CBATH/BATHN BA1...............101 H5
RDLND/MONT BS6................55 H2
Shaftesbury Cl NAIL BS48.......79 E1
Shaftesbury Rd BATHSE BA2......2 D7
WSM BS23..........................121 G3
Shaft Rd BATHSE BA2...........111 E4
Shakespeare Av BATHSE BA2..108 C3
Shaldon Rd HORF/LLZ BS7.....46 C4
The Shallows KEYN BS31.........99 G1
Sham Castle La BATHSE BA2......3 K5
Shamrock Rd EVILLE/WHL BS5..47 F5
Shanklin Dr BRSTK/PCHW BS34..32 D3
Shannon Ct CBRIS/FH BS1 *......5 G4
THNB/SVB BS35......................9 E4
Shapcott Cl
BRSG/KWL/STAPK BS4..........74 A5
Shaplands
HNLZ/SM/SNYPK/WT BS9......44 D4
Sharland Gv
BMSTRD/HC/WWD BS13.........95 H1
Shaw Cl EVILLE/WHL BS5.......56 D3
MANG/FISH BS16...................49 H5
Shaw Gdns HGRV/WHIT BS14...85 G4
Shaws Wy BATHSE BA2..........107 E2
Shearmore Cl HORF/LLZ BS7...46 C1
Sheene La BMSTR BS3............72 D3
Sheene Rd BMSTR BS3...........72 D3
Sheene Wy BMSTR BS3...........72 D3
Sheeps Cft
BMSTRD/HC/WWD BS13.........84 A5
Sheepway PTSHD/EG BS20......40 C4
Sheepwood Cl
HNBRY/STHM BS10................31 E4
Sheepwood Rd
HNBRY/STHM BS10................31 E4
Sheldare Barton
EVILLE/WHL BS5...................58 B4
Sheldon Cl CLVDN BS21..........65 F3
Sheldrake Dr MANG/FISH BS16..49 H2
Shellard Rd
BRSTK/PCHW BS34................32 C2
Shellards Rd
OLD/WMLY/WICK BS30..........76 C3
Shelley Av CLVDN BS21...........65 F3
Shelley Cl EVILLE/WHL BS5......57 F3
Shelley Rd BATHSE BA2.........108 C3
WSM BS23..........................125 F2
Shelley Wy HORF/LLZ BS7.......32 C5
Shellmor Av
BRSTK/PCHW BS34................20 D1
Shellmor Cl BRSTK/PCHW BS34..21 E1
Shepherds Cl MANG/FISH BS16..35 E5
Shepherds Wk ALMDB BS32.....21 E2
Sheppard Rd MANG/FISH BS16..48 C2
Sheppy's Mi YTN/CONG BS49..114 D1
Shepton Wk BMSTR BS3..........73 F3
Sherbourne Av ALMDB BS32....21 H2
Sherbourne Cl
KGWD/HNM BS15..................59 F1
Sherbourne St
EVILLE/WHL BS5...................57 G3
Sheridan Rd BATHSE BA2.......107 E2
Sheridan Wy
OLD/WMLY/WICK BS30..........76 C1
Sherperds Wy MTN/WRL BS22..123 F1
Sherrin Wy
BMSTRD/HC/WWD BS13.........94 C4
Sherston Cl MANG/FISH BS16...48 B3
NAIL BS48..........................67 H5
Sherston Rd HORF/LLZ BS7.....32 A5

Sherwell Rd BRSG/KWL/STAPK BS4 ......74 D3
Sherwood Cl KEYN BS31 ......88 B4
Sherwood Crs MTN/WRL BS22 ......117 C5
Sherwood Rd KEYN BS31 ......88 B4
KGWD/HNM BS15 ......58 A2
Shetland Rd HNBRY/STHM BS10 ......31 H4
Shetland Wy NAIL BS48 ......67 H5
Shickle Gv BATHSE BA2 ......110 A1
Shields Av HORF/LLZ BS7 ......32 C5
Shiels Dr ALMDB BS32 ......21 F3
Shilton Cl KGWD/HNM BS15 ......59 F4
Shimsey Cl MANG/FISH BS16 ......86 A4
Shiners Elms YTN/CONG BS49 ......112 A3
Shipham Cl CFTN/FAIL WHIT BS14 ......86 A4
NAIL BS48 ......79 C1
Ship La CBRIS/FH BS1 ......5 C7
Shipley Mow MANG/FISH BS16 ......49 H2
Shipley Rd HNLZ/SM/SNYPK/WT BS9 ......31 E5
Shipnan Ct MANG/FISH BS16 ......49 E4
Shire Gdns AVONM BS11 ......28 D5
Shirehampton Rd AVONM BS11 ......43 F1
Shires Yd CBATH/BATHN BA1 ......3 F3
Shire Wy YATE/CS BS37 ......25 G4
Sickerwick La CBATH/BATHN BA1 ......91 C5
Shophouse Rd BATHSE BA2 ......107 G2
Shorthill Rd YATE/CS BS37 ......37 G1
Shortlands Rd AVONM BS11 ......29 G4
Short La LGASH BS41 ......70 C4
Short St CBRISNE BS2 ......73 H1
Short Wy CFTN/FAIL BS8 ......69 C3
THNB/SVB BS35 ......9 H5
Shortwood Hl MANG/FISH BS16 ......50 B3
Shortwood Rd BMSTRD/HC/WWD BS13 ......96 B1
MANG/FISH BS16 ......51 E4
Shortwood Vw KGWD/HNM BS15 ......59 F5
Shortwood Wk BMSTRD/HC/WWD BS13 ......96 B1
Showering Cl HGRV/WHIT BS14 ......86 C4
Showering Rd HGRV/WHIT BS14 ......86 C4
Shrewsbury Bow OMX/HUT/LCK BS24 ......122 D3
Shrubbery Av WSM BS23 ......120 D2
Shrubbery Cots RDLND/MONT BS6 ......55 F1
Shrubbery Rd MANG/FISH BS16 ......48 D3
WSM BS23 ......6 B1
Shrubbery Ter WSM BS23 ......6 B1
Shrubbery Wk West WSM BS23 * 6 C1
Shuter Rd BMSTRD/HC/WWD BS13 ......83 H4
Sibland Rd THNB/SVB BS35 ......9 E4
Sibland Cl THNB/SVB BS35 ......9 E4
Sibland Rd THNB/SVB BS35 ......9 E4
Sibland Wy THNB/SVB BS35 ......9 E4
Sidcot BRSG/KWL/STAPK BS4 ......75 E4
Sideland Cl HGRV/WHIT BS14 ......86 D3
Sidelands Rd MANG/FISH BS16 ......48 C2
The Sidings BRSTK/PCHW BS34 ......33 C5
KGWD/HNM BS15 ......59 G4
Sidmouth Gdns BMSTR BS3 ......73 E4
Sidmouth Rd BMSTR BS3 ......73 E4
Signal Rd MANG/FISH BS16 ......49 E4
Silbury Ri KEYN BS31 ......98 B2
Silbury Rd BMSTR BS3 ......71 H4
Silcox Rd BMSTRD/HC/WWD BS13 ......84 B1
Siklands Gv HNLZ/SM/SNYPK/WT BS9 * 44 A2
Silverberry Rd MTN/WRL BS22 ......122 D2
Silver Birch Cl BRSTK/PCHW BS34 ......21 F5
Silvercourt NAIL BS48 ......66 D4
Silverhill Rd HNBRY/STHM BS10 ......30 C2
Silverlow Rd NAIL BS48 ......67 E4
Silver Md YTN/CONG BS49 ......114 D4
Silverstone Wy YTN/CONG BS49 ......114 D3
Silver St CBRIS/FH BS1 ......5 F2
NAIL BS48 ......67 E4
YTN/CONG BS49 ......114 D4
Silverthorne La CBRISNE BS2 ......5 K5
Silverton Ct BRSG/KWL/STAPK BS4 * 73 C5
Simmonds Vw BRSTK/PCHW BS34 ......21 H5
Simons Cl MTN/WRL BS22 ......122 D1
Singapore Rd WSM BS23 ......124 D5
Sion Hl CBATH/BATHN BA1 ......102 A3
CFTN/FAIL BS8 ......54 D4
Sion Hill Pl CBATH/BATHN BA1 ......102 B3
Sion Hill Rd CBATH/BATHN BA1 ......102 B3
Sion La CFTN/FAIL BS8 ......54 D4
Sion Pl BATHSE BA2 ......3 K4
CFTN/FAIL BS8 ......54 D4
Sir John's La EVILLE/WHL BS5 ......46 D4
Sir Johns Wd NAIL BS48 * 67 C5
Siskin Cl PTSHD/EG BS20 ......40 B2
Siston Cl KGWD/HNM BS15 ......59 C1
Siston Common OLD/WMLY/WICK BS30 ......59 H2
Siston La OLD/WMLY/WICK BS30 ......60 C2
Six Streams KGWD/HNM BS15 ......59 C1
Sixth Av HORF/LLZ BS7 ......32 C4
Sixty Acres Cl CFTN/FAIL BS8 ......53 E3
Skippon Ct KGWD/HNM BS15 ......76 B1
Skylark Av CLVDN BS21 ......63 F1
Sladebrook Av BATHSE BA2 ......107 H4
Sladebrook Rd BATHSE BA2 ......107 C5
Slade La NAIL BS48 ......79 H4
Slade Rd PTSHD/EG BS20 ......39 H5

Slades Ct NAIL BS48 ......79 H5
Sleep La HGRV/WHIT BS14 ......97 C1
Slimbridge Cl YATE/CS BS37 ......26 B5
Sloan St EVILLE/WHL BS5 ......57 F5
Sloe Cl MTN/WRL BS22 ......122 A4
Slymbridge Av HNBRY/STHM BS10 ......31 E1
Small La MANG/FISH BS16 ......47 C3
Small St CBRIS/FH BS1 ......4 E5
CBRISNE BS2 ......73 H1
Smallway YTN/CONG BS49 ......114 D1
Smarts Gn YATE/CS BS37 ......27 E2
Smeaton Rd CBRIS/FH BS1 ......72 A1
Smithcourt Dr BRSTK/PCHW BS34 ......21 E4
Smithmead BMSTRD/HC/WWD BS13 ......84 C4
Smoke La AVONM BS11 ......16 C4
Smythe Cft HGRV/WHIT BS14 ......96 D1
Smyth Rd BMSTR BS3 ......72 B3
Smyths Cl AVONM BS11 ......28 B4
Sneyd Park Ms HNLZ/SM/SNYPK/WT BS9 * 44 B5
Snowberry Cl ALMDB BS32 ......21 G2
Snowberry Wk EVILLE/WHL BS5 ......57 G3
Snowdon Cl MANG/FISH BS16 ......47 H4
Snowdon Rd MANG/FISH BS16 ......47 H4
Snowdon V WSM BS23 ......7 J1
Snowdrop Cl MANG/FISH BS16 ......47 H5
Snow Hl CBATH/BATHN BA1 ......102 D3
Solent Wy THNB/SVB BS35 ......9 E5
Solsbury La CBATH/BATHN BA1 ......90 D5
Somberby Cl ALMDB BS32 ......21 F3
Somerdale Av BATHSE BA2 ......108 A5
BRSG/KWL/STAPK BS4 ......74 B5
MTN/WRL BS22 ......121 H5
Somerdale Cl MTN/WRL BS22 ......121 H5
Somerdale Rd KEYN BS31 ......88 C2
Somerdale Rd North KEYN BS31 ......88 C2
Somerdale Vw BATHSE BA2 ......107 H5
Somermead BMSTR BS3 ......72 D5
Somerset Av OMX/HUT/LCK BS24 ......122 C4
WSM BS23 ......14 B4
Somerset Crs BRSTK/PCHW BS34 ......21 H5
Somerset La CBATH/BATHN BA1 ......102 B3
Somerset Pl CBATH/BATHN BA1 ......102 B3
Somerset Rd BRSG/KWL/STAPK BS4 ......73 H5
CLVDN BS21 ......65 E2
PTSHD/EG BS20 ......38 D5
Somerset Sq CBRIS/FH BS1 ......5 C7
Somerset St CBATH/BATHN BA1 ......3 H5
CBRIS/FH BS1 ......5 H5
CBRISNE BS2 ......55 H1
Somerset Ter BMSTR BS3 ......73 F3
Somerton Cl KGWD/HNM BS15 ......59 E4
Somerton Rd CLVDN BS21 ......64 D1
HORF/LLZ BS7 ......46 A2
Somerville Cl KEYN BS31 ......99 F2
Sommerville Rd HORF/LLZ BS7 ......46 A5
Sommerville Rd South RDLND/MONT BS6 ......56 B1
Soper Gdns BRSG/KWL/STAPK BS4 ......84 D2
Sophia Gdns MTN/WRL BS22 ......118 A4
Sorrel Cl THNB/SVB BS35 ......9 E2
Southwell Rd KGWD/HNM BS15 ......58 C2
Southampton Gdns HORF/LLZ BS7 * 46 B3
Southampton Ms HORF/LLZ BS7 * 46 B3
South Av BATHSE BA2 ......2 A6
PTSHD/EG BS20 ......39 H7
YATE/CS BS37 ......25 F1
Southbourne Gdns CBATH/BATHN BA1 ......103 E3
Southcot Pl BATHSE BA2 ......3 H7
South Crs WSM BS23 ......6 C2
South Cft HNLZ/SM/SNYPK/WT BS9 ......45 C1
South Dene HNLZ/SM/SNYPK/WT BS9 ......44 C2
Southdown MTN/WRL BS22 ......117 G4
Southdown Av BATHSE BA2 ......107 G4
Southdown Rd BATHSE BA2 ......107 G3
HNLZ/SM/SNYPK/WT BS9 ......45 C1
Southend Rd WSM BS23 ......124 D2
Southernhay CFTN/FAIL BS8 * 4 A5
MANG/FISH BS16 ......48 C4
Southernhay Av CFTN/FAIL BS8 ......4 A5
Southernhay Crs CFTN/FAIL BS8 ......4 A5
Southern Wy CLVDN BS21 ......64 B3
Southey Av KGWD/HNM BS15 ......58 D2
Southey Rd CLVDN BS21 ......64 D3
Southey St CBRISNE BS2 ......56 B2
Southfield Av KGWD/HNM BS15 ......59 E2
Southfield Cl WSM BS23 ......124 C5
Southfield Ct HNLZ/SM/SNYPK/WT BS9 ......45 E1
Southfield Rd HNLZ/SM/SNYPK/WT BS9 ......45 E1
NAIL BS48 ......67 F3
RDLND/MONT BS6 ......55 H2
Southfield Wy YATE/CS BS37 ......14 C3
Southgate CBATH/BATHN BA1 * 3 G6
South Green St CFTN/FAIL BS8 ......54 D5
South Gv PTSHD/EG BS20 ......42 C4
HORF/LLZ BS7 ......46 A4
South Hayes EVILLE/WHL BS5 ......46 D4
Southlands CBATH/BATHN BA1 ......101 F3
Southlands Wy YTN/CONG BS49 ......114 D1
South Lawn OMX/HUT/LCK BS24 ......126 C2
South Lawn Cl OMX/HUT/LCK BS24 ......126 C2
South Lea Rd CBATH/BATHN BA1 ......101 F4

Southleigh Rd CFTN/FAIL BS8 ......4 A1
South Liberty La BMSTR BS3 ......72 B5
Southmead Rd HNBRY/STHM BS10 ......31 C5
HNLZ/SM/SNYPK/WT BS9 ......45 F1
MTN/WRL BS22 ......121 C4
Southmead Wy HNBRY/STHM BS10 ......31 H5
Southover Cl HNLZ/SM/SNYPK/WT BS9 ......31 E5
South Pde BATHSE BA2 ......3 H5
WSM BS23 ......6 D5
South Rd ALMDB BS32 ......11 F1
BMSTR BS3 * 72 D3
KGWD/HNM BS15 ......58 D3
PTSHD/EG BS20 ......39 H2
RDLND/MONT BS6 ......55 C1
WSM BS23 ......120 B2
Southsea Rd BRSTK/PCHW BS34 ......20 C3
Southside WSM BS23 ......6 E2
South Side YTN/CONG BS49 ......115 E1
Southside Cl HNLZ/SM/SNYPK/WT BS9 ......43 H1
Southside Crs MTN/WRL BS22 ......116 D3
Southstoke La BATHSE BA2 ......110 D3
Southstoke Rd BATHSE BA2 ......110 D1
South Ter RDLND/MONT BS6 ......55 E1
South Vw FRCTL/WBN BS36 ......26 E3
MANG/FISH BS16 ......49 E3
PTSHD/EG BS20 ......39 C3
Southview Cl OMX/HUT/LCK BS24 ......126 B4
South View Crs FRCTL/WBN BS36 ......24 B4
South View Ri FRCTL/WBN BS36 ......24 B4
South View Rd BATHSE BA2 ......2 A5
South View Ter YTN/CONG BS49 ......112 B2
Southville Pl BMSTR BS3 ......73 E2
Southville Rd BMSTR BS3 ......72 D2
Southway Dr OLD/WMLY/WICK BS30 ......77 G1
Southwell St CBRISNE BS2 ......4 D1
Southwood Av HNLZ/SM/SNYPK/WT BS9 ......30 A5
Southwood Dr HNLZ/SM/SNYPK/WT BS9 ......29 H5
Southwood Dr East HNLZ/SM/SNYPK/WT BS9 ......30 A5
Spa La CBATH/BATHN BA1 ......103 F2
Spalding Cl HORF/LLZ BS7 ......46 C5
Spar Rd AVONM BS11 ......28 C1
YATE/CS BS37 ......13 H5
Spartley Dr BMSTRD/HC/WWD BS13 ......84 A3
Spartley Wk BMSTRD/HC/WWD BS13 ......84 A3
Speedwell Av EVILLE/WHL BS5 ......57 F4
Speedwell Cl THNB/SVB BS35 ......9 E2
Speedwell Rd EVILLE/WHL BS5 ......57 H2
Spencer Dr MTN/WRL BS22 ......118 A5
Spencers Belle Vue CBATH/BATHN BA1 ......2 E1
Spey Cl THNB/SVB BS35 ......8 D4
Spindleberry Gv NAIL BS48 ......67 H4
Spinners End MTN/WRL BS22 ......118 A4
Spinney Rd OMX/HUT/LCK BS24 ......127 G2
The Spinney ALMDB BS32 ......21 G3
MANG/FISH BS16 ......23 H5
OMX/HUT/LCK BS24 ......127 C2
PTSHD/EG BS20 ......39 C5
Spires Vw MANG/FISH BS16 * 47 C3
Spring Crs BATHSE BA2 ......3 H6
Springfield THNB/SVB BS35 ......9 E4
Springfield Av AVONM BS11 ......42 D2
HORF/LLZ BS7 ......46 B3
MANG/FISH BS16 ......49 C2
MTN/WRL BS22 ......121 H4
Springfield Cl BATHSE BA2 ......107 C2
MANG/FISH BS16 ......49 C2
Springfield Gv RDLND/MONT BS6 ......45 F3
Springfield Pl CBATH/BATHN BA1 ......102 C3
Springfield Rd MANG/FISH BS16 ......49 C1
PTSHD/EG BS20 ......42 C4
PTSHD/EG BS20 ......39 F3
RDLND/MONT BS6 ......55 H2
Springfields BRSTK/PCHW BS34 ......32 C3
Spring Gdns BRSG/KWL/STAPK BS4 ......73 H5
Spring Gardens Rd BATHSE BA2 ......3 C3
Spring Hl KGWD/HNM BS15 ......59 E1
MTN/WRL BS22 ......121 H1
RDLND/MONT BS6 ......55 F1
Spring Hill Dr MTN/WRL BS22 ......122 A3
Spring La CBATH/BATHN BA1 ......89 F5
LGASH BS41 ......95 F3
Springleaze BRSG/KWL/STAPK BS4 ......85 C1
MANG/FISH BS16 ......49 C1
Springly Ct KGWD/HNM BS15 * 59 C5
Spring Ri PTSHD/EG BS20 ......39 H5
Spring St BMSTR BS3 ......73 F2
Spring Street Pl BMSTR BS3 ......73 F2
Spring Ter MTN/WRL BS22 ......121 H1
Spring V CBATH/BATHN BA1 ......103 E2
Springville Cl OLD/WMLY/WICK BS30 ......76 D3
Springwood Dr HNBRY/STHM BS10 ......30 B2
Spring Wood Gdns OMX/HUT/LCK BS24 ......126 D3
Spruce Wy BRSTK/PCHW BS34 ......20 A3
MANG/FISH BS16 ......122 B3
The Square BATHSE BA2 ......2 E6
BRSG/KWL/STAPK BS4 ......85 C1
MANG/FISH BS16 * 5 D5
MANG/FISH BS16 * 49 E4

Squires Ct OLD/WMLY/WICK BS30 ......76 C2
Squires Leaze THNB/SVB BS35 ......9 E2
Stabbins Cl MTN/WRL BS22 ......118 A3
Stable Yd BATHSE BA2 ......2 A3
Stackpool Rd BMSTR BS3 ......72 D2
Stadium Rd RDLND/MONT BS6 ......45 C3
Stafford Crs THNB/SVB BS35 ......8 C3
Stafford Pl WSM BS23 ......7 F2
Stafford Rd CBRISNE BS2 ......56 C1
EVILLE/WHL BS5 ......57 E3
WSM BS23 ......6 D5
Staffords Ct OLD/WMLY/WICK BS30 ......59 C5
Stafford St BMSTR BS3 ......73 E2
Stainer Cl BRSG/KWL/STAPK BS4 ......84 B1
Stainer Rd MANG/FISH BS16 ......49 H5
Stall St CBATH/BATHN BA1 ......3 C4
Stambrook Pk CBATH/BATHN BA1 ......91 E4
Stanbridge Cl MANG/FISH BS16 ......48 B3
Stanbridge Rd MANG/FISH BS16 ......49 F2
Stanbury Av MANG/FISH BS16 ......48 B3
Stanbury Rd BMSTR BS3 ......73 F3
Stancombe La NAIL BS48 ......80 D2
Standfast Rd HNBRY/STHM BS10 ......30 D2
Standish Av BRSTK/PCHW BS34 ......20 D1
Standish Cl HNBRY/STHM BS10 ......30 D4
Standon Wy HNBRY/STHM BS10 ......31 C5
Stane Wy AVONM BS11 ......42 C1
Stanfield Cl HORF/LLZ BS7 ......46 C2
Stanford Cl FRCTL/WBN BS36 ......23 F2
Stanford Pl BRSG/KWL/STAPK BS4 * 85 C2
Stanhope Pl CBATH/BATHN BA1 * 2 D4
Stanhope Rd OLD/WMLY/WICK BS30 ......76 C4
WSM BS23 ......124 D3
Stanhope St CBRISNE BS2 ......73 H1
Stanley Av BRSTK/PCHW BS34 ......32 C5
HORF/LLZ BS7 ......46 A5
Stanley Cha EVILLE/WHL BS5 ......57 E3
Stanley Gdns OLD/WMLY/WICK BS30 ......77 E2
Stanley Gv WSM BS23 ......7 C4
Stanley Hl BRSG/KWL/STAPK BS4 ......73 H2
Stanley Md ALMDB BS32 ......11 E1
Stanley Pk EVILLE/WHL BS5 ......56 D2
Stanley Park Rd MANG/FISH BS16 ......49 E5
Stanley Rd RDLND/MONT BS6 ......55 C1
WSM BS23 ......7 H4
Stanley Rd West BATHSE BA2 ......2 A4
Stanley St BMSTR BS3 ......73 E2
Stanley St North BMSTR BS3 ......72 D3
Stanley St South BMSTR BS3 ......72 D3
Stanley Ter BMSTR BS3 ......73 E3
Stanshalls Cl BLAG/CWMG/WR BS40 ......92 D4
Stanshalls Dr BLAG/CWMG/WR BS40 ......92 D4
Stanshalls La BLAG/CWMG/WR BS40 ......92 D4
Stanshawe Crs YATE/CS BS37 ......26 A1
Stanshawes Court Dr YATE/CS BS37 ......26 A2
Stanshawes Dr YATE/CS BS37 ......25 H2
Stanshaws Rd MANG/FISH BS16 ......48 A1
Stanshaws Cl ALMDB BS32 ......10 D5
Stanton Cl KGWD/HNM BS15 ......59 F2
Stanton Rd HNBRY/STHM BS10 ......32 A4
Stanway OLD/WMLY/WICK BS30 ......77 E5
Stanway Cl BATHSE BA2 ......110 B1
Staple Gv KEYN BS31 ......88 A4
Staple Grove Crs EVILLE/WHL BS5 ......58 A4
Staplehill Rd MANG/FISH BS16 ......48 B4
Staples Cl CLVDN BS21 ......65 E4
Staples Gn MTN/WRL BS22 ......118 A5
Staples Rd YATE/CS BS37 ......13 H5
Stapleton Cl MANG/FISH BS16 ......47 H5
Stapleton Rd EVILLE/WHL BS5 ......56 D1
Star Barn Rd FRCTL/WBN BS36 ......24 A1
Starcross Rd MTN/WRL BS22 ......122 D1
Star La MANG/FISH BS16 ......47 H5
PTSHD/EG BS20 ......42 C4
Starling Cl MTN/WRL BS22 ......122 D3
Station Ap CBRIS/FH BS1 ......5 J6
WSM BS23 ......7 F5
Station Av MANG/FISH BS16 ......60 A3
WSM BS23 ......79 C2
YATE/CS BS37 ......27 F2
YTN/CONG BS49 ......114 C2
Station La HORF/LLZ BS7 ......46 C4
Station Rd AVONM BS11 ......42 D3
BRSG/KWL/STAPK BS4 ......74 B4
BRSTK/PCHW BS34 ......32 C2
CBATH/BATHN BA1 ......101 H5
CLVDN BS21 ......64 D2
FRCTL/WBN BS36 ......35 E1
HNBRY/STHM BS10 ......30 C2
KEYN BS31 ......88 B3
MANG/FISH BS16 ......48 A4
MTN/WRL BS22 ......122 C1
NAIL BS48 ......67 E3
OLD/WMLY/WICK BS30 ......60 C3
PTSHD/EG BS20 ......39 H2
WSM BS23 ......6 E5
YATE/CS BS37 ......12 D4
YTN/CONG BS49 ......114 C2
Station Road Link HNBRY/STHM BS10 ......59 C1
Staunton Flds HGRV/WHIT BS14 ......97 F1
Staunton La HGRV/WHIT BS14 ......86 D5
Staunton Wy HGRV/WHIT BS14 ......86 C5
Staveley Crs HNBRY/STHM BS10 ......31 G3

Stavordale Gv HGRV/WHIT BS14 ......86 A3
Staynes Crs KGWD/HNM BS15 ......59 E3
Steanbridge Rd ALMDB BS32 ......21 F4
Steel Ct OLD/WMLY/WICK BS30 ......76 C4
Steel Mills KEYN BS31 ......88 C5
Stella Gv BMSTR BS3 ......72 B4
Stephens Dr OLD/WMLY/WICK BS30 ......76 C1
Stephen St EVILLE/WHL BS5 ......57 E3
Stepney Rd EVILLE/WHL BS5 ......57 E3
Stepney Wk EVILLE/WHL BS5 ......57 E3
The Stepping Stones BRSG/KWL/STAPK BS4 * 57 C5
Sterncourt Rd MANG/FISH BS16 ......48 A1
Stevens Crs BMSTR BS3 ......73 G2
Stevens Wk ALMDB BS32 ......21 F2
Steway La CBATH/BATHN BA1 ......91 H1
Stibbs Ct OLD/WMLY/WICK BS30 ......76 C2
Stibbs Hl EVILLE/WHL BS5 ......58 A4
Stickland CLVDN BS21 ......64 C4
Stile Acres AVONM BS11 ......29 C4
Stillhouse La BMSTR BS3 ......73 E2
Stillingfleet Rd BMSTRD/HC/WWD BS13 ......84 D4
Stillman Ct BMSTRD/HC/WWD BS13 ......83 H5
Stinchcombe YATE/CS BS37 ......26 A1
Stirling Cl YATE/CS BS37 ......13 H3
Stirling Rd BRSG/KWL/STAPK BS4 ......74 B2
Stirling Wy KEYN BS31 ......88 B5
Stirtingale Av BATHSE BA2 ......107 H4
Stirtingale Rd BATHSE BA2 ......107 H4
Stock La YTN/CONG BS49 ......115 F5
Stockton Cl HGRV/WHIT BS14 ......85 C5
KGWD/HNM BS15 ......58 D3
Stock Wy North NAIL BS48 ......67 F4
Stock Wy South NAIL BS48 ......67 F4
Stockwell Av MANG/FISH BS16 ......49 F1
Stockwell Cl MANG/FISH BS16 ......49 E1
Stockwell Dr MANG/FISH BS16 ......49 G2
Stockwood Crs BRSG/KWL/STAPK BS4 ......73 C4
Stockwood Hl KEYN BS31 ......87 H2
Stockwood La HGRV/WHIT BS14 ......86 D4
Stockwood Ms BRSG/KWL/STAPK BS4 ......75 E1
Stockwood Rd BRSG/KWL/STAPK BS4 ......75 E5
HGRV/WHIT BS14 ......86 D4
Stoeleigh Ct MTN/WRL BS22 ......118 A5
Stoke Bridge Av BRSTK/PCHW BS34 ......21 F4
Stokefield Cl THNB/SVB BS35 ......8 C3
Stoke Gv HNLZ/SM/SNYPK/WT BS9 ......44 C2
Stoke Hamlet HNLZ/SM/SNYPK/WT BS9 ......44 C4
Stoke Hl HNLZ/SM/SNYPK/WT BS9 ......44 C4
Stoke La BRSTK/PCHW BS34 ......21 E2
HNLZ/SM/SNYPK/WT BS9 ......44 D2
MANG/FISH BS16 ......33 C5
Stokeleigh Wk HNLZ/SM/SNYPK/WT BS9 ......44 A3
Stokemead BRSTK/PCHW BS34 ......21 E2
Stoke Mdw ALMDB BS32 ......21 F1
Stoke Paddock Rd HNLZ/SM/SNYPK/WT BS9 ......44 B2
Stoke Park Rd South HNLZ/SM/SNYPK/WT BS9 ......44 C5
Stoke Rd HNLZ/SM/SNYPK/WT BS9 ......44 C5
PTSHD/EG BS20 ......39 H3
Stokes Cl OLD/WMLY/WICK BS30 ......76 D2
Stokes Cft CBRIS/FH BS1 ......56 A3
Stoke View Rd MANG/FISH BS16 ......47 H5
Stoneberry Rd HGRV/WHIT BS14 ......96 D1
Stonebridge CLVDN BS21 ......64 C4
Stonebridge Pk EVILLE/WHL BS5 ......57 F1
Stonebridge Rd WSM BS23 ......125 E2
Stonechat Gdns MANG/FISH BS16 ......47 G2
Stonechat Gv PTSHD/EG BS20 ......40 C2
Stone Cl FRCTL/WBN BS36 ......35 E1
Stonehill KGWD/HNM BS15 ......76 B2
Stonehouse Cl BATHSE BA2 ......111 F1
Stonehouse La BATHSE BA2 ......109 C5
Stone La FRCTL/WBN BS36 ......35 E1
Stoneleigh Crs BRSG/KWL/STAPK BS4 ......73 H4
Stoneleigh Dr OLD/WMLY/WICK BS30 ......76 C1
Stoneleigh Rd BRSG/KWL/STAPK BS4 ......73 H4
Stoneleigh Wk BRSG/KWL/STAPK BS4 ......73 H4
Stonewell Dr YTN/CONG BS49 ......114 D3
Stonewell Gv YTN/CONG BS49 ......114 D3
Stonewell La YTN/CONG BS49 ......114 D3
Stonewell Park Rd YTN/CONG BS49 ......114 D3
Stoneyfield Cl PTSHD/EG BS20 ......42 B4
Stoneyfields PTSHD/EG BS20 ......42 B4
Stoney Steep NAIL BS48 ......67 H1
PTSHD/EG BS20 ......39 C2
Stores Rd AVONM BS11 ......43 E4
Stormont Cl WSM BS23 ......125 E3
Stormont Ct OMX/HUT/LCK BS24 ......122 B4
Stothard Rd HORF/LLZ BS7 ......46 D1
Stottbury Rd HORF/LLZ BS7 ......46 C4
Stoulton Gv HNBRY/STHM BS10 ......31 E2
Stourden Cl MANG/FISH BS16 ......48 A1
Stourton Dr OLD/WMLY/WICK BS30 ......76 C2
Stover Rd YATE/CS BS37 ......13 F5
Stowell Pk YTN/CONG BS49 ......112 D4

Stowey Rd YTN/CONG BS49 .....112 B2
Stowick Crs AVONM BS11 ....30 A4
Stradbrook Av
　EVILLE/WHL BS5.................58 B4
Stradling Av WSM BS23 ....125 E1
Stradling Rd AVONM BS11 ....30 A5
Stradling Ter WSM BS23 * 125 E1
Straight St CBRISNE BS2............5 J4
Stratford Cl HGRV/WHIT BS14 ....96 C1
Strathearn Dr
　HNBRY/STHM BS10 ....31 F5
Strathmore Rd HORF/LLZ BS7 ...46 A2
Stratton Pl
　OLD/WMLY/WICK BS30 ....76 C4
Stratton Rd KEYN BS31 ....99 F1
Strawberry Cl NAIL BS48............67 E5
Strawberry Hi CLVDN BS21........65 E1
Strawberry La LGASH BS41 ....94 D1
Strawbridge Rd
　EVILLE/WHL BS5.................56 D4
Stream Cl HNBRY/STHM BS10 ...31 H2
Streamcross YTN/CONG BS49 ...113 E1
Streamleaze THNB/SVB BS35 .....8 D4
Streamside CLVDN BS21 ....65 F2
Stream Side MANG/FISH BS16....49 F2
Streamside Rd YATE/CS BS37 ....26 C1
The Stream MANG/FISH BS16 ....34 B3
Stretford Av EVILLE/WHL BS5 ....57 F3
Stretford Rd EVILLE/WHL BS5 ....57 F3
Strode Rd CLVDN BS21 ....64 B4
Strode Wy CLVDN BS21 ....64 B4
Stroud Rd AVONM BS11.............43 E3
　BRSTK/PCHW BS34 ....20 A2
Stroud Wy
　OMX/HUT/LCK BS24 ....122 B4
Stuart Pl BATHSE BA2 ....2 A5
Stuart Rd WSM BS23 ....113 E1
Stuart St EVILLE/WHL BS5..........57 E4
Sturden La MANG/FISH BS16.....34 C2
Sturdon Rd BMSTR BS3.............72 B3
Sturmer Cl YATE/CS BS37 ....14 A3
Sturmey Wy PTSHD/EG BS20.....42 D5
Sturminster Cl
　HGRV/WHIT BS14 ....86 C3
Sturminster Rd
　HGRV/WHIT BS14 ....86 B4
Sulis Manor Rd BATHSE BA2 ....110 B2
Sullivan Cl
　BRSG/KWL/STAPK BS4.........85 E3
Sumerlin Dr CLVDN BS21...........65 F2
Summerfield
　MTN/WRL BS22.................118 A5
Summerfield Rd
　CBATH/BATHN BA1 ....102 D3
Summerfield Ter
　CBATH/BATHN BA1 * 102 D3
Summer Ground Dr
　BMSTRD/HC/WWD BS13......84 B4
Summerhayes
　OLD/WMLY/WICK BS30 ....77 G1
Summer Hl
　BRSG/KWL/STAPK BS4.........73 H2
Summerhill Rd
　CBATH/BATHN BA1 ....102 A3
　EVILLE/WHL BS5.................57 H3
Summerhill Ter
　EVILLE/WHL BS5.................57 H4
Summer House Wy
　OLD/WMLY/WICK BS30 ....59 H4
Summerlands NAIL BS48............80 A4
Summerlands Rd WSM BS23 ......7 J3
Summer La BATHSE BA2 ....111 F1
　BNWL BS29......................127 H2
　MTN/WRL BS22.................123 E2
Summer La North
　MTN/WRL BS22.................122 D1
Summerleaze MANG/FISH BS16 .51 H1
　MANG/FISH BS16 ....48 D1
Summerleaze Ct BATHSE BA2 .....3 J5
Summers Md YATE/CS BS37 ......14 A2
Summers Rd CBRISNE BS2 ....56 C2
Summer St BMSTR BS3 ....72 D2
Summit Cl KGWD/HNM BS15 .....59 E3
Sundays Hi ALMDB BS32...........10 C3
Sunderland Pl CFTN/FAIL BS8.....4 B4
Sunderland St BATHSE BA2 ....3 H3
Sundridge Pk YATE/CS BS37 .....26 A2
Sunningdale CFTN/FAIL BS8......55 F3
　YATE/CS BS37...................26 A2
Sunningdale Cl NAIL BS48 ....67 H5
Sunningdale Dr
　OLD/WMLY/WICK BS30 ....59 H5
Sunningdale Rd
　MTN/WRL BS22.................117 G5
Sunnybank BATHSE BA2 ....109 E5
Sunny Bank KGWD/HNM BS15...58 B2
　MANG/FISH BS16 * 49 E2
Sunny Bank Wy
　OMX/HUT/LCK BS24 ....123 E2
Sunnydene
　BRSG/KWL/STAPK BS4.........74 C2
Sunnyhill Dr AVONM BS11 ....43 H1
Sunnymead KEYN BS31 ....98 A1
Sunnymede Rd NAIL BS48 ....67 E4
Sunnyside FRCTL/WBN BS36.....23 H3
　HNLZ/SM/SNYPK/WT BS9 .....44 C3
Sunnyside Crs CLVDN BS21........64 D2
Sunnyside La MANG/FISH BS16...34 B3
　YATE/CS BS37...................13 H5
Sunnyside Rd CLVDN BS21.........64 D2
　WSM BS23 ....7 F7
Sunnyside Rd North WSM BS23 ...7 F7
Sunnyvale Dr
　OLD/WMLY/WICK BS30 ....77 G3
Sunny Wk KGWD/HNM BS15 .....58 B2
Sunridge MANG/FISH BS16 ....48 D2
Sunrise Gv
　BRSG/KWL/STAPK BS4.........74 C2
Surrey Rd HORF/LLZ BS7...........46 A5
Surrey St CBRISNE BS2...............5 H1
Suspension Br CFTN/FAIL BS8 ....54 C4
Sussex Pl BATHSE BA2 * 3 H7
Sussex St CBRISNE BS2.............56 C5
Sutherland Av
　MANG/FISH BS16 ....49 E1
　YATE/CS BS37...................13 H5

Sutherland Dr
　OMX/HUT/LCK BS24 ....126 A4
Sutherland Pl CFTN/FAIL BS8 ....55 E1
Sutton Av
　BRSG/KWL/STAPK BS4.........74 C2
Sutton Cl MTN/WRL BS22 ....122 B3
Sutton St BATHSE BA2 ....3 J5
Swainswick HGRV/WHIT BS14....85 G3
Swainswick Gdns
　CBATH/BATHN BA1 ....103 F2
Swainswick La
　CBATH/BATHN BA1 ....103 G1
Swaish Dr
　OLD/WMLY/WICK BS30 ....76 C2
Swallow Dr BRSTK/PCHW BS34 ..20 A2
Swallow Gdns MTN/WRL BS22..122 A3
Swallow Pk THNB/SVB BS35 ......8 D1
Swallows Ct
　BRSTK/PCHW BS34 ....33 G1
The Swallows
　MTN/WRL BS22.................122 A4
Swallow St CBATH/BATHN BA1 ...3 G5
Swan Cl MTN/WRL BS22 ....122 A3
Swane Rd HGRV/WHIT BS14.....87 E3
Swan Fld YATE/CS BS37............14 B5
Swanmoor La FRCTL/WBN BS36.22 C2
Swanmore Crs
　HNBRY/STHM BS10 ....31 E1
Sweetgrass Rd
　OMX/HUT/LCK BS24 ....122 C4
Sweets Rd KGWD/HNM BS15.....59 E1
Swift Cl MTN/WRL BS22 ....122 A3
Swiss Rd BMSTR BS3................72 A4
　WSM BS23 ....7 J3
Sycamore Cl EVILLE/WHL BS5 ....57 G2
　KGWD/HNM BS15 ....75 G3
　NAIL BS48........................67 F4
　OMX/HUT/LCK BS24 ....126 B1
　WSM BS23 ....7 J3
Sycamore Dr
　BRSTK/PCHW BS34 ....20 A3
　THNB/SVB BS35 ....8 D3
Sydenham Blds BATHSE BA2 * 3 J5
Sydenham Hl
　RDLND/MONT BS6..............55 H2
Sydenham La
　RDLND/MONT BS6..............55 H2
Sydenham Rd BATHSE BA2 ....2 D5
　BRSG/KWL/STAPK BS4.........73 H3
　RDLND/MONT BS6..............55 H2
Sydenham Wy
　KGWD/HNM BS15 ....75 H3
Sydney Blds BATHSE BA2 ....3 J3
Sydney Pl BATHSE BA2 ....3 J3
Sydney Rd BATHSE BA2 ....3 J3
Sydney Rw CBRIS/FH BS1 ....4 A7
Sydney Whf BATHSE BA2 ....3 K4
Sylvan Wy
　HNLZ/SM/SNYPK/WT BS9 .....43 H2
Sylvia Av BMSTR BS3................73 G3
Symes Pk CBATH/BATHN BA1 ...101 F2
Symington Rd
　MANG/FISH BS16 ....48 B3
Syston Wy KGWD/HNM BS15.....58 D2

T

Tabernacle Rd
　KGWD/HNM BS15 ....58 C5
Tackley Rd EVILLE/WHL BS5 ......46 D5
Tadwick La CBATH/BATHN BA1...90 A4
Tailors Ct CBRIS/FH BS1 ....5 F5
Talbot Av KGWD/HNM BS15......58 B2
Talbot Rd
　BRSG/KWL/STAPK BS4.........74 A4
Talgarth Rd HORF/LLZ BS7........46 B4
Tallis Gv BRSG/KWL/STAPK BS4..85 E3
Tamar Cl THNB/SVB BS35 ....9 E5
Tamar Dr KEYN BS31................88 D5
Tamar Rd CBRISNE BS2.............57 E5
　MTN/WRL BS22.................122 C1
Tamworth Rd KEYN BS31..........88 B5
Tankard's Cl CFTN/FAIL BS8 ....4 D2
Tanner Cl
　OLD/WMLY/WICK BS30 ....76 C1
Tanners St THNB/SVB BS35 ....8 C4
Tanners Wk BATHSE BA2 ....107 E2
Tanorth Cl HGRV/WHIT BS14 .....96 C1
Tanorth Rd HGRV/WHIT BS14....96 C1
Tansy La PTSHD/EG BS20..........40 B3
The Tanyard
　OLD/WMLY/WICK BS30 * 77 E4
Tapsters
　OLD/WMLY/WICK BS30 * 76 D2
Tara Ct FRCTL/WBN BS36..........23 F1
Tarnock Av HGRV/WHIT BS14....85 H2
Tarragon Pl ALMDB BS32 ....21 H3
Taunton Rd MTN/WRL BS22 ....118 A4
Taunton Wk HORF/LLZ BS7........46 C4
Taveners Wk NAIL BS48 * 67 G3
Taverna Cl WSM BS23 ....125 E2
Taverner Cl
　BRSG/KWL/STAPK BS4.........85 E2
Tavistock Rd
　BRSG/KWL/STAPK BS4.........73 G5
　RDLND/MONT BS6..............55 G1
Tavistock Wk
　BRSG/KWL/STAPK BS4.........73 G5
Tawny Wy MTN/WRL BS22 ......122 A4
Taylor Cl KGWD/HNM BS15.......59 F3
Taylor Ct MTN/WRL BS22 ....122 C1
Taylor Gdns
　BMSTRD/HC/WWD BS13......84 A5
Tayman Cl HNBRY/STHM BS10...44 A2
Tayman Rdg
　OLD/WMLY/WICK BS30 ....89 G1
Taynton Cl
　OLD/WMLY/WICK BS30 ....77 E4
Teal Cl ALMDB BS32.................21 H3
　MTN/WRL BS22.................122 C2
Teasel Md ALMDB BS32 ....21 G3
Teasel Wk MTN/WRL BS22 ......122 A4
Teddington Cl BATHSE BA2 ......107 H3
Teesdale Cl MTN/WRL BS22 ....122 A3

Teewell Av MANG/FISH BS16 .....49 E4
Teewell Cl MANG/FISH BS16......49 E4
Teewell Hl MANG/FISH BS16......49 E4
Teignmouth Rd
　BRSG/KWL/STAPK BS4.........73 G5
　CLVDN BS21......................65 E2
Telephone Av CBRIS/FH BS1 ....4 E4
Telford Wk EVILLE/WHL BS5 ......58 A2
Templar Rd YATE/CS BS37.........14 A4
Temple Back CBRIS/FH BS1 ....5 H5
Temple Back East CBRIS/FH BS1 ..5 J5
Temple Ga CBRIS/FH BS1 ....5 H6
Templeland Rd
　BMSTRD/HC/WWD BS13......84 A4
Temple Rose St CBRIS/FH BS1 .....5 H5
Temple St BMSTR BS3 ....72 C4
　CBRIS/FH BS1 ....5 H5
　KEYN BS31 ....88 B4
Temple Wy CBRIS/FH BS1 ....5 H5
Temple Way U/P CBRISNE BS2....5 J3
Tenby Rd KEYN BS31 ....88 A5
Tenby St EVILLE/WHL BS5 ....56 D4
Tennessee Gv
　RDLND/MONT BS6..............45 G3
Tenniscourt Rd
　KGWD/HNM BS15 ....59 G2
Tennis Rd
　BRSG/KWL/STAPK BS4.........73 G4
Tennyson Av KEYN BS31 ....88 B5
Tennyson Rd CBATH/BATHN BA1..3 H1
　HORF/LLZ BS7...................46 A5
　WSM BS23 ....125 E3
Tenth Av HORF/LLZ BS7............32 D4
Tereslake Gn
　HNBRY/STHM BS10 ....31 H1
Terrace Wk CBATH/BATHN BA1 * .3 G5
Terrell Gdns EVILLE/WHL BS5.....57 F4
Terrell St CBRISNE BS2...............4 E2
Tetbury Cl BRSTK/PCHW BS34....21 E2
Tetbury Gdns NAIL BS48 ....67 H5
Tetbury Rd KGWD/HNM BS15....58 B3
Teviot Rd KEYN BS31................88 D5
Tewkesbury Rd CBRISNE BS2......56 C1
Tewther Rd
　BMSTRD/HC/WWD BS13......95 H1
Teyfant Rd
　BMSTRD/HC/WWD BS13......96 B1
Teyfant Wk
　BMSTRD/HC/WWD BS13......85 H5
Thackeray HORF/LLZ BS7 ....32 C5
Thackeray Av CLVDN BS21.........64 D1
Thackeray Rd CLVDN BS21 ....64 D1
Thanet Rd BMSTR BS3..............72 C4
Thatcher Cl PTSHD/EG BS20......39 H4
Thatchers Cl EVILLE/WHL BS5.....58 B5
There-And-Back-Again La
　CFTN/FAIL BS8 * 4 C3
Theresa Av HORF/LLZ BS7 ....46 A4
Theynes Cft LGASH BS41 ....71 E5
Thicket Av MANG/FISH BS16......48 C4
Thicket Rd MANG/FISH BS16......48 C4
Thicket Wk THNB/SVB BS35........8 C5
Thiery Rd
　BRSG/KWL/STAPK BS4.........74 B4
Thingwall Pk MANG/FISH BS16...47 G5
Third Av BATHSE BA2 ....2 C5
　HORF/LLZ BS7...................32 C4
Third Wy AVONM BS11..............28 C3
Thirlmere Ct
　OLD/WMLY/WICK BS30 ....60 B5
Thirlmere Rd
　BRSTK/PCHW BS34 ....20 C2
　WSM BS23 ....125 F2
Thistle St BMSTR BS3................72 C3
Thomas Av MANG/FISH BS16.....35 H5
Thomas Cl CBRIS/FH BS1............5 G4
Thomas Pring Wk
　EVILLE/WHL BS5.................58 A2
Thomas St CBATH/BATHN BA1 ..102 D4
Thomas St North
　RDLND/MONT BS6..............55 H2
Thomas Wy MANG/FISH BS16....47 G1
Thomson Rd
　HGRV/WHIT BS14 ....86 D3
Thomson Rd EVILLE/WHL BS5....56 D5
Thornbank Pl BATHSE BA2 ....2 D6
Thornbury Dr WSM BS23 ....124 B4
Thornbury Rd WSM BS23 ....124 B4
Thorn Cl MTN/WRL BS22 ....123 E1
　YATE/CS BS37...................25 H1
Thorndale CFTN/FAIL BS8 ....55 E2
Thorndale Ms CFTN/FAIL BS8.....55 E3
Thornmayes Cr
　FRCTL/WBN BS36...............23 G2
The Thornhills
　MANG/FISH BS16 ....48 B2
Thornleigh Rd HORF/LLZ BS7.....46 A3
Thornmead Gv
　HNBRY/STHM BS10 ....31 E3
Thorns Farm YATE/CS BS37 * 26 A1
Thorncroft Cl HORF/LLZ BS7......46 D1
Three Oaks Cl MANG/FISH BS16.48 C4
Three Peaks Wk LGASH BS41.....95 H5
Three Queens La CBRIS/FH BS1 ...5 G5
Three Wells Rd
　BMSTRD/HC/WWD BS13......84 A5
Thrissell St EVILLE/WHL BS5 ......56 C3
Throgmorton Rd
　BRSG/KWL/STAPK BS4.........85 G2
Thrush Cl MTN/WRL BS22 ....122 B3
Thurlestone HGRV/WHIT BS14....85 G2
Thurlow Rd EVILLE/WHL BS5......57 E1
Thurstons Barton
　EVILLE/WHL BS5.................57 F1
Thyme Cl PTSHD/EG BS20.........40 B3
Tibberton KGWD/HNM BS15......59 G2
Tibbott Rd HGRV/WHIT BS14.....86 B4
Tibbott Wk HGRV/WHIT BS14....86 B4
Tichborne Rd EVILLE/WHL BS5....56 D5
　WSM BS23 ....125 E4
Tickenham Hl CLVDN BS21 ....67 E2
Tickenham Rd CLVDN BS21........65 H1
Tide Gv AVONM BS11 ....29 H4
Tidenham Wy
　BRSTK/PCHW BS34 ....20 B1
Tilley Cl KEYN BS31.................98 B2
Tilling Rd HNBRY/STHM BS10.....46 A1

Tilling Wk HNBRY/STHM BS10....46 A1
Tilting Rd THNB/SVB BS35...........8 C1
Timber Dene MANG/FISH BS16 ...47 F4
Timbercombe Wk
　HGRV/WHIT BS14 ....86 A4
Timsbury Rd BMSTR BS3 ....73 F4
Tindell Ct
　OLD/WMLY/WICK BS30 ....76 C2
Tintern Av EVILLE/WHL BS5 ....57 F3
Tintern Cl
　OLD/WMLY/WICK BS30 ....59 F5
Tippetts Rd KGWD/HNM BS15....58 D5
Tirley Wy MTN/WRL BS22 ....121 G1
Titan Barrow
　CBATH/BATHN BA1 ....104 D2
Tiverton Gdns
　MTN/WRL BS22.................122 D1
Tiverton Rd CLVDN BS21 ....65 E4
Tiverton Wk MANG/FISH BS16....58 A1
Tivoli La WSM BS23 ....6 E2
Tockington La ALMDB BS32.......10 C1
Toll Bridge Rd
　CBATH/BATHN BA1 ....103 H1
Tone Rd CLVDN BS21 ....64 D4
Tor Cl MTN/WRL BS22.............122 D1
Tormarton Crs
　HNBRY/STHM BS10 ....30 D1
Tormynton Rd
　MTN/WRL BS22.................122 B1
Toronto Rd HORF/LLZ BS7 ....32 C5
Torpoint Rd BMSTR BS3............73 E4
Torrance Cl
　OLD/WMLY/WICK BS30 ....60 B5
Torridge Rd KEYN BS31............88 D5
Torrington Av
　BRSG/KWL/STAPK BS4.........85 G1
Torrington Crs
　MTN/WRL BS22.................117 H5
Tortworth Rd HORF/LLZ BS7......46 A3
Totnes Cl MTN/WRL BS22........122 D1
Totshill Dr
　BMSTRD/HC/WWD BS13......85 F5
Totshill Gv
　BMSTRD/HC/WWD BS13......85 F5
Tottenham Pl CFTN/FAIL BS8 ......4 A3
Totterdown La
　OMX/HUT/LCK BS24 ....125 E5
Totterdown Rd WSM BS23.........7 H5
Touchstone Av
　BRSTK/PCHW BS34 ....21 E1
Tovey Cl MTN/WRL BS22 ....117 F4
Tower Hi CBRISNE BS2...............5 H4
Tower House La NAIL BS48 ....67 G2
Tower La CBRIS/FH BS1..............5 F5
　OLD/WMLY/WICK BS30 ....59 G5
Towerleaze
　HNLZ/SM/SNYPK/WT BS9 .....44 B5
Tower Rd KGWD/HNM BS15......58 C2
Tower Rd North
　OLD/WMLY/WICK BS30 ....59 H5
Tower Rd South
　OLD/WMLY/WICK BS30 ....59 H5
Tower St CBRIS/FH BS1 ....5 H5
Tower Wk WSM BS23..............120 C2
Townsend ALMDB BS32 ....10 B5
Townsend Cl HGRV/WHIT BS14..87 E4
Townsend Rd
　HGRV/WHIT BS14 ....87 E4
Townshend Rd
　MTN/WRL BS22.................117 H3
Tozers Hl
　BRSG/KWL/STAPK BS4.........74 B4
Tracy Cl HGRV/WHIT BS14 ....85 G2
Trafalgar Cl
　CBATH/BATHN BA1 ....101 G3
Trafalgar Ter BMSTR BS3...........72 B5
Tramway Rd
　BRSG/KWL/STAPK BS4.........73 E5
Tranmere Av
　HNBRY/STHM BS10 ....31 E1
Tranmere Gv
　HNBRY/STHM BS10 ....31 E2
Tratman Wk
　HNBRY/STHM BS10 ....30 D2
Travers Cl
　BRSG/KWL/STAPK BS4.........85 E3
Travers Wk BRSTK/PCHW BS34..21 G5
Trawden Cl WSM BS23 ....121 F2
Tredegar Rd MANG/FISH BS16...48 B5
Treefield Pl CBRISNE BS2...........56 C1
Treefield Rd CLVDN BS21 ....64 D3
Tree Leaze YATE/CS BS37..........14 B5
Tregarth Rd BMSTR BS3............72 A5
Trelawn Cl MTN/WRL BS22 ......123 G1
Trelawney Av EVILLE/WHL BS5 ...57 F2
Trelawney Pk
　BRSG/KWL/STAPK BS4.........74 C3
Trelawney Rd
　RDLND/MONT BS6..............55 G2
Trellisick Gdns
　OMX/HUT/LCK BS24 ....122 C3
Trellick Wk MANG/FISH BS16.....33 G5
Tremlett Ms MTN/WRL BS22....118 A4
Trenchard Rd KEYN BS31 ....99 E2
　OMX/HUT/LCK BS24 ....127 G2
Trenchard St CBRIS/FH BS1 ....4 D4
Trench La ALMDB BS32 ....11 F4
　FRCTL/WBN BS36...............11 H5
Trendlewood Pk
　MANG/FISH BS16 ....47 G4
Trendlewood Wy NAIL BS48.......67 H5
Trenleigh Dr MTN/WRL BS22 ....122 C1
Trent Dr THNB/SVB BS35 ....9 E5
Trent Gv KEYN BS31................88 D5
Trentham Cl CBRISNE BS2..........56 C1
Trescothick Cl KEYN BS31..........88 A3
Trescothick Dr
　OLD/WMLY/WICK BS30 ....77 G3
Tresham Cl ALMDB BS32...........11 F5
Trevanna Rd BMSTR BS3 ....72 A5
Trevelyan Rd WSM BS23.............7 G5
Trevelyan Wk
　BRSTK/PCHW BS34 ....22 A5
　HNBRY/STHM BS10 ....30 D2
Treverdowe Wk
　HNBRY/STHM BS10 ....30 B2

Trevethin Cl
　KGWD/HNM BS15 ....58 C4
Trevisa Gv HNBRY/STHM BS10...31 C1
Trewartha Cl WSM BS23.............7 J2
Trewartha Pk WSM BS23 ....7 J2
Trewint Gdns
　BRSG/KWL/STAPK BS4.........85 G1
Triangle East BATHSE BA2...........2 A6
Triangle North BATHSE BA2 ....2 A6
Triangle South CFTN/FAIL BS8 .....4 B3
Triangle Vis BATHSE BA2.............2 A6
Triangle West BATHSE BA2..........2 A6
Trident Cl MANG/FISH BS16.......35 G4
Trim Br BATHSE BA1 * 3 F4
Trim St CBATH/BATHN BA1 ....3 F4
Trinder Rd PTSHD/EG BS20........42 D4
Trinity Cl CBATH/BATHN BA1 ....2 A6
Trinity Ct KGWD/HNM BS15.......59 E3
Trinity La YATE/CS BS37............15 H5
Trinity Ms CBRISNE BS2..............5 J3
Trinity Rd BATHSE BA2 ....109 E5
　CBRISNE BS2....................56 B4
　NAIL BS48........................67 E5
　WSM BS23 ....120 B2
Trinity St CBATH/BATHN BA1 ....3 F4
　CBRIS/FH BS1 * 4 C4
　CBRISNE BS2....................56 C4
Trinity Wk CBRISNE BS2............5 J3
Trin Mills CBRIS/FH BS1 ....5 F6
Tripps Cnr YTN/CONG BS49 .....112 D4
Tripps Rw LGASH BS41.............71 H5
Troon YATE/CS BS37.................26 A2
Troon Dr
　OLD/WMLY/WICK BS30 ....59 H5
Troopers' Hill Rd
　BRSG/KWL/STAPK BS4.........57 H5
Trossachs Dr BATHSE BA2 ....103 C4
Trowbridge Rd
　HNBRY/STHM BS10 ....31 G4
Trowbridge Wk
　HNBRY/STHM BS10 ....31 C4
Trubshaw Cl HORF/LLZ BS7.......46 B2
Trumpet La EVILLE/WHL BS5.....58 B4
Truro Rd BMSTR BS3................72 B3
　NAIL BS48........................79 H1
Trym Cross Rd
　HNLZ/SM/SNYPK/WT BS9 .....44 A3
Trym Leaze
　HNLZ/SM/SNYPK/WT BS9 .....44 A3
Trym Rd
　HNLZ/SM/SNYPK/WT BS9 .....45 E1
Trym Side
　HNLZ/SM/SNYPK/WT BS9 .....44 A3
Trymwood Cl
　HNBRY/STHM BS10 ....30 D3
Trymwood Pde
　HNLZ/SM/SNYPK/WT BS9 .....44 C1
Tucker St CBRISNE BS2.............5 H3
Tuckett La MANG/FISH BS16......48 C1
Tucking Mill Cots BATHSE BA2 ..111 H5
Tuckmill CLVDN BS21...............64 A4
Tudor Cl OLD/WMLY/WICK BS30..77 F3
Tudor Rd KGWD/HNM BS15......59 H1
　MTN/WRL BS22.................117 H4
　PTSHD/EG BS20.................39 H4
Tuffley Rd HNBRY/STHM BS10....31 G4
Tufton Av AVONM BS11.............29 G5
Tugela Rd
　BMSTRD/HC/WWD BS13......84 A2
Tunbridge Wy
　MANG/FISH BS16 ....35 G5
Tunstall Cl
　HNLZ/SM/SNYPK/WT BS9 .....44 C4
Turley Rd EVILLE/WHL BS5 ....57 F2
Turnberry
　OLD/WMLY/WICK BS30 ....59 H5
　YATE/CS BS37...................26 A2
Turnbridge Cl
　HNBRY/STHM BS10 ....31 G1
Turnbridge Rd
　HNBRY/STHM BS10 ....31 G1
Turnbury Av NAIL BS48............67 H5
Turnbury Cl MTN/WRL BS22.....117 G5
Turner Cl KEYN BS31...............99 F2
Turner Ct MTN/WRL BS22........117 G5
Turner Dr YATE/CS BS37...........25 H1
Turner Gdns HORF/LLZ BS7.......46 D2
Turners Ct
　OLD/WMLY/WICK BS30 ....76 C2
Turner Wk
　OLD/WMLY/WICK BS30 ....60 B4
Turner Wy CLVDN BS21............64 B4
Turnpike Cl YATE/CS BS37.........14 B5
Turtlegate Av
　BMSTRD/HC/WWD BS13......83 H5
Turtlegate Wk
　BMSTRD/HC/WWD BS13......83 H5
Tutton Wy CLVDN BS21.............65 F3
Tweed Cl THNB/SVB BS35...........9 E4
Tweed Rd CLVDN BS21 ....64 C4
Tweeny La
　OLD/WMLY/WICK BS30 ....60 B5
Twenty Acres Rd
　HNBRY/STHM BS10 ....31 E3
Twerton Farm Cl BATHSE BA2 ...107 G3
Twickenham Rd
　RDLND/MONT BS6..............45 G3
Two Acres Rd
　HGRV/WHIT BS14 ....85 H3
Two Mile Ct KGWD/HNM BS15 * .58 C3
Twomile Hill Rd
　KGWD/HNM BS15 ....58 B3
Two Rivers Wy
　BLAG/CWMG/WR BS40........115 G3
　KEYN BS31 ....98 A1
　YTN/CONG BS49................115 E2
The Twynings
　KGWD/HNM BS15 ....59 E1
Tybalt Wy BRSTK/PCHW BS34 ...21 G5
Tydeman Rd PTSHD/EG BS20.....40 B2
Tyler Cl KGWD/HNM BS15 ....59 H3
Tyler Gn MTN/WRL BS22 ....118 A4
Tyler's La MANG/FISH BS16 ......48 D3
Tyler's La MANG/FISH BS16 ......48 D3
Tylers Wy YATE/CS BS37............14 B1
Tyndale Av MANG/FISH BS16 ....48 C4
　YATE/CS BS37...................13 H4

Tyndale Rd KGWD/HNM BS15 ...... 59 E1
Tyndale Vw THNB/SVB BS35 ...... 8 C4
Tyndall Av CFTN/FAIL BS8 .... 4 C2
Tyndall Rd EVILLE/WHL BS5 ...... 56 D3
Tyndalls Park Ms CFTN/FAIL BS8 ... 4 C1
Tyndalls Park Rd CFTN/FAIL BS8 ... 4 B1
Tyndalls Wy
 HNBRY/STHM BS10 .... 32 A5
Tyne Gv PTSHD/EG BS20 .... 40 B2
Tyne Rd HORF/LLZ BS7 .... 45 H5
Tyne St CBRISNE BS2 .... 56 C1
Tyning Cl HGRV/WHIT BS14 .... 85 H2
 YATE/CS BS37 .... 14 A5
Tyning End BATHSE BA2 .... 3 K7
Tyning La CBATH/BATHN BA1 ..... 103 E3
Tyning Rd BATHSE BA2 .... 109 F5
 BATHSE BA2 .... 104 A3
 BMSTR BS3 .... 73 G3
 KEYN BS31 .... 99 F2
Tynings Ms WSM BS23 .... 124 D2
The Tynings CLVDN BS21 .... 64 A4
Tyning Ter CBATH/BATHN BA1 .... 102 D3
The Tyning BATHSE BA2 .... 3 K7
Tynte Av
 BMSTRD/HC/WWD BS13 .... 84 C5
Tyntesfield Rd
 BMSTRD/HC/WWD BS13 .... 84 B2
Tyrone Wk
 BRSG/KWL/STAPK BS4 .... 85 F1
Tyrrel Wy BRSTK/PCHW BS34 ..... 21 G4

U

Ullswater Cl
 OLD/WMLY/WICK BS30 .... 60 B5
 WSM BS23 .... 125 F2
 YATE/CS BS37 .... 14 A4
Ullswater Dr
 CBATH/BATHN BA1 .... 102 D2
Ullswater Rd
 HNBRY/STHM BS10 .... 31 F4
Uncombe Cl NAIL BS48 .... 80 C3
Underbanks PTSHD/EG BS20 .... 42 D4
Underhill Dr WSM BS23 .... 124 C4
Underwood Av
 MTN/WRL BS22 .... 121 G2
Underwood Rd
 PTSHD/EG BS20 .... 39 G5
Unicorn Business Pk
 BRSG/KWL/STAPK BS4 .... 74 C1
Union Gallery CBRIS/FH BS1 * 5 G2
Union Pas CBATH/BATHN BA1 ...... 3 G4
Union Pl WSM BS23 * 6 D4
Union Rd CBRISNE BS2 .... 5 K3
Union St CBATH/BATHN BA1 .... 3 F4
 CBRIS/FH BS1 .... 5 F4
 NAIL BS48 .... 66 D5
 WSM BS23 .... 6 D5
Unity Rd KEYN BS31 .... 88 D4
Unity St CBRIS/FH BS1 .... 5 E3
 CBRISNE BS2 .... 5 J3
 KGWD/HNM BS15 .... 58 C3
University Cl
 HNLZ/SM/SNYPK/WT BS9 .... 44 D4
University Hall
 HNLZ/SM/SNYPK/WT BS9 .... 44 D4
University Rd CFTN/FAIL BS8 .... 4 E3
University Wk CFTN/FAIL BS8 ...... 4 E3
Uphill Dr CBATH/BATHN BA1 ...... 103 G2
Uphill Rd North WSM BS23 .... 124 C3
Uphill Rd South WSM BS23 .... 124 C4
Uphill Wy WSM BS23 .... 124 C5
Upjohn Crs
 BMSTRD/HC/WWD BS13 .... 96 A1
Uplands Dr KEYN BS31 .... 99 G2
Uplands Rd KEYN BS31 .... 99 F2
 MANG/FISH BS16 .... 48 C5
The Uplands NAIL BS48 .... 78 D2
Upper Bath Rd THNB/SVB BS35 .... 8 C4
Upper Belgrave Rd
 CFTN/FAIL BS8 .... 55 E1
Upper Belmont Rd
 HORF/LLZ BS7 .... 46 A5
Upper Bloomfield Rd
 BATHSE BA2 .... 110 B1
Upper Borough Walls
 CBATH/BATHN BA1 .... 3 F4
Upper Bristol Rd WSM BS23 .... 7 K1
Upper Byron Pl CFTN/FAIL BS8 .... 4 B3
Upper Camden Pl
 CBATH/BATHN BA1 * 102 D2
Upper Chapel La
 FRCTL/WBN BS36 .... 24 A3
Upper Cheltenham Pl
 RDLND/MONT BS6 .... 56 A2
Upper Church La CBRISNE BS2 .... 4 D3
Upper Church Rd WSM BS23 .... 6 C1
Upper Church St
 CBATH/BATHN BA1 .... 2 E2
Upper Conham V
 CBATH/BATHN BA1 * 75 F1
Upper Cranbrook Rd
 RDLND/MONT BS6 .... 45 H4
Upper East Hayes
 CBATH/BATHN BA1 .... 103 E3
Upper Hedgemead Rd
 CBATH/BATHN BA1 .... 3 F1
Upper Lambridge St
 CBATH/BATHN BA1 .... 103 E2
Upper Lansdown Ms
 CBATH/BATHN BA1 .... 102 C3
Upper Maudlin St CBRIS/FH BS1 .. 4 E2
Upper Oldfield Pk BATHSE BA2 .... 2 B6
Upper Perry Hi BMSTR BS3 .... 72 D3
Upper Sandhurst Rd
 BRSG/KWL/STAPK BS4 .... 74 C2
Upper Station Rd
 MANG/FISH BS16 .... 48 C4
Upper Stone Cl
 FRCTL/WBN BS36 .... 24 A1
Upper St BRSG/KWL/STAPK BS4 ... 73 H2
Upper Sydney St BMSTR BS3 .... 72 C3
Upper Town La
 BLAG/CWMG/WR BS40 .... 92 D4
Upper Wells St CBRIS/FH BS1 * 4 D4

Upton La LGASH BS41 .... 95 E3
Upton Rd BMSTR BS3 .... 72 C2
Urchinwood La
 YTN/CONG BS49 .... 115 F2
Urfords Dr MANG/FISH BS16 .... 48 C2

V

Vaida Rd MTN/WRL BS22 .... 121 H1
Vale Crs MTN/WRL BS22 .... 123 F1
Vale End NAIL BS48 .... 67 E5
Vale La BMSTR BS3 .... 84 D1
Vale Mill Wy
 OMX/HUT/LCK BS24 .... 122 C3
Valentine Cl HGRV/WHIT BS14 .... 86 A4
Valerian Cl AVONM BS11 .... 43 F2
Vale St BRSG/KWL/STAPK BS4 ..... 73 H3
The Vale MANG/FISH BS16 .... 50 D1
Valetta Ct WSM BS23 .... 125 E3
Vale View Pl
 CBATH/BATHN BA1 .... 103 E3
Vale View Ter
 CBATH/BATHN BA1 .... 104 A1
Valley Cl NAIL BS48 .... 67 F4
Valley Gdns MANG/FISH BS16 ..... 35 F5
 NAIL BS48 .... 67 F4
Valley View Cl
 CBATH/BATHN BA1 .... 103 E2
Valley View Rd
 CBATH/BATHN BA1 .... 103 F1
Valley Way Rd NAIL BS48 .... 67 F3
The Valls ALMDB BS32 .... 11 H1
Valma Rocks EVILLE/WHL BS5 ..... 57 H5
Vanbrugh La MANG/FISH BS16 .... 47 G1
Van Diemen's La
 CBATH/BATHN BA1 .... 102 B2
Vandyck Av KEYN BS31 .... 88 C3
Vane St BATHSE BA2 .... 3 J5
Varsity Wy
 OMX/HUT/LCK BS24 .... 123 E5
Vassall Ct MANG/FISH BS16 .... 48 B3
Vassall Rd MANG/FISH BS16 ...... 48 B3
Vaughan Cl HNBRY/STHM BS10 ... 30 D2
Vauxhall Ter BMSTR BS3 * 72 B2
Vayre Cl YATE/CS BS37 .... 27 E1
Vee La BLAG/CWMG/WR BS40 ..... 93 E4
Vellore La BATHSE BA2 .... 3 K3
Ventnor Rd BRSTK/PCHW BS34 .... 32 C2
 EVILLE/WHL BS5 .... 57 H2
Venus St YTN/CONG BS49 .... 115 E4
Vera Rd MANG/FISH BS16 .... 57 H1
Verbena Wy MTN/WRL BS22 ..... 122 D2
Vereland Rd
 OMX/HUT/LCK BS24 .... 126 B4
Verlands YTN/CONG BS49 .... 115 E1
Vernham Gv BATHSE BA2 .... 110 A1
Vernhampond Cl
 BATHSE BA2 .... 110 A1
Vernon Cl KEYN BS31 .... 99 E1
Vernon Pk BATHSE BA2 .... 107 H1
Vernon St
 BRSG/KWL/STAPK BS4 .... 73 G2
Vernon Ter BATHSE BA2 * 107 H1
Vernslade CBATH/BATHN BA1 .... 101 F2
Verrier Rd EVILLE/WHL BS5 .... 57 E4
Verwood Dr
 OLD/WMLY/WICK BS30 .... 77 F5
Vian End MTN/WRL BS22 .... 117 G4
Vicarage Ct MTN/WRL BS22 ..... 117 G5
Vicarage Ct KGWD/HNM BS15 .... 75 G1
Vicarage La NAIL BS48 .... 81 H3
Vicarage Rd BMSTR BS3 .... 72 C2
 BMSTRD/HC/WWD BS13 .... 84 A3
 CFTN/FAIL BS8 .... 55 E1
 EVILLE/WHL BS5 .... 57 E3
 FRCTL/WBN BS36 .... 24 A5
 KGWD/HNM BS15 .... 75 G1
Vicars Cl MANG/FISH BS16 .... 48 B4
Victoria Av EVILLE/WHL BS5 .... 57 E3
Victoria Bridge Rd BATHSE BA2 ... 2 C4
Victoria Blds BATHSE BA2 .... 2 B4
Victoria Cl BATHSE BA2 .... 107 H2
 PTSHD/EG BS20 .... 39 H3
 THNB/SVB BS35 .... 8 C1
Victoria Gdns
 CBATH/BATHN BA1 .... 104 A1
 RDLND/MONT BS6 .... 55 H2
Victoria Gv BMSTR BS3 .... 73 F2
Victoria Ms BMSTR BS3 * 72 C3
Victoria Pde EVILLE/WHL BS5 * 57 E3
Victoria Pk KGWD/HNM BS15 ..... 58 D3
 WSM BS23 .... 6 C1
Victoria Pl BMSTR BS3 * 103 F3
 CBATH/BATHN BA1 .... 103 F3
Victoria Qd WSM BS23 .... 6 E2
Victoria Rd AVONM BS11 .... 28 B5
 CBRISNE BS2 .... 73 H1
 CLVDN BS21 .... 64 C2
 KEYN BS31 .... 99 E1
 KGWD/HNM BS15 .... 58 D3
 OLD/WMLY/WICK BS30 .... 77 G1
Victoria Sq CFTN/FAIL BS8 .... 55 E4
 PTSHD/EG BS20 .... 39 H3
 WSM BS23 .... 6 C4
Victoria St CBRIS/FH BS1 .... 5 G3
 MANG/FISH BS16 .... 48 D4
Victoria Ter BATHSE BA2 .... 2 B5
 CBRISNE BS2 .... 74 A1
 CFTN/FAIL BS8 .... 54 B5
Victoria Wk RDLND/MONT BS6 .... 55 H2
Victor Rd BMSTR BS3 .... 72 D3
Victor St CBRISNE BS2 .... 73 G2
 CBRISNE BS2 .... 56 C5
Vigor Rd
 BMSTRD/HC/WWD BS13 .... 84 C4
Village Cl YATE/CS BS37 .... 13 E4
The Village MANG/FISH BS16 * 50 A1
Villiers Rd EVILLE/WHL BS5 .... 56 D4
The Villings BMSTR BS3 * 71 H5

Vilner La THNB/SVB BS35 .... 8 C5
Vimpany Cl HNBRY/STHM BS10 ... 30 D2
Vimpennys La THNB/SVB BS35 .... 18 B1
Vincent Cl AVONM BS11 .... 30 A3
Vincent Gdns MTN/WRL BS22 .... 122 D1
Vineyards CBATH/BATHN BA1 * 3 F2
Vining Wk EVILLE/WHL BS5 .... 56 D3
Vinny Av MANG/FISH BS16 .... 7 H5
Vintery Leys
 HNLZ/SM/SNYPK/WT BS9 .... 45 F1
Virginia Cl YATE/CS BS37 .... 26 C1
Vivian St BMSTR BS3 .... 73 E3
Vowell Cl
 BMSTRD/HC/WWD BS13 .... 84 C5
Vowles Cl NAIL BS48 .... 67 H3
Voyager Cl BRSTK/PCHW BS34 .... 34 A1
Vynes Cl NAIL BS48 .... 67 H5
Vynes Wy NAIL BS48 .... 68 A5
Vyvyan Rd CFTN/FAIL BS8 .... 55 E4
Vyvyan Ter CFTN/FAIL BS8 .... 55 E4

W

Wade Rd YATE/CS BS37 .... 13 E4
Wades Rd BRSTK/PCHW BS34 ..... 32 D2
Wade St CBRISNE BS2 .... 5 J1
Wadham Dr MANG/FISH BS16 .... 34 B4
Wadham Gv MTN/WRL BS16 ...... 49 H3
Wadham St WSM BS23 .... 6 B3
Wagtail Gdns MTN/WRL BS22 ... 122 B3
Wainbrook Dr EVILLE/WHL BS5 ... 57 F1
Wains Cl CLVDN BS21 .... 64 C3
Wainwright Cl
 MTN/WRL BS22 .... 118 A4
Wakedean Gdns
 YTN/CONG BS49 .... 112 A2
Wakeford Rd MANG/FISH BS16 ... 35 G5
Wakeford Wy
 OLD/WMLY/WICK BS30 .... 60 B4
Walcot Blds
 CBATH/BATHN BA1 * 102 D4
Walcot Ga CBATH/BATHN BA1 ..... 3 G1
Walcot Pde
 CBATH/BATHN BA1 * 102 D4
Walcot St CBATH/BATHN BA1 ..... 3 G3
Walcot Ter
 CBATH/BATHN BA1 * 3 G3
Waldegrave Rd
 CBATH/BATHN BA1 .... 102 B3
Walden Rd KEYN BS31 .... 88 D5
Walford Av MTN/WRL BS22 ...... 118 C5
Walker Cl EVILLE/WHL BS5 .... 57 E1
 MANG/FISH BS16 .... 49 G1
Walkers Dr
 OMX/HUT/LCK BS24 .... 122 C4
Walker St CBRISNE BS2 .... 4 D1
Walker Wy THNB/SVB BS35 .... 8 C5
Wallace Rd
 CBATH/BATHN BA1 .... 103 E3
Wallingford Rd
 BRSG/KWL/STAPK BS4 .... 85 E2
Walliscote Av
 HNLZ/SM/SNYPK/WT BS9 .... 45 G2
Walliscote Rd
 HNLZ/SM/SNYPK/WT BS9 .... 45 G2
 WSM BS23 .... 6 E4
Walliscote Rd South
 WSM BS23 .... 124 C2
Wallscourt Rd
 BRSTK/PCHW BS34 .... 32 D3
Wallscourt Rd South
 HORF/LLZ BS7 .... 32 D4
Walmesley Ter
 CBATH/BATHN BA1 * 102 D3
Walnut Av YATE/CS BS37 .... 14 D4
Walnut Cl FRCTL/WBN BS36 .... 24 A4
 KEYN BS31 .... 88 B5
 NAIL BS48 .... 79 F1
 OMX/HUT/LCK BS24 .... 122 D3
 THNB/SVB BS35 .... 8 E3
Walnut Crs
 BLAG/CWMG/WR BS40 .... 93 G4
Walnut Dr CLVDN BS21 .... 63 F3
Walnut Heath YATE/CS BS37 ...... 14 D4
Walnut Ri
 HNLZ/SM/SNYPK/WT BS9 .... 31 E5
Walnut Rd AVONM BS11 .... 42 D2
 CLVDN BS21 .... 63 F3
Walnut Tree Cl ALMDB BS32 ..... 10 C2
Walnut Wk
 BMSTRD/HC/WWD BS13 .... 84 B3
Walsh Av HGRV/WHIT BS14 .... 85 H2
Walsh Cl OMX/HUT/LCK BS24 ... 122 A4
Walshe Av YATE/CS BS37 .... 27 E1
Walsingham Rd
 RDLND/MONT BS6 .... 56 A1
Walter St BMSTR BS3 .... 72 B2
Waltham End
 OMX/HUT/LCK BS24 .... 122 D3
Walton Av
 BRSG/KWL/STAPK BS4 .... 74 C1
Walton Cl KEYN BS31 .... 88 A5
 OLD/WMLY/WICK BS30 .... 76 B5
Walton Crs
 BLAG/CWMG/WR BS40 .... 93 G4
Walton Dr CLVDN BS21 .... 63 F3
Walton Heath YATE/CS BS37 ...... 14 D4
Walton Ri
 HNLZ/SM/SNYPK/WT BS9 .... 31 E5
Walton Rd AVONM BS11 .... 42 D2
 CLVDN BS21 .... 63 F3
Walton St EVILLE/WHL BS5 .... 56 C2
Walwyn Cl BATHSE BA2 .... 107 F1
Wansbeck Rd KEYN BS31 .... 88 D5
Wansbrough Rd
 MTN/WRL BS22 .... 118 A4
Wanscow Wk
 HNLZ/SM/SNYPK/WT BS9 .... 45 F2
Wansdyke Rd BATHSE BA2 .... 110 A1
Wapping Rd CBRIS/FH BS1 .... 4 E6
Warden Rd BMSTR BS3 .... 72 D2
Wardour Rd
 BRSG/KWL/STAPK BS4 .... 85 E1
Wareham Cl NAIL BS48 .... 67 E5
Warleigh Dr
 CBATH/BATHN BA1 .... 104 B1
Warleigh La
 CBATH/BATHN BA1 .... 104 C4
Warleys La
 OMX/HUT/LCK BS24 .... 123 F2
Warman Cl HGRV/WHIT BS14 ..... 87 E3

Warman Rd HGRV/WHIT BS14 .... 87 E3
Warmington Rd
 HGRV/WHIT BS14 .... 86 A5
Warminster Rd BATHSE BA2 ..... 103 F4
 CBRISNE BS2 .... 56 C1
Warne Ct KGWD/HNM BS15 .... 59 F5
 YTN/CONG BS49 .... 113 G4
Warne Rd
 OLD/WMLY/WICK BS30 .... 76 D2
Warren Cl ALMDB BS32 .... 11 F4
 OMX/HUT/LCK BS24 .... 126 A4
Warren Gdns HGRV/WHIT BS14 ... 87 F4
Warren La LGASH BS41 .... 82 B1
Warren Rd BRSTK/PCHW BS34 .... 32 D2
Warren Wy YATE/CS BS37 .... 14 A4
Warrilow Cl MTN/WRL BS22 ..... 118 A5
Warrington Rd
 BRSG/KWL/STAPK BS4 .... 74 C4
Warry Cl NAIL BS48 .... 68 A4
Warwick Av EVILLE/WHL BS5 ..... 56 D2
Warwick Cl MTN/WRL BS22 ..... 121 H5
 OLD/WMLY/WICK BS30 .... 77 E4
Warwick Pl THNB/SVB BS35 .... 8 B3
Warwick Rd
 CBATH/BATHN BA1 .... 101 G5
 KEYN BS31 .... 88 A5
 RDLND/MONT BS6 .... 55 F2
Washingpool La AVONM BS11 ..... 17 E3
Washing Pound La
 HGRV/WHIT BS14 .... 66 C2
Washington Av
 EVILLE/WHL BS5 .... 57 E2
Washpool La BATHSE BA2 .... 107 E5
Watch Elm Cl ALMDB BS32 .... 21 G4
Watch House Pl
 PTSHD/EG BS20 .... 40 A2
Watchhouse Rd
 PTSHD/EG BS20 .... 38 B4
Watchill Av
 BMSTRD/HC/WWD BS13 .... 84 A3
Watchill Cl
 BMSTRD/HC/WWD BS13 .... 84 A3
Watcombe Cl MTN/WRL BS22 ... 122 B2
Waterbridge Rd
 BMSTRD/HC/WWD BS13 .... 83 H3
Watercress Cl NAIL BS48 .... 67 E4
Watercress Rd HORF/LLZ BS7 .... 46 B5
Waterdale Cl
 HNLZ/SM/SNYPK/WT BS9 .... 45 G1
Waterdale Gdns
 HNLZ/SM/SNYPK/WT BS9 .... 45 G1
Waterford Cl THNB/SVB BS35 ...... 8 C5
Waterford Rd
 HNLZ/SM/SNYPK/WT BS9 .... 45 F2
Water La BMSTR BS3 .... 73 G5
 CBRIS/FH BS1 .... 5 H4
 PTSHD/EG BS20 .... 42 C4
Waterloo Blds BATHSE BA2 ...... 107 H1
Waterloo Pl CBRISNE BS2 .... 5 K3
Waterloo Rd CBRISNE BS2 .... 5 K3
Waterloo St CFTN/FAIL BS8 .... 54 D4
 CFTN/FAIL BS8 .... 5 G4
 WSM BS23 .... 6 E3
Watermore Cl
 FRCTL/WBN BS36 .... 24 A3
Waterside Dr ALMDB BS32 .... 20 C1
Waterside Pk
 PTSHD/EG BS20 .... 38 B4
Water's La
 HNLZ/SM/SNYPK/WT BS9 .... 45 E1
Waters Rd KGWD/HNM BS15 ..... 58 C3
Waters La BATHSE BA2 .... 107 F1
 NAIL BS48 .... 79 F1
Wathen Rd RDLND/MONT BS6 .... 46 B5
Watkins V
 HNLZ/SM/SNYPK/WT BS9 .... 31 E5
Watleys End Rd
 FRCTL/WBN BS36 .... 24 A1
Watling Wy AVONM BS11 .... 42 D1
Watson Av
 BRSG/KWL/STAPK BS4 .... 74 C2
Watson's Rd
 OLD/WMLY/WICK BS30 .... 76 B5
Watters Cl FRCTL/WBN BS36 ...... 24 B4
Wavell Cl YATE/CS BS37 .... 13 H5
Waveney Rd KEYN BS31 .... 99 E1
Waverley Rd AVONM BS11 .... 43 E2
 NAIL BS48 .... 67 H4
 RDLND/MONT BS6 .... 55 G2
 WSM BS23 .... 124 C5
 YATE/CS BS37 .... 13 F5
Waverley St EVILLE/WHL BS5 ..... 56 C1
Wayfield Gdns
 CBATH/BATHN BA1 .... 91 E5
Wayford Cl KEYN BS31 .... 99 E1
Wayleaze FRCTL/WBN BS36 .... 24 D3
Wayside MTN/WRL BS22 .... 122 A1
Wayside Dr CLVDN BS21 .... 62 C5
Weal Ter CBATH/BATHN BA1 * ... 101 G2
The Weal CBATH/BATHN BA1 .... 101 G2
Weatherley Dr PTSHD/EG BS20 ... 38 D5
Weatherly Av BATHSE BA2 .... 110 C1
Webbs Heath
 OLD/WMLY/WICK BS30 .... 60 B4
Webb St EVILLE/WHL BS5 .... 56 B5
Webbs Wood Rd ALMDB BS32 .... 21 H5
Wedgewood Rd
 MANG/FISH BS16 .... 34 D4
Wedgwood Cl
 HGRV/WHIT BS14 .... 86 A4
Wedgwood Rd BATHSE BA2 ...... 107 E2
Wedlock Wy BMSTR BS3 * 72 A3
Wedmore Cl BATHSE BA2 .... 107 F1
 KGWD/HNM BS15 .... 59 F4
Wedmore Pk BATHSE BA2 .... 107 E4
Wedmore Rd CLVDN BS21 .... 64 C2
 KEYN BS31 .... 89 G5
 NAIL BS48 .... 79 F1
Wedmore V BMSTR BS3 .... 73 G2
Wedmore Vale BMSTR BS3 * 73 G2
Weetwood Rd
 YTN/CONG BS49 .... 115 E1
Weight Rd EVILLE/WHL BS5 .... 57 E4
The Weind MTN/WRL BS22 ...... 122 A1
Weir La CFTN/FAIL BS8 .... 70 B1

Weir Rd YTN/CONG BS49 .... 115 E3
Welland Rd KEYN BS31 .... 88 C5
Wellard Cl MTN/WRL BS22 * 118 A4
Well Cl LGASH BS41 .... 71 E5
Well Cl WSM BS24 .... 125 G4
Wellgarth Rd
 BRSG/KWL/STAPK BS4 .... 73 H4
Wellgarth Wk
 BRSG/KWL/STAPK BS4 .... 73 H5
Well House Cl
 HNLZ/SM/SNYPK/WT BS9 .... 54 C1
Wellington Av
 RDLND/MONT BS6 .... 56 A2
Wellington Blds
 CBATH/BATHN BA1 .... 101 G2
Wellington Crs HORF/LLZ BS7 .... 46 A2
Wellington Dr
 HNLZ/SM/SNYPK/WT BS9 .... 45 F2
 YATE/CS BS37 .... 13 F5
Wellington Hl HORF/LLZ BS7 ..... 46 A2
Wellington Hl West
 HNLZ/SM/SNYPK/WT BS9 .... 45 G1
Wellington La
 RDLND/MONT BS6 .... 56 A2
Wellington Ms AVONM BS11 ...... 42 D3
Wellington Pk CFTN/FAIL BS8 * ... 55 E4
Wellington Rd CBRISNE BS2 .... 5 J2
 KGWD/HNM BS15 .... 58 D1
 YATE/CS BS37 .... 13 F5
Wellington Ter CFTN/FAIL BS8 .... 54 D5
 CLVDN BS21 .... 62 A5
Wellington Wk
 HNBRY/STHM BS10 .... 45 G1
Well La BNWL BS29 .... 127 H3
Well Pk YTN/CONG BS49 .... 115 E2
Wells Cl HGRV/WHIT BS14 .... 86 B4
 NAIL BS48 .... 68 A5
Wellsea Gv WSM BS23 .... 121 G4
Wells Rd BATHSE BA2 .... 2 E7
 BRSG/KWL/STAPK BS4 .... 73 G2
 HGRV/WHIT BS14 .... 86 A1
 LGASH BS41 .... 94 D3
Wells St BMSTR BS3 .... 72 B2
Wellstead Av YATE/CS BS37 ...... 25 H1
Wellsway BATHSE BA2 .... 110 B2
 KEYN BS31 .... 88 C5
Wellsway Pk BATHSE BA2 .... 110 B2
Wellsway Rd KEYN BS31 .... 98 A1
Welsford Av MANG/FISH BS16 .... 47 E4
Welsford Rd MANG/FISH BS16 ... 47 E4
Welsh Back CBRIS/FH BS1 .... 5 F6
Welton Wk KGWD/HNM BS15 ..... 58 C2
Wemberham Crs
 YTN/CONG BS49 .... 112 A2
Wemberham La
 YTN/CONG BS49 .... 112 A3
Wenmore Cl MANG/FISH BS16 ... 34 D4
Wentforth Dr
 KGWD/HNM BS15 .... 58 C1
Wentwood Dr
 OMX/HUT/LCK BS24 .... 125 F5
Wentworth
 OLD/WMLY/WICK BS30 .... 59 G5
 YATE/CS BS37 .... 13 H1
Wentworth Cl MTN/WRL BS22 ... 117 G5
Wentworth Rd HORF/LLZ BS7 .... 45 H5
Wescott Gv AVONM BS11 * 30 A3
Wesley Cl KGWD/HNM BS15 ...... 76 A1
Wesley Cl EVILLE/WHL BS5 .... 57 F2
 MANG/FISH BS16 .... 48 D5
Wesley Dr MTN/WRL BS22 ...... 117 H5
Wesley Hl KGWD/HNM BS15 ..... 58 D2
Wesley La
 OLD/WMLY/WICK BS30 .... 77 E1
Wesley Pl CFTN/FAIL BS8 .... 55 E1
Wesley Rd HORF/LLZ BS7 .... 46 A4
Wesley St BMSTR BS3 .... 72 D3
Wesley Wk
 OMX/HUT/LCK BS24 .... 122 B3
Wessex Av HORF/LLZ BS7 .... 46 B1
Wessex Ct HORF/LLZ BS7 * 46 B1
Wessex Rd
 OMX/HUT/LCK BS24 .... 125 G4
Westacre Cl
 HNBRY/STHM BS10 .... 31 E3
West Ar CBRIS/FH BS1 * 5 F4
West Av BATHSE BA2 .... 107 H2
Westaway Cl YTN/CONG BS49 ... 112 C4
Westaway Pk
 YTN/CONG BS49 .... 112 D4
Westbourne Av CLVDN BS21 ...... 64 B3
 KEYN BS31 .... 88 B4
Westbourne Cl
 MANG/FISH BS16 .... 49 F1
Westbourne Crs CLVDN BS21 ..... 64 B3
Westbourne Pl CFTN/FAIL BS8 .... 4 A1
Westbrook Pk
 CBATH/BATHN BA1 .... 101 F2
Westbrook Rd
 BRSG/KWL/STAPK BS4 .... 86 C1
 MTN/WRL BS22 .... 122 A2
Westbury Court Rd
 RDLND/MONT BS6 .... 44 D1
Westbury Crs WSM BS23 .... 125 E4
Westbury Hl
 HNLZ/SM/SNYPK/WT BS9 .... 45 E1
Westbury La
 HNLZ/SM/SNYPK/WT BS9 .... 43 H1
Westbury Ms
 HNLZ/SM/SNYPK/WT BS9 .... 45 E1
Westbury Pk
 RDLND/MONT BS6 .... 45 E1
Westbury Rd
 RDLND/MONT BS6 .... 55 E1
West Cl BATHSE BA2 .... 107 F2
West Coombe
 HNLZ/SM/SNYPK/WT BS9 .... 44 B2
Westcourt Dr
 OLD/WMLY/WICK BS30 .... 77 G2
West Cft CLVDN BS21 .... 64 B3
 HNLZ/SM/SNYPK/WT BS9 .... 45 G1

West Dene
HNLZ/SM/SNYPK/WT BS9 44 C2
West Dundry La LGASH BS41 94 D2
West End BMSTR BS3 72 D2
CBRISNE BS2 4 E1
West End La NAIL BS48 78 A2
Westering Cl MANG/FISH BS16 49 G3
Westerleigh Cl
MANG/FISH BS16 49 F1
Westerleigh Rd BATHSE BA2 111 F1
CLVDN BS21 64 B3
MANG/FISH BS16 51 F2
MANG/FISH BS16 49 E2
MANG/FISH BS16 37 G5
YATE/CS BS37 37 E2
Western Av FRCTL/WBN BS36 23 G2
Western Ct BRSTK/PCHW BS34 34 A1
Western Dr
BRSG/KWL/STAPK BS4 85 F2
Western Rd HORF/LLZ BS7 46 A2
Westfield CLVDN BS21 64 D5
Westfield Cl BATHSE BA2 108 B4
KEYN BS31 87 H4
KGWD/HNM BS15 76 A1
NAIL BS48 79 H3
WSM BS23 124 C4
Westfield Dr NAIL BS48 79 H3
Westfield La
BRSTK/PCHW BS34 33 G2
Westfield Pk
CBATH/BATHN BA1 101 F5
RDLND/MONT BS6 55 F2
Westfield Pl CFTN/FAIL BS8 54 D4
Westfield Rd
HNLZ/SM/SNYPK/WT BS9 31 E5
NAIL BS48 79 H3
Westfield Wy ALMDB BS32 11 F5
Westgate CBRIS/FH BS1 * 4 B6
Westgate Blds
CBATH/BATHN BA1 3 F4
Westgate St CBATH/BATHN BA1 3 F4
West Gv RDLND/MONT BS6 56 B2
Westhall Rd CBATH/BATHN BA1 2 A2
West Hl PTSHD/EG BS20 39 G3
West Hill Ct PTSHD/EG BS20 39 G2
West Hill Gdns PTSHD/EG BS20 39 G3
Westland Av
OLD/WMLY/WICK BS30 77 F2
West La BLAG/CWMG/WR BS40 92 C4
West Lea Rd
CBATH/BATHN BA1 101 F4
West Leaze Pl ALMDB BS32 21 G4
Westleigh Cl
HNBRY/STHM BS10 31 H4
YATE/CS BS37 25 G1
Westleigh Pk HGRV/WHIT BS14 85 H5
Westleigh Rd
HNBRY/STHM BS10 31 G4
West Links Cl MTN/WRL BS22 116 C5
West Ml CFTN/FAIL BS8 54 D4
Westmarch Wy
MTN/WRL BS22 117 H4
Westmead Gdns
CBATH/BATHN BA1 101 F2
Westmead Rd EVILLE/WHL BS5 58 B4
Westminster Cl
HNLZ/SM/SNYPK/WT BS9 * 45 E1
Westminster Rd
EVILLE/WHL BS5 57 F3
Westmoreland Dr BATHSE BA2 2 D5
Westmoreland Rd BATHSE BA2 2 D6
RDLND/MONT BS6 45 E5
Westmoreland Station Rd
BATHSE BA2 2 C6
Westmoreland St BATHSE BA2 2 D6
Weston Av EVILLE/WHL BS5 57 F4
Weston Cl
HNLZ/SM/SNYPK/WT BS9 44 A1
Weston Crs HORF/LLZ BS7 46 A2
Weston Farm La
CBATH/BATHN BA1 101 G2
Weston La CBATH/BATHN BA1 101 H3
Weston Ldg WSM BS23 * 6 D2
Weston Pk CBATH/BATHN BA1 101 H3
Weston Pk East
CBATH/BATHN BA1 102 A4
Weston Pk West
CBATH/BATHN BA1 101 H3
Weston Rd CBATH/BATHN BA1 2 A1
CFTN/FAIL BS8 69 H3
LGASH BS41 70 C5
NAIL BS48 82 A1
YTN/CONG BS49 114 A1
Westons Brake
MANG/FISH BS16 35 G4
Westons Hill Dr
MANG/FISH BS16 35 G5
Westons Wy
KGWD/HNM BS15 59 F4
Weston Wy
OMX/HUT/LCK BS24 126 B4
Weston Wood Rd
PTSHD/EG BS20 39 G5
Westover Cl
HNLZ/SM/SNYPK/WT BS9 30 D4
Westover Dr
HNLZ/SM/SNYPK/WT BS9 31 E5
Westover Gdns
HNLZ/SM/SNYPK/WT BS9 30 D5
Westover Ri
HNLZ/SM/SNYPK/WT BS9 31 E4
Westover Rd
HNLZ/SM/SNYPK/WT BS9 31 E5
West Pde
HNLZ/SM/SNYPK/WT BS9 44 A1
West Pk CFTN/FAIL BS8 55 F3
West Park Rd MANG/FISH BS16 49 E3
West Priory Cl
HNLZ/SM/SNYPK/WT BS9 45 E1
West Rdg FRCTL/WBN BS36 23 H3
West Rd YTN/CONG BS49 112 B4
West Rocke Av
HNLZ/SM/SNYPK/WT BS9 44 B1
West Shrubbery
RDLND/MONT BS6 55 F1
West St BMSTR BS3 72 C4
CBRISNE BS2 5 K3
KGWD/HNM BS15 58 D3
OLD/WMLY/WICK BS30 77 F2
WSM BS23 6 D3
West Town Dr
BRSG/KWL/STAPK BS4 86 C1
West Town Gv
BRSG/KWL/STAPK BS4 86 C1
West Town La
BRSG/KWL/STAPK BS4 74 C5
HGRV/WHIT BS14 86 A1
West Town Pk
BRSG/KWL/STAPK BS4 74 C5
West Town Rd AVONM BS11 42 C1
NAIL BS48 79 H4
West View Rd BMSTR BS3 72 C3
CBATH/BATHN BA1 104 B1
KEYN BS31 88 B4
Westward Dr PTSHD/EG BS20 42 C4
Westward Gdns LGASH BS41 71 E4
Westward Rd
BMSTRD/HC/WWD BS13 84 A2
West Wy CLVDN BS21 64 C2
HNBRY/STHM BS10 32 A1
Westway NAIL BS48 67 E4
West Wick
OMX/HUT/LCK BS24 123 F3
Westwood Cl MTN/WRL BS22 122 C1
Westwood Crs
BRSG/KWL/STAPK BS4 74 C1
Westwood Rd
BRSG/KWL/STAPK BS4 86 C1
Westwoods
CBATH/BATHN BA1 104 C1
Wetherby Ct MANG/FISH BS16 35 F4
Wetherell Pl CFTN/FAIL BS8 4 A3
Wetlands La PTSHD/EG BS20 39 G5
Wexford Rd
BRSG/KWL/STAPK BS4 85 E1
Weymouth Rd BMSTR BS3 73 E4
Weymouth St
CBATH/BATHN BA1 103 E4
Wharfedale THNB/SVB BS35 9 E4
Wharf La PTSHD/EG BS20 40 D3
Wharf Rd MANG/FISH BS16 47 H4
Wharnecliffe Cl
HGRV/WHIT BS14 86 A4
Wharnecliffe Gdns
HGRV/WHIT BS14 86 A4
Whatley Rd CFTN/FAIL BS8 55 E2
Wheatfield Dr ALMDB BS32 21 F1
MTN/WRL BS22 117 H3
Wheathill Cl KEYN BS31 87 H4
Wheelers Patch
MANG/FISH BS16 49 H3
Whinchat Gdns
MANG/FISH BS16 47 H2
Whippington Ct
CBRIS/FH BS1 * 5 G2
Whistle Rd KGWD/HNM BS15 59 H1
Whitby Rd
BRSG/KWL/STAPK BS4 74 B1
Whitchurch La
BMSTRD/HC/WWD BS13 84 B4
LGASH BS41 95 G3
Whitecross Av
HGRV/WHIT BS14 86 B3
Whitecross Rd WSM BS23 124 D1
Whitefield Av EVILLE/WHL BS5 58 A2
KGWD/HNM BS15 76 A1
Whitefield Cl
CBATH/BATHN BA1 91 G5
Whitefield Rd EVILLE/WHL BS5 58 A1
Whitefields YATE/CS BS37 27 E1
Whitehall Av EVILLE/WHL BS5 57 G2
Whitehall Gdns
EVILLE/WHL BS5 57 F2
Whitehall Rd EVILLE/WHL BS5 57 E3
Whitehouse La BMSTR BS3 73 E2
Whitehouse Pl BMSTR BS3 73 F2
White House Rd
YTN/CONG BS49 113 F3
Whitehouse St BMSTR BS3 73 F2
Whiteladies Ga
CFTN/FAIL BS8 * 55 F2
Whiteladies Rd CFTN/FAIL BS8 4 B1
Whiteleaze HNBRY/STHM BS10 31 G5
White Lodge Pk
PTSHD/EG BS20 39 H2
White Lodge Rd
MANG/FISH BS16 49 F4
Whiteoak Wy NAIL BS48 79 E1
Whitesfield Rd NAIL BS48 67 E5
Whites Hl EVILLE/WHL BS5 58 A5
Whiteshill MANG/FISH BS16 34 D2
White St EVILLE/WHL BS5 5 K1
Whitethorn V
HNBRY/STHM BS10 31 G2
White Tree Rd
HNLZ/SM/SNYPK/WT BS9 45 F4
Whitewall La THNB/SVB BS35 9 G2
Whiteway Cl
BRSG/KWL/STAPK BS4 57 G5
EVILLE/WHL BS5 58 A3
Whiteway Ct EVILLE/WHL BS5 58 A3
Whiteway Ms EVILLE/WHL BS5 58 A3
Whiteway Rd BATHSE BA2 107 E2
EVILLE/WHL BS5 58 A2
Whitewells Rd
CBATH/BATHN BA1 102 D2
Whitewood Rd
EVILLE/WHL BS5 57 H2
Whitfield Cl MANG/FISH BS16 48 D5
Whitfield Rd THNB/SVB BS35 8 D2
Whiting Rd
BMSTRD/HC/WWD BS13 84 B5
Whitland Av
BMSTRD/HC/WWD BS13 84 C4
Whitland Rd
BMSTRD/HC/WWD BS13 84 C4
Whitley Cl YATE/CS BS37 13 G4
Whitley Md BRSTK/PCHW BS34 33 G2
Whitmead Gdns
BMSTRD/HC/WWD BS13 84 D5
Whitmore Av
BRSG/KWL/STAPK BS4 75 F3
Whitson St CBRIS/FH BS1 5 F1
Whitting Rd WSM BS23 124 D2
Whittington Dr
MTN/WRL BS22 122 A1
Whittington Rd
MANG/FISH BS16 48 C2
Whittock Rd HGRV/WHIT BS14 86 C4
Whittock Sq HGRV/WHIT BS14 86 C2
Whittucks Cl KGWD/HNM BS15 76 A2
Whittucks Rd
KGWD/HNM BS15 75 H2
Whitwell Rd HGRV/WHIT BS14 86 A1
Whytes Cl
HNLZ/SM/SNYPK/WT BS9 31 E5
Wick Crs BRSG/KWL/STAPK BS4 74 C3
The Wickets HORF/LLZ BS7 32 B4
KGWD/HNM BS15 58 D1
Wickfield CLVDN BS21 64 C4
Wickham Cl YATE/CS BS37 27 F2
Wickham Ct MANG/FISH BS16 47 F3
Wickham Gln MANG/FISH BS16 47 F3
Wickham Hl MANG/FISH BS16 47 F3
Wickham Vw MANG/FISH BS16 47 F4
Wick House Cl KEYN BS31 99 E1
Wicklow Rd
BRSG/KWL/STAPK BS4 85 F1
Wick Rd BRSG/KWL/STAPK BS4 74 C2
MTN/WRL BS22 117 H1
OMX/HUT/LCK BS24 119 E3
Wicks Rd MTN/WRL BS22 118 A1
Wickwar Rd YATE/CS BS37 14 C4
Wick Wick Cl FRCTL/WBN BS36 35 G4
Widcombe HGRV/WHIT BS14 85 H4
Widcombe Cl EVILLE/WHL BS5 58 A4
Widcombe Crs BATHSE BA2 3 J7
Widcombe Hl BATHSE BA2 3 J7
Widcombe Pde BATHSE BA2 * 3 H7
Widcombe Ri BATHSE BA2 3 J7
Widcombe Ter BATHSE BA2 3 K7
Widmore Gv
BMSTRD/HC/WWD BS13 * 84 C4
Wight Rw PTSHD/EG BS20 40 B2
Wigmore Gdns
MTN/WRL BS22 121 H1
Wigton Crs HNBRY/STHM BS10 31 G3
Wilbye Gv
BRSG/KWL/STAPK BS4 85 E2
Wilcox Cl KGWD/HNM BS15 58 C4
Wildcountry La NAIL BS48 82 B4
Wildcroft Rd
HNLZ/SM/SNYPK/WT BS9 45 F3
Willada Cl BMSTR BS3 72 C4
William Mason Cl
EVILLE/WHL BS5 56 D4
Williams Cl
OLD/WMLY/WICK BS30 76 C4
Williamson Rd HORF/LLZ BS7 46 B5
William St BATHSE BA2 3 H3
BMSTR BS3 73 F2
CBRISNE BS2 56 B2
MANG/FISH BS16 48 B5
Willianstowe BATHSE BA2 111 G1
Willinton Rd
BRSG/KWL/STAPK BS4 85 G2
Willis Rd KGWD/HNM BS15 59 F1
Williton Crs WSM BS23 125 E4
Willment Wy AVONM BS11 28 D4
Willmott Cl HGRV/WHIT BS14 96 C1
Willoughby Cl
BMSTRD/HC/WWD BS13 84 B2
Willoughby Rd HORF/LLZ BS7 46 A3
Willow Bed Cl MANG/FISH BS16 48 B2
Willow Cl BATHSE BA2 110 B2
BRSTK/PCHW BS34 20 A3
CLVDN BS21 65 E2
LGASH BS41 70 C5
MTN/WRL BS22 123 G1
OLD/WMLY/WICK BS30 60 B5
PTSHD/EG BS20 39 G4
WSM BS23 124 D4
Willowdown MTN/WRL BS22 117 F4
Willow Dr OMX/HUT/LCK BS24 126 B4
The Willowfalls
CBATH/BATHN BA1 103 H1
Willow Gdns MTN/WRL BS22 123 G1
Willow Gn BATHSE BA2 108 B3
Willow Gv MANG/FISH BS16 58 C1
Willow Rd KGWD/HNM BS15 75 H2
The Willows ALMDB BS32 21 F2
NAIL BS48 67 G3
YATE/CS BS37 13 H5
Willow Wk HNBRY/STHM BS10 31 F2
KEYN BS31 88 A5
Willow Wy FRCTL/WBN BS36 24 A4
Willsbridge Hl
OLD/WMLY/WICK BS30 76 D4
Wills Dr EVILLE/WHL BS5 56 C3
Wills Wy
BMSTRD/HC/WWD BS13 85 E3
Willway St BMSTR BS3 73 F2
CBRISNE BS2 5 K3
Wilmot Ct
OLD/WMLY/WICK BS30 59 G5
Wilmots Wy PTSHD/EG BS20 42 D4
Wilshire Av KGWD/HNM BS15 76 A1
Wilson Pl CBRISNE BS2 56 B3
Wilson St CBRISNE BS2 5 H1
Wilton Cl HNBRY/STHM BS10 31 G5
Wilton Gdns WSM BS23 6 E6
Wiltshire Av YATE/CS BS37 14 C4
Wiltshire Pl MANG/FISH BS16 49 E5
Wiltshire Wy
CBATH/BATHN BA1 102 D2
Wimbledon Rd
RDLND/MONT BS6 45 G3
Wimborne Rd BMSTR BS3 72 D5
Winash Cl HGRV/WHIT BS14 86 C1
Wincanton Cl MANG/FISH BS16 35 F4
NAIL BS48 68 A5
Winchcombe Cl NAIL BS48 79 H1
Winchcombe Rd
FRCTL/WBN BS36 23 H2
Winchester Av
BRSG/KWL/STAPK BS4 74 C3
Winchester Rd BATHSE BA2 2 B6
BRSG/KWL/STAPK BS4 74 C3
Wincroft
OLD/WMLY/WICK BS30 77 F2
Windcliff Crs AVONM BS11 29 E5
Windermere
HNBRY/STHM BS10 * 31 H3
Windermere Av WSM BS23 125 E2
Windermere Rd
BRSTK/PCHW BS34 20 C2
Windermere Wy
OLD/WMLY/WICK BS30 60 B5
Windmill Cl BMSTR BS3 73 F2
Windmill Hl BMSTR BS3 73 E3
OMX/HUT/LCK BS24 126 D4
Windmill La
HNBRY/STHM BS10 30 B2
Windmill Rd CLVDN BS21 65 E5
Windrush Cl BATHSE BA2 107 E3
Windrush Ct THNB/SVB BS35 8 D4
Windrush Rd KEYN BS31 88 D5
Windscreens Av CBRISNE BS2 5 K3
Windsor Av EVILLE/WHL BS5 58 B5
KEYN BS31 88 B5
Windsor Bridge Rd
CBATH/BATHN BA1 2 A3
Windsor Cl BRSTK/PCHW BS34 33 G1
CLVDN BS21 64 C3
Windsor Ct MANG/FISH BS16 49 E1
Windsor Crs
HNBRY/STHM BS10 30 A1
Windsor Dr NAIL BS48 67 F4
YATE/CS BS37 13 H4
Windsor Gv EVILLE/WHL BS5 56 D3
Windsor Pl
CBATH/BATHN BA1 * 101 H5
CFTN/FAIL BS8 54 D5
MANG/FISH BS16 49 G3
Windsor Rd MTN/WRL BS22 121 H1
OLD/WMLY/WICK BS30 76 C4
RDLND/MONT BS6 56 A1
Windsor Ter BMSTR BS3 73 G2
CFTN/FAIL BS8 54 D5
Windsor Vls
CBATH/BATHN BA1 101 H5
Windwhistle Cir WSM BS23 125 E2
Windwhistle La WSM BS23 124 D3
Windwhistle Rd WSM BS23 124 C3
Wineberry Cl EVILLE/WHL BS5 57 F2
Wine St CBRIS/FH BS1 5 F3
Winfield Rd
OLD/WMLY/WICK BS30 60 A4
Winford Cl PTSHD/EG BS20 40 A4
Winford Gv
BMSTRD/HC/WWD BS13 84 B1
Winford La
BLAG/CWMG/WR BS40 94 A4
Wingard Cl WSM BS23 124 C4
Wingard Ct WSM BS23 124 D1
Wingfield Rd BMSTR BS3 73 F4
Winifred's La
CBATH/BATHN BA1 102 B3
Winkworth Pl CBRISNE BS2 56 B2
Winsbury Wy ALMDB BS32 21 E2
Winscombe Cl KEYN BS31 88 A3
Winscombe Rd WSM BS23 7 H5
Winsford St EVILLE/WHL BS5 * 56 C3
Winsham Cl HGRV/WHIT BS14 86 A4
Winsley Rd RDLND/MONT BS6 55 H2
Winterbourne Hl
FRCTL/WBN BS36 22 D5
Winterbourne Rd
BRSTK/PCHW BS34 21 H4
Winterstoke Cl BMSTR BS3 72 C4
Winterstoke Rd BMSTR BS3 72 A3
OMX/HUT/LCK BS24 125 G4
WSM BS23 7 J7
Winton St
BRSG/KWL/STAPK BS4 73 G2
Wistaria Av YATE/CS BS37 26 C1
Wisteria Av
OMX/HUT/LCK BS24 126 A4
Witchell Rd EVILLE/WHL BS5 57 E4
Witch Hazel Rd
BMSTRD/HC/WWD BS13 96 B1
Witcombe YATE/CS BS37 25 G3
Witcombe Cl KGWD/HNM BS15 59 E2
Witham Rd KEYN BS31 98 B1
Witherlies Rd
MANG/FISH BS16 47 H2
Withey Cl West H
NLZ/SM/SNYPK/WT BS9 44 C3
The Witheys HGRV/WHIT BS14 86 B5
Withington Cl
OLD/WMLY/WICK BS30 77 F4
Withleigh Rd
BRSG/KWL/STAPK BS4 74 A4
Withy Cl NAIL BS48 67 G3
Withy Cl East
HNLZ/SM/SNYPK/WT BS9 44 D3
Withymead YTN/CONG BS49 113 F2
Withypool Gdns
HGRV/WHIT BS14 86 A4
The Withys PTSHD/EG BS20 42 D4
Withywood Gdns
BMSTRD/HC/WWD BS13 * 84 A5
Withywood Rd
BMSTRD/HC/WWD BS13 84 A5
Witney Cl KEYN BS31 99 E1
Witney Md FRCTL/WBN BS36 23 H2
Woburn Cl
OLD/WMLY/WICK BS30 76 C1
Woburn Rd EVILLE/WHL BS5 46 D5
Wolferton Rd HORF/LLZ BS7 56 B1
Wolfridge Gdns
HNBRY/STHM BS10 31 E1
Wolseley Rd HORF/LLZ BS7 45 H5
Wolvers Hill Rd
OMX/HUT/LCK BS24 123 F3
Woodacre PTSHD/EG BS20 40 A1
Woodbine Rd EVILLE/WHL BS5 57 E3
Woodborough St
EVILLE/WHL BS5 56 D2
Woodbridge Rd
BRSG/KWL/STAPK BS4 73 H4
Woodchester
KGWD/HNM BS15 49 E5
YATE/CS BS37 26 A4
Woodchester Rd
HNBRY/STHM BS10 45 G1
Woodcliff Rd MTN/WRL BS22 121 H2
Woodcote KGWD/HNM BS15 58 D5
Woodcote Rd MANG/FISH BS16 58 B1
Woodcote Wk
MANG/FISH BS16 58 B1
Woodcroft Av EVILLE/WHL BS5 57 F3
Woodcroft Cl
BRSG/KWL/STAPK BS4 74 D2
Woodcroft Rd
BRSG/KWL/STAPK BS4 74 D2
Woodend KGWD/HNM BS15 58 D5
Woodend Rd FRCTL/WBN BS36 23 H3
Wood End Wk
HNLZ/SM/SNYPK/WT BS9 44 A2
Woodfield Rd
RDLND/MONT BS6 55 F2
Woodford Cl NAIL BS48 67 H5
Woodgrove Rd
HNBRY/STHM BS10 30 B3
Woodhall Cl MANG/FISH BS16 49 F2
Wood Hl YTN/CONG BS49 112 D5
Woodhill Av PTSHD/EG BS20 39 H2
Wood Hill Pk PTSHD/EG BS20 39 H1
Woodhill Rd PTSHD/EG BS20 39 H2
Woodhill Views NAIL BS48 67 G3
Woodhouse Gv HORF/LLZ BS7 46 A2
Woodhouse Rd BATHSE BA2 107 F1
Woodhurst Rd WSM BS23 7 J3
Woodington Ct
OLD/WMLY/WICK BS30 76 C2
Woodington Rd CLVDN BS21 64 C4
The Wood Kilns
YTN/CONG BS49 112 A2
Woodland Av
KGWD/HNM BS15 58 D1
Woodland Cl CFTN/FAIL BS8 69 G2
KGWD/HNM BS15 58 C1
Woodland Ct
MANG/FISH BS16 * 48 C2
Woodland Gld CLVDN BS21 62 C5
Woodland Gv BATHSE BA2 109 H2
HNLZ/SM/SNYPK/WT BS9 44 B2
Woodland Pl BATHSE BA2 109 G2
Woodland Rd CFTN/FAIL BS8 4 C2
NAIL BS48 67 F3
WSM BS23 124 C2
Woodlands ALMDB BS32 11 F4
CLVDN BS21 64 C1
MANG/FISH BS16 49 E2
Woodlands La ALMDB BS32 10 D5
Woodlands Pk
ALMDB BS32 10 D4
CBATH/BATHN BA1 103 F2
Woodlands Ri
MANG/FISH BS16 48 D2
Woodland Ter
KGWD/HNM BS15 58 D4
RDLND/MONT BS6 55 F1
Woodland Wy CFTN/FAIL BS8 69 G2
KGWD/HNM BS15 58 C1
Wood La WSM BS23 7 H1
Woodleaze
HNLZ/SM/SNYPK/WT BS9 43 H2
Woodleigh THNB/SVB BS35 8 D3
Woodleigh Gdns
HGRV/WHIT BS14 86 B3
Woodmancote YATE/CS BS37 25 H2
Woodmancote Rd
RDLND/MONT BS6 56 A2
Woodmans Cl YATE/CS BS37 26 D2
Woodmans Rd YATE/CS BS37 26 D2
Woodmans V YATE/CS BS37 27 E2
Woodmarsh Cl
HGRV/WHIT BS14 85 H5
Woodmead Gdns
BMSTRD/HC/WWD BS13 84 D5
Woodmill YTN/CONG BS49 112 A2
Woodpecker Crs
MANG/FISH BS16 51 G4
Woodpecker Dr
MTN/WRL BS22 122 B3
Wood Rd KGWD/HNM BS15 58 D3
Woodside
HNLZ/SM/SNYPK/WT BS9 * 44 B5
Woodside Av
OMX/HUT/LCK BS24 125 G4
Woodside Gdns
PTSHD/EG BS20 38 C3
Woodside Gv
HNBRY/STHM BS10 30 B2
Woodside Rd
BRSG/KWL/STAPK BS4 57 G5
CLVDN BS21 62 C5
FRCTL/WBN BS36 24 B3
KGWD/HNM BS15 58 C3
Woodspring Av
MTN/WRL BS22 116 B5
Woodspring Crs
MTN/WRL BS22 116 B5
Woodstock Av
RDLND/MONT BS6 55 G2
Woodstock Cl
KGWD/HNM BS15 59 F3
Woodstock Rd
KGWD/HNM BS15 59 F3
MTN/WRL BS22 121 G3
RDLND/MONT BS6 55 F1
Wood St BATHSE BA2 2 E6
CBATH/BATHN BA1 3 F4
EVILLE/WHL BS5 56 D1
Woodview CLVDN BS21 65 F2
Woodview Cl AVONM BS11 43 E1
Woodview Dr
YTN/CONG BS49 113 G3
Woodview Ter NAIL BS48 67 G4
WSM BS23 7 H6
Woodward Av YATE/CS BS37 25 F1
Woodward Dr
OLD/WMLY/WICK BS30 76 C2
Woodwell Rd AVONM BS11 43 E2
Woodyleaze Dr
KGWD/HNM BS15 58 C5
Wookey Cl NAIL BS48 79 G1
Woolcot St RDLND/MONT BS6 55 F1
Wooler Rd WSM BS23 7 F3
Woollard La HGRV/WHIT BS14 97 G2
Woolley Rd HGRV/WHIT BS14 86 D4
Woolvers Hill Rd BNWL BS29 127 H1
Woolvers Wy
OMX/HUT/LCK BS24 123 E5
Wootton Crs
BRSG/KWL/STAPK BS4 57 G5
Wootton Pk HGRV/WHIT BS14 74 A5
Wootton Rd
BRSG/KWL/STAPK BS4 57 G5
Worcester Blds
CBATH/BATHN BA1 103 E2
Worcester Cl MANG/FISH BS16 58 B1
Worcester Crs CFTN/FAIL BS8 54 D3
Worcester Gdns NAIL BS48 78 C1
Worcester Pk
CBATH/BATHN BA1 103 E3
Worcester Pl
CBATH/BATHN BA1 * 103 E2

Worcester Rd *CFTN/FAIL* BS8...... 55 E3
KGWD/HNM BS15............ 58 D2
Worcester Ter
CBATH/BATHN BA1.......... 103 E3
CFTN/FAIL BS8................. 55 E3
Worcester Vls
CBATH/BATHN BA1 *.......... 103 E2
Wordsworth Rd *CLVDN* BS21.... 64 C3
HORF/LLZ BS7..................... 46 C1
WSM BS23........................ 125 F3
Workshop Rd *AVONM* BS11...... 28 C1
World's End La *KEYN* BS31...... 89 F4
Worlebury Cl *MTN/WRL* BS22.. 116 C5
Worlebury Hill Rd
MTN/WRL BS22................. 121 F1
WSM BS23........................ 121 E1
Worlebury Park Rd
MTN/WRL BS22................. 116 B5
Worle Ct *MTN/WRL* BS22........ 117 C5
Worle Moor Rd
OMX/HUT/LCK BS24.......... 122 B4
Worrall Ms *CFTN/FAIL* BS8...... 55 E1
Worrall Rd *CFTN/FAIL* BS8....... 55 E1
Worre's La *MANG/FISH* BS16..... 34 D2
Worsley St *EVILLE/WHL* BS5..... 57 F4
Worthing Rd
BRSTK/PCHW BS34............. 20 E2
Worthy Cl *KGWD/HNM* BS15..... 59 E5
Worthy La *WSM* BS23.............. 6 D5
Worthy Pl *WSM* BS23................ 6 D3
Worthy Rd *AVONM* BS11........... 16 D3
The Worthys *ALMDB* BS32........ 22 A4
Wotton Rd *YATE/CS* BS37........ 12 C3
Wrangle Farm Gn *CLVDN* BS21.. 65 E3

The Wrangle
OMX/HUT/LCK BS24.......... 122 C4
Wraxall Gv
BMSTRD/HC/WWD BS13...... 84 A1
Wraxall Hi *NAIL* BS48............... 68 B1
Wraxall Rd *KGWD/HNM* BS15... 59 C5
Wrenbert Rd
MANG/FISH BS16................ 48 D3
Wren Cl *MANG/FISH* BS16........ 47 C1
MTN/WRL BS22.................. 122 A3
Wren Dr *MANG/FISH* BS16....... 47 H2
Wright Wy *MANG/FISH* BS16.... 33 C5
Wrington Cl
BRSTK/PCHW BS34............. 21 E3
Wrington Crs
BMSTRD/HC/WWD BS13...... 84 B2
Wrington La
YTN/CONG BS49................ 115 E1
Wrington Md
YTN/CONG BS49................ 115 E1
Wrington Rd *YTN/CONG* BS49.. 115 F2
Wroughton Dr
BMSTRD/HC/WWD BS13...... 85 E5
Wroughton Gdns
BMSTRD/HC/WWD BS13...... 85 E5
Wroxham Dr
BRSTK/PCHW BS34............. 21 E2
Wyatt Av
BMSTRD/HC/WWD BS13...... 84 A4
Wyatt Cl
BMSTRD/HC/WWD BS13...... 84 A4
Wyatt's Cl *NAIL* BS48.............. 67 E4
Wyatts Vw
BRSG/KWL/STAPK BS4........ 57 C4

Wychwood
KGWD/HNM BS15............... 58 D5
Wyck Beck Rd
HNBRY/STHM BS10............. 31 E1
Wycliffe Rd
HNLZ/SM/SNYPK/WT BS9..... 45 F1
Wycliffe Rw
WSM BS23 *......................... 73 C2
Wycombe Gv
BRSG/KWL/STAPK BS4........ 74 C4
Wye Ct *THNB/SVB* BS35............ 8 D4
Wye Croft Ct
HNBRY/STHM BS10............. 31 H2
Wyedale Av
HNLZ/SM/SNYPK/WT BS9..... 43 H1
Wykis Ct
KGWD/HNM BS15 *............... 76 B1
Wyllie Ct *MTN/WRL* BS22....... 117 H5
Wymbush Crs
BMSTRD/HC/WWD BS13...... 84 D4
Wymbush Gdns
BMSTRD/HC/WWD BS13...... 84 D4
Wyndham Crs
BRSG/KWL/STAPK BS4........ 75 E3
PTSHD/EG BS20................. 42 B3
Wyndham Wy
PTSHD/EG BS20................. 39 H2
The Wynstones
KGWD/HNM BS15............... 58 C4
Wynter Cl *MTN/WRL* BS22...... 117 H5
Wytherlies Dr
FRCLT/WBN BS16............... 47 H2
Wyvern Cl
WSM BS23.......................... 7 H5

Wyvern Ms *WSM* BS23 *............ 7 J5

Y

Yanleigh Cl
BMSTRD/HC/WWD BS13....... 83 F3
Yanleigh Est *LGASH* BS41 *...... 83 E1
Yanley La *LGASH* BS41............. 83 E1
Yarbury Wy
OMX/HUT/LCK BS24.......... 123 E2
The Yard *CBRISNE* BS2............ 46 C5
Yate Rd *YATE/CS* BS37............. 12 B5
Yeates Ct *CLVDN* BS21............ 65 E2
Yeo Cl *WSM* BS23................... 125 F1
Yeolands Dr *CLVDN* BS21......... 64 B4
Yeo La *LGASH* BS41................. 70 C5
Yeomans Cl
HNLZ/SM/SNYPK/WT BS9..... 44 B3
Yeomanside Cl
HGRV/WHIT BS14................ 86 B4
Yeomead *NAIL* BS48................ 67 C3
Yeomeads *LGASH* BS41............ 70 C5
Yeo Moor *CLVDN* BS21............ 65 E3
Yeo Valley Wy *NAIL* BS48........ 68 A4
Yeoward Rd *CLVDN* BS21......... 65 E4
Yeo Wy *CLVDN* BS21................ 64 B3
Yewcroft Cl *HGRV/WHIT* BS14... 85 H5
Yew Tree Cl *NAIL* BS48............. 66 D5
Yew Tree Dr *KGWD/HNM* BS15.. 49 F5
OMX/HUT/LCK BS24.......... 123 E3
Yew Tree Gdns *NAIL* BS48........ 66 D5

PTSHD/EG BS20 *.................. 42 C4
Yew Tree Pk *YTN/CONG* BS49.. 114 D3
Yomede Pk
CBATH/BATHN BA1............ 101 F5
York Av *HORF/LLZ* BS7............ 46 B4
York Cl *BRSTK/PCHW* BS34....... 33 F1
MANG/FISH BS16................ 35 F4
MTN/WRL BS22.................. 117 H4
YATE/CS BS37................... 14 A3
York Ct *CBRISNE* BS2 *............. 56 A3
York Gdns *CFTN/FAIL* BS8........ 55 B3
FRCTL/WBN BS36............... 23 F2
York Pl *CBATH/BATHN* BA1 *... 103 E4
CFTN/FAIL BS8..................... 4 A3
York Rd *BMSTR* BS3................ 73 H3
EVILLE/WHL BS5................. 57 F2
EVILLE/WHL BS5................. 48 E4
RDLND/MONT BS6............... 56 A2
York St *CBATH/BATHN* BA1........ 3 C5
CBRISNE BS2........................ 5 C1
CFTN/FAIL BS8..................... 55 E1
EVILLE/WHL BS5................. 57 E4
WSM BS23............................ 6 D4
Youngs Ct *MANG/FISH* BS16.... 35 H5
Youngwood La *NAIL* BS48........ 78 D3

Z

Zetland Rd *RDLND/MONT* BS6... 55 H1
Zig Zag *CLVDN* BS21................ 64 D1
Zinc Rd *AVONM* BS11............... 28 C2

Index – featured places

Abbey Wood Business Park
BRSTK/PCHW BS34............. 32 D3
Abbotswood Primary School
YATE/CS BS37..................... 25 H3
Acton Court
YATE/CS BS37..................... 12 B2
Air Balloon Hill J & I School
EVILLE/WHL BS5.................. 58 A4
Alien School House
BMSTR BS3......................... 76 D1
All Saints East Clevedon CE
Primary School
CLVDN BS21........................ 65 F1
All Saints Exhibition Centre
CFTN/FAIL BS1..................... 5 F3
Almondsbury Business Centre
ALMDB BS32........................ 11 F4
Almondsbury Cemetery
ALMDB BS32........................ 10 C1
Almondsbury CE Primary
School
ALMDB BS32........................ 10 C2
Almondsbury Town FC
ALMDB BS32........................ 10 C3
Amelia Nutt Clinic
BMSTRD/HC/WWD BS13...... 84 A5
Amf Bowling
WSM BS23............................ 6 D5
Anchor Business Centre
CFTN/FAIL BS8..................... 55 F2
Anchor Head Hotel
WSM BS23............................ 6 A1
Andalusia Academy Bristol
CBRISNE BS2...................... 56 B3
Aretians RFC
BRSTK/PCHW BS34............. 20 D5
Arnolfini
CBRIS/FH BS1....................... 4 E6
Arnos Manor Hotel
BRSG/KWL/STAPK BS4........ 74 B3
Arnos Vale Cemetery
BRSG/KWL/STAPK BS4........ 74 A3
The Arosfa Hotel
WSM BS23............................ 6 D2
Arts Centre Cinema
CBRISNE BS2...................... 55 H3
Ashbrook House School
WSM BS23............................ 6 D6
Ashcombe Primary School
WSM BS23............................ 7 K4
Ashley Down J & I School
HORF/LLZ BS7..................... 46 A3
Ashley Down Old Boys
RFC
HORF/LLZ BS7..................... 32 D5
Ashley Trading Estate
RDLND/MONT BS6............... 56 B1
Ashmead Industrial Estate
KEYN BS31......................... 89 E4
Ashton Court Estate
LGASH BS41....................... 71 F2
Ashton Gate Primary School
BMSTR BS3......................... 72 B2
Ashton Gate Trading Estate
BMSTR BS3......................... 71 H3
Ashton Park School
BMSTR BS3......................... 71 H3
Ashton Vale Primary School
BMSTR BS3......................... 72 A4
Atlantic Business Park
WSM BS23............................ 6 A1
Avonbank Industrial Centre
AVONM BS11....................... 42 B1
Avonbridge Trading Estate
AVONM BS11....................... 28 C5
Avondale Business Centre
MANG/FISH BS16................ 47 H5
Avon Friends of the Earth
Depot
CBRISNE BS2...................... 98 C3
Avon Gorge Industrial Estate
AVONM BS11....................... 42 C1
Avon Gorge Nature Reserve
CFTN/FAIL BS8................... 54 B4

Avonmouth CE Primary
School
AVONM BS11....................... 28 C5
Avonmouth Medical Centre
AVONM BS11....................... 28 C5
Avon Primary School
AVONM BS11....................... 28 D5
Avon Riverside Estate
AVONM BS11....................... 42 B1
Avonside Industrial Park
CBRISNE BS2...................... 57 E5
Avon Trading Estate
CBRISNE BS2...................... 73 H1
Avon Valley Country Park
KEYN BS31......................... 89 G3
Avon Valley Railway
OLD/WMLY/WICK BS30........ 89 F1
Avon View Cemetery
EVILLE/WHL BS5................. 57 G4
Aztec Hotel
ALMDB BS32........................ 10 D5
B6 Sixth Form Centre
KEYN BS31.......................... 88 A3
Backwell CE Junior School
NAIL BS48........................... 80 B4
Backwell Leisure Centre
NAIL BS48........................... 80 A3
Backwell Medical Centre
NAIL BS48........................... 80 A3
Backwell RFC
NAIL BS48........................... 79 H3
Backwell School
NAIL BS48........................... 80 A3
Badminton Road Trading
Estate
YATE/CS BS37..................... 25 F1
Badminton School
HNLZ/SM/SNYPK/WT BS9..... 45 E3
Badocks Wood Primary
School
HNBRY/STHM BS10............. 31 F5
Bailbrook House Hotel
CBATH/BATHN BA1............ 103 G2
Baileys Court Primary School
BRSTK/PCHW BS34............. 21 H4
Balaclava Industrial Estate
MANG/FISH BS16................ 47 H5
Bank Leaze Primary School
AVONM BS11....................... 29 H2
Bannerman Road
Primary School
EVILLE/WHL BS5................. 56 D2
Barley Close Primary School
MANG/FISH BS16................ 49 G2
Barnack Trading Centre
BMSTR BS3......................... 72 D5
Barrow Hospital
NAIL BS48........................... 82 D3
Barrs Court Primary School
OLD/WMLY/WICK BS30........ 76 C1
Barton Hill Infant School
CBRISNE BS2...................... 56 D5
Barton Hill Primary School
EVILLE/WHL BS5................. 56 D5
Barton Hill Trading Estate
EVILLE/WHL BS5................. 56 D5
Bath Abbey
CBATH/BATHN BA1.............. 3 G4
Bathampton Primary School
BATHSE BA2...................... 104 A2
Bath Boating Station
BATHSE BA2...................... 103 E4
Bath CC
BATHSE BA2........................ 3 J5
Bath City FC
BATHSE BA2...................... 107 G1
The Bath Clinic
BATHSE BA2...................... 109 H5
Bath College of Higher
Education
CBATH/BATHN BA1............ 102 B5
Batheaston CE Primary
School
CBATH/BATHN BA1............. 91 E5
Batheaston Medical Centre
CBATH/BATHN BA1............. 91 E5

Bathford Primary School
CBATH/BATHN BA1............ 104 D2
Bath Golf Club
BATHSE BA2...................... 109 G1
Bath Media College
CBATH/BATHN BA1.............. 3 F3
Bath Natural Health Clinic
CBATH/BATHN BA1.............. 2 D4
Bath Postal Museum
CBATH/BATHN BA1.............. 3 F3
The Bath Priory Hotel
CBATH/BATHN BA1............ 101 H4
Bath Rugby
(Recreation Ground)
BATHSE BA2........................ 3 H4
Bath Spa University
(Newton Park Campus)
BATHSE BA2...................... 106 A2
Bath Sports & Leisure Centre
BATHSE BA2........................ 3 H4
Bathwick Cemetery
BATHSE BA2...................... 109 F2
Bathwick St Mary
CE Primary School
BATHSE BA2...................... 103 F4
Baytree School
MTN/WRL BS22.................. 121 H5
Beachlands Hotel
WSM BS23......................... 124 C2
Beacon Rise Primary School
KGWD/HNM BS15............... 58 D5
Beazer Garden Maze
BATHSE BA2........................ 3 H4
Becket Primary School
MTN/WRL BS22.................. 122 D1
Becks Business Park
WSM BS23............................ 7 K5
Bedminster Down School
BMSTRD/HC/WWD BS13...... 84 A2
Beechen Cliff School
BATHSE BA2...................... 108 D3
Beeches Trading Estate
YATE/CS BS37..................... 13 E5
Beehive Trading Estate
EVILLE/WHL BS5................. 57 G4
Begbrook Primary School
MANG/FISH BS16................ 47 H2
Belgrave School
CFTN/FAIL BS8................... 54 D1
Berkeley Square Hotel
CFTN/FAIL BS8.................... 4 B3
Best Western Abbey Hotel
CBATH/BATHN BA1.............. 3 G5
Best Western
Victoria Square Hotel
CFTN/FAIL BS8................... 55 E4
Best Western Walton Park
Hotel
CLVDN BS21....................... 62 B4
Birdwell Primary School
LGASH BS41....................... 82 D1
Bishopston
Primary School
HORF/LLZ BS7..................... 45 H4
Bishopston House Clinic
HORF/LLZ BS7..................... 46 A4
Bishopsworth CE Junior School
BMSTRD/HC/WWD BS13...... 84 A3
Bishopsworth Swimming Pool
BMSTRD/HC/WWD BS13...... 84 A3
Bitton Station
OLD/WMLY/WICK BS30........ 77 E5
Blackberry Hill Hospital
MANG/FISH BS16................ 47 H3
Blackhorse Primary School
MANG/FISH BS16................ 35 G5
Blaise Hamlet (NT)
HNBRY/STHM BS10............. 30 B3
Blaise Primary School
HNBRY/STHM BS10............. 30 D3
Bonville Business Centre
BRSG/KWL/STAPK BS4........ 75 F4
Bonville Trading Estate
BRSG/KWL/STAPK BS4........ 75 F4
Book Museum
CBATH/BATHN BA1.............. 3 H6

Bournville Junior School &
Community Infant School
WSM BS23......................... 125 E1
Bowling Hill Business Park
YATE/CS BS37..................... 26 C1
The Bowl Inn Hotel
ALMDB BS32........................ 10 C2
Bowsland Green Primary
School
ALMDB BS32........................ 11 F5
Bradley Stoke Community
School *ALMDB* BS32........... 21 G2
Bradley Stoke Leisure Centre
ALMDB BS32........................ 21 G1
Brassmill Lane Trading Estate
CBATH/BATHN BA1............ 101 F5
Brentry Hospital
HNBRY/STHM BS10............. 31 F3
Brentry Primary School
HNBRY/STHM BS10............. 31 F2
Briarwood Special School
MANG/FISH BS16................ 48 B5
Bridge Farm Primary School
HGRV/WHIT BS14................ 85 H5
Bridge Road Business Park
WSM BS23............................ 7 H6
Brimsham Green School
YATE/CS BS37..................... 13 H3
Brislington
Enterprise College
BRSG/KWL/STAPK BS4........ 87 E1
Brislington Retail Park
BRSG/KWL/STAPK BS4........ 74 D5
Brislington Trading Estate
BRSG/KWL/STAPK BS4........ 74 D4
Bristol & Clifton Golf Club
CFTN/FAIL BS8................... 70 B1
Bristol Baptist College
CFTN/FAIL BS8................... 54 D3
Bristol Business Park
MANG/FISH BS16................ 33 G4
Bristol Cathedral
CBRIS/FH BS1....................... 4 D5
Bristol Cathedral School
CBRIS/FH BS1....................... 4 D5
Bristol City FC (Ashton Gate)
BMSTR BS3......................... 72 A3
Bristol
Civil Service Sports Club
HORF/LLZ BS7..................... 46 B2
Bristol County Sports Club
CBRIS/FH BS1....................... 4 D3
Bristol Dental Hospital
CBRIS/FH BS1....................... 4 F2
Bristol Eye Hospital
CBRIS/FH BS1....................... 5 F2
Bristol Gateway School
CBRISNE BS2...................... 56 C1
Bristol General Hospital
CBRIS/FH BS1....................... 5 F5
Bristol Golf Club
HNBRY/STHM BS10............. 19 F3
Bristol Grammar Lower School
CFTN/FAIL BS8..................... 4 B2
Bristol Grammar School
CFTN/FAIL BS8..................... 4 C2
Bristol Harlequins RFC
BRSG/KWL/STAPK BS4........ 75 F4
Bristol Homeopathic Hospital
CFTN/FAIL BS8................... 55 G3
Bristol Ice Rink
CBRIS/FH BS1....................... 4 D3
Bristol International Airport
NAIL BS48........................... 92 B5
Bristol Marriott Hotel
CBRIS/FH BS1....................... 5 H3
Bristol Marriott Royal Hotel
CBRIS/FH BS1....................... 4 D5
Bristol North Baths
HORF/LLZ BS7..................... 45 H5
Bristol & North Somerset
Sports Club
CBRISNE BS2...................... 70 A3
Bristol Old Vic (New Vic
Theatre & Theatre Royal)
CBRIS/FH BS1....................... 4 E4

Bristol Rovers FC & Bristol RFC
(Memorial Stadium)
HORF/LLZ BS7..................... 46 B2
Bristol Rovers FC
BRSG/KWL/STAPK BS4........ 75 E5
Bristol Royal Hospital for
Children
CBRISNE BS2........................ 4 D2
Bristol Royal Infirmary
CBRISNE BS2........................ 4 E1
Bristol's Blaise Castle House
Museum
HNBRY/STHM BS10............. 30 C5
Bristol's City Museum & Art
Gallery
CFTN/FAIL BS8..................... 4 C3
Bristol's Georgian House
CBRIS/FH BS1....................... 4 C4
Bristol South Swimming Pool
BMSTR BS3......................... 72 D2
Bristol's Red Lodge
CBRIS/FH BS1....................... 4 D3
Bristol Vale Trading Estate
BMSTR BS3......................... 72 C5
Bristol Zoo Gardens
CFTN/FAIL BS8................... 54 D2
British Empire &
Commonwealth Museum
CBRIS/FH BS1....................... 5 H6
Broadlands School
KEYN BS31......................... 88 A3
Broadmead Lane Industrial
Estate
KEYN BS31......................... 88 D2
Broadoak Maths & Computing
College
WSM BS23......................... 124 C3
Broadwalk Shopping Centre
BRSG/KWL/STAPK BS4........ 74 A4
Broadway Infant School
YATE/CS BS37..................... 14 C5
Brockenridge Infant School
FRCTL/WBN BS36............... 24 A3
Brock Street Clinic
CBATH/BATHN BA1.............. 2 E2
Brockway Medical Centre
NAIL BS48........................... 67 G4
Bromley Heath J & I School
MANG/FISH BS16................ 35 E5
Brooklea Clinic
BRSG/KWL/STAPK BS4........ 74 D1
Broomhill J & I School
BRSG/KWL/STAPK BS4........ 75 E3
Browns Folly Nature Reserve
CBATH/BATHN BA1............ 104 D3
Brunel's SS Great Britain
CBRIS/FH BS1....................... 4 B6
The Building of Bath Museum
CBATH/BATHN BA1.............. 3 F2
Burnbush Primary School
HGRV/WHIT BS14................ 86 C4
Burnett Business Park
KEYN BS31......................... 98 D3
Bush Industrial Estate
EVILLE/WHL BS5................. 57 F3
The Business Park
BMSTRD/HC/WWD BS13...... 96 B1
Butcombe Pre-Preparatory
School
CFTN/FAIL BS8................... 54 D3
BW Estates
OMX/HUT/LCK BS24.......... 125 F3
Cabot Circus
CBRIS/FH BS1....................... 5 H2
Cabot Primary School
CBRISNE BS2...................... 56 B3
Cabot Tower
CFTN/FAIL BS8..................... 4 B4
Cadbury Camp
PTSHD/EG BS20.................. 66 B1
Cadbury Heath Health Centre
OLD/WMLY/WICK BS30........ 76 D1
Cadbury Heath Primary School
OLD/WMLY/WICK BS30........ 59 H5
Cadbury House Hotel
YTN/CONG BS49................ 112 D4

Callicroft Primary School
BRSTK/PCHW BS34 .... 20 A2

Canford Cemetery
HNLZ/SM/SNYPK/WT BS9 .... 44 C1

Canford Crematorium
HNLZ/SM/SNYPK/WT BS9 .... 44 D1

Canons House
CBRIS/FH BS1 .... 4 D6

Canon's Marsh Amphitheatre
CBRIS/FH BS1 .... 4 D6

Carla Trading Estate
BMSTR BS3 .... 72 A3

Carlyle Business Centre
CBRISNE BS2 .... 56 C5

Carmel Christian Centre &
School
BRSG/KWL/STAPK BS4 ...... 74 D5

Carrick Business Park
BRSG/KWL/STAPK BS4 ...... 75 E5

Castle Batch Primary School
MTN/WRL BS22 .... 117 H3

Castlemead Shopping Centre
MTN/WRL BS22 .... 117 H3

Central Health Clinic
CBRISNE BS2 .... 5 H4

Central Trading Estate
BRSG/KWL/STAPK BS4 .... 74 A2

Chandag J & I School
KEYN BS31 .... 88 D5

Chandos Trading Estate
CBRISNE BS2 .... 73 H1

Charborough Road Primary
School
BRSTK/PCHW BS34 .... 32 B3

Charlotte Keel Health Clinic
EVILLE/WHL BS5 .... 56 C2

Chatterton House
CBRIS/FH BS1 .... 5 G6

Cheddar Grove Primary School
BMSTRD/HC/WWD BS13 ... 84 B1

Cherry Garden Primary School
OLD/WMLY/WICK BS30 ...... 77 E4

Chesterfield Hospital
CFTN/FAIL BS8 .... 55 E5

Chester Park J & I School
MANG/FISH BS16 .... 48 A5

Chipping Edge Estate
YATE/CS BS37 .... 26 D1

Chipping Sodbury Cemetery
YATE/CS BS37 .... 26 D2

Chipping Sodbury Golf Club
YATE/CS BS37 .... 15 E4

Chipping Sodbury School
YATE/CS BS37 .... 26 D2

Chittening Industrial Estate
AVONM BS11 .... 16 D3

Christchurch CE Junior School
MANG/FISH BS16 .... 48 D3

Christchurch CE Primary
School
KGWD/HNM BS15 .... 75 G2

Christ Church CE VC Infant
School
MANG/FISH BS16 .... 48 D3

Christ Church Primary School
WSM BS23 .... 7 F3

Christ the King RC Primary
School
THNB/SVB BS35 .... 8 D3

Church Farm Business Park
BATHSE BA2 .... 99 H5

Churchill Business Park
WSM BS23 .... 7 J5

Cinema de Lux
CBRIS/FH BS1 .... 5 H2

Cineworld
HGRV/WHIT BS14 .... 85 F3

The City Academy Bristol
EVILLE/WHL BS5 .... 57 E3

City Business Park
CBRIS/FH BS1 .... 5 F3

City of Bath College
CBATH/BATHN BA1 .... 3 F5

City of Bristol College
(Bedminster Centre)
BMSTR BS3 .... 73 E4

City of Bristol College
(Brunel Centre)
HORF/LLZ BS7 .... 46 B4

City of Bristol College
(College Green Centre)
CBRIS/FH BS1 .... 4 B5

City of Bristol College
(Downend Centre)
MANG/FISH BS16 .... 35 G5

City of Bristol College
(Folly Lane Centre)
CBRISNE BS2 .... 56 C5

City of Bristol College
(Hartcliffe Centre)
BMSTRD/HC/WWD BS13 ... 85 E5

City of Bristol College
(Kingswood Centre)
KGWD/HNM BS15 .... 59 E3

City of Bristol College
(Lawrence Weston Centre)
AVONM BS11 .... 29 H3

City of Bristol College
(Parkway Transport
Technology Centre)
BRSTK/PCHW BS34 .... 33 F2

City of Bristol College
(Soundwell Centre)
MANG/FISH BS16 .... 59 E1

City & Port of Bristol Social &
Sports Club
AVONM BS11 .... 43 E3

Civil Service Sports Club
BATHSE BA2 .... 109 H5

Claremont Special School
RDLND/MONT BS6 .... 45 G3

Claverham CC
YTN/CONG BS49 .... 112 D4

Clevedon Army Training Corps
Squadron
CLVDN BS21 .... 64 C1

Clevedon Cemetery
CLVDN BS21 .... 64 A3

Clevedon Community School
CLVDN BS21 .... 62 D5

Clevedon Court (NT)
CLVDN BS21 .... 65 G1

Clevedon Craft Centre
CLVDN BS21 .... 65 G3

Clevedon Fruit Market
CLVDN BS21 .... 64 D2

Clevedon Golf Club
CLVDN BS21 .... 62 D3

Clevedon Health Centre
CLVDN BS21 .... 65 E2

Clevedon Hospital
CLVDN BS21 .... 65 E2

Clevedon Pier
CLVDN BS21 .... 62 A5

Cleve House School
BRSG/KWL/STAPK BS4 ..... 74 A3

Clifton Cathedral Church
CFTN/FAIL BS8 .... 55 E3

Clifton Clinic
CFTN/FAIL BS8 .... 55 E4

Clifton College Preparatory
School
CFTN/FAIL BS8 .... 54 D2

Clifton College Sports Club
CFTN/FAIL BS8 .... 53 H4

Clifton Down Shopping Centre
CFTN/FAIL BS8 .... 55 E4

Clifton High School & Lower
School
CFTN/FAIL BS8 .... 54 D4

Clifton Hotel
CFTN/FAIL BS8 .... 4 A2

Clifton RFC
HNBRY/STHM BS10 .... 18 D5

Clifton Tutors
CFTN/FAIL BS8 .... 55 E3

Coates Industrial Estate
NAIL BS48 .... 67 G3

College House
MANG/FISH BS16 .... 48 A3

Colston Hall
CBRIS/FH BS1 .... 4 E3

Colstons Collegiate School
MANG/FISH BS16 .... 47 E4

Colstons Girls School
RDLND/MONT BS6 .... 56 A2

Colstons Primary School
RDLND/MONT BS6 .... 55 G2

Combe Down CE Primary
School
BATHSE BA2 .... 111 F1

Combe Down RFC
BATHSE BA2 .... 109 E5

Commodore Hotel
MTN/WRL BS22 .... 116 A5

The Compton Clinic
KGWD/HNM BS15 .... 45 E4

Coniston Primary School
BRSTK/PCHW BS34 .... 20 B1

Connaught Primary School
BRSG/KWL/STAPK BS4 ..... 85 F1

Congyre Medical Centre
BRSTK/PCHW BS34 .... 32 C2

Corbett House Clinic
EVILLE/WHL BS5 .... 56 D4

Corpus Christi RC Primary
School
WSM BS23 .... 6 D7

Cossham Memorial Hospital
KGWD/HNM BS15 .... 58 C1

Cotham Park RFC
CFTN/FAIL BS8 .... 53 G5

Cotham School
RDLND/MONT BS6 .... 55 H4

Country View Holiday Park
MTN/WRL BS22 .... 116 C2

Court De Wyck Primary School
YTN/CONG BS49 .... 113 F2

Courtney Primary School
KGWD/HNM BS15 .... 59 F4

Cranleigh Court Infant School
YATE/CS BS37 .... 13 H4

Create Centre
CBRIS/FH BS1 .... 72 A1

Cribbs Causeway Regional
Shopping Centre
BRSTK/PCHW BS34 .... 19 H4

Cribbs Causeway Retail Park
BRSTK/PCHW BS34 .... 19 G4

Cricket Pavilion
BATHSE BA2 .... 3 H4

Crockerne CE Primary School
PTSHD/EG BS20 .... 42 C5

Crofts End Industrial Estate
EVILLE/WHL BS5 .... 57 G2

The Cross Bath
CBATH/BATHN BA1 .... 3 F5

Crossways J & I School
THNB/SVB BS35 .... 9 E3

Crown Industrial Estate
OLD/WMLY/WICK BS30 .... 59 H5

Culverhay School
BATHSE BA2 .... 107 G5

Culverhay Sports Centre
BATHSE BA2 .... 107 G5

Culverhill School
YATE/CS BS37 .... 25 H3

Curzon Cinema
CLVDN BS21 .... 64 C2

Custom House
CBRIS/FH BS1 .... 5 F5

Daunceys Hotel
WSM BS23 .... 120 A2

Days Inn
PTSHD/EG BS20 .... 41 H4

Deers Wood Primary School
KGWD/HNM BS15 .... 59 G1

Devon Road Trading Estate
EVILLE/WHL BS5 .... 57 E2

Dixon Business Centre
BRSG/KWL/STAPK BS4 ..... 75 E4

Docks Industrial Estate
AVONM BS11 .... 17 E2

Dolphin Square Shopping
Centre
WSM BS23 .... 6 D5

Douglas Road Industrial Park
KGWD/HNM BS15 .... 58 D3

Downend CC
MANG/FISH BS16 .... 48 D2

Downend School
MANG/FISH BS16 .... 49 F1

Downs Fitness & Health Centre
RDLND/MONT BS6 .... 55 E1

Drove Road Hospital
WSM BS23 .... 125 E1

Duckmoor Road Industrial
Estate
BMSTR BS3 .... 72 B2

Dukes Hotel
BATHSE BA2 .... 3 H5

Dundry CE Primary School
LGASH BS41 .... 94 C2

Eagles Wood Business Park
ALMDB BS32 .... 11 E4

Eastgate Retail Park
EVILLE/WHL BS5 .... 56 D1

Easton Business Centre
EVILLE/WHL BS5 .... 56 D3

Easton CE Primary School
EVILLE/WHL BS5 .... 56 C3

Easton Leisure Centre
EVILLE/WHL BS5 .... 56 C3

Eastpark Trading Estate
EVILLE/WHL BS5 .... 57 F2

Eastville Health Centre
EVILLE/WHL BS5 .... 56 D1

Eldonwall Trading Estate
CBRISNE BS2 .... 74 B1

Elmfield Special School
HNBRY/STHM BS10 .... 31 F5

Elmlea Junior School
HNLZ/SM/SNYPK/WT BS9 .. 44 D3

Elm Park Primary School
FRCTL/WBN BS36 .... 23 E4

Entry Hill Golf Course
BATHSE BA2 .... 108 C5

Explore-At-Bristol
CBRIS/FH BS1 .... 4 D5

Express by Holiday Inn
BATHSE BA2 .... 2 C5
BRSTK/PCHW BS34 .... 33 E2
CBRIS/FH BS1 .... 5 H6

The Eye Clinic
CBRIS/FH BS1 .... 5 G2

Fairfield High School
RDLND/MONT BS6 .... 56 B1

Fairfield Park Health Centre
CBATH/BATHN BA1 .... 103 E3

Fairfield PNEU School
NAIL BS48 .... 80 B3

Fair Furlong Primary School
BMSTRD/HC/WWD BS13 ... 84 B5

Fairway Industrial Centre
BRSTK/PCHW BS34 .... 32 B2

Falconride Primary School
EVILLE/WHL BS5 .... 59 E2

Fashion Museum
CBATH/BATHN BA1 .... 3 F2

Fashion Research Centre
CBATH/BATHN BA1 .... 2 E3

Ferry Steps Industrial Estate
CBRISNE BS2 .... 73 H2

Filton Airfield
HNBRY/STHM BS10 .... 19 H5

Filton Avenue
J & I School
HORF/LLZ BS7 .... 46 C1

Filton Cemetery
MANG/FISH BS16 .... 33 G5

Filton Clinic
HORF/LLZ BS7 .... 32 C3

Filton College
BRSTK/PCHW BS34 .... 32 C1

Filton Golf Club
BRSTK/PCHW BS34 .... 32 A1

Filton High School
BRSTK/PCHW BS34 .... 33 F2

Filton Hill Primary School
BRSTK/PCHW BS34 .... 32 D1

Filton Recreation Centre
BRSTK/PCHW BS34 .... 32 D1

Filwood Swimming Baths
BRSG/KWL/STAPK BS4 ..... 85 F1

Fishponds Health Centre
MANG/FISH BS16 .... 48 B4

Fishponds Trading Estate
EVILLE/WHL BS5 .... 57 H1

Five C Business Centre
CBRISNE BS2 .... 64 B4

Flax Bourton CE Primary
School
NAIL BS48 .... 81 E1

Florence Brown Community
School
BRSG/KWL/STAPK BS4 ..... 85 E1

Folk House
CBRIS/FH BS1 .... 4 D3

Fonthill Primary School
HNBRY/STHM BS10 .... 32 A3

Foster Almshouses
CBRIS/FH BS1 .... 4 E3

Four Acres Primary School
BMSTRD/HC/WWD BS13 ... 83 H5

Frampton Cotterell
CE Primary School
FRCTL/WBN BS36 .... 23 G2

Frenchay CE Primary School
MANG/FISH BS16 .... 48 B1

Frenchay Hospital
MANG/FISH BS16 .... 34 B5

Frenchay Village Museum
MANG/FISH BS16 .... 34 A5

Frome Bank Junior School
YATE/CS BS37 .... 13 H4

Fromeside Clinic
MANG/FISH BS16 .... 47 H3

Gay Elms Primary School
BMSTRD/HC/WWD BS13 ... 84 A5

Gillingstool Primary School
THNB/SVB BS35 .... 8 C4

The Glebe Infant School
YTN/CONG BS49 .... 114 C2

Glencoe Business Park
WSM BS23 .... 7 K5

Glenfrome Primary School
EVILLE/WHL BS5 .... 46 D4

Gloucestershire CCC
(County Ground)
HORF/LLZ BS7 .... 46 A4

Glynne Wickham Studio
Theatre
CFTN/FAIL BS8 .... 4 D3

Golden Valley Primary School
NAIL BS48 .... 67 G4

Gordano RFC
PTSHD/EG BS20 .... 41 E5

Gordano School
PTSHD/EG BS20 .... 39 H5

Gracefield Preparatory School
MANG/FISH BS16 .... 48 B3

Granby House Clinic
BMSTR BS3 .... 72 D3

Grand Pier
WSM BS23 .... 6 C4

The Grange Hotel
MANG/FISH BS36 .... 22 B1

The Grange School & Sports
College
OLD/WMLY/WICK BS30 .... 59 H4

Great Western Business Park
YATE/CS BS37 .... 13 F4

Greenbank Cemetery
EVILLE/WHL BS5 .... 57 F1

Greenfield Primary School
BRSG/KWL/STAPK BS4 ..... 84 D2

Green Park Station Market
CBATH/BATHN BA1 .... 2 D4

Greystoke Business Centre
PTSHD/EG BS20 .... 39 H4

Grove Industrial Estate
BRSTK/PCHW BS34 .... 20 D3

Grove Junior School
NAIL BS48 .... 79 E1

Grove Road Day Hospital
RDLND/MONT BS6 .... 55 E1

Grove Sports Centre
NAIL BS48 .... 79 E1

Hambrook Primary School
MANG/FISH BS16 .... 34 D2

Hambrook Sports Club
MANG/FISH BS16 .... 34 D2

Hampset CC
BATHSE BA2 .... 108 A5

Hannah Abbots Junior School
KGWD/HNM BS15 .... 75 H2

Hanham Business Park
KGWD/HNM BS15 .... 75 G1

Hanham High School
KGWD/HNM BS15 .... 75 H2

Hannah More Infant School
NAIL BS48 .... 79 E1

Hannah More Primary School
CBRISNE BS2 .... 5 K4

Harbour Road Trading Estate
PTSHD/EG BS20 .... 40 A2

Hareclive Primary School
BMSTRD/HC/WWD BS13 ... 84 D5

Haringtons Hotel
CBATH/BATHN BA1 .... 3 F4

Hartcliffe Engineering
Community College
BMSTRD/HC/WWD BS13 ... 85 F5

Hartcliffe Health Centre
BMSTRD/HC/WWD BS13 ... 84 D5

Harveys Wine Museum
CBRIS/FH BS1 .... 4 D4

Haslemere Industrial Estate
AVONM BS11 .... 28 C2

Hawkfield Business Park
HGRV/WHIT BS14 .... 84 E5

Hawkins Clinic
CBATH/BATHN BA1 .... 3 F4

Haycombe Cemetery
BATHSE BA2 .... 107 E3

Haycombe Crematorium
BATHSE BA2 .... 107 E3

Hayesfield School Technology
College
BATHSE BA2 .... 2 C5

Hayward Road Industrial
Estate
MANG/FISH BS16 .... 48 D5

Headley Park Primary School
BMSTRD/HC/WWD BS13 ... 84 C3

Heath House Priory Hospital
HORF/LLZ BS7 .... 46 D4

The Helicopter Museum
OMX/HUT/LCK BS24 .... 126 B1

Henbury Court Primary School
HNBRY/STHM BS10 .... 30 C2

Henbury Golf Club
HNBRY/STHM BS10 .... 30 C3

Henbury Lodge Hotel
HNBRY/STHM BS10 .... 30 C3

Henbury Old Boys AFC
HNBRY/STHM BS10 .... 30 D3

Henbury School
HNBRY/STHM BS10 .... 30 C2

Henbury Swimming Pool
HNBRY/STHM BS10 .... 30 D2

Henfield Business Park
FRCTL/WBN BS36 .... 36 B3

Hengrove Community Arts
College
HGRV/WHIT BS14 .... 86 A2

Hengrove Leisure Park
HGRV/WHIT BS14 .... 85 F3

Henleaze J & I School
RDLND/MONT BS6 .... 45 G3

Heritage Centre
WSM BS23 .... 6 D5

Herons Moor Community
Primary School
OMX/HUT/LCK BS24 .... 122 D5

The Herschel Museum of
Astronomy
CBATH/BATHN BA1 .... 2 E4

Heywood Health Centre
PTSHD/EG BS20 .... 42 C4

Highcroft Junior School
PTSHD/EG BS20 .... 42 C4

High Down Infant School
PTSHD/EG BS20 .... 39 E4

Highridge Infant School
BMSTRD/HC/WWD BS13 ... 84 A3

Hillcrest Primary School
BRSG/KWL/STAPK BS4 ..... 73 H3

Hillfield Primary School
MANG/FISH BS16 .... 48 C5

Hillside First School
MTN/WRL BS22 .... 122 B1

Hippodrome Theatre
CBRIS/FH BS1 .... 4 E4

Hither Green Industrial Estate
CLVDN BS21 .... 65 F2

HM Prison
HORF/LLZ BS7 .... 45 H3

Holburne Museum of Art
BATHSE BA2 .... 3 J2

Holloway Dental Health Centre
HGRV/WHIT BS14 .... 86 B1

Hollywood Bowl
CBRISNE BS2 .... 74 B1

Holy Cross Primary School
BMSTR BS3 .... 72 D2

Holy Family RC Primary School
BRSTK/PCHW BS34 .... 20 D2

Holymead Infant School
BRSG/KWL/STAPK BS4 ..... 74 C4

Holymead Junior School
BRSG/KWL/STAPK BS4 ..... 74 C4

Homefield Industrial Estate
OMX/HUT/LCK BS24 .... 126 D1

Horfield Health Centre
HORF/LLZ BS7 .... 46 C2

Horfield Primary School
HNBRY/STHM BS10 .... 45 H1

Horfield Sports Centre
HORF/LLZ BS7 .... 46 B1

Hornets RFC
MTN/WRL BS22 .... 121 H4

Horseworld
HGRV/WHIT BS14 .... 97 G1

Hot Bath Gallery & College
of Art
CBATH/BATHN BA1 .... 3 F5

Hotel du Vin & Bistro
CBRIS/FH BS1 .... 4 E4

Hotspots Indoor Sports
Centre
BRSG/KWL/STAPK BS4 ..... 75 E4

Hotwells Primary School
CFTN/FAIL BS8 .... 54 D5

Hutton Moor Leisure Centre
WSM BS23 .... 121 G4

Hutton Primary School
OMX/HUT/LCK BS24 .... 126 B4

Hydro Estate
AVONM BS11 .... 28 B2

IKEA Bristol *EVILLE/WHL* BS5 ... 46 D5

Ilminster Avenue Primary
School
BRSG/KWL/STAPK BS4 ..... 85 H1

Iron Acton CE Primary School
YATE/CS BS37 .... 12 C3

The Jane Austen Centre
CBATH/BATHN BA1 .... 3 F3

John Cabot Academy
KGWD/HNM BS15 .... 58 C4

The John Milton Health Clinic
HNBRY/STHM BS10 .... 31 E2

Jorrocks Estate
YATE/CS BS37 .... 13 F3

Jubilee Public Baths
BRSG/KWL/STAPK BS4 ..... 74 A4

Jurys Bristol Hotel
CBRIS/FH BS1 .... 4 E5

The Kendleshire Golf Club
FRCTL/WBN BS36 .... 36 A1

Kenn Business Park
CLVDN BS21 .... 65 E5

Kewstoke Primary School
MTN/WRL BS22 .... 116 C5

Keynsham Cemetery
KEYN BS31 .... 88 B5

Keynsham Hospital
KEYN BS31 .... 88 C5

Keynsham Leisure Centre
KEYN BS31 .... 88 C4

Keynsham RFC
KEYN BS31 .... 88 A2

Keynsham Town FC
KEYN BS31 .... 88 A2

King Edmund Community
School
YATE/CS BS37 .... 25 H1

King Edward Pre Preparatory
School
CBATH/BATHN BA1 .... 101 H4

King Edwards Junior School
BATHSE BA2 .... 103 F5

King Edwards School
BATHSE BA2 .... 103 F5

Kings Business Park
CBRISNE BS2 .... 57 E5

Kings Chase Shopping Centre
KGWD/HNM BS15 .... 58 D3

Kings Court Primary School
YATE/CS BS37 .... 26 A2

Kingsfield School
RDLND/MONT BS6 .... 55 G2

Kingshill CE Primary School
NAIL BS48 .... 67 E3

Kingsland Trading Estate
CBRISNE BS2 .... 56 C4

Kingsweston Special School
AVONM BS11 .... 29 G5

Kingswood Health Centre
KGWD/HNM BS15 .... 59 E3

Kingswood Leisure Centre
MANG/FISH BS16 .... 48 D5

Kingswood Preparatory School
CBATH/BATHN BA1 .... 102 B3

Kingswood School
CBATH/BATHN BA1 .... 102 B2

Kingswood Trading Estate
KGWD/HNM BS15 .... 58 D2

Knowle Golf Club
BRSG/KWL/STAPK BS4 ..... 86 C1

Knowle Park J & I School
BRSG/KWL/STAPK BS4 ..... 73 H5

Lambretta Scooter Museum
CBRIS/FH BS1 .... 7 F5

Lancaster House School
WSM BS23 .... 7 F3

Lansdown Cemetery
CBATH/BATHN BA1 .... 102 A1

Lansdown CC
  CBATH/BATHN BA1 ....101 G4
Larkhall FC
  CBATH/BATHN BA1 ....103 E1
Laura Place Fountain
  BATHSE BA2 ....3 H3
Lawnwood Road Industrial
  Estate
  EVILLE/WHL BS5 ....56 D3
Lawrence Hill Health Centre
  CBRISNE BS2 ....56 C4
Lawrence Hill
  Industrial Estate
  EVILLE/WHL BS5 ....57 E3
Lawrence Hill Industrial Park
  EVILLE/WHL BS5 ....56 D3
Leigh Court Business Centre
  CFTN/FAIL BS8 ....53 C1
Liberty Industrial Park
  BMSTR BS3 ....72 A5
Lime Grove Special School
  BATHSE BA2 ....3 J5
The Link Centre
  BATHSE BA2 ....110 C2
Little Mead Primary School
  HNBRY/STHM BS10 ....31 F4
Little Stoke Primary School
  BRSTK/PCHW BS34 ....21 F4
Little Theatre
  CBATH/BATHN BA1 ....3 F4
Locking Farm Industrial
  Estate
  OMX/HUT/LCK BS24 ....126 D1
Locking Primary School
  OMX/HUT/LCK BS24 ....127 E2
Locking Road Business Park
  WSM BS23 ....7 J5
Lockleaze Primary School
  HORF/LLZ BS7 ....46 D2
Locksbrook Cemetery
  BATHSE BA2 ....101 H5
Locksbrook Road Trading
  Estate
  BATHSE BA2 ....107 H1
Lodge Causeway Trading
  Estate
  MANG/FISH BS16 ....47 H5
Long Ashton Business Park
  LGASH BS41 ....71 E5
Long Ashton Golf Club
  LGASH BS41 ....70 B3
Longbrook Trading Estate
  BMSTR BS3 ....71 H3
Longton Industrial Estate
  WSM BS23 ....7 J6
Longwell Green CP School
  OLD/WMLY/WICK BS30 ....76 C3
Lonsdale Business Centre
  KCWD/HNM BS15 ....58 C1
Luckwell Primary School
  BMSTR BS3 ....72 B3
Macdonald Bath Spa Hotel
  BATHSE BA2 ....103 F5
Maes Knoll Fort
  HGRV/WHIT BS14 ....96 D3
Malago Vale Trading Estate
  BMSTR BS3 ....73 E3
The Mall *CBRIS/FH* BS1 ....5 G2
The Maltings
  Industrial Estate
  CBATH/BATHN BA1 ....101 F5
Mangotsfield Cemetery
  MANG/FISH BS16 ....49 F1
Mangotsfield CE Primary
  School
  MANG/FISH BS16 ....49 H2
Mangotsfield School
  MANG/FISH BS16 ....49 H4
Mangotsfield United FC
  MANG/FISH BS16 ....49 H5
Manor Brook Primary School
  THNB/SVB BS35 ....8 C1
The Manor CE Primary School
  FRCTL/WBN BS36 ....24 A4
Manor Farm Associated FC
  HNLZ/SM/SNYPK/WT BS9 ....43 H3
Maritime Heritage Centre
  YTN/CONG BS49 ....112 B2
Market Industrial Estate
  YTN/CONG BS49 ....112 B2
Mary Elton Primary School
  CLVDN BS21 ....64 B4
May Park Primary School
  EVILLE/WHL BS5 ....57 E1
Mayshill Cemetery
  FRCTL/WBN BS36 ....24 D1
Meadowbrook Primary School
  ALMDB BS32 ....21 G2
Meadow School
  OLD/WMLY/WICK BS30 ....89 G1
Mead Vale Primary School
  MTN/WRL BS22 ....122 B2
Mendip Green First School
  MTN/WRL BS22 ....122 B2
Mendip Leisure Centre
  PTSHD/EG BS20 ....39 H4
Menzies Waterside Hotel
  BATHSE BA2 ....3 H6
Mercure Brigstow Hotel
  CBRIS/FH BS1 ....5 G5
Mercure Francis Hotel
  CBATH/BATHN BA1 ....3 F4
Mercure Holland House Hotel
  CBRIS/FH BS1 ....5 F7
Midland Way Business Park
  THNB/SVB BS35 ....8 C4
Millennium Exhibition Centre
  CBRIS/FH BS1 ....4 D6
Millennium Square
  CBRIS/FH BS1 ....4 D6
Millipond Primary School
  EVILLE/WHL BS5 ....56 C2
Milson Street Clinic
  CBATH/BATHN BA1 ....3 F3
Milton Infant School
  MTN/WRL BS22 ....121 H2
Milton Junior School
  MTN/WRL BS22 ....121 H2
Milton Road Cemetery
  WSM BS23 ....7 H2

Minto Road Industrial Centre
  CBRISNE BS2 ....56 B1
Mizzymean
  Recreation Centre
  NAIL BS48 ....67 F5
Model Yacht Centre
  WSM BS23 ....6 C3
Monks Park School
  HORF/LLZ BS7 ....32 B4
Monkton Combe Junior
  School
  BATHSE BA2 ....111 H1
Monkton Combe Pre
  Preparatory School
  BATHSE BA2 ....111 G1
Monkton Farleigh & South
  Wraxall CE Primary School
  BOAV BA15 ....105 F5
Montpelier Health Centre
  RDLND/MONT BS6 ....56 A2
Moorlands J & I School
  BATHSE BA2 ....108 A4
The Mount
  CBATH/BATHN BA1 ....91 H4
Museum of Bath at Work
  CBATH/BATHN BA1 ....3 F1
Museum of East Asian Art
  CBATH/BATHN BA1 ....2 E2
Nailsea Health Centre
  NAIL BS48 ....67 F4
Nailsea School
  NAIL BS48 ....67 G5
Netham Industrial Estate
  EVILLE/WHL BS5 ....57 F4
Netham Industrial Park
  EVILLE/WHL BS5 ....57 F4
New Birchfield Hotel
  WSM BS23 ....6 B1
Newbridge Industrial Estate
  BRSG/KWL/STAPK BS4 ....75 E5
Newbridge Junior School
  CBATH/BATHN BA1 ....101 G5
Newbridge Primary School
  CBATH/BATHN BA1 ....101 G5
Newbridge Trading Estate
  BRSG/KWL/STAPK BS4 ....57 F5
New Fosseway Special School
  HGRV/WHIT BS14 ....86 A2
New Oak Primary School
  HGRV/WHIT BS14 ....86 A2
New Ocean Hotel
  WSM BS23 ....6 A1
New Siblands Special School
  THNB/SVB BS35 ....9 E3
Newton Mill Caravan &
  Camping Park
  BATHSE BA2 ....107 E1
No 1 Royal Crescent
  CBATH/BATHN BA1 ....2 E2
Norland College
  CBATH/BATHN BA1 ....103 E4
Northavon Business Centre
  YATE/CS BS37 ....13 C4
North Bristol RFC
  ALMDB BS32 ....10 C4
Northleaze Primary School
  LGASH BS41 ....71 E4
Northridge Business Centre
  YATE/CS BS37 ....13 G5
North Road Primary School
  YATE/CS BS37 ....13 F3
North Somerset Museum
  WSM BS23 ....6 E3
North Worle Shopping Centre
  MTN/WRL BS22 ....118 A5
Novers Hill Trading Estate
  BMSTR BS3 ....72 D5
Novotel
  CBRIS/FH BS1 ....5 H5
Oakfield Business Park
  KCWD/HNM BS15 ....58 D4
The Oaklands Business Park
  YATE/CS BS37 ....13 E4
Oatley Trading Estate
  KCWD/HNM BS15 ....58 D2
Odd Down FC
  BATHSE BA2 ....110 A2
Odeon Cinema
  CBATH/BATHN BA1 ....2 E5
  CBRIS/FH BS1 ....5 F3
  WSM BS23 ....6 E4
Old Bristolians Sports Club
  BATHSE BA2 ....70 C2
Oldbury Court Primary School
  MANG/FISH BS16 ....48 C1
Old Culverhaysians RFC
  BATHSE BA2 ....110 A1
Oldfield Old Boys RFC
  BATHSE BA2 ....2 D6
Oldfield Park Infant School
  BATHSE BA2 ....2 B5
Oldfield Park Junior School
  BATHSE BA2 ....107 H3
Oldfield School
  CBATH/BATHN BA1 ....101 E3
Old Knightstone Theatre
  WSM BS23 ....6 A2
Oldmixon Primary School
  OMX/HUT/LCK BS24 ....125 F4
Open University
  CBRIS/FH BS1 ....5 G6
Optimax Laser Eye Clinic
  CBRIS/FH BS1 ....4 E4
Oral Health Centre
  CBATH/BATHN BA1 ....3 F3
The Orchard Medical Centre
  KCWD/HNM BS15 ....58 D3
Orchard View
  (Ham Green Hospital)
  PTSHD/EG BS20 ....43 E4
Our Lady of Lourdes RC
  Primary School
  KCWD/HNM BS15 ....59 E4
Our Lady of the Rosary RC
  Primary School
  AVONM BS11 ....29 G4
Outline Fitness Club
  WSM BS23 ....7 F6
Paragon School
  BATHSE BA2 ....108 D4

Parish Wharf Leisure Centre
  PTSHD/EG BS20 ....40 A2
The Park School
  YATE/CS BS37 ....59 E3
Parkwall Primary School
  OLD/WMLY/WICK BS30 ....76 D1
Parkway Trading Estate
  CBRISNE BS2 ....56 B1
Parnall Road Industrial Estate
  MANG/FISH BS16 ....48 A5
Parson Street Primary School
  BMSTR BS3 ....72 D4
Patchway Community College
  ALMDB BS32 ....20 C1
Patchway Health Clinic
  ALMDB BS32 ....20 C2
Patchway Trading Estate
  BRSTK/PCHW BS34 ....19 H2
Pembroke Road Surgery
  CFTN/FAIL BS8 ....55 E2
Perry Court Junior School
  HGRV/WHIT BS14 ....85 H3
Phoenix Business Park
  BMSTR BS3 ....72 B4
Picturedrome Cinema
  RDLND/MONT BS6 ....45 E4
The Picture House
  CBRIS/FH BS1 ....5 G1
Picture This
  CBRIS/FH BS1 ....4 A7
Pines Way Industrial Estate
  BATHSE BA2 ....2 D5
Pizey Avenue
  Industrial Estate
  CLVDN BS21 ....64 D3
Playhouse Theatre
  WSM BS23 ....6 D2
The Podium
  Shopping Centre & Library
  CBATH/BATHN BA1 ....3 G3
Portbury Sawmills Industrial
  Estate
  PTSHD/EG BS20 ....41 H1
Portishead Business Park
  PTSHD/EG BS20 ....39 H2
Portishead Cemetery
  PTSHD/EG BS20 ....39 G5
Portishead Health Centre
  PTSHD/EG BS20 ....39 H3
Portishead Lifeboat Station
  PTSHD/EG BS20 ....38 D2
Portishead Primary School
  PTSHD/EG BS20 ....40 A2
Portishead Trading Estate
  AVONM BS11 ....28 B5
Portway Community School
  AVONM BS11 ....43 E1
Portway Trading Estate
  AVONM BS11 ....42 C1
Pratt's Hotel
  BATHSE BA2 ....3 H5
Premier Inn
  BRSTK/PCHW BS34 ....32 C2
  PTSHD/EG BS20 ....40 A3
Prior Park College
  BATHSE BA2 ....109 F5
Prior Park Landscape
  Garden (NT)
  BATHSE BA2 ....109 F4
Priory Community School
  MTN/WRL BS22 ....118 A5
Priory Farm Trading Estate
  PTSHD/EG BS20 ....41 F5
Pucklechurch CE Primary
  School
  MANG/FISH BS16 ....51 G2
Pucklechurch Trading Estate
  MANG/FISH BS16 ....51 F2
QEH Theatre
  CFTN/FAIL BS8 ....4 A3
Quakers Friars
  CBRIS/FH BS1 ....5 H2
Queen Elizabeth Hospital
  CFTN/FAIL BS8 ....4 B4
Queen Elizabeths Hospital
  School
  CFTN/FAIL BS8 ....4 A3
The Queensberry Hotel
  CBATH/BATHN BA1 ....2 E2
Radnor Business Centre
  HORF/LLZ BS7 ....46 A3
Ralph Allen School
  BATHSE BA2 ....109 H5
Ramada Plaza Bristol
  CBRIS/FH BS1 ....5 H6
Ravenswood Special School
  NAIL BS48 ....67 E3
Raysfield J & I School
  YATE/CS BS37 ....26 B2
Redfield Edge Primary School
  OLD/WMLY/WICK BS30 ....77 G2
Redfield Leisure Centre
  EVILLE/WHL BS5 ....57 E4
Redgrave Theatre
  BATHSE BA2 ....54 D3
Redland Green School
  RDLND/MONT BS6 ....45 G3
Redland High Junior School
  RDLND/MONT BS6 ....55 G1
Redland High School for Girls
  RDLND/MONT BS6 ....55 G1
The Red Maids Junior School
  HNLZ/SM/SNYPK/WT BS9 ....45 F1
The Red Maids School
  HNLZ/SM/SNYPK/WT BS9 ....45 E1
Redwood Hotel
  CFTN/FAIL BS8 ....70 C2
Ridge Junior School
  YATE/CS BS37 ....14 B5
Ridgeway Industrial Estate
  EVILLE/WHL BS5 ....57 G1
Ridgeway Park Cemetery
  EVILLE/WHL BS5 ....47 F5
The Ridings High School
  FRCTL/WBN BS36 ....22 D4
Riverbank Medical Centre
  MTN/WRL BS22 ....118 A5
Riverside Business Park
  BATHSE BA2 ....2 E5
  EVILLE/WHL BS5 ....57 F5

Riverside Leisure Centre
  BATHSE BA2 ....56 B3
Robin Cousins Sports Centre
  AVONM BS11 ....28 C5
Rodford Primary School
  YATE/CS BS37 ....25 C3
Rodney Hotel
  CFTN/FAIL BS8 ....54 D4
Roman Baths & Pump Room
  CBATH/BATHN BA1 ....3 G5
The Royal Crescent Hotel
  BATHSE BA2 ....2 D2
Royal High School Bath
  GDST Senior School
  CBATH/BATHN BA1 ....102 C2
The Royal High School
  (Junior Department)
  CBATH/BATHN BA1 ....102 C4
The Royal Hotel
  WSM BS23 ....6 C3
Royal National Hospital for
  Rheumatic Diseases
  CBATH/BATHN BA1 ....3 F4
Royal Navy &
  Royal Marines Careers
  Information Office
  CBRIS/FH BS1 ....4 E3
Royal United Hospital
  CBATH/BATHN BA1 ....101 G4
Royal Victoria Park Bandstand
  CBATH/BATHN BA1 ....2 D3
Royal Victoria Park Pavilion
  CBATH/BATHN BA1 ....2 E3
RSPCA & Dogs Home
  CBRISNE BS2 ....73 H2
Russell Town Industrial Park
  EVILLE/WHL BS5 ....57 E4
St Andrews CE Primary
  School
  CBATH/BATHN BA1 ....2 E1
St Andrews Junior School
  YTN/CONG BS49 ....114 C2
St Annes CE Primary School
  OLD/WMLY/WICK BS30 ....77 F3
  OMX/HUT/LCK BS24 ....119 G3
St Annes J & I School
  BRSG/KWL/STAPK BS4 ....74 C1
St Annes Park
  Primary School
  BRSG/KWL/STAPK BS4 ....74 D1
St Augustine of Canterbury
  RC Primary School
  MANG/FISH BS16 ....49 F1
St Barnabas CE Primary
  School
  RDLND/MONT BS6 ....56 B2
St Bedes Catholic College
  AVONM BS11 ....29 G3
St Bernadettes Catholic
  Secondary School
  HGRV/WHIT BS14 ....86 A3
St Bernadettes RC Primary
  School
  HGRV/WHIT BS14 ....86 A3
St Bernards RC Primary School
  AVONM BS11 ....43 E2
St Bonaventures RC Primary
  School
  RDLND/MONT BS6 ....45 G4
St Brendans Trading Estate
  AVONM BS11 ....28 B3
St Catherines Industrial Estate
  BMSTR BS3 ....73 E2
St Chads Patchway CE Primary
  School
  BRSTK/PCHW BS34 ....21 E1
St Christophers School
  RDLND/MONT BS6 ....45 E5
St Francis Catholic Primary
  School
  NAIL BS48 ....67 G5
St Gabriel's Business Park
  EVILLE/WHL BS5 ....56 D3
St George Health Centre
  KCWD/HNM BS15 ....58 A3
St Georges CE Primary School
  CFTN/FAIL BS8 ....4 B5
St Georges Industrial Estate
  AVONM BS11 ....28 B2
St Georges VA Primary School
  MTN/WRL BS22 ....118 B5
St Gregorys Catholic College
  BATHSE BA2 ....110 B2
St James Cemetery
  BATHSE BA2 ....2 C5
St Johns CE Primary School
  CFTN/FAIL BS8 ....55 E1
St Johns Church & Old City Gate
  CBRIS/FH BS1 ....5 F3
St Johns Lane Health Centre
  BMSTR BS3 ....73 F4
St Johns Mead CE Primary
  School
  YATE/CS BS37 ....26 D2
St Johns Primary School
  KEYN BS31 ....88 B4
St Johns RC Primary School
  BATHSE BA2 ....3 J4
St John the Evangelist CE
  Primary School
  CLVDN BS21 ....64 C4
St Josephs Catholic Primary
  School
  PTSHD/EG BS20 ....39 H5
St Joseph's RC Primary School
  MANG/FISH BS16 ....48 B5
St Katharine's Primary School
  BLAG/CWMG/WR BS40 ....92 B5
St Katherines School
  PTSHD/EG BS20 ....43 G5
St Keyna Primary School
  KEYN BS31 ....88 C3
St Marks CE School
  CBATH/BATHN BA1 ....103 E2
St Mark's Community Centre
  BATHSE BA2 ....3 G7
St Marks VA Primary School
  MTN/WRL BS22 ....117 G4
St Martins CE Junior School
  MTN/WRL BS22 ....122 A2

St Martins Garden
  Primary School
  BATHSE BA2 ....110 C1
St Martins Hospital
  BATHSE BA2 ....110 C1
St Mary Redcliffe Cemetery
  BRSG/KWL/STAPK BS4 ....74 A2
St Mary Redcliffe CE VC Primary
  School
  BMSTR BS3 ....73 F2
St Mary's Catholic Primary
  School
  ALMDB BS32 ....22 A3
St Marys CE VA Primary School
  PTSHD/EG BS20 ....41 G5
St Marys Hospital
  CFTN/FAIL BS8 ....4 B3
St Marys RC Primary School
  CBATH/BATHN BA1 ....101 G3
St Mary's Redcliffe Church
  CBRIS/FH BS1 ....5 G6
St Marys RFC
  FRCTL/WBN BS36 ....11 H5
St Matthias & Dr Bells CE
  Primary School
  MANG/FISH BS16 ....48 A4
St Michael on the Mount
  Primary School
  CFTN/FAIL BS8 ....4 D3
St Michaels CE Junior School
  BATHSE BA2 ....107 E1
St Michael's Cemetery
  CBATH/BATHN BA1 ....101 H5
St Michaels CE Primary
  School
  BRSTK/PCHW BS34 ....21 G5
St Michaels CE VC Primary
  School
  FRCTL/WBN BS36 ....22 D4
St Michaels Hill Clinic
  CBRISNE BS2 ....4 E2
St Michaels Hospital
  CBRISNE BS2 ....4 D1
St Nicholas Chantry Primary
  School
  CLVDN BS21 ....65 E1
St Nicholas Market
  CBRIS/FH BS1 ....5 F4
St Nicholas of Tolentine RC
  Primary School
  EVILLE/WHL BS5 ....5 K1
St Patricks RC Primary School
  EVILLE/WHL BS5 ....57 F4
St Pauls Catholic Primary
  School
  YATE/CS BS37 ....26 A2
St Peter & Paul RC Primary
  School
  RDLND/MONT BS6 ....55 G3
St Peters CE Primary School
  PTSHD/EG BS20 ....39 H3
St Philips CE Primary School
  BATHSE BA2 ....108 A5
St Pius X RC Primary School
  BMSTRD/HC/WWD BS13 .....84 B4
St Saviours Infant School
  CBATH/BATHN BA1 ....103 E2
St Saviours Junior School
  CBATH/BATHN BA1 ....103 E2
St Stephens Business Centre
  OLD/WMLY/WICK BS30 ....77 F1
St Stephens CE Primary School
  BATHSE BA2 ....102 C3
St Stephens J & I School
  KCWD/HNM BS15 ....58 D1
St Teresas Catholic Primary
  School
  HORF/LLZ BS7 ....32 A4
St Teresas Private Hospital
  BATHSE BA2 ....100 A4
St Ursulas High School
  HNLZ/SM/SNYPK/WT BS9 ....45 E2
St Vincents Trading Estate
  CBRISNE BS2 ....57 E5
St Werburgh's Primary School
  CBRISNE BS2 ....56 C1
Sally Lunn's Refreshment
  House & Museum
  CBATH/BATHN BA1 ....3 G5
Saltford CE Primary School
  KEYN BS31 ....99 E2
Saltford Golf Club
  KEYN BS31 ....99 F3
Sampson House Business Park
  HNBRY/STHM BS10 ....18 B3
Samuel Whites Infant School
  KCWD/HNM BS15 ....75 H1
Saracens RFC
  HNBRY/STHM BS10 ....18 D5
Satellite Business Park
  EVILLE/WHL BS5 ....57 F4
Saville Court Business Centre
  CFTN/FAIL BS8 ....55 E4
Sawclose Health
  CBATH/BATHN BA1 ....3 F4
School of Christ the King
  BRSG/KWL/STAPK BS4 ....85 F2
Scotch Horn Community &
  Sports Centre
  NAIL BS48 ....67 G4
Sea Mills Infant School
  HNLZ/SM/SNYPK/WT BS9 ....44 A1
Sea Mills Junior School
  HNLZ/SM/SNYPK/WT BS9 ....43 H3
SeaQuarium
  WSM BS23 ....6 C6
Sefton Park J & I School
  HORF/LLZ BS7 ....46 B5
Severnvale Trading Estate
  AVONM BS11 ....28 C4
Sham Castle
  BATHSE BA2 ....109 G1
Sheene Court Industrial Estate
  BMSTR BS3 ....72 D3
The Sheiling School
  THNB/SVB BS35 ....8 B3
The Shield Retail Centre
  BRSTK/PCHW BS34 ....32 C2
Shield Road Primary School
  HORF/LLZ BS7 ....32 C4

Shirehampton Cemetery
AVONM BS11 .... 42 D2
Shirehampton CC
AVONM BS11 .... 43 F1
Shirehampton Health Centre
AVONM BS11 .... 43 E2
Shirehampton Park Golf Club
AVONM BS11 .... 43 F2
Shirehampton Primary School
AVONM BS11 .... 42 D2
Shirehampton
Swimming Pool
AVONM BS11 .... 43 E2
Shortwood Lodge Golf Club
MANG/FISH BS16 .... 50 A5
Showcase Cinema
CBRISNE BS2 .... 74 B1
Silverhill School
FRCTL/WBN BS36 .... 23 E3
Simplex Trading Estate
OLD/WMLY/WICK BS30 .... 77 G2
The Sir Bernard Lovell School
OLD/WMLY/WICK BS30 .... 77 F2
Soaphouse Industrial Estate
EVILLE/WHL BS5 .... 57 G3
Solsbury Hill Hill Fort
CBATH/BATHN BA1 .... 90 C5
South Bristol Business Park
BRSC/KWL/STAPK BS4 .... 85 E2
South Bristol Cemetery
BMSTRD/HC/WWD BS13 .... 83 H1
South Bristol Crematorium
BMSTRD/HC/WWD BS13 .... 84 A1
South Bristol Retail Park
BMSTR BS3 .... 72 B3
Southdown J & I School
BATHSE BA2 .... 107 G4
Southfield Road Trading
Estate
NAIL BS48 .... 67 G3
Southgate
CBATH/BATHN BA1 .... 3 G6
Southmead Health Centre
HNBRY/STHM BS10 .... 31 G3
Southmead Hospital
HNBRY/STHM BS10 .... 45 H1
South Street Primary School
BMSTR BS3 .... 72 C3
South View Business Centre
MANG/FISH BS16 .... 49 E3
South View Business Park
MANG/FISH BS16 .... 49 E3
Southville Primary School
BMSTR BS3 .... 72 D2
Sovereign Shopping Centre
WSM BS23 .... 6 D4
Speedwell Industrial Estate
CLVDN BS21 .... 64 C3
Speedwell Swimming Baths
EVILLE/WHL BS5 .... 57 H2
Speedwell Technology College
EVILLE/WHL BS5 .... 58 A2
Spike Island Centre of
Contemporary Art & Design
CBRIS/FH BS1 .... 4 A7
Springfield School
RDLND/MONT BS6 .... 56 A1
Springwater Park
Trading Estate
EVILLE/WHL BS5 .... 57 G4
Stafford Business Centre
WSM BS23 .... 7 G4
Stanbridge Primary School
MANG/FISH BS16 .... 49 F2
Staple Hill Primary School
MANG/FISH BS16 .... 48 D4
Sterling College International
CBATH/BATHN BA1 .... 3 G2

Stock Exchange
CBRIS/FH BS1 .... 4 E4
Stockwood Green Primary
School
HCRV/WHIT BS14 .... 86 D5
Stockwood Open Space Nature
Reserve
HCRV/WHIT BS14 .... 87 E3
Stockwood Vale Golf Club
KEYN BS31 .... 87 F3
Stoke Bishop CE Primary
School
HNLZ/SM/SNYPK/WT BS9 .... 44 B3
Stoke Gifford Medical Centre
BRSTK/PCHW BS34 .... 33 G1
Stoke Lodge Primary School
BRSTK/PCHW BS34 .... 21 E2
Stokes Medical Centre
BRSTK/PCHW BS34 .... 21 E3
Stoke View Business Park
MANG/FISH BS16 .... 47 H4
Stone Hill Business Centre
KGWD/HNM BS15 .... 76 B2
Storybox Theatre
YTN/CONG BS49 .... 113 G3
Stover Trading Estate
YATE/CS BS37 .... 25 F1
Summerhill J & I School
EVILLE/WHL BS5 .... 57 G3
Sun Life Sports Club
BRSTK/PCHW BS34 .... 30 D1
Sunnyside Farm
Trading Estate
PTSHD/EG BS20 .... 52 C1
Swainswick Primary School
CBATH/BATHN BA1 .... 90 A4
Temple Quay
CBRIS/FH BS1 .... 5 J5
Temple Trading Estate
CBRISNE BS2 .... 74 A1
Teyfant Community School
BMSTRD/HC/WWD BS13 .... 85 F5
Theatre Royal
CBATH/BATHN BA1 .... 2 E4
Thermae Bath Spa
CBATH/BATHN BA1 .... 3 F5
Thistle Hotel
CBRIS/FH BS1 .... 5 F3
Thornbury Castle Hotel
THNB/SVB BS35 .... 8 B2
Thornbury Cemetery
THNB/SVB BS35 .... 8 B3
Thornbury Golf Lodge Hotel &
Centre
THNB/SVB BS35 .... 8 A5
Thornbury Health Centre
THNB/SVB BS35 .... 8 D3
Thornbury Hospital
THNB/SVB BS35 .... 8 D3
Thornbury Leisure Centre
THNB/SVB BS35 .... 8 C5
Three Ways School
BATHSE BA2 .... 3 J4
BATHSE BA2 .... 110 C2
CBATH/BATHN BA1 .... 102 A5
Tickenham Primary School
CLVDN BS21 .... 66 A2
Time Machine Museum
WSM BS23 .... 6 E3
Toll House Clinic
YATE/CS BS37 .... 27 E1
Torwood House School
RDLND/MONT BS6 .... 45 E5
Totterdown Bridge Industrial
Estate *CBRISNE* BS2 .... 73 H2
Travelodge
CBATH/BATHN BA1 .... 3 G3
HNBRY/STHM BS10 .... 19 E4

Trinity Theological College
HNLZ/SM/SNYPK/WT BS9 .... 44 C4
TT Trading Estate
YATE/CS BS37 .... 27 E1
Tudor Lodge Health Centre
WSM BS23 .... 124 D2
Twerton Cemetery
BATHSE BA2 .... 107 H1
Twerton Infant School
BATHSE BA2 .... 107 E2
Two Mile Hill J & I School
KGWD/HNM BS15 .... 58 B3
Twyford House CC
AVONM BS11 .... 43 F1
The Tynings Primary School
MANG/FISH BS16 .... 49 F4
Tyntesfield House (NT)
NAIL BS48 .... 68 D2
Unicorn Business Park
CBRISNE BS2 .... 74 B1
University of Bath
BATHSE BA2 .... 109 H2
University of Bristol
CFTN/FAIL BS8 .... 4 C1
University of Bristol Childrens
Hospital
CFTN/FAIL BS8 .... 4 C2
University of the West of
England
BMSTR BS3 .... 71 H2
CBRIS/FH BS1 .... 5 F4
University of the West of
England (Frenchay Campus)
MANG/FISH BS16 .... 33 G5
University of the West of
England (Glenside Campus)
MANG/FISH BS16 .... 47 G3
University of the West of
England
(St Matthias Campus)
MANG/FISH BS16 .... 48 A3
Uphill Primary School
WSM BS23 .... 124 C4
Upper Horfield
Primary School
HORF/LLZ BS7 .... 32 B5
Victoria Art Gallery
BATHSE BA2 .... 3 G4
Victoria Monument
CBATH/BATHN BA1 .... 2 C2
Victoria Park
Business Centre
CBATH/BATHN BA1 .... 2 A3
Victoria Park Community
Infant School
BMSTR BS3 .... 73 F3
Vines Industrial Estate
NAIL BS48 .... 67 H3
Vue Cinema
HNBRY/STHM BS10 .... 19 C4
Wadehurst Industrial Park
CBRISNE BS2 .... 56 C4
Walliscote Primary School
WSM BS23 .... 6 B5
Wallis Estate
CBRISNE BS2 .... 46 B5
Wansdyke Business Centre
BATHSE BA2 .... 108 A3
Wansdyke Primary School
HCRV/WHIT BS14 .... 85 G5
Warmley CE School
OLD/WMLY/WICK BS30 .... 60 A5
Warmley Park School
OLD/WMLY/WICK BS30 .... 59 H4
Watershed Cinema
CBRIS/FH BS1 .... 4 E5
Watershed Media Centre
CBRIS/FH BS1 .... 4 E5

Waycroft Primary School
HCRV/WHIT BS14 .... 86 D4
Wellesley Primary School
YATE/CS BS37 .... 25 H4
Wellsway School
KEYN BS31 .... 88 D4
Wentworth House Hotel
BATHSE BA2 .... 108 B3
Westbourne Hotel
CFTN/FAIL BS8 .... 4 A1
Westbury on Trym
CE Primary School
HNLZ/SM/SNYPK/WT BS9 .... 31 E5
Westbury Park Primary
School *RDLND/MONT* BS6 ..... 45 E4
Westcliff College of Further
Education *WSM* BS23 .... 120 A2
West Country Water Park
FRCTL/WBN BS36 .... 11 H5
Westerleigh Crematorium
YATE/CS BS37 .... 37 G4
Westhaven Special School
WSM BS23 .... 124 B4
Westland Business Centre
OMX/HUT/LCK BS24 .... 125 G3
West Leigh Infant School
NAIL BS48 .... 79 G3
Weston All Saints Primary
School
CBATH/BATHN BA1 .... 101 F2
Weston Business Park
BNWL BS29 .... 127 G3
OMX/HUT/LCK BS24 .... 126 B1
Weston College
WSM BS23 .... 6 C2
WSM BS23 .... 125 E4
Weston Express Business
Park
MTN/WRL BS22 .... 121 H5
Weston Park Primary School
MTN/WRL BS22 .... 29 F5
Weston Retail Park
WSM BS23 .... 7 J7
Weston St Johns
Associated FC
WSM BS23 .... 125 E3
Weston-super-Mare AFC
(Woodspring Stadium)
OMX/HUT/LCK BS24 .... 125 F2
Weston-super-Mare Borough
Employees Sports Club
WSM BS23 .... 7 G5
Weston-super-Mare Cemetery
MTN/WRL BS22 .... 117 F4
Weston-super-Mare
Crematorium
MTN/WRL BS22 .... 117 F4
Weston-super-Mare CC
WSM BS23 .... 124 D3
Weston-super-Mare General
Hospital
WSM BS23 .... 124 D4
Weston-super-Mare
Golf Club
WSM BS23 .... 124 B2
Weston-super-Mare RFC
WSM BS23 .... 7 F6
Westpoint Trading Estate
KGWD/HNM BS15 .... 58 D4
West Town Lane Primary
School
BRSC/KWL/STAPK BS4 .... 74 B5
Wheatfield Primary School
ALMDB BS32 .... 21 F1
Whitchurch Health Centre
HCRV/WHIT BS14 .... 85 H4
Whitchurch Primary School
HCRV/WHIT BS14 .... 86 B5

Whitchurch Sports Centre
HCRV/WHIT BS14 .... 85 G4
Whitefield Fishponds
Community School
MANG/FISH BS16 .... 47 H4
Whitehall Primary School
EVILLE/WHL BS5 .... 57 F2
Whitehall Trading Estate
EVILLE/WHL BS5 .... 57 E3
Wick CE Primary School
OLD/WMLY/WICK BS30 .... 61 F5
Widcombe
CE Junior School
BATHSE BA2 .... 3 J6
Widcombe Infant School
BATHSE BA2 .... 3 H6
William Budd Health Centre
BRSC/KWL/STAPK BS4 .... 85 E1
Willisbridge Mill Museum &
Nature Reserve
OLD/WMLY/WICK BS30 .... 77 E4
Wilverley Trading Estate
BRSC/KWL/STAPK BS4 .... 74 D5
Wincombe Trading Estate
CBRISNE BS2 .... 73 H2
Windmill Farm
Business Centre
BMSTR BS3 .... 73 E2
Windmill Hill City Farm
BMSTR BS3 .... 73 E2
Window Arts Centre
CBATH/BATHN BA1 .... 3 F5
Windwhistle Primary School
WSM BS23 .... 125 E3
Winford CE Primary School
BLAG/CWMG/WR BS40 .... 93 G5
Winter Gardens & Pavilion
WSM BS23 .... 6 C3
Withywood Community
School
BMSTRD/HC/WWD BS13 .... 84 B4
Woodlands Golf & Country
Club
ALMDB BS32 .... 11 H4
Wood Road Industrial Centre
KGWD/HNM BS15 .... 58 D3
Woodspring Golf & Country
Club
LGASH BS41 .... 83 F5
Woodstock Special School
HNBRY/STHM BS10 .... 30 C3
Worlebury Golf Club
MTN/WRL BS22 .... 116 C5
Worlebury St Pauls
CE VA First School
MTN/WRL BS22 .... 121 G1
Worle Health Centre
MTN/WRL BS22 .... 122 B1
Wraxall CE Primary School
NAIL BS48 .... 68 A2
Wyvern Community School
WSM BS23 .... 125 E1
Wyvern Sports Centre
WSM BS23 .... 125 E1
Yate Leisure Centre
YATE/CS BS37 .... 14 A5
Yate Outdoor
Sports Complex
YATE/CS BS37 .... 13 H2
Yate Town FC
YATE/CS BS37 .... 13 F4
Yatton J & I School
YTN/CONG BS49 .... 112 C5
Yeo Moor J & I School
CLVDN BS21 .... 65 E3

Acknowledgements

Schools address data provided by Education Direct.

Petrol station information supplied by Johnsons.

Garden centre information provided by:

Garden Centre Association  Britains best garden centres

Wyevale Garden Centres

The statement on the front cover of this atlas is sourced, selected and quoted
from a reader comment and feedback form received in 2004

Speed camera locations

Speed camera locations provided in association with RoadPilot Ltd

RoadPilot is the developer of one of the largest and most accurate databases of speed camera locations in the UK and Europe. It has provided the speed camera information in this atlas. RoadPilot is the UK's pioneer and market leader in GPS (Global Positioning System) road safety technologies.

microGo (pictured right) is RoadPilot's latest in-car speed camera location system. It improves road safety by alerting you to the location of accident black spots,

fixed and mobile camera sites. RoadPilot's microGo does not jam police lasers and is therefore completely legal.

RoadPilot's database of fixed camera locations has been compiled with the full co-operation of regional police forces and the Safety Camera Partnerships.

For more information on RoadPilot's GPS road safety products, please visit **www.roadpilot.com** or telephone 0870 240 1701

RoadPilot

ALARM MODE

GPS Antenna
microGo is directional, it only alerts you to cameras on your side of the road

Visual Countdown
To camera location

Your Speed
The speed you are travelling when approaching camera

Camera Types Located
Gatso, Specs, Truvelo, TSS/DSS, Traffipax, mobile camera sites, accident black spots, congestion charges, tolls

Voice Warnings
Only if you are exceeding the speed limit at the camera

Plug and Go
Easy to move from vehicle to vehicle

64 Colour Options
To match vehicle's illumination

Speed Limit at Camera
Screen turns red as additional visual alert

Single Button Operation
For easy access to speed display, camera warning, rescue me location, trip computer, congestion charge, max speed alarm, date and time

SPEED READING

AA Street by Street QUESTIONNAIRE

Dear Atlas User
Your comments, opinions and recommendations are very important to us.
So please help us to improve our street atlases by taking a few minutes
to complete this simple questionnaire.

You do not need a stamp (unless posted outside the UK). If you do not want to remove
this page from your street atlas, then photocopy it or write your answers on a plain sheet
of paper.

Send to: Marketing Assistant, AA Publishing, 14th Floor Fanum House,
Freepost SCE 4598, Basingstoke RG21 4GY

ABOUT THE ATLAS...

Please state which city / town / county you bought:

_____

Where did you buy the atlas? (City, Town, County)

_____

For what purpose? (please tick all applicable)

To use in your local area ☐   To use on business or at work ☐

Visiting a strange place ☐   In the car ☐   On foot ☐

Other (please state)

_____

Have you ever used any street atlases other than AA Street by Street?

Yes ☐   No ☐

If so, which ones?

_____

Is there any aspect of our street atlases that could be improved?
(Please continue on a separate sheet if necessary)

_____
_____
_____
_____
_____

Please list the features you found most useful:

_____
_____
_____

Please list the features you found least useful:

_____
_____
_____

LOCAL KNOWLEDGE...

Local knowledge is invaluable. Whilst every attempt has been made to make the information contained in this atlas as accurate as possible, should you notice any inaccuracies, please detail them below (if necessary, use a blank piece of paper) or e-mail us at *streetbystreet@theAA.com*

_____
_____
_____

ABOUT YOU...

Name (Mr/Mrs/Ms) _____

Address _____

                                                Postcode _____

Daytime tel no _____

E-mail address _____

Which age group are you in?

Under 25 ☐   25-34 ☐   35-44 ☐   45-54 ☐   55-64 ☐   65+ ☐

Are you an AA member?   YES ☐   NO ☐

Do you have Internet access?   YES ☐   NO ☐

Thank you for taking the time to complete this questionnaire. Please send it to us as soon as possible, and remember, you do not need a stamp (unless posted outside the UK).

We may use information we hold about you to telephone or email you about other products and services offered by the AA, we do NOT disclose this information to third parties.

Please tick here if you do not wish to hear about products and services from the AA. ☐

ML060y